Morocco

Travellers' Guide

Morocco

by Christopher Kininmonth
revised by John Richmond

Jonathan Cape London

By the same author

The Children of Thetis
Rome Alive
The Brass Dolphins
The Travellers' Guide to Malta and Gozo
The Travellers' Guide to Sicily
Frontiers
Maze

First published 1972
Reprinted 1974
Second edition 1981
Revised second edition 1986
Text and maps © Copyright Helga Greene 1972, 1981, 1986
Maps by Janet Landau and John R. Hunt
General Editors: Judith Greene and June Gordon-Walker

Jonathan Cape Ltd
32 Bedford Square, London WC1B 3EL

British Library Cataloguing in Publication Data

Kininmonth, Christopher
    Morocco. – Rev. 2nd ed. – (Travellers' guide)
    1. Morocco – Description and travel – 1981–   – Guide-books
    I. Title   II. Richmond, John   III. Series
    916.4′045   DT304

ISBN 0-224-02393-4

Typeset by Computape (Pickering) Ltd, North Yorkshire
and printed in Great Britain by
Thomson Litho, East Kilbride, Scotland

CONTENTS

MAPS AND CHARTS

Acknowledgments

It is always impossible properly to thank all those who have helped one to an understanding of a country, however insufficient that may be. Often, you never even learn the names of people whose chance remarks you will particularly remember. This is more than ever the case with Moroccans because they are so forthcoming a people.

I received much intelligent aid from Moroccan officials. I hope they will feel it to have been worth their while to have given it me. But I would like also explicitly to thank those who, understanding the problems of a would-be guide-book writer, put themselves to much trouble to help me make it as good as possible. Moroccans and, as it were, 'old Moroccan hands' – what was always delightful about their help was its grounding in their pride for the country. Of these, the late A. Benjelloun-Touimi, A. Hajouji, A. Ouriaghli, Miss R. Bennis, Anthony Bent, Sydney Cooper and Christopher Wanklyn must claim special mention. It is a pleasure to own a debt of gratitude to Dr Thor Heyerdahl for advice and instruction on the megalithic structures at and near Lixus. And I would like John Shepherd to accept this book as a token of my gratitude for his sustaining enthusiasm and unending kindness.

The revision of 1981 called for renewed thanks to A. Hajouji, the Moroccan Ministry of Tourism and British Caledonian Airways.

CK

I hope that the reader will not find my amendments to Christopher Kininmonth's text too obtrusive. I should like to add my own acknowledgment of the assistance given by Rob Saunders of the British Embassy in Rabat and of the advice of Doug Scott.

JR

Chart of Excursions

City	Principal sights in city Major	Minor
TANGIER (1 day)	Dar el-Makhzen (Museum of Moroccan Arts) (Museum of Antiquities) Medina	Cape Malabata Cape Spartel Ksar es-Seghir Cotta
RABAT (2 days)	Casbah des Oudaïa (Museum of Moroccan Arts) Hassan Mosque and Tower Bab er-Rouah Bab ez-Zaër Chella Archaeological Museum Salé	Medina Great Mosque Dar el-Makhzen Bab el-Had
CASABLANCA (½ day)		Aquarium
MARRAKECH (2 days)	Koutoubia Mosque Medrassa ben Yussef Koubba el-Baroudiyin Saadi Necropolis el-Badi Palace Museum of Moroccan Arts (Dar Si' Saïd) Bab Aguenau Menara Gardens Markets Jemaa el-Fna	Casbah Mosque ben Salih Mosque el-Mouassine Mosque Bab Doukkala Mosque 'La Bahia' Palace Tanneries Agdal Gardens Walls
FES (2 days)	Dar el-Makhzen Dar Batha (Museum of Moroccan Arts) Medrassa 'bu Inania Medrassa el-Attarine Medrassa el-Misbahiya Medrassa es-Sebbayin Medrassa es-Sahrij el-Kairouyyin Mosque Zawiya Moulay Idriss Merinid Tombs	Medrassa es-Seffarin Medrassa ech-Cherratin el-Andalus Mosque Tanneries Walls Mellah Makina Msalla es-Sultan

INTRODUCTION

Any visitor travelling for a first time in Morocco is likely to be struck most by its unlikeliness to anywhere else he has been. Even should he be familiar with other North African countries he will find it so. This is mostly due to the extent to which, between at least the seventeenth and the twentieth centuries, Morocco has been isolated not only from Europe but from the rest of the Moslem world also. It was largely ignored even by that general and often romantic awareness of the world which Europeans developed during the nineteenth century. Hence its name does not conjure for us so precise and evocative an image as names like 'Siam', 'Afghanistan' or 'Montenegro' still can do

The customary shorthand references of guide-books − for instance, 'baroque' or 'bourgeois' − have scarcely any aptness to describe Moroccan things. Morocco has fallen out of step with European development since the expulsion from Spain of the Moslems and even such expressions as 'medieval' mean something rather different there; it is questionable whether such a term as 'aristocratic' could ever have been applied to the feudal masters of the country; 'southern' carries quite a different bouquet of images in Morocco from those it does in Europe. Not only this, but, since my guide must presuppose a readership drawn from a Christian culture and of European or American habits of thought − or experience − it has been necessary to revise somewhat the usual conventions for guide-books. Instead of accepting that the reader will be well informed as to background and in need only of gentle prods to his memory − 'since the descent of the Huns' is a favourite of this kind − I have had to attempt far more than is customary to explain how and why the country and its people are what they now are.

Morocco is a land of great and even extravagant scenic beauty. Mountains and plains on a huge scale; ocean coasts and Saharan wastes: these features have an explicit relevance to everything about the country in addition to their intrinsic fascination. In this magnificent and significant setting a quite strange − to *us* strange − and rather tumbledown society slowly expires while another, quite new, very individualistic and contemporary one develops to take the other's place. The new is vivid, at once evolutionary and revolutionary − not yet stable − and the old is extremely picturesque. The old is also now finally and irretrievably archaistic. It was not necessarily retrogressive while Morocco still preserved its isolation; then it was merely static, and perhaps inevitably atrophic. But since the French protectorate became established through the first four decades of this century the old ways were doomed. The vices of traditionalism were counterbalanced by its qualities; it is our good fortune that a measured revolution which aims to preserve the best while discarding the worst allows us to examine today the living past of Morocco. For us this must at present be the main 'touristic' attraction of that country.

The unlikeliness to other places brings out the explorer in one. The impact of all you find there is so exciting that it almost seems a pity to blunt it all by preparing oneself with a guide. But once he is there the interested traveller must be prompted to ask a host of questions deserving answers if for no other reason than that, in fairness to the Moroccans — who are of ancient civilization, proud, fierce, sensitive and sharply intelligent; not at all quaint — no myths or legends should be allowed to accrue because of their visitors' ignorance. In order to answer questions about Morocco I have had to try to learn — and sometimes to resort to awaiting inspiration — so that I could arrive at the answers which at least seem satisfactory to me. Therefore I have written this guide more personally than is usual — if you have any quarrel with what I have written it is with me alone.

The questions I have asked myself, and those that I am capable of imagining others may ask, have been too numerous all to be answered here. I have noticed, though, that in Morocco I tend more often to ask 'why' than 'what is that?' and because I believe the why-questions to be the more important I have concentrated upon answering them rather than the others. My suggested explanations are scattered throughout this volume — they could not be repeated each time they might be pertinent and, this being so, I have had to assume you will have the patience to read the introductory sections.

Of the transliteration of Arabic names into Roman script in a manner meaningful and phonetically correct, T. E. Lawrence commented, 'Arabic names won't go into English, exactly, for their consonants are not the same as ours, and their vowels, like ours, vary from district to district. There are some "scientific systems" of transliteration helpful to people who know enough Arabic not to need helping, but a wash-out for the world. I spell my names anyhow ...'

I have tried to adopt those spellings which newspapers have

made us familiar with — 'Nasser' (rather than 'Nusair'); 'Hussein' (although *The Times* has it 'Husain'); 'Mohammed' (rather than 'Muhammad') — but there are plenty of doubtful cases. A French rendering sometimes approximates better than English but I have tried to avoid using it since English-speaking readers cannot know when they are supposed to slip into it. Beyond this I can only do as Lawrence, spell them anyhow. Moroccan place-names are often of Berber origin (and the Berbers speak three dialects, two of which are mutually incomprehensible), so where a name of this kind will be quite unfamiliar I have followed the spelling used on the Michelin map most generally in use. This may not be quite the same as the signposts' spelling — both of course are gallicized versions — but they will not be so different as to cause you too much confusion.*

Both in my spelling of personal names and that of Frenchified place-names you should sound each vowel except in the case of 'ou', which sounds as 'oo' (e.g. in 'Essaouira'; 'Mediaouina'). The French cannot make up their minds how to spell a consonant in Berber which is sometimes halfway between a gutteral 'l' and an 'r': 'Tarhlremt' or 'Taghremt'; 'Tinerhir' or 'Tineghir' — in both cases the first version comes nearer, but is still miles off. 'Irgherm' has a warning, guttural look which seems to work. In general, you will not go far wrong if you sound 'a' nicely and roundly; 'Rabat' does not rhyme with 'hay bat', but with 'nab at' — so long, that is, as you speak the Queen's English, not Oxford vintage of the 'thirties; or Brooklynese or Yorkshire.

As everywhere else, perhaps the best way to travel in Morocco is by your own car. Buses are cheap and widespread but, apart from those linking the larger towns, they are too time-consuming a means of exploring the side-turnings for most people. So this guide has on the whole been written to be of most use to the motor-borne. The one disadvantage of driving your own car is that it tends to encourage one to stay aloof from the people: the *ideal* way to travel would be to bus over the major stages — for the sake of the company — and recklessly to hire cars for detours.

Have courage and do not be too afraid of indifferent road-surfaces; your car may be stronger than you tend to believe. Do not be afraid you will miss your bathing if you go into the interior. There are swimming-pools (*piscines*) practically everywhere

---

* Just at present, the signpost situation is a sorry one. Age is breaking up those set up in colonial times and their replacement by smart new ones has been halted by the exigencies of the desert war.

larger than a village, all the better hotels have them, and there are lakes in the mountains too. Be wary of the rivers, however; it is uncertain in which, exactly, the disease carrying bilharzia lurks.

It must be emphasized that this is not a complete guide to the country. The interesting, accessible places are described in some detail, the less interesting more briefly; the difficult parts to reach are touched upon; the practically inaccessible ones ignored. Not all roads are described in the itinerary sections, only those which are the most interesting or, like that comparatively dull one between Casablanca and Marrakech, those which you will be quite likely to travel for the sake of convenience.

Only brief mention is made of the two squalid Spanish colonies of Ceuta and Melilla, small intrusive enclaves upon Moroccan soil, trading-posts, useful ports and smuggling centres — but not yet parts of Morocco.

Finally, I should emphasize the great climatic changes which occur across the country. The north coast is purely Mediterranean in climatic type, though you are there on the receiving end of the wintry gales from which, generally, on the European coasts you are somewhat protected. The plains of 'inner' Morocco, where the big cities lie, have on the whole milder winters than the coast, certainly so down at Marrakech, but their summers are really hot and only on the Atlantic coast are there sea winds to temper the weight of the sun. The far south — the Sous valley and the Draa and Ziz — are clement in winter, summery in spring and a furnace in summer, usually; high places like Tinerhir can sometimes be blasted by icy winter winds which burn the palms. Snow fell on Erfoud in 1973, astonishing the inhabitants. Agadir, though, on the Atlantic, has a genuinely wonderful climate. It is, even, less windy than the more northerly ports though summer breezes can be counted on to keep the worst heat at bay. The high mountains of course have a climate all their own: fierce winters and wonderful, rather late springs, tempestuous autumn storms and still, diamond-sharp summers when the air at a centre such as Ifrane is like a benediction after the dry staleness of the plains.

The foregoing stands virtually unchanged since first this guide was written, yet the years between then and now have brought great changes to Morocco. The population has increased to an estimated seventeen million. A large proportion of this increase is ascribed to the new and prospering bourgeoisie — itself an expression of changed Morocco. It is therefore urban-based, or at least orientated towards the bigger towns, all of which have become greatly extended and industrialized. These people are less traditional in their outlook than their forebears, though they still respect the conventions of their Islamic society, at any rate outwardly. The old ruling class actively turns itself into a meritocracy (and continues in office), very much, incidentally, on the model of King Hassan II, a professional and practical monarch if ever there was one. Expanding industry, the modernization of agriculture and exploitation of natural resources, tourism – increased contact with foreigners – these all foster a change in mores among the people. In this Morocco shares with all the other developing, Moslem countries; theirs can be a cruel dilemma. Yet Islam is perhaps the religion which most encourages those civic virtues so needed during times of social transition. King Hassan is assiduous in emphasizing Morocco's Islamic character, and as yet there is no sign of any fundamentalist backlash, the traditional reaction to change in Islamic countries. And I think one should honour the fact that Moroccans have shown the least hostility towards their once large Jewish community of any Moslem country. Many rich Jews identify themselves with the country and flourish, though the poorer took fright and emigrated – it was less easy for them, probably, to make a clear distinction in their own minds (as in those of others less than well-educated amongst their neighbours) between Judaism and Zionism. King Hassan has actually invited their return and offered to assist it, their intelligence and skills being as welcome now as in the past.

In particular the creation of dams and newly irrigated areas, and extensive re-afforestation, has been altering the landscape in many parts (always hearteningly); industrialization and urbanization has created a kind of jeans-wearing artisan and proletarian section of the population; Morocco may be scenically even more beautiful than it was, but it is less obviously picturesque to our eyes. Deep in the medinas, or in the countryside (where, however, new and more commodious housing replaces the old *ksour*, which are sadly left for the weather to rot) is where the old Morocco is still to be found. Fortunately the bulk of foreigners visiting the country are either those new, tax-exempt demi-gods, the businessmen cloistered in the best hotels, or – to borrow Freya Stark's unkind definition – 'tourists, not travellers'. These come packaged together, insulated as if, otherwise, they might catch something shaming, riding high above the streets behind tinted windows and impassively staring at the natives they have no desire to understand while being conveyed from 'sight' to 'folkloric' event and back to the hotels whose pools they prefer to the open sea — cocooned in a sunny safety very dear to them. All that is done very well now, and at generally competitive prices: also it has the great advantage of keeping them out of the hair of those more bent upon travelling in this still intensely fascinating — moving, changing — country. Our guide-book is primarily designed for the latter category of visitor although we have left the really adventurous to get on with it unaided, as adventurers should.

At the time of writing, the Moroccan government is still engaged in a war with the Polisario over what was formerly Spanish Sahara (although skirmishing on the northern border between Algeria and Morocco suggests otherwise). While in 1979 Mauritania was obliged to agree terms and withdraw from the southern part of the territory, with so much prestige attached to the issue following the Green March of 1975, Morocco has built a system of defensive sand walls and patrols the area beyond the *cordon sanitaire* extensively. As long as Algeria continues to support Polisario, and the United States and France to support Morocco, this deadlock is likely to persist. Although travellers regularly visit Tan Tan and Laayoune, it would be prudent to take advice from the Foreign Office before setting out for the extreme south and south-east.

GETTING TO MOROCCO

AIR

Royal Air Maroc operates four times a week from London (Heathrow) to Agadir, Casablanca, Marrakech and Tangier with many connections to inland destinations. Royal Air Maroc shares routes with European carriers to most European capitals and also flies to the Americas, the Middle East and parts of Africa. British Caledonian ordinarily serves Morocco but does not exercise that right at present.

Cheap flights and packages are offered by many British firms whose names can be found in the classified section of the newspapers. Late booking may secure a bargain but in high season you may be disappointed. Take care to confirm your return flight 72 hours prior to leaving as R.A.M. flies aeroplanes at capacity. Flying to Gibraltar and taking a ferry or flight to Tangier is often cheaper than a direct flight (for Gib-Air, Gibraltar Travel Ltd., 24 New Broadway, London W5).

SEA

Direct sea connections between the U.K. and Morocco, and the U.S.A. and Morocco are now very few and far between. Fred Olsen Lines run a service from the U.K. which calls at Agadir approximately twice monthly from September through to May. It is also worth inquiring about passenger-carrying cargo boats.

Morocco's sea connections with Spain and Gibraltar are frequent and varied: Limadet run a twice-weekly ferry between Malaga and Tangier; Bland Line between Gibraltar and Tangier; Transmediterranea run several daily sailings between Algeciras and Tangier or Ceuta; all these carry cars. There is a Spanish ship which plies between Malaga and Melilla, calling at the tiny islands which Spain still holds.

There are also regular sailings between Marseilles and Casablanca, and between Sete and Tangier.

It is always a good thing to book well in advance for the longer sea hauls, but the ferries run what are virtually walk-on walk-off services. If you are taking a car, however, it is best to book ahead in high season through Melia Travel, 12 Dover Street, London W1 (tel. 01-409 1884).

RAIL

The most convenient rail connection between Morocco and the Continent has its terminal at Paris (Gare d'Austerlitz). This Sud Express takes forty-eight hours to reach Casablanca, going by Bordeaux, Madrid, Algeciras and Tangier.

ROAD

It is a long way — about 2,000 miles — from Britain to Tangier, but a pleasant drive. Anyone in a hurry will scarcely make it under four days, since the water crossings cause delays. There are, of course, various ways of ferrying your car over part of the journey: by flying from Britain to France, taking car-sleeper passage to Biarritz, and from Madrid to Algeciras; see Sea (above) for car ferries. The crossing from Gibraltar is usually the most convenient, though one can also cross from Algeciras or Malaga.

Those who intend to travel in a heavy vehicle, including Land Rovers, may encounter difficulties on entry at Ceuta and Tangier and it is advisable to consult the Moroccan Embassy in London prior to departure.

Coach services do operate to Morocco but are in general not a bargain compared even with air travel. Of more interest are some overland packages using Land Rovers and, occasionally, converted buses, camping en route. This makes possible access to remote regions without the attendant expense and risk of an individual expedition.

DOCUMENTS

A currently valid passport is required, though no visa is necessary for citizens of the United States or bearers of British passports inscribed at the bottom *United Kingdom of Great Britain and Northern Ireland*, or *Jersey*, *Guernsey and its Dependencies*, or the *Isle of Man*, or *Gibraltar*.

Moroccan immigration officials may refuse entry to holders of passports with evidence of travel to Israel or South Africa. In Britain a Regional Passport Office will usually issue a fresh passport to those affected.

If you take your car with you, you will need your international driving licence and green card insurance certificate, including a reference to Morocco. Personal and vehicle documentation must correspond perfectly.

VACCINATION

No certificates are required for entry to Morocco. It is sensible for travellers to consult their family doctor about immunization. Morocco is considered by the World Health Organization to be within the malaria risk area but few travellers take precautions, nor is the threat of bilharzia (*schistosomiasis*) in southern waters regarded with concern. It would be wise though to guard against typhoid.

TRAVEL IN MOROCCO

AIR

Royal Air-Inter links Agadir, Al-Hoceima, Casablanca, Fes, Laayoune, Meknes, Marrakech, Ouarzazate, Oujda, Rabat, Tangier, Tan Tan and Tetuan — at quite moderate rates.

There are numerous airfields open to private aircraft; for information apply to La Fédération Aéronautique du Maroc, 8 Rue de la Seine, Le Polo, Casablanca.

RAIL

Travel by rail is comfortable as the faster trains are air-conditioned, though the lines are few. Trains run from Tangier to Rabat and Casablanca, branching at Sidi Kacem to Meknes, Fes, Taza and Oujda — then on into Algeria. Also there is a line from Casablanca to Marrakech with branch lines to Oued Zem and Safi. There is a bar of some sort on most trains. Fares are very reasonable indeed. Apart from the normal reductions on Transalpino fares to and from Morocco, travellers under 26 can use Inter-Rail Cards for travel within Morocco and most sea crossings (Transalpino, 71–5 Buckingham Palace Road, London SW1, and at large British Rail stations with Travel Centres).

BUSES

In general these leave one main town for another at least twice a day, with more frequent connections between the principal towns and fewer between out-of-the-way places. Time-tables are available at bus stations. Fares are cheap; on some services there are Pullman coaches for which the price is slightly higher — one such is the overnight Pullman du Sud from Casablanca to Goulimine. The services are generally fast, the vehicles comfortable and journeys well organized. It is an excellent way to travel the country.

We give the addresses of the C.T.M. bus station in the principal towns. Lesser bus companies' garages are usually near by.

TAXIS

A sensible division has been made between mini and major taxis in all the larger towns. The cheap mini (*petit*) taxis may only ply within the city limits and not carry more than three passengers; the bigger ones carry five passengers and go any distance, and are quite a bit more expensive. All are metered, but not all the meters always work. Always negotiate the fare beforehand, and if you intend to spend any time in the city inquire at the local office of O.N.M.T. for a tariff. There is the usual, international racket at airports and arriving passengers should beat the sharks by taking the airport bus. Where horse cabs are available, these are not metered; the fare is comparable to that for a *petit taxi*. Tipping is not customary.

GUIDES

Official guides can be had on application to the local tourist offices, and for reasonable rates, though these vary from one town to another. Beyond leading you to the right places during opening hours, too few are adequate. (One is reminded that until recently nepotism was the sole principle of recruitment to all grades of the old *makhzen* civil services.) But recently young men of education and special training have been recruited for this work; ask for one of these. Often the bright children who offer themselves prove more entertaining guides than the official old retainers, but their information is suspect. The motorcycling tourist-trappers should be avoided at all cost.

MOTORING

Car Hire
To hire a self-drive car is quite possible in Morocco, but also quite

unusually expensive; the deposits and kilometre rates are high. Some people find it useful to make a private deal with a taxi owner-driver. It might also be worth inquiring about the possibility of hiring a Land-Rover, especially in Marrakech, for expeditions into the Sahara.

PETROL
Super-grade petrol costs about as much as in Britain.

ROADS
Roads are mostly of good quality and well engineered. Driving is on the right and road signs conform to international usage. The traffic police and highway patrols are strict and make no distinctions between native and foreigner. The rule giving precedence to vehicles entering a flow of traffic to its right from uncontrolled turnings is implicitly − not to say aggressively − observed. Vehicles entering the flow on roundabouts enjoy priority.

Travel on these roads is surprisingly fast. In a reasonably heavy and ordinarily fast car one can drive from Tangier to Marrakech by Casablanca in a day (Casablanca to Marrekech, 230 kilometres, can be driven in under two hours in a really fast car, while the sea at Essaouira can be reached from Marrakech in one and a half hours). Marrakech to Fes by Beni Mellal, and from Fes to Oujda, are also a day's not difficult drive.

Naturally all the mountain-roads are slower than those on the plains. Real care should be taken on curving mountain-roads if there is gravel on the bends − it gets washed down from the friable rock − since this is as easy to skid upon as ice. Should a pass be blocked by snow or landslide the police put up notices at the start of the road leading to it. Although petrol is not a problem, it is best always to fill up when one can in wilder parts.

TRACKS
In the far south it is tempting to visit the oases. They are mostly very beautiful to see. But the tracks are bad − worst when they have been laid with broken rocks. They can, however, be taken by a stout car with a good clearance, though a wise driver will have water, rations, compass, plenty of tools, wire, rubber piping, extra petrol cans and tyres in case of emergencies on such little-frequented *pistes*. A four-wheel drive would be altogether more confidence-inspiring. It is advisable to report to the local authorities as you set off and ask them to telephone ahead so that

if you do not turn up they can go looking for you. There are usually guest quarters in the civil authorities' buildings where you can stay, sometimes very primitively. Some oases have rudimentary inns also. Treks of this kind are exciting, fairly tough and not to be undertaken rashly. While the desert war continues, travel among the southern oases may prove more dangerous than exciting. The Polisario have captured foreign travellers, and, in the past, released them in Algeria. While the Moroccan government insists that no part of the country is closed to tourists, you will require (and almost invariably receive) written permission from the local military command for travel beyond southern checkpoints, for example Tan Tan and Zagora.

While some of the roads in the pre-Sahara are still unmetalled, it is necessary to hold strictly to them in wet weather, though when dry the going is apt to be easier on the parallel earth-tracks — take the one with the freshest heavy-lorry tracks. These are, however, sometimes pitted with mantrap-size pot-holes often invisible under the dust. Never allow yourself to lose speed or driving-power in mud or loose sand. Rain, by the way, though very rare in this part, usually comes alarmingly in cloud-bursts when it does appear.

MAPS

The O.N.M.T. provide free pamphlets on Fes, Meknes, Marrakech, Agadir, Casablanca and Rabat-Sale with a plan of major routes and sights. Unfortunately they lack the detail of the 1979 Éditions Gauthey series, now rather hard to come by. Even armed with an accurate map, a complex medina, like that of Fes, where many of the streets are unnamed, will defeat the most competent navigator. Follow the plans in this book and where necessary employ a guide.

There are useful large-scale road maps. Michelin, sheet 169 (1:1 million), is good but currently unobtainable. Within Morocco, the General Tyre and Rubber Co. *Carte Routière Maroc* (1:1·5 million) is all that is available and is definitely inferior to *Roger Lascelles' Morocco* (1:800,000/1:2·5 million), Hallwag's *Maroc Canaries* (1:1 million) or Kümmerly & Frey's *Morocco* (1:1 million). For travel to remote parts on *piste*, the *Moroccan Survey Sheets* (1:50,000 or 1:100,000) can be obtained from Stanford's Map Centre, 12 Long Acre, Covent Garden, London WC2, or McCarta, 122 King's Cross Road, London WC1.

HOTELS AND RESTAURANTS

HOTELS AND OTHER ACCOMMODATION

From luxury hotels — really luxurious — to caravanserais where you take your mat and find stalling for your animals, all of them are beautifully clean in Morocco. As a tourist you will be expected to want to stay your side of the fence, though there is nothing to prevent your 'going native' if you want. There are economic advantages in doing so, but a loss in creature comforts. The very good hotels compare with their peers elsewhere. I quarrel with the price of drinks in them — as I do with those in all places in Morocco where they expect the bulk of the custom to be foreign.

All the acceptable hotels in the country are classified. Those whose names appear in this guide-book (under the entry for the towns in which they are situated) are taken from the official lists at the time of printing and it is more than likely that these will have very shortly been added to, while others may have been reclassified. There is considerable variation within categories; the names of several hotels worth avoiding have been omitted here, but on the other hand a few unclassified *pensions* (such as the *Hôtel Continental* in Tangier) have been given a special mention. (Arm yourself with the latest lists from the Moroccan National Tourist Office, though these no longer list lower category lodgings.) Official classification carries with it acceptance of maximum prices chargeable according to the rooms chosen — single, double, with or without bath, demi- and full pension or room only — and an agreement on the part of the management that those prices shall be inclusive of taxes and service. Only the category of five-star hotels is absolved from these restrictions but the publication of official lists has persuaded the managements of these to publicize their prices also — though these are *less* tax and service of course.

For some time it was possible to criticize the quality of service and food in the general category of first-class hotels — now ****A or B — but the Moroccan Government has been taking very severe measures to remedy this. One does not want to be a difficult visitor, but in cases like this it is a genuine public service to complain where the complaint is justified. Much attention is currently being paid to the provision of far more new three- and two-star hotels so that Morocco will become opened up to a less

Maximum prices for hotel accommodation including service, in Dirhams

GRADE OF HOTEL	ROOM WITH BATH OR SHOWER				ROOM WITH DOUCHE AND WASHBASIN		WASHBASIN ONLY		EXTRA BED	BREAK-FAST	3-COURSE MENU
	With W.C.		Without W.C.								
	1 person	2 people	1 person	2 people	1 person	2 people	1 person	2 people			
****A	167	214	137	179	107	130	–	–	45	18	65
****B	140	174	114	141	89	111	–	–	45	18	60
***A	107	130	84	106	63	81	–	–	40	14	50
***B	92	114	73	92	53	71	–	–	40	14	50
**A	77	90	60	72	45	59	36	45	25	10	40
**B	60	74	49	60	40	49	35	41	25	10	40
*A	55	64	43	55	35	43	30	40	22	9	35
*B	44	56	38	46	30	40	29	38	22	9	35

well-off kind of visitor – and particularly to families who want things to be nice but who cannot afford to stay *en masse* in the more expensive hotels. From all points of view, the Moroccan tourist authorities are proving very imaginative in the ways they are developing the industry without ruining the countryside or the seashores. They show themselves quick to learn by mistakes already made elsewhere and no less quick to recognize their own.

Hoteliers have to maintain good service; otherwise their establishments may be downgraded, in which case they are obliged to apply the maximum price fixed for the lower-grade hotel. It must be emphasized that the Government has fixed the maximum prices, not the prices themselves. This means that actual prices will generally be below the maximum because of the competition which exists between hotels of the same standard.

PENSIONS

These exist in the new quarters of the new towns. They should be sought *in situ*.

VILLAS AND PRIVATE HOUSES

In the larger towns these are available to rent, or indeed to buy. It is far more sensible and economical to find them on the spot.

Though agents (e.g. Brompton Travel, 206 Walton Street London sw3) handle villas in Tangier and elsewhere in Morocco, if you ask the waiters in the more obvious cafés of a town they will soon produce mysterious middlemen whose business it is to put vendor and lessor in touch with potential clients. A deal can be fixed in a very few days if only a short renting is involved, and you know exactly what you are getting.

Self-catering accommodation (twin bed studios and apartments) is available in Agadir, Tangier, Restinga Smir (near Tetouan) and Al-Hoceima. Information from the Moroccan Tourist Office. Hire of servants is cheap and easy to arrange.

HOLIDAY VILLAGES

These establishments are on the increase, the Government encouraging them. We list them under those towns near which they exist at present.

YOUTH HOSTELS

Youth hostels in Morocco offer very inexpensive accommodation to visitors. There are hostels in Asni, Azrou, Casablanca, Fes, Ifrane, Meknes, Marrakech and Rabat.

CAMPING

This once gipsy-like, insouciant way of spending a holiday is in Morocco, as everywhere else, now ghetto-ed into encampments anywhere in the region of civilization. Camping grounds proliferate in the main tourist resorts. New ones are also being equipped. Information available from Moroccan Tourist Office.

Away from these organized 'campings' there is still plenty of room in Morocco for a caravan to stop or a tent to be pitched. But where there is water there are usually houses and the would-be solitary is perforce involved in society. Experienced campers advise others always to put themselves under the protection of the local police (who will want you to fill out their wretched *fiches* in any case). They are helpful, have water and often shower-baths, and will keep the curious from pestering you. The vicinity of police stations is rarely, however, sylvan.

RESTAURANTS AND FOOD

Apart from the hotels there are some very excellent restaurants in Morocco. These are usually run by Frenchmen who have not as yet lowered their standards and upped their prices drastically as their compatriots at home have. There are restaurants in the modern quarters of Rabat, Casablanca and Marrakech that are particularly good, as are those in Meknes, Mohammedia, Beni Mellal, Midelt, Taza and Oujda. There are also several restaurants on the coasts which serve delicious fish dishes. The fish restaurant by the beach at Essaouira is still memorable, the smaller hotel at Oualidia not a bad second to it. But specific recommendations can be invidious; who knows when something will happen to change a place? And there may be many others which we have not had occasion to try. In both Ceuta and Melilla there are excellent Spanish restaurants.

The Moroccan kitchen is the least known of the world's great and subtle cuisines. It is the visitor's misfortune that most of the tourist-baited, so-called 'Moroccan' restaurants are traps of the sorriest sort, while the ordinary little restaurants in the old towns neither boast nor set out to provide *la haute cuisine marocaine*. They do, however, often provide interesting and appetizing meals, and they should certainly be tried, particularly in Fes, where cooking reflects the city's long leadership of the country's cultural life. Other good spots for sampling local food — kebabs and other savoury things to nibble — are near bus stations, railway stations and markets. It is in Marrakech that the best Moroccan food is available to the well-heeled tourist. *La Maison Arabe*, where you must book ahead and preferably discuss the menu, is good. It is expensive, and you get scant value unless you go in a fairly large party since the proprietress, a French lady, charges a set price per head and serves one dish per head less one — i.e. one dish between two, two between three and so on — when a good dinner requires at least four dishes from which all diners eat their portions. The setting is bogus, the cooking, although somewhat adapted from the genuine Fasi,* can be excellent, although recently the standard has become uncertain. The Moroccan restaurant in the Hotel Mamounia is currently considered the best.

* Adjective derived from Fes; also a man of Fes.

Meal-times in French restaurants are pleasantly late, in Moroccan ones practically round the clock — the *Maison Arabe* by appointment, evenings only.

Moroccan food must have come from as many places as the people themselves and it is most necessary to differentiate between country cooking, with the poorer townsman's too, and the sophisticated *haute cuisine* of the rich.

The former is naturally simple, generally mutton or chicken (sometimes camel) for the meat, *couscous* and bread for bulk, beans, root vegetables, greens and rice for special occasions. It is rarely thrown together anyhow, however, but slowly cooked, spiced and made interesting with herbs. Contrasted tastes are often featured in the same dish, most often piquant or bitter with something very bland.

Not very adventurous food of this kind is what you will most likely find in cheap native restaurants like those near markets in the medinas. And good it often is, too, even though, unless it is offal, the meat is more often tough than not. To this category belong the ubiquitous '*brochettes*' of which there are three main sorts. *Boulfaf* is bits of veal or sheep's liver skewered and grilled over charcoal and strewn with cummin. You will meet this on street stalls where it is invariably served with a hot sauce for dipping into, and it is usually better done there than in restaurants, being somehow fresher and more briskly done. *Kebab* is a grander version of boulfaf, being made of fillet of beef or lamb, marinated, spiced, grilled with interlarding fat and onion; *kefta* (grilled rissoles) is the third variety, which, to be really good, should properly come from a superior kind of kitchen.

The *haute cuisine* primarily represents a memory of el-Andalus in its luxurious days. See above for your chances of sampling it. Mme Guinaudeau's *Fes Vu Par Sa Cuisine* (See Bibliography) gives scores of recipes for *touajen*, the stewed or steamed dishes which are the staples of this kitchen. Traditionally cooked over a small charcoal brazier in a thick, shallow earthenware, covered plate, the ingredients of a *tajine* — olive oil or butter and very little liquid, spiced meat to which vegetables are added when their times come — are very gently rendered tender and then usually added to piled-up couscous (a freshly made, granulated pasta) or rice, and kept hot under a basket-weave cone covered with red leather. Since the spices and herbs in active use in a Moroccan kitchen run into dozens, the possibilities for diversification among *touajen* are almost limitless and, indeed, there are humble countryman's sorts and every gradation upwards in cost and complexity thereafter.

Rich cooking in Morocco is even more notable for the trimmings. The starter dish for parties, for instance, is the *b'stilla*, a pie of pigeon meat cooked with cinnamon in a crisp crust of finest flaky pastry thoroughly sprinkled with icing sugar: unbelievably delicious. Sweets play an important part, a basis of honey and almonds being a favourite. You should shop in a pastrycook's if you get the chance. Excellent soups, fruit drinks, the tea that ends the meal, distillations of flowers, *majoun*: this kitchen is as grand and has been as inventively, carefully and lovingly thought about as any in the world.

In 'European' restaurants you seem rarely to find any but hack *touajen*, but more or less authentic versions of chicken with almonds or chicken with lemons are often on the menu. The last is generally more successful since it is simple to do and chiefly depends for its taste on the use of salted lemons — a very great culinary invention.

You might just strike it lucky in the mountains and get a chance to eat *mishoui*, a whole roast animal, most often a sheep, such as is prepared for festivals.

Festivals, in fact, are generally celebrated with special dishes, each traditional to the season, and even with a succession of meals over the festive period; but it is a sad thing that because you are probably not a Moslem few Moroccans can be persuaded to believe you would like to eat foods closely associated in their minds with religious feasts. An exception to be found in many simple food shops is *harira*, soup. There is an infinite number of variations of *harira*, but one of the most soothing to the tired is always what the establishment reckons to be its Ramadan soup — the dish with which the day's fasting is traditionally broken at nightfall. Usually based upon lamb and coriander-flavoured, laced with lemon, it is creamy and very digestible.

DRINK

Water is invariably nice to taste — marvellous often in the mountains — and safe to drink. There is, however, a great sale of excellent local mineral waters, drinking which constitutes a harmless and profitable *snobbisme*. *Oulmes* is sparkling and, so the label boasts, radioactive. *Sidi Ali* and *Sidi Harazem* are still and neutral in taste but still welcome when neither alcohol nor coffee will provide sufficient volume to quench desiccating thirst.

The drink of the country is mint tea, made with plenty of sugar in a pot stuffed with fresh sprigs of mint. It is most refreshing and very cheap. Moroccans are also addicted to revoltingly sweet fizzy drinks; however, there is a pleasant, not too sweet orange drink called Judor.

There is schizophrenia in the country about alcoholic drinks. Good Moslems will not drink them; rebellious ones adore them; lapsing ones do not see why they should not drink them. By law, no alcoholic beverages may be sold by the bottle to *Moroccan* Moslems, although a Moroccan Moslem may now hold a licence to sell them. The French and Spanish occupying powers both drank and produced alcoholic beverages. They have left a legacy of manly drinking among service personnel and the ruling classes that is at odds with the policies these uphold. Cafés are numerous, often even in small places, at quite a lot of which Moroccans are served alcohol without question. As a foreigner you will have no difficulty in being served wherever drink is availabe, but in the remoter parts it grows scarce. South of Agadir it is best to travel well provided, although here and there Jewish grocer shops sell beer, wine and *pastis* when not shut because of religious holidays. As a foreigner, too, there is no difficulty about your buying bottles at grocers' shops.

Moroccan wine is of a remarkably good quality if in general a little heavy. It is comparatively cheap and it should never be necessary to drink the cheapest and poorest brands. Among the red wines, Cabernet is quite drinkable, if tart; Bled and Tarik are better. Better yet are the very light rosé wines, Gris de Gerrouane and Gris de Boulaouane. The local lager-type beers are agreeable enough and the Moroccan-made *pastis* as good as that made anywhere. All imported drinks are comparatively expensive, although, bought by the bottle, they are still cheaper than in self-punitive Britain; tots work out about the same in bars, though not those of hotels.

There is no clear ruling about licensing hours, many places being open all day and closing at 23.00 hours − after which you must repair to discos or night clubs and almost always pay very dearly for your persistence.

PRACTICAL INFORMATION

CLIMATE AND CLOTHES

Something has been said about climate from the visitor's point of view in the Introduction (see p. 18).

Since Morocco is a country of mountains, plains, seaboards and deserts, the climate is extremely diverse. In general, all the land north and west of the Atlas Mountains, including the Rif massif, conforms to the Mediterranean type of climate. This is, of course, locally modified by latitude, altitude, proximity to or distance from the Atlantic coast (sea winds make this a fresher part in summer). The interior grows really hot and stifling — though very dry — in midsummer, while the seaboards and the mountain resorts remain delightful. South and east of the mountains the climate is Saharan — very dry and very hot indeed, but in winter cold at night. Though snow lies thickly on the high mountains in winter, there is little permanent snow. In the late autumn and through the short winter one must be prepared for rain.

It follows that you should judge what clothing to take according to the season and the parts you intend to visit. In summer dress lightly, though if you intend going up the mountains take a cardigan or pullover. Some sort of head-covering is sensible in the Saharan regions, if not elsewhere. In spring and autumn you may need protection against rain and sudden chill. In winter you do not need heavy clothing, but may occasionally want to wrap up — naturally so if you are making for the ski resorts.

HEALTH

Except in the remotest parts you need not fear there will be no doctor should you require one. Perhaps the most skilled are more likely to be found in the larger towns, as also the best-equipped hospitals. If you are ailing it may be wise to make for the local provincial capital at least. There is no reciprocal arrangement with the British National Health Service, so you must pay for medical attention. Inexpensive insurance schemes exist to cover this contingency.

In the event of ill health, the local tourist office should be able to provide a list of English- or French-speaking doctors and the address of a duty pharmacy.

TOURIST INFORMATION

The exploitation of Morocco's very great tourist potential is controlled by the Government through the energetic and imaginative Ministry of Tourism. The ministry has set up the O.N.M.T. (Office National Marocain du Tourisme) which has branches in the major cities and abroad where inquiries on all aspects of tourism in the country can be made. O.N.M.T. addresses are given under the entries for the towns where they are situated: the London office is at 174 Regent Street, W1R 6HB, the New York at 521 Fifth Avenue, N.Y. 10017.

MUSEUMS AND MONUMENTS

The individual times of admission and prices of entry are given under the appropriate entries for these. In general, the prices are minimal and no concessions are offered to students or large parties.

MOSQUES

To anyone used to travel in the rest of the Moslem world, saving only Saudi Arabia, it is tantalizing not to be allowed to enter any of the mosques or shrines in Morocco. This is particularly trying to a student of architecture, but bear it he must. It is not at all wise to attempt even to venture into the doorway of a mosque in the process of building; in the countryside it could be suicidal to enter a shrine.

However, the Merinid Medersa 'bu Inania in Fes (p. 251), the prayer-hall of which is still in use as a mosque, *is* open to infidel visitors as far as the lattice screen across the hall. And for some reason the Fasi is less averse than other Moroccans to being seen at prayer; the doors of the great and beautiful mosques of Fes stand open and it is possible to see much of their interiors even without seeming too inquisitive or impious while lingering on their thresholds.

The old *medrassa* of Fes and elsewhere, when not being restored, are open to visitors since they are no longer in use as theological colleges.

It is customary to give something (a dirham is usual) to the keepers of places for which no entrance charge is made.

BANKS AND CURRENCY

The Moroccan dirham is not freely exchangeable. Its current rate is therefore artificial, and expensively so to foreigners. As in France, people are still apt to be reluctant to count in anything except 'old' francs — with consequent fluttering in innocent breasts at times, as when a thousand francs is demanded in place of a hundred. In effect 1·65 DH will be called either '165 francs' or '1 dirham 65 francs'. You should check exchange rates with your bank as they are subject to considerable fluctuation. Better hotels, of course, change travellers' cheques — some restaurants and shops will too — but generally it is better to go to a bank. These are open from 8.30 to 11.30 in the mornings and again in the afternoons from 15.00 to 17.30. They shut on Saturdays and Sundays, and on many holidays, Moslem, Jewish, Christian and national. Do not count on it that there will be a bank in the smaller towns. The Banque Commerciale du Maroc is less time-consuming than the Banque Nationale du Maroc as a place to change money, while some others have special exchange counters and *bureaux de change* exist in the bigger tourist centres. Credit cards still cause consternation. American Express, Visa and Diners Club are accepted in roughly descending order. Access has almost no currency outside a few hotels, restaurants and shops, mostly in Tangier — it cannot be used to secure a cash advance. B.M.C.E. will advance cash against Visa however. A further irritation is a supplement of up to 7 per cent charged by some traders on credit transactions. The Eurocheque system is widely understood and even in the south, which is poorly served by banks, it is a useful source of money (currently a maximum of 1,000 DH a day). As a crude guide to finding banks, look for the main street in the new town, often as not named after Mohammed V.

On entering the country one is handed a foreign-currency declaration-form on which all amounts changed must be entered by the changer if the exchange value of his money is 5,000 DH or more. This is claimed from you upon departure. It is illegal to import or export Moroccan currency, and it should be realized that nobody will change dirhams officially into any other currency outside Morocco. Even the Gibraltarian black market gives derisory prices. Change any you have, therefore, before leaving the country. The *bureaux de change* at airports, by the way, rarely open outside ordinary business hours and will usually only sell you French francs. As only 25 per cent of currency exchanged can be reconverted, keep your bank receipts or declaration form.

SHOPPING AND SOUVENIRS

Shops on the whole open early and keep pretty late hours. They take a good siesta, however.

Locally made cigarettes are cheap (about 50p for twenty) and good, especially if you like 'black' tobacco. Imported brands — the most popular English, American and French are available in all sizeable places — are considerably more expensive.

The needs of traditional Moroccan life are supplied, as they have always been, by local craftsmen, only luxury goods being imported. These traditional crafts are supported by the Government and perhaps rather too much pushed under the noses of visitors. The attraction of the markets — *souks* — whether the permanent ones in the towns (where, too, there are whole quarters devoted to one craft or another and one may shop direct from the makers) or the country ones that are usually held once a week, is such that it is inconceivable that any visitor should ignore them. However, there is extra profit to be made in many ways, by hotel-keepers whose entrance halls are cluttered with poufs and camel saddles and by the owners of large, brazenly glittering stores made richly colourful with displays of carpets and caftans, not to mention itinerant vendors who never take no for an answer. It takes character to pass the tourist shops in the markets — your guide, official or not, will lead your steps inexorably to them since he hopes for his cut. Needless to say, buy where your fancy takes you, but if you can make some respectable local friend he may help you to find good-quality stuff and drive an honest bargain. You will in any case pay more than a Moroccan would. It is a very poor country where competition is lethal and your most honest friend owes his compatriots a stronger loyalty than he does you.

There is a seemingly endless optimism about all this output of handicrafts; its basis is not your trade but the lively local market. It follows that there is in all trades a range of products of varied quality and cost. What is shoved under your nose is rarely of high quality, though often highly priced. A not very observant eye can immediately discern this, although too few evidently do. It must be said too that workmanship of a princely quality grows sadly rare since the old, aristocratic, let alone the moneyed, market has been dwindling in the face of occidentalization. And the tradition behind these crafts has for too long been too static; doing the same thing for centuries is inevitably stultifying and boring, and the workmanship loses its edge. There is too much sense of deadening repetition about most of these products, and scarcely ever a sense of creation — save with the carpets. Among these, with patience, you can find examples of creativity within the framework of the various, often very local traditions.

Many shops purport to be antiquarian. Very little among their wares is older than the century — but then only sixty years ago Morocco was living in the seventeenth century. The ubiquitous long-barrelled rifles, the silver-chased pistols, were used forty years ago; all southerners still wear silver-sheathed daggers and carry decorated leather pouches under their outer garments, their women wear heavy silver jewellery inset with amber and gold filigree earrings or bracelets. But it is rare indeed to find objects belonging to the old days when really fine quality was demanded by the better-off. Attentive visits to the folk art museums of Fes, Meknes, Marrakech, Tangier and Rabat will train your eye to spot these. None the less, such things are discoverable; the hunt is worth while. Fine barbaric jewellery can still be had in the far south. Most of the big amber beads are plastic and none save experts seem to be able to tell one from t'other.

The sale in the high mountains, usually by vociferous children, of lumps of crystal, amethyst and other semi-precious stones can be a snare. Such is the gullibility of many that these stones are often preposterously dyed. Some are cunningly tinted. But it is not really very hard to spot the true from the false, and pointless to make a fool of yourself even for a few pence mis-spent. For a couple of dollars or a pound sterling you can acquire a reasonable piece of amethyst.

Good buying must be a matter of some knowledge and considerable patience, certainly of bargaining. Find the best craftsmen if you want anything made to your order — and if you must wear native clothes, have them made to measure by good tailors; I am afraid you will be unlikely to be able to wear them with the conviction and grace you have admired in Moroccans.

If all this sounds discouraging, take heart that the materials are excellent; leather, wool, beautiful cedar-wood, some marvellous silks from Fes (where the most traditional designs are still the best), very serviceable earthenware, splendid matting of various kinds (that used for lining the walls of mosques particularly perhaps), brass, copper, soft silver.

Carpets made and sold at the several regional Government-sponsored centres are excellent. They are sold by the density of the knotting and at regulated prices. No need to bargain here.

Co-opartim and official *Artinisat* shops also exist; the goods sold in them are of officially guaranteed quality, and their prices fixed and marked.

Spices are a temptation in the markets redolent with their heavy smells. They do not keep well for long, so do not buy in bulk. It is quite hard to find genuine saffron, and not outstandingly cheap when you do. A delicious, useful and exotic thing to buy, difficult to obtain elsewhere, is *ras el-hanout*, hard, irregular-shaped nuts like root ginger powdered with saffron yellow. It is made of pepper, curry, cinnamon, bird's tongue, saffron, egg white and aubergine, and you grate it to use. This does keep well.

Well worth seeking out are tins of white truffles which cost only a few pounds for a kilogramme, tins of *argan* oil in the south, as well as the usual olive oil, and the delectable fat olives of all shades preserved with lemon, garlic and chili.

Country markets are often held in compounds set away from, though centred upon, the villages they serve. These are often called after the days of the week upon which they are held, thus:

> *Souk* el-had, i.e. the first: Sunday,
> *Souk et-tnine*, i.e. the second: Monday,
> *Souk et-tleta*, i.e. the third: Tuesday,
> *Souk el-arba*, i.e. the fourth: Wednesday,
> *Souk el-khemis*, i.e. the fifth: Thursday,
> *Souk es-sebt*, i.e. the sixth: Saturday.

On Friday, the Moslem day of rest, markets are rarely held, with the notable exception of *Souk el-Gour* near Meknes (see p. 267). (Friday is called, as mosques are, 'the assembly' — *el-djemaa*.)

These *souks* are delightful to visit. In many cases also, of course, a village is big enough to have its own weekly market, or the market has become the rallying-point about which a village has grown. Wherever possible we give the day of the week on which these villages hold their markets since they constitute one

---

* Meaning 'market'.

of the very real pleasures of travel in the countryside. Many of the wares offered may be fairly uniform, but there are none the less quite considerable regional differences, both of type and local products, which it is fascinating to note.

TIPPING

The Continental habit of adding service to bills and expecting a supplementary tip in cash prevails except in hotels. Where someone renders you a service outside the course of his duty it is easy and kind to be generous — and in a country where a man can live on five dirhams a day, and where very many have the greatest difficulty in finding them, your small change is a windfall to him. Two or three dirhams for the hotel porter, any small change to waiters (on top of the 15 per cent service charge) and a dirham for airport and railway porters should suffice.

Islam attaches a special importance to giving alms and it seems churlish not to be charitable, while as a foreign visitor one is wealthy beyond the dreams of Morocco's poor.

PHOTOGRAPHY

Simple Moroccans have as strong an aversion to being photographed as the sophisticated have a passion for it. In the countryside one should be ready to desist with a quick apology if need be. And never, ever, attempt to photograph a woman. In the towns where tourists are everyday phenomena it is different.

Equipment, films of all sorts, are available in the big towns and simple requirement can be found in the smaller.

SPORT

Football is the national passion. And swimming, and basket-ball. Opportunities for out-door sports are encouraged by the authorities who seek constantly to attract international events to this country which by climate and variety of terrain can provide perfect conditions for almost all types of sport.

BATHING

The types of beaches and the kinds of amenities available on certain of these are given in the town descriptions. All sizeable towns in the interior have municipal swimming-pools; the better hotels also.

It must be said that bathing off the Atlantic coast is not safe in the way that it is off the Mediterranean coast. It is no more dangerous than Atlantic bathing off the British Isles or France, Spain or Portugal, and no less so. But because it is so warm people are apt to forget about ocean currents and big swells, to their peril.

UNDERWATER FISHING

The Moroccan waters are rich in fish of all sorts since the colder-water fish travel down so far south on cool currents while tropical ones move up on warmer currents. There are spear-fishing clubs at Rabat, Casablanca, Tetouan, Meknes and Agadir. Compressed air can be had in these towns. Special facilities for the sport are provided at the newly created Mediterranean resort of M'diq (p. 292). On the whole, the Mediterranean coast under the Rif is the best for this sport. For additional information apply to Fédération Royale Marocaine d'Études et Sports Sous-Marines, BP 368, Rabat.

YACHTING

All Moroccan ports are open to private yachts and several basins are projected or under construction. The Mediterranean coast is covered by the Admiralty's *Mediterranean Pilot*, vol. 1; the Atlantic by *African Pilot*, vol. 1. But any yacht club will be able to supply information on conditions along the Moroccan coast.

HUNTING

You can hunt anywhere in Morocco, though you may be most comfortable if you confine yourself to the Tourist Zone, an immense (and recently enlarged to 118,000 hectares) triangle of country between Kénitra, Larache and Ouezzane. The high season is from November to the end of February, with a week or two at either end when certain game is to be had. Parties employ a guide and porters, trackers and beaters. Wild sheep and gazelle are prohibited game, but not wild boar.

A would-be hunter should notify the National Tourist Office, BP 19, Rabat, of his means of transport and time of arrival so that customs arrangements can be made to clear his guns, the reference numbers and complete descriptions of which should be stated. He must present a valid national shooting permit and three passport photographs in order to obtain an import permit, third-party insurance and a hunting permit. The address of both chief hunting associations, Fédération des Associations Cynégétiques and Fédération Royale Marocaine de Chasse, is 36 Boulevard Omar Ibn Khattab, BP 724, Rabat. Full information can be supplied by them.

FISHING

All fishing rights are reserved to the state, and permits are granted by the Administration des Eaux et Forêts. These have regional offices in the various provincial capitals. An annual permit costs 35 DH, a daily one 3 DH; a special permit to fish certain artificial lakes stocked with trout costs between 30 and 60 DH annually, and between 3 and 5 DH daily. These fees are subject to change. With them one is free to fish by whatever method one likes, short of dynamiting. Salmon and trout are to be had in the provinces of Rabat, Beni Mellal, Marrakech, Ouarzazate, Agadir and Oujda. The waters of the following rivers and their tributaries are particularly recommended: Hachef, Loukkos, Moulouya, Sebou, Inaouene, Ouerha, Beth. Many local clubs offer reserved reaches for their members.

SKI-ING

The heights of the Rif, the Middle and High Atlas all lend themselves to ski-ing. Centres are at Ketama, for the Rif; Ifrane, for Mischliffen in the Jebel Hebri and the Jebel Bou Iblane, in the Middle Atlas; and Oukaîmeden, near Marrakech, in the High Atlas. One should check the condition of the snow, preferably with the Fédération Royale Marocaine de Ski et de Montagne (Haut Commissariat à la Jeunesse et aux Sports, Boulevard Mohammed V, Rabat) before leaving as, though the snow lies commonly through the winter, occasional warm years reduce it, or curtail the season.

CLIMBING

This sport is not much developed as yet in Morocco. The Club Alpin has its headquarters at 'Les Belles Images' bookshop, Boulevard Mohammed V, Rabat.

RIDING

With so very much fine country for riding it is rather sad that more facilities do not exist for a visitor to obtain a mount. Some country hotels do have stables; polo and racing is quite popular in the biggest cities, where horses are available for hire. The Club Équestre Bayard, Rue Schumann, Casablanca, organizes a ride through the Middle Atlas every September, for about twelve days, with daily stages of about twenty miles and *folklorique* entertainments in the evenings. It is quite feasible to buy or hire horses, mules and donkeys and to find a suitable guide to explore the mountains yourself. A good horse can be had for a few thousand dirhams and a donkey for as little as two hundred; the hire of mules on the approaches to Mt Toubkal is well established and costs about 45 DH a day.

GOLF

On the outskirts of Rabat is the magnificent forty-five-hole course of Skhirat. The eighteen-hole course at Mohammedia is the scene of international tournaments; the other eighteen-hole courses are at Marrakech and Tangier. A nine-hole course of good standard is at Casablanca with another belonging to the Tidighine Hotel at Ketama.

TENNIS

Tennis clubs exist in the bigger towns. Apply for temporary membership *in situ*. Many hotels also have courts.

BODYBUILDING

This sport, or preoccupation, has recently taken a hold on the imagination of Moroccan youth and clubs or commercial gymnasiums can be found in most of the towns of any size. Visitors seem welcome without formalities.

ENTERTAINMENT

THEATRES AND CINEMAS

There is little theatrical activity in the country, but cinemas flourish. English-speaking films are usually dubbed into French. Egyptian films are often screened — their comedians are very funny. The stars of the world of Arab entertainment occasionally give concerts in the main centres, but Western talents are less often seen.

NIGHT CLUBS

These are features of the larger towns and more popular resorts only. They are much the same as anywhere else, though perhaps somewhat more lacking in heart than in the frenetic good-time places. There is insufficient local support for them to be able to afford front-rank cabaret artists or bands. Most fun are the Casablanca discotheques; they knock spots off anything Tangier can provide. The appropriate gear is just about anything which covers essentials, but even if merchant seamen are at ease in jeans and sweat-shirts, you may yourself feel happier in something more stylish, no matter how casual. And there are places where ties are *de rigueur*; you will hardly be likely not to sense them.

All the good hotels have their own night clubs, though generally too few patrons to make them very attractive — but see under Drink (p. 32).

CANNABIS

A word about this drug: its sale is prohibited in Morocco, though the law must be admitted to be more honoured in the breach. Mankind needs something to take him out of himself and in one form or another cannabis is probably the most universally used agent for doing so in the world. Moslems who do not use alcohol commonly use it instead. Like alcohol, it is not as physically addictive as 'hard' drugs are, though a man may have a psychological need of it to excess. One scarcely ever sees a Moroccan alcoholic, but sometimes a sad *hashisheur* who smokes his tiny pipefuls with obsessive frequency. To those unused to it it can have unpredictable effects and it is unwise as well as aesthetically wrong to take it in any quantity with alcohol. Since it is unlawful, it is anyway advisable for a visitor to be most discreet about his use of it. Even if, as you may very well do, you see children openly smoking in the side streets, do not follow suit.

It is an offence, punishable by a heavy fine and/or prison, for a foreigner to possess drugs. Additional draconian penalties are payable to the tobacco monopoly and customs authorities, and vehicles used for the transport of drugs are liable to confiscation. It is in the interest of the Moroccan seller of *kif* to inform the police, because he is thereby eligible for 10 per cent of the fines and can continue in business. Do not think that you are in some relaxed backwater because of the manners and music of the sixties and seventies; *kif* is big business (see special note about travel in the Rif Mountains near Ketama, p. 297).

Moroccans are extremely tolerant about their visitors' quirks and vices, but as tourism greatly increases in volume it is inevitable that they impose limits to the scope of their hospitality.

PUBLIC HOLIDAYS AND OTHER FESTIVALS

OFFICIAL HOLIDAYS

January 1st	New Year's Day
March 3rd	Fête du Trône (Independence Day and accession of King Hassan II)
May 1st	Labour Day
November 6th	Green March
November 18th	Accession of King Mohammed V

RELIGIOUS HOLIDAYS

Aîd es-Seghir (ending the fast of Ramadan)
Aîd el-Kebir (commemorating Abraham's sacrifice)
Mouloud (in honour of the Prophet's birth)

The dates of these three religious holidays vary since the Moslem calendar does not coincide with the Georgian, being for a year of 354 days with eleven leap years in a cycle of thirty years. Thus the feasts move backwards against our calendar by some ten or eleven days each year. Mouloud now falls in February. It will be better, however, to confirm these with the Moroccan National Tourist Office if you are anxious to assist at one; and, besides, all banks and places of business are closed on these religious holidays.

MOUSSEMS
These are festivals held in honour of a past saint or marabout (see p. 86) during which pilgrims congregate about the shrine enclosing the holy man's tomb. They last from one day to several, depending on their importance and the crowds they attract. There are market booths, entertainers, usually a fantasia on horse- or camel-back ridden by many armed men. The opening exhortation to Chapter 100 of the Koran brilliantly, if obscurely, describes the scene,

> By the snorting chargers,
>   the fire-strikers,
>   the plunder-raiders at daybreak,
>   the dust-raisers
>   centring in it all together!*

There can be good dancing to watch too. (But during the last ten years the larger moussems have become 'tourist attractions' and their once genuine folkloric aspects are vanishing — along with the piety of the occasion.) Notables set up their tents to receive visitors, and a deal of trading — from arranged marriages to the cabals of local politics — is conducted on these occasions. Some, like that at Tan Tan in the Sahara, are important markets for people who have little occasion to visit many others in the year, while some — Moulay Idriss, for instance, the greatest of all, which the King himself attends — are predominantly holiday affairs while having also a more marked element of piety. You should see one if you can. Few of them are held on fixed dates of the Moslem calendar, and those usually in the far south where the weather can be more surely counted upon. The rest are announced by the regional governor on suitable dates during the summer months and at best we can tell you only that such and such is held 'about September' when mention is made of the more accessible moussems under the entries for their locations. The local tourist office will, however, know the current year's dates within a few weeks of their taking place, though probably only for those held within the province.

Festivals and Moussems
For the religious festivals of the Islamic year and their dating see above. This list is not a complete one; it comprises all those festivals mentioned in the text, with one or two others.

Government-sponsored festivals

June	Festival of Folklore	Marrakech
May/June	Rose Festival	El-Kelaa des M'Gouna
June	Cherry Festival	Sefrou
October	Date Festival	Erfoud

A festival providing a platform for Third World artists has been established at Asilah.

* Translated by James Kritzeck, as are all quotations given from the Koran.

Moussems

(1) Held in connection with religious festivals (for dating see under Religious Holidays):

Mouloud	Sidi Abdullah ben Hassoun	Salé
	Sidi Loughlimi	Settat
	Sidi Mohammed ben Aîssa	Meknes
	Sidi Yussef	Ouaouizarht
One week after Mouloud	Sidi Ali ben Hamdoud	Jebel Zerhoun (near Meknes)
Two weeks after Mouloud	Moulay 'Brahim	Asni
	El-Ouina	near Marrakech

(2) Held around general dates, often in connection with local harvests:

April	Sidi Harazem	near Fes
April/May	Sebatou Rijal	Jebel Habid (near Essaouira)
May	Sidi Achmed el-Bernoussi	Fes
	Tan Tan	Tan Tan
	Rbi Abraham Moul'Niss	Azemmour
	Moulay Abdessalam ben Mchich*	near Chechaouen
June/July	Moulay Bouselham	near Ksar el-Kebir
July	Aît Omghar	near Marrakech
	Sidi ben Ali Harazem	Fes
	Et-Tleta de Oued Laou	near Tetouan
August	Sidi Ali ben Brahim	near Beni Mellal
	Setti Fatma	near Marrakech
	Sidi Lachen	near Rabat
August/ September	Moulay Adbullah	near El-Jadida
	Tissa	Rif Mountains
September	Sidi Achmed ou Moussa	near Agadir
	Moulay Idriss (el-Akhbar)	Moulay Idriss
	Moulay Idriss (II)	Fes
	Imilchil	Imilchil
	Sidi Bouzekri	Meknes
	Skhirat	near Bouznika
	Taounate	Rif Mountains
	Tedders	Tedders
	Sidi 'bu Amar	Rommani

* Officially a December festival though usually now held in May.

October	Sidi Ali bou Ghaleb	Fes
	Moulay Bouchta	Moulay Bouchta
	Sidi Kacem	Sidi Kacem
November	Sidi Bennour	Sidi Bennour

POSTAL INFORMATION

Airmail letters of up to 20 grammes cost 3 DH to the United States, 2·40 DH to the United Kingdom and Europe excepting France, Spain and Portugal which are all 2 DH. Postcards are 2 DH, 1·60 DH and 1·40 respectively. Internal telegrams, which are useful for advance reservation of hotels, cost 0·50 DH per word.

Much of the Moroccan telephone system is now automated and it is possible to dial abroad direct from most major towns. European destinations cost on average 25 DH for a three-minute call, and the United States, 78 DH. Local and national calls can be made from call-boxes which accept 10-, 20- and 50-centime pieces and one-dirham coins. If you wish to use a hotel telephone to make an international call, negotiate the rate beforehand.

WEIGHTS AND MEASURES

The metric system of weights and measures is in general use in Morocco.

ELECTRICITY

220 volts AC has now largely superseded the 110 volt system.

TIME

Greenwich Mean Time, Summer time has been introduced (G.M.T. + 1 hour). The dates of changed hours differ from those in more northerly countries.

GEOGRAPHIC DESCRIPTION

Morocco occupies the westernmost portion of North Africa. Its area is greater than that of France. Where the land masses of Europe and Africa close to form the Straits of Gibraltar, the Mediterranean coast of Morocco faces that of south-eastern Spain. Its eastern border lies approximately along the third meridian east, marching with Algeria. The country also borders the Atlantic, its coast-line running in a generally north-eastern to south-western direction as far south as the Canary Islands, or about latitude 27·5 N. Its south-eastern frontier runs at a more acute angle to the Equator than does this coast. With the agreement of the then Spanish government in 1976 Morocco occupied the northern sector of Spain's Saharan colony of Rio d'Oro, Mauritania occupying the southern part. This area lies south of the old Moroccan frontier and along the Atlantic coast. As yet, Algeria does not recognize this action and supports the Polisario in this conflict. Reports of border skirmishes in the north suggest more direct confrontation and make relations between the two sufficiently sour to cause problems for third parties. In 1978, Mauritania withdrew all claims upon its position, to which Morocco then staked a further claim for itself. At the time of going to press it is difficult to be sure to what extent any or all of the erstwhile Rio d'Oro can be said, whether in international law or practical fact, to be an integral part of the Kingdom of Morocco.

Within this fairly compact shape, acting as a spine to the country, there rises the chain of the High Atlas Mountains. This divides the territory into an inner and an outer Morocco, the one a land of mountains and plains sloping to the sea and lying north-west to the mountain barrier, the other one of stony slopes channelled by torrent beds running to extinction in the wastes of the Sahara Desert, which is to all intents and purposes another 'sea'. Here the 'coast' could be well enough defined by those areas which are inhabitable − promontories of watered land following the bigger rivers, a scatter of islands formed by oases − but since the desert is potentially rich in minerals and oil the artificial frontiers drawn across the emptiness of sand and gravel are important and, see above, in dispute.

The Atlas Mountains are the culmination of that chain of heights which separates the rich littoral of western North Africa − the Maghreb − from the Sahara. Here it divides into three ranges: the longest, highest and central one being the High Atlas with peaks rising to over 4,000 metres, the shortest and lowest being the Anti-Atlas and the most northerly, knotted against the heights of the High Atlas, being the Middle Atlas. Standing back from the Mediterranean coast is the isolated succession of massifs called the Rif Mountains. These are not connected to the Atlas and in fact belong to the European system of mountains. Between the Rif and the Middle Atlas is a long pass held at the col by the town of Taza. This is usually called the Taza Gap, though it is really more of a corridor leading between Morocco and Algeria and also between inner and outer Morocco, for here an arm of the desert runs almost to the Mediterranean coast and the frontier town of Oujda is virtually an oasis settlement. Far to the south of Oujda, and to its west, lies the comparatively easy pass called the Tizi n'Talrhemt connecting the rich desert territory of the Tafilelt, by Er Rachidia and Midelt, with Fes and the central plains. Between these passes only a few tracks cross the mountains and very few again between the Tizi n'Talrhemt and the two passes south of Marrakech. Of these the more easterly, the Tizi n'Tichka, is the highest and most used. It leads to Ourzazate, while the Tizi n'Test gives more directly to the valley of the Sous and Taroudant and to the coast at Agadir. A third and easier pass connects the western Sous valley and Chichaoua, west of Marrakech; this has been made into a fast road (P10) leading by Imi-n-Tanout to Agadir. It will be seen therefore that outer Morocco, linked to inner only by a few, mostly high and difficult passes snowbound in winter, is necessarily an isolated region. It is almost as far from Oujda to the Atlantic mouth of the Draa as it is from Zagora, centre of habitation on the upper Draa, on the most southerly of the Saharan 'promontories', to Timbuctou — right across the Sahara. Thus the fact that Oujda is accessible from inner Morocco has absolutely no effect upon control of the populous Tafilelt or the settlements along the Draa and the Sous. The Anti-Atlas, which separates the courses of these last two rivers, is sparsely populated and even more cut off.

FLORA

Anyone at all interested in flowers or trees, wild or cultivated, must delight in Morocco. There are between 3,500 and 4,000 native varieties growing under the differing conditions afforded by mountain and plain reaching from the Mediterranean to the barren Sahara. However, most of these species belong to Mediterranean types and it is in their profusion rather than their rarity that they make so great an impression. Heralded by wintry drifts of narcissi, spring blossoms with tracts of orange-gold reminding you that we call the marigold 'African', with miles of delicate asphodel, dark-crimson stains over the young wheat where the gladioli bloom, and camomile like snow along the railway lines. The valleys sloping to the Sahara turn pink, blue and lemon-yellow with statice — never mixed but always separated.

Everywhere the plains have been transformed by the introduction of the eucalyptus, Australia's gracious gift to the rest of the world. The various soils are rich, though their productivity depends on their humidity. Irrigation, actively being extended over many parts, brings a flourish of intensive cultivation that can make a notable contrast to its unwatered surroundings. The higher plains are mostly the driest and it is in the lower regions like that stretching from Fes to the Atlantic that you can see what munificence the country is capable of. Most heartening of sights, re-afforestation is being undertaken on an immense scale. It will modify the extremes of the climate within a foreseeable future.

A key to the distribution of Moroccan flora, as much dependent upon rainfall as on altitude and type of soil, is briefly thus:

littorals	cork and evergreen;
forests	cedar, juniper, thuya (*arbor-vitae*), cypress;
lower slopes of mountains	olive, lentisk, mastic, kermes oak, arbutus, myrtle, heather, broom, bean-trefoil, wormwood, rosemary;
valleys	oleander, willow, tamarisk;
higher slopes to tops	saxifrages, lavender, mint, thyme, chrysanthemum;
dry pasturages	esparto, mugwort, asphodel, cadow saffron, squill, dwarf palm, jujube, buckthorn, lotus tree; with terebinth, betoum and pistachio in the valleys;
far south-west (tropical)	argan, *euphorbia cacoides*;
irrigated pre-Sahara	dates, rubbers.

The argan (sometimes called argana) tree (*Arganis sideroxylon*) is a spiny, knotted tree rather like an olive which bears fruit, larger than the olive, from which a rich oil is extracted. Growing as a sparse forest on the steppe, it is a considerable curiosity. The goats of the district between Essaouira and Agadir, and thereabouts only it seems, have the picturesque habit of climbing the argan trees to eat the leaves. The oil is very good in salads. The many thousands of acres which are densely clothed with *euphorbia cacoides* are also strange to see. This is an extremely tough and brutal-looking cactus of a dark grey-green, viciously spiked.

The interested should consult *Catalogue des Plantes du Maroc* by E. Jahandiez and R. Negre, and *Flore de l'Afrique du Nord* by R. Marie — which is illustrated.

FAUNA

One must be surprised by the birds of Morocco. They stand out so remarkably against the landscape — storks (they migrate away from August to January) and flocks of ibis are dramatically white and large; ravens are huge; eagles and falcons stoop among lesser birds of prey; the brown African sparrow ventures into your room where his European fellow keeps to the courtyard — these seem always to capture your notice. Less often to be seen, though not uncommon, are the colourful bee-eater (*Merops apiaster*) and roller (*Coracias garrulus*), lapwing, pigeon, turtle-dove, red-legged partridge, duck, quail, bustard, sand-grouse. Morocco lies on one of the two major migratory routes of the very many species of birds travelling annually back and forth between Europe and Africa. This traffic between southern Spain and the Tangerine tip of Morocco is dense and at times spectacular.

The land animals prove disappointing by comparison. The camel is rapidly being superseded by the motor; fine Arab horses are a rare sight — though neither of course is native. Prolonged hunting and the worsening climate have exterminated many species such as the lion (twenty languish in the zoo between Rabat and Casablanca), in the first century A.D. the neighbourhood of Rabat was infested by elephant. But wild boar, gazelle, Barbary apes and a kind of baboon and even panthers still exist in their appropriate habitats; the leopard may still exist. Ostrich only disappeared in living memory; the bubal hartebeest during the Second World War, while lion were recorded in the Middle Atlas as recently as 1922. A charming little sand squirrel inhabits the hot rock faces and both snakes and lizards wax large and fat.

Insects are rarely troublesome in Morocco except in the mountains and oases. At the same time, the sight of so many butterflies sporting in the glades of the Middle Atlas must be compensation for a few pests.

HISTORY

PREHISTORY

When most of Europe was covered by ice of the Quaternary period the Sahara Desert was probably a region of grassy steppes and wooded mountains where rivers flowed abundantly and the valleys were peopled. Elephants, rhinoceroses, hippopotami, giraffe and zebra grazed up to the southern slopes of the Atlas Mountains, Gradually the climate of the region worsened to its present state, while that of the lands north of the mountain barrier improved. During the Paleolithic period an intelligent sort of man hunted the primeval forests of the latter territory — where he had been preceded by Mousterian man and a Neanderthal type also. The primitive culture of these Paleolithic northerners possibly had its origin in Egypt. In the form developed in north-west Africa — the Maghreb, we will call it — this is called the *Mousillian* culture after the pilot site of Mousillah on the Algero-Moroccan frontier. From this indigenous culture there developed, under the influences spreading from the Near East, an agricultural, Neolithic culture which in places lasted into the historical era. It was these people, remote in culture, though less so in time, who carved the reliefs of animals — and sometimes of men — on the rock faces of river gorges running into the wastes of the desert. There are many examples of these to be seen today if one is willing to put up with the rigours of travel in the remoter parts. Less adventurous visitors can see some specimens in the Rabat museum or, *in situ*, at Oukaïmeden (p. 231), where, since this is a high and lonely mountain valley, now a ski resort, one wonders whether the carvers worked in honour of a sky or mountain deity long worshipped there or whether, poor primitives, this was one of their last retreats against the advance of a civilization scores of hundreds of years of incomprehensible development ahead of their own. The Neolithic Moroccans also built the great cromlech or circle of standing stones to the north-east of Larache (p. 156).

Historical Chart

DATES	PERIOD/EVENTS	RULERS
	Prehistoric era	
c. 1100	*? Phoenician colonization*	
	Capture of isolated ports	
c. 550	Carthagian domination of Punic settlements; development of gold route to West Africa	
c. 200	Rise of Berber Kingdom of Mauritania	
146	Fall of Carthage to Rome and decline of Punic influence	
	Growth of Roman influence	
c. 110	Bocchus king of Mauritania	Bocchus
*c.*104	Death of Jugurtha of Numidia	
82	Sertorius in Tangier	
46	Battle of Thapsus; Numidia taken under direct Roman rule	
25	Juba II restored to Numidian throne as a client king	
20	Juba II translated to Mauritanian throne, ruling also all Numidia not excluded in the Roman province of Africa	Juba II
B.C.		
A.D.		
c. 19	Ptolemy succeeds Juba II	Ptolemy
41	Ptolemy's death	
44	*Direct Roman rule*	Roman emperors
	Mauritania annexed	(Claudius to
c. 253	Roman withdrawal to Tangier	Diocletian)
	Moroccan Dark Age	
429	Genseric the Vandal crosses Morocco	
535	Belisarius garrisons Ceuta	
	Arab conquest	
682	Uqba ben Nafi's exploratory raid	
788–923	*Idrissid dynasty*	Idriss I (d. 791/2)
791/2		Rashid (regent 791/2–804)
809	Foundation of Fes	Idriss II (792–828)
		Mohammed (826–36)
c. 836	*Ommayed and Fatimid influence*	Ali (836–48)
	Fragmentation of authority	Yahya I
		Yahya II (848)
969	Fatimid removal to Cairo	Ali ben Omar
		Yahya III (880–905)
		Yahya IV (905–23)

CAPITAL CITIES	SITES AND MAJOR BUILDINGS
	Neolithic rock carvings at Oukaïmeden and desert edges
? Lixus	Punic sites at Essaouira and Tetouan
? Tangier or ? unknown site	
	Volubilis Babba Campestris Banasa
	Rabat (bronzes, etc., in museum) Tetouan (museum) Rabat (Chella; forum)
Volubilis Moulay Idriss Fes	

DATES	PERIOD/EVENTS	RULERS
A.D. *c.* 1050	*Sanhajan conquest* (Completed *c.* 1075)	
1060–1147 1062 *c.* 1130	*Almoravid dynasty* Foundation of Marrakech Mohammed ibn Tumart dies	Yussef ibn Tashfin (1060–1107) Ali ben Yussef (1107–43) Ibrahim ibn Tashfin (1145) Isaac ben Ali (1145–7)
1147–1244	*Almohad dynasty*	Abd el-Mumin (1133–63) Abu Yaacub Yussef (1163–84) Yaacub el-Mansur (1184–99) el-Nasser (1199–1213) el-Mustansir (1213–24) el-Makhlu (1224) el-'Adil (1224–7) Yahya (1227–9) el-Mamun (1227–32) er-Rashid (1232–42) es-Saïd (1242–8)
1248	Merinids capture Fes	el-Mutarda (1248–66) Abu Dabbus (1266–9)
1269 1244–*c.* 1450	Marrakech taken by the Merinids *Merinid dynasty* Wattasid viziers were dominant between 1358 and 1374, and again between 1393 and 1421	Abu Yahya (1244–58) Abu Yussef Yaacub (1258–86) Abu Yaacub Yussef (1286–1307) Abu Thabit (1307–8) Abu Rabia (1307–8) Abu Saïd Uthman (1310–31) Abu el-Hassan (1331–51) Abu Inan Faris (1351–8) es-Saïd I (1358–9) Abu Salim (1359–61) Abu Zaiyan (1361–6) Abd el-Aziz (1366–72) es-Saïd II (1372–4) Abu el-Abbes (1374–84) Abu Faris Musa (1834–6) el-Wathiq (1386–7) Abu el-Abbes (second reign 1387–93) Abus Faris Abd el-Aziz (1393–6) Abu Emir Abdullah (1396–8)
c. 1400	Beginning of Portuguese aggression against Morocco	Abu Saïd Uthman II (1398–1421) Abd el-Haqq (1421–65)
1492	Fall of Granada Rise of the Marabouts	Wattasids

CAPITAL CITIES	SITES AND MAJOR BUILDINGS

Marrakech	
Fes	
Seville	Koubba el-Baroudiyin
	(Marrakech)
	Walls, gates, Koutoubia and
	Casbah mosques at Marrakech
Marrakech	Walls, gates, Tower and Mosque
Seville	of Hassan at Rabat
	Tinmel
	Tit (Giralda Tower and other
Fes	Spanish monuments);
Marrakech	Tlemcen

Fes	Chella (Rabat)
Marrakech, Meknes	

	Medrassa at Fes; Fes el-Jedid;
	ben Yussef Medersa at Marra-
	kech (Alhambra of Granada;
	Tlemcen)

DATES	PERIOD/EVENTS	RULERS
A.D.		
1458–1554	The Wattasids, first regents, then usurpers, controlled little of the country save the cities, the rural areas being dominated by the Marabouts	
c. 1510	Among these the Saadi family emerged as rulers of the Sous	
1520	Saadi capture Marrakech (the Two Kingdoms of Morocco)	
1541	Saadi capture Agadir	
1554–1659	*Saadi dynasty*	Mohammed esh-Sheikh (1554–7)
1554	Saadi capture Fes	Abdullah el-Ghalib (1557–7
		Mohammed el-Masluh (1574–6)
		Abd el-Malik (1576–8)
1578	Battle of 'the Three Kings'	Achmed el-Mansur (1578–1603)
		Zaydan (1603–28)
		el-Mamun (1610–13)
		Abdullah ibn Mamun (1613–24)
		Abd el-Malik ibn Mamun (1624–6)
	Republic of Bou Regreg	Abd el-Malik (1628–31)
1630–40	Alaouite family establishing itself in the Tafilelt	el-Walid (1631–6)
1650	Marabouts of Djila take Fes	Mohammed esh-Sheikh II (1636–54)
1662–84	British ownership of Tangier	Achmed el-Abbes (1654–9)
1659–present	*Alaouite dynasty*	Rashid (1654–72)
1666	Alaouites retake Fes	
1669	Alaouites take Marrakech	Moulay Ismaïl (1672–1727) (1727–46; eleven 'rulers' during a period of anarch
		Abdullah ben Ismaïl (1745–57)
		Mohammed (Sidi) ibn Abdullah (1757–90)
		Yazid (1790–92)
		Suleiman (1792–1822)
		Abd er-Rahman (1822–59)
		Mohammed (1859–73)
		Moulay Hassan (1873–94)
		Abd el-Aziz (1894–1908)
1912	French and Spanish colonial rule	Abd el-Hafid (1908–12)
		Moulay Yussef (1912–27)
1956	Independence of Morocco	Mohammed V (1927–61)
		Hassan II (1961–present)

CAPITAL CITIES	SITES AND MAJOR BUILDINGS

Saadi: Marrakech
Wattasids: Fes

Marrakech

Badi Palace; mosques of Bab
Doukkala and el-Mouassine;
Saadi tombs at Marrakech

At Fes only

Marrakech

Meknes

Meknes

Pavilions and palaces of Marrakech

Rabat/Fes

el-Baïda Palace, Marrakech
Palais Jamaï Hotel, Fes

Rabat

PHOENICIAN COLONIZATION (c. 1100–146 B.C.)

The Moroccan Bronze Age was introduced by the Phoenicians who, coming from the eastern Mediterranean seaboard called Caanan, were the first people to establish known trading-posts on the Atlantic coasts of Europe and Africa, doing so around 1100 B.C. Earliest of all their posts were Gadera (now Cadiz) on the Spanish coast, and Liks on the hill lying on the northern side of the mouth of the River Likkus, opposite the modern Larache. From such a small beginning the enormous Moroccan hinterland was slowly drawn into contact with Mediterranean civilization. Liks was later joined by other Punic settlements along the sea routes leading first eastwards to Carthage, the great Phoenician base where Tunis now stands, and then homewards to Palestine: Tingis (Tangier), Tamuda (near Tetouan), Rusadir (Melilla); and by still more adventurous Atlantic-coast settlements like Chella, which is outside Rabat, and another on the islands of Essaouira. The Phoenicians of Carthage became independent of the founder cities of Caanan during the first half of the sixth century B.C., following upon the destruction of the Caananitish city of Tyre by Nebuchadnezzar. The Carthagians then remained the major civilizing influence on the Maghreb until long after the Romans destroyed their state in 146 B.C.

Jérôme Carcopino, in a remarkable feat of sustained deduction,* has shown that the Phoenicians' interest in the far west was gold, ivory and slaves, in that order; also that the Atlantic settlements on the bay at Essaouira being the southernmost, were little exploited until almost a hundred years after the fall of Tyre, when Carthage had established both its independence and its hegemony over the western colonies. E. W. Bovill† accepts instead more recent thinking about the Phoenicians' trade and dismisses Carcopino's elucidation of the mysterious *periplous* of Hauna, a voyage claiming to have reached as far as the north of the Niger. Carthage was not particularly rich in gold (when in 241 B.C. the Romans extorted a huge fine from that state, it was in silver) and there was gold nearer at hand in the Fezzan. Elephants abounded in Inner Morocco, it is true. The Phoenicians had no need to raid, or trade, for slaves so far away as beyond the

---

* Jérôme Carcopino, *Le Maroc Antique* (Gallimard, Paris, 1943; revised edition, 1947).
† E. W. Bovill, *The Golden Trade of the Moors* (Oxford University Press, 2nd edition 1968).

Sahara. There are, however, indications that a trickle of gold did reach them from West Africa by way of the Atlantic coast. During the fifty century B.C. Herodotus heard of the 'silent' gold trade conducted in the upper Niger and Senegal riverine area. His version of its operation is rather garbled, but he could not have obtained it unless some contact existed between the north and south of the Sahara at a time when the land routes were not in use.

Procopius notes that Punic was still spoken in the Maghreb in the first half of the sixth century A.D. Certainly the Punic cities of Morocco were minting coins with Punic inscriptions during the first half of the first century B.C. although they were then surrounded by, and perhaps subject to, the Berber Kingdom of Mauritania established some hundred years earlier.

BERBER KINGDOM OF MAURITANIA (*c*. 200 B.C.–A.D. 44)
The Berber Kingdom of Mauritania occupied the northern half of present-day Morocco; it was allied to Numidia, also a Berber kingdom, which occupied northern Algeria and Tunisia. The rulers of these kingdoms were of the same family — a circumstance which is perhaps a tribute to Berber solidarity since the two territories are naturally divided by the intrusive arm of desert which I have called the 'Oujda corridor' and by the range of the High Atlas, the same barrier which dictates the position of the present Algero–Moroccan border in the north.

GROWTH OF ROMAN INFLUENCE (146 B.C.–A.D. 44)

Moroccan isolation thus for the first time became a significant fact after the fall of Carthage in 146 B.C. During the Second Punic War Numidia supported Rome against Carthage and was rewarded by the grant of all the land round that defeated city. This, however, brought Numidia under strong Roman influence and when its king, Jugurtha, murdered his two cousins and co-heirs to the throne, Rome unsuccessfully attacked the country (111 B.C.). Seven years later Marius finally defeated Jugurtha. Bocchus, king of Mauritania, who was Jugurtha's father-in-law, had first supported though later betrayed him. In this way Mauritania too was drawn into the Roman civil wars. Jugurtha died in a Roman prison; the Numidian state was greatly reduced in size and its rulers to the status of vassal kings. In 72 B.C. the Roman general Sertorius, who had been defeated in Spain, crossed southwards over the Straits of Gibraltar and occupied Tangier for a few months. When civil war was resumed between Pompey and Caesar, Juba I of diminished Numidia supported the former. He was trounced at the battle of Thapsus in 46 B.C. and committed suicide afterwards. This time Numidia was placed under direct Roman rule. Juba's son, also called Juba, and still a child, walked ahead of Caesar's chariot during his subsequent triumph at Rome. Nevertheless the boy was given a princely education and was to become one of the most learned men of his time. As a writer he was considered important for the breadth of his interests and erudition and for the wealth of the sources he was able to command; unfortunately his work now survives only in references to it made by subsequent authors, in particular Pliny the Younger. It is also possible that Juba was a rather hack scholar in the manner of the other ancients, merely compiling endless quotations from other authors into general works of reference — whose loss is still our misfortune.

Meanwhile the civil war between Augustus (Gaius Octavius) and Mark Antony again affected Mauritania.

The joint kings of the country took opposing sides. Of these two brothers one delivered Tangier to Augustus, who rewarded it with the rights of a Roman city in 28 B.C.; the other, Bogud, supported the loser, Antony, and was killed in 31 B.C. when Agrippa captured Methone. Tangier had already been annexed to Rome in 33 B.C. during Augustus's consolidation of his hold on the west of the empire, but it still could have declared for Antony.

The young Juba was admired by Augustus for his ability and in 25 B.C. was appointed to succeed to his father's throne, five years after the civil wars at last ended with the defeat of Antony at Actium, his suicide and that of Cleopatra. They had left behind them a daughter, Cleopatra Silene, whom Augustus gave in marriage to Juba. She had appeared in Augustus's triumph at Rome with her younger brother, Alexander Helios. On her marriage, she took charge of his brother and also the youngest, Ptolemy Philadelphus. All three were scarcely more than children and the boys disappear from history at this point. Five years later Juba II was translated to the throne of Mauritania, to which was annexed the greater part of Numidia. The cities of Tangier, Asilah, Banasa and Babba Campestris appear to have been under direct Roman rule within this large vassal kingdom. Juba's western capital would seem to have been Volubilis (p. 276), while Caesarea (now Cherchel, in Algeria) was his eastern. Juba reigned many years — his portrait as a reflective young man, an exceptionally fine bronze, is in the Rabat museum. He was succeeded by his son Ptolemy at his death in about A.D. 19. Juba's reign had not been an entirely peaceful one; there had been several uprisings against his Romanized and Roman-dominated rule and it is possible that Ptolemy was not in fact confirmed on his throne until A.D. 24, when his coins show triumphal insignia in honour of a Roman victory over insurgents who had begun their revolt in his father's time. Seventeen years later Ptolemy was summoned to Lyons to attend Gaius Caligula, the unstable young emperor whom absolute power soon rendered wholly insane. The story is that the very rich Ptolemy — Mauritania had grown exceedingly prosperous — was received by the crowds with an ovation which out-clamoured that for the emperor who, from spite, had the Mauritanian assassinated. It was, however, the policy of Rome to control borderlands like Mauritania through puppet kings until such time as she was ready to annex them to direct rule.

DIRECT ROMAN RULE (A.D. 44–c. 253)

Succeeding his murdered nephew, the emperor Claudius regularized this annexation in A.D. 44. One of Ptolemy's ministers replied by raising a rebellion which took the Romans three years of campaigning and 20,000 troops to subdue. Morocco had in fact already embarked, indeed was established, upon the invidualistic course that it was to hold until the twentieth century. A Moroccan is his own master unless a better man can master him. The Romans proved the better men in this instance and, once firmly established, they made a first expedition across the Atlas. Yet of the two North African provinces, both of which were of immense value to Rome, only Numidia — presently to be called Mauritania Caesariensis — was ever seriously developed.

As a continental island, Morocco has usually been something of a Cinderella region: this was the first significant period of the sort. The sea was used as its chief means of communication with Italy and the rest of the Empire. There were few, unpaved roads in the country, the main one being from Tangier to Salé with a branch leading to Volubilis. Repeated revolts by the people harassed the Government until, under Diocletian (about A.D. 253), the Romans withdrew behind a frontier stretching from north of Larache to Tetouan, thus abandoning the cities of Salé and Volubilis. Even this small territory seems to have been retained only in order to protect Tangier and the southern flank of the Straits of Gibraltar.

MOROCCAN DARK AGE (c. A.D. 253–682)

Throughout the period of direct Roman rule Christianity seems to have made considerable headway in the country. There appears too to have been a large influx of Jews. Barely controlled as much of the area was, it may well have been a place of refuge for the Jews whose exclusive beliefs ran so against official Roman thought and policy and thus incurred persecution. For both sects Morocco may well have become a sanctuary after the Roman withdrawal. Always, perhaps, something of an island of urban civilizations, Volubilis remained a Romanized city until the coming of the Arabs, three hundred years after its abandonment by Rome. (In this, of course, it was not unlike contemporary Rome herself.)

Genseric the Vandal and his 80,000 troops crossed into Morocco from Spain but, with the possible exception of Ceuta and, less likely, of Tangier, he does not appear to have occupied any of the territory, merely passing through to Algeria and Tunisia. This was in A.D. 429. He may have claimed suzerainty over all the old Roman parts although, since his hold over the western Algerian littoral is known to have been tenuous, his claim was not likely to have been at all effective in Morocco.

We are apt to regard history as a fait accompli, not asking ourselves why it happened as it did. Genseric's reason for crossing into Morocco and moving on eastwards is illuminating. Large and flourishing cities had grown up in Spain during the Roman occupation, particularly in Andalusia. These prospered on the export of oil, wine, grapes and cloth, not growing grain for their own use, but depending on imported North African harvests. Eastern Algeria and Tunisia, Tripoli, were the main grain producers, and rich prizes in themselves. But the ruler of still richer Spain needed absolute control of them for the sake of Spain's food supply. This situation remained unchanged during the subsequent Byzantine occupation of North Africa, though somewhat in reverse since possession of the grain lands allowed them to dominate, without extending themselves to occupy, Spain. In the same way, after the Arab conquest of the Maghreb the Andalusians all but invited them into Spain, offering no resistance to their advance. Thus Morocco was to become Arabized and Islamic almost as a side effect of its rich neighbour's need for a stable supply of wheat.

Already, by the time of the Vandals, Morocco had become a home for anachronistic ideas and ways of life. There were, perhaps, no longer true neoliths in the remote mountains, but Punic was spoken on the plains; Volubilis was Roman (as Tangier too most probably was); there were pagans in the hills — animists whose traditions were Neolithic — and settlements of early Christians and Jews of an ancient orthodoxy who, indeed, survive there even today. This may seem odd when one looks at a map of the country and sees it as an obvious link between Spain and the rest of North Africa, yet in those days it was merely a wild part lying along a dangerous Mediterranean sea route with few, indifferent ports for which a vessel, risking pirates and wreckers, could run in a storm. On land the Rif mountain range was virtually impassable, while the route by the Taza Gap and across the Oujda corridor was both perilous and slow.

When Count Belisarius recaptured North Africa for the 'Roman' Byzantine emperor of Constantinople, Justinian, in A.D. 535, the only part of Morocco he garrisoned was Ceuta, best of the Mediterranean ports and at the entrance of the Straits. There he built a fortress and dedicated a church to the Virgin. The town was to remain Byzantine until some unknown time after the arrival of the Arabs.

ARAB CONQUEST (A.D. 682–788)

This warlike people reached Tripolitania in A.D. 647, only twenty-five years after the Prophet Mohammed, with his followers, moved from Mecca to Medina and, in doing so, inaugurated the Moslem era — on July 16th, A.D. 622. Twenty-three years later again Uqba ben Nafi, the Arab governor of Tunisia, founded the city of Kairouan. His successor made a raid as far as Tlemcen near the present frontier between Algeria and Morocco. But the Berbers were proving as stubborn an obstacle to Arab expansion as they had been to Roman.

Berber resistance was led by a remarkable woman, Kahina 'the Prophetess' and queen of the Aurès, a camel-herding tribe from the Sahara. Reappointed to the governorship of the west (A.D. 682), Uqba ben Nafi made an extended raid into Morocco. The records are vague. He is credited either with having merely made a foray into the country, not reaching the Atlantic or, having made terms with the Byzantine Count Julian of Ceuta, proceeding to the capture of Tangier, penetrating to the Tafilelt by way of Volubilis, destroying the chief towns of the Haouz plain (where Marrakech lies today) and visiting the Sous valley. He returned by a more southerly route and was surprised by Kahina's men at Biskra where he was killed with most of his force. His tomb in the Biskra oasis is still a centre of pilgrimage.

The Berbers did not like — and in the wilder parts are still reluctant — to be under any rule save that of their own loose, elective confederations. Sometimes this has led to their being conquered because divided, but more often it has contributed to their strength when outside threats have emotionally united them. At this time, with the Byzantines in decadence and the Arabs mustering only comparatively small columns seeking to establish footholds in the country, the flexibility of Berber social organization gave them a remarkable cohesion and strength. Arab historians claim that Uqba Ben Nafi's raid resulted in the conversion to Islam of many Berbers. This is most probably an apocryphal claim though it may well symbolize the truth about the Arab conquest of Morocco, which was through the Berbers' enthusiasm for the new religion. In their extreme isolation and the monotony of their agricultural existence, religion represents — it still does — the one means of exercising the imagination, the only opportunity for expressing the people's spirituality. Religious festivals are the Berbers' only diversions. None the less it is probably too simple an explanation merely to suggest that a new religion was accepted for the sake of its novelty. Like the Arabs, the Berbers appear to have a real talent for religion, a bent towards spiritual discipline and a gusto for rebelling against its constraints. At least in the first centuries of the era, Christianity (though to what extent it was embraced by the Berbers we cannot now tell) seems to have asked a great deal of the individual while not helping him with that enforced discipline which, particularly, the Roman Church later developed. One can imagine that the Berbers liked Christianity, that they were poorly instructed in its teaching and that it failed to strike any permanent roots among them because it lacked a firm enough social and moral discipline to add zest to any revolt against its code. Mohammed's teaching rests to a great extent on experience of Christianity's mistakes. His message was delivered intact — aspirations, promises and restraints virtually all at one time. The basic simplicity of Islam's demands on the individual makes its appeal to the simple very strong while its opportunities for the most sophisticated thought and spiritual exercise have proved virtually limitless. If anything it demands a still greater act of faith than Christianity does, but a more direct one. There is little doubt that it was the attraction of Islam for the Berber temperament that slowly allowed the Arabs to dominate the region. Another contributory factor may have been the Arabs' need for mercenary troops and the successes they met with in Spain.

This Arab ascendancy was not established so fast as devout historians would have us believe. Yet the story is told of Uqba ben Nafi that he rode his horse into the Atlantic until the sea reached around his own neck before he called, 'O God, I take you to witness that there is no ford here. If there was I would cross it.' — this only thirty years before Musa ben Nasser had so far established Arab control over the northern plains of Morocco that he was able to take the alternative route that offered and launch from Tangier his rapid conquest of Spain. He must already have been sure of his Moroccan base and, beginning in A.D. 711, this advance into Spain and Europe was halted by Charles Martel at Poitiers in France, in A.D. 732. Ben Nasser had already certainly made an expedition throughout Morocco, probably starting in A.D. 705.

However well received they may eventually have been by the Berber tribes, we must suppose that the Arab invaders had an extraordinarily dynamic force of their own. This was obviously grounded in their inspirational faith (they were not at this time aggressive zealots, but ardent believers in the worth of the message they carried), and it must too have had some foundation in those quite other, mysterious forces which occasionally cause astonishing outbreaks of vigour among the people of remote and hitherto quiescent regions. Whereas Genghis Khan and Tamerlane, with their fanatic followers, brought nothing with them across the world, the Arabs, like the Greeks under Alexander the Great, were bearers of a positive element which consolidated their victories. The Arabs swept across the exhausted world of the abandoned Roman provinces, sustained more by their ardour and their vigour than by military ability. And as conquerors they were just. They were respectful of Christians and Jews, on the whole,* and, perhaps because they were themselves so recently

* Say: O unbelievers!
  I do not worship what you worship

pagan, more insistent on converting the pagans. These, in Morocco, were largely Berbers. Proud, independent and conservative, however great the appeal of Islam may have been, the Berbers accepted the Arabs' religion more easily than direct Arab rule or — elsewhere an important unifying factor in the Moslem territories — their language. Twelve hundred years later it is still possible to find Berbers who do not speak Arabic, though they grow few these days. It was not long before Berber Moslem dynasties were arising in the area and, though the two races lived side by side and the ruling class has for centuries been predominantly Arab, a certain almost token animosity between them is even still noticeable today. (It is perhaps not more than an expression of racial identity, but it is there. The fact that in Morocco, Arabism is still identified with urbanism, whereas the Berber tradition remains above all rural, also emphasizes the division.)

The pioneering Arabs and their troops (augmented by Libyan, Tunisian and Algerian Berber converts) have since received many and considerable reinforcements at various times. All the same it is perhaps most remarkable that the country should now be so Arabic. From the start of the Arab era Morocco was remote from the centre of power. It was governed by a delegate of the viceroy of Kairouan, himself remote from and barely controlled by the Caliphs. Kairouan in fact became independent of the Caliphs about twenty-five years after the invasion of Spain; Morocco was virtually independent of both Kairouan and Spain. The Caliphate was itself in trouble. Islam was divided between differing interpretations of its teaching — it was too early, even, for orthodoxy to have become firmly distinguishable from heresy — and the Prophet's heirs disputed their legacy of expanding empire (see also p. 285). The Alids soon lost the Caliphate to the Ommayeds of Damascus, and they in their turn gave way to the Abbasids. Members of defeated houses took refuge in the remoter parts of the Moslem world. Some of them had the good fortune to be able to set up principalities of their own, based on the immense respect they commanded as descendants of the Prophet or his companions. One such was established in the

and you do not worship what I worship;
and I shall not worship what you worship
and you will not worship what I worship.
You have your religion and I have mine.
— such is the tolerant Meccan Chapter 109 of the Koran.

Tafilelt, with Sigilmassa as its capital. This endured as an enclave of the Shiite heresy for many years. What is now Morocco was then divided between a number of virtually independent principalities of the kind still existing in the Gulf States. El-Muradi, an independent-minded governor of the area, raided the Sous valley in A.D. 739 and in doing so provoked revolts elsewhere. The viceroy of Kairouan managed to re-establish his control over the north, though farther south the great Berber tribe of the Barghawata maintained their political independence. This was based on their adherence to a strange sect originally founded in the north, in A.D. 742, by a Berber called Salih who proclaimed himself prophet and produced a sacred book in Berber which closely resembled the Koran. The southern plains were then well populated, the people living in large villages, and this Salihian state prospered for three hundred years before, upon its conquest, vanishing without trace.

IDRISSID DYNASTY AND OMMAYED AND FATIMID INFLUENCE (A.D. 788–c. 1050)

Another, though this time an orthodox, state was founded in 788 at Volubilis. It was to prove the germ from which, despite all vicissitudes, the state of Morocco was soon to grow and to endure. Moulay* Idriss was a great-grandson of Ali, the Prophet's cousin and original disciple to whom he gave his daughter Fatima as wife; it is the most illustrious lineage in Islam. But the Alids had lost the battle for power and Idriss became a refugee who with one attendant made the perilous journey to the Maghreb from the east. When he arrived at Volubilis the local tribe — Aouraba — received him with the honour due to his birth and a deep, superstitious respect for his *baraka*. *Baraka* is a mystic, charismatic power of benediction which, though the great may assume it and saints acquire it, has its real source in the Prophet's heredity. In the view of the Aouraba Idriss had it to an exceptional degree since he was not only a sherif but also a man of exceptional merit — a term which in this case denotes conspicuous devoutness. His servant Rashid, too, was evidently a man of exceptional ability. The Aouraba elected Moulay Idriss to be their *imam*, which in those days, and in the Berbers' sense of the

---

* 'Moulay' is a Maghrebi title of respect denoting a member of a sherifian family: a descendant of the Prophet.

word, meant he was to be their political and military leader as well as their spiritual mentor and leader of their prayers. Idriss and Rashid were doubtless devout men, but they combined the practical with the spiritual. They set about creating themselves a kingdom. Neighbouring areas inhabited by Jews. Christians and pagans were attacked and forced to accept Moulay Idriss as Moslem, Arab overlord. The Idrissid kingdom prospered; its growth alarmed the Caliph Harun er-Rashid for it could have proved the focal point for an Alid revival. The Caliph sent an agent to curry favour with Idriss in order to approach him closely enough to poison him — which was accomplished in 791 or 792. Idriss was buried in a mausoleum at a neighbouring settlement to Volubilis, farther up the hills, to which he may already have moved his base. A town grew up about the mausoleum, which is today the principal shrine in Morocco; it is called, simply, Moulay Idriss (see p. 285). Idriss had married a Berber woman who was with child at the time of his death; the infant proved to be a boy, Idriss II, in whose name Rashid acted as regent. If the Caliph had been alarmed by the growth of Idriss's principality, others were attracted by it. There was a steady flow of Arab immigrants into it. On Rashid's death one such succeeded him as regent until Idriss II was seventeen, at which age he assumed control. Idriss the elder had given the kingship its mystique, his son — most probably basing his policies upon Rashid's foundations — gave it its characteristically Arab administration. Neville Barbour* describes it thus,

This is a Muslim administration of which the methods are Arab, the official language is Arabic, and Arab arts and literature are encouraged. In this way Morocco was set on the path of becoming, by gentle and almost perceptible stages, Muslim and Arabic-speaking. Not that the Arabs ever proclaimed that Morocco was Arab in the way that the French were later to proclaim that Algeria was French. On the contrary, the Berber-speaking basis of the country was always recognized, and newly assimilated Berber areas for a time retained their customary law. Nevertheless the country became increasingly Muslim; the fact that the Qur'an was delivered in Arabic and that Islam arrived from the Arab East had the effect of emphasizing the Arab element in Morocco rather as

* Neville Barbour, *Morocco* (Thames and Hudson, London, 1965).

the practice of the Catholicism of Rome inevitably promotes a certain degree of the Latin outlook and civilization.

It was Idriss II who made Fes his capital. This was a move of great importance. A small and probably Berber settlement existed on the site before the move, on the right-hand, Andalus bank of the River Fes. It guarded a ford and had perhaps been established by Idriss I. Well-watered, in the heart of the politically all-important, most fertile district of northern Morocco, Fes is also on the natural cross-roads between the east-west route from the Atlantic to Algeria by the Taza Gap and that running south from the Mediterranean across the foothills of the Middle Atlas to the southern plains (from which the Sous is most easily approached) and over the least difficult pass across the High Atlas to the Tafilelt and the Saharan routes. Idriss's Fes consisted of his el-Aliya Palace, in what is now the Kairouyyin Quarter, perhaps also of barracks and officials' houses as well as administrative buildings, situated on the left bank of the river. This formed the nucleus of the new city which was to remain quite separate from the older settlement for two hundred years. It housed Idriss's 500-strong Arab guard. But the real making of the great city came in 818 when several thousand refugees arrived from Cordoba, whence they had been expelled, and, seven years later, by many others coming from Kairouan. Both those cities were leading centres of Arab civilization — indeed of all civilization at that time — and the refugees' arrival transformed Fes into one too, almost overnight. Ever since then Fes has been the spiritual and intellectual capital of Morocco whose influence has been felt throughout the Arab and Moslem world. Yet, like most other medieval cities, it was a self-centred town, distrustful of the different, rural community surrounding it and communicating only with other similar cities by means of trade, embassies and the movements of scholars, preachers and master craftsmen. Even today townsman and countryman seem like different beings and, behind its beautiful saffron-coloured walls, Fes is an island in an agrarian sea — the most beautiful city in the most beautiful setting in the West, surpassing even Edinburgh.

Idriss II died in 828 and was buried in his capital, where his shrine has a very real importance, almost as if he were the city's titular deity.

By about 836, authority became fragmented as the Idrissid kingdom began to dissolve swiftly into principalities once more, some of them Arab and Idrissid themselves, others Berber. North and east of Morocco, two great powers developed; the Caliphate of Cordoba in Spain and the Fatimid Kingdom of Kairouan. The last was Shiite and, in its strength, sought to dominate and to proselytize Morocco. In 917 the Fatimids annexed Alhucemas, a little state centring on the Mediterranean port of that name, and imposed their supremacy on Yahya IV of Fes. The Cordobans occupied the remaining Mediterranean ports, Ceuta, Melilla and Tangier, in order to counter the growing threat to themselves that they saw in the Fatimid advance. Serious conflict was, however, avoided since the Fatimids conquered Egypt in 969 and removed their capital to Cairo, and with it their western interests to the extent even of presently relinquishing their hold on Tunisia. For sixty years Cordoba's influence tended to grow over the Moroccan states. While this contained, or implied, a political threat, it was certainly of benefit from a cultural point of view. But Cordoba was rich, luxurious, and had strayed from rather than revolted against the ascetic paths of its founders. The small and greedy principalities of Morocco too tended to forsake all high ideals for reasons of practical expediency and to celebrate their successes with all sorts of departures from the Islamic code in favour of forbidden luxuries such as wine-drinking. This is a very necessary point to understand about Morocco: its history alternates violently between puritanical reform and lapses into sinful, sensual, moral backsliding.

Chapter 96 of the Koran, known as 'the Clot', is traditionally believed to have been the first of the Prophet's revelations. As handed down, it is a palimpsestic chapter; the first verse is thought original,

> Recite: In the name of your Lord who created,
> created man from a clot,
> Recite: and your Lord is most generous, who taught by the pen,
> taught man what he did not know.

This is orthodoxy. The next verse is perhaps an addition,

> No, but man is rebellious
> because he sees himself grown rich.
> Indeed, the return is to your Lord.

This states the antithesis and the remedy: the two verses together prophesy the history of all Islam and of Morocco with it.

The Fatimid withdrawal to Egypt led to a terrible catastrophe over all the Maghreb. Primitive and aggressive herdsmen, the Hilali Arab tribe from the Arabian peninsula, uprooted by nobody knows what agency, moved into Egypt and set about wreaking havoc there. The Fatimids' response to this was to induce them to move westwards. With an inexplicable, raging hatred of settled civilization and all its ways, the Hilali simply destroyed all they could of what men had done to make the Maghreb rich and civilized. They ruined the water supply systems, the irrigation works, the immense olive yards, the fields, villages, cities — anything that could not be defended against them. They fetched up in southern Morocco and were to prove important agents in the Arabization of the rural areas and the adoption of the Arabic language. Religious zeal, however, played no part in their raging progress.

SANHAJAN CONQUEST (c. A.D. 1050–c. 1075)

The sudden collapse of Cordoban power in 1031 cleared Morocco for the first of its great, puritan and unificatory revivals. The impulse to this and its leadership came from the far south, in the western Sahara which is now called Mauritania. There, there lived a Berber or Berber-speaking tribe of nomads of the Sanhaja family. Like the Tuaregs of today (who are also Berbers), the Sanhaja wore veils across the lower part of their faces, a not uncommon habit among the 'Blue men' of the south even now. The Sanhaja still flourish in Senegal and indeed that country derives its name from them. Around 1050 a sheikh of the tribe made a pilgrimage to Mecca and there discovered to his horror how very debased was the form of Islam practised by his fellow-tribesmen. They had been 'converted' in the ninth century, though neither, it seems, very able nor thoroughly. The sheikh determined to secure an instructor for his people and succeeded in persuading a narrowly pious Moroccan from the Sous called Abdullah Yasin to accept this perhaps not over-attractive task. Yasin was a *faqih*, an expert practitioner in religious law. Reform in Islam seems, in some inexplicable way, necessarily to be not merely militant but allied to militarism. The Prophet found it a necessary alliance though, since he was a genuine innovator, his circumstances do not form an exact precedent for subsequent reformers. However, Yasin began his mission mildly, contenting himself with preaching against such breaches of the law as wine-drinking, wives in excess of the statutory four and the practice of music — an art which, among the tentmen of the Arab world is always associated with licentiousness. The easygoing Sanhaja took violent exception to his strictures and became so threatening that Yasin was on the point of giving up his mission; but there were some who had been fired by his puritanism and with these he retired to an island. Its position is unknown; it could have been in the Senegal or Niger rivers, or off the Mauritanian coast. There they founded a *ribat*, a fortified, monastic institution not unlike a Templar castle whose inmates shared with the knights a similarly combative and aggressive piety. The very improbability that such a germ, planted off shore in that way, should grow to become a great empire is somehow entirely typical of Morocco; the fact that it was an irrational expectation could be just that element about it which was capable of touching Moroccan imaginations.

Yasin's disciples submitted to a fiercely sadistic discipline imposed with terrible lashings awarded for the least infringement of the letter of orthodox law. None the less they attracted recruits. Soon they were able to make sorties from the *ribat* forcibly to impose their asceticism on others. Though presumably their nearest neighbours were the first to be coerced, their first recorded success was the overthrow of the heretic state of Sigilmassa.*

By now Yasin remained at base, retaining religious and administrative control while Yahya ibn Omar, his lieutenant, commanded the military arm. The zealots worked fast: only four years after the pious sheikh had made his pilgrimage, with Sigilmassa already purged, they turned to the kingdom of Ghana and sacked its towns, reducing the population to a proper sobriety. Yahya died and was succeeded by his brother Abu Bekr. He attacked the Sous valley in 1056, where another small

---

* Islamic orthodoxy was pretty well established by the end of the first millennium A.D. It followed upon the critical acceptance of all relevant *sunna* – that body of anecdote and hearsay about the Prophet and his sayings originally supplied by his companions after his death, to fill the various crucial (mainly juridical) lacunae in the Koran. Had Mohammed lived longer, it was presumed he would have filled those gaps with pronouncements along the lines indicated by these traditional accounts. *Sunna* means 'tradition' and a *Sunni* Moslem is an orthodox Moslem. To what extent Morocco was then *Sunni* is not known, but that Yasin's followers were *Sunni* is certain.

Shiite state had sprung up based upon Taroudant. This too was reclaimed for strict orthodoxy. And Abu Bekr passed on over the High Atlas to the Haouz, the plain of Marrakech, where Aghmat had replaced Nifs as the chief town. There he married the first woman in Moroccan history to emerge as a personality — its beautiful and intelligent queen, Zeinab. From this base the Sanhaja attacked the heretical kingdom of the Barghawata. Yasin himself came up to take part in the campaign and was killed in the course of it, in 1059. However, Abu Bekr succeeded at least in cowing the Barghawata before dissensions following Yasin's death called him back to the Sahara in 1071. The command in the north was passed to his cousin Yussef ibn Tashfin together with Zeinab whom, rather touchingly, Abu Bekr deemed too delicate to be exposed to the rigours of the desert. However, with her experience and urban intelligence she may well have been judged essential to Sanhajan control of the sedentary tribes of their new territories, foreign in ways and manner of thought as these must have been to them. Enormously able as Yussef was to prove, one cannot avoid supposing that Zeinab's advice was crucial to him while he learned how to handle people and problems new in his experience. She last appears when Abu Bekr returned from the desert in 1072 or 1073 and she advised Yussef to meet him with presents pointedly chosen so that 'he would lack for nothing in the desert'. Finding the couple so well established beyond the Atlas, Abu Bekr wisely accepted the gifts in the spirit they were offered and returned again to the southern dominions which the Sanhaja had won themselves.

Yussef first united the bulk of Morocco. It has since fallen apart on more than one occasion while yet its inherent unity was recognized by its inhabitants. He founded Marrakech, the 'capital of the south', or, if Abu Bekr ordered its founding, its building fell to Yussef. It is a totally different town from Fes, a desert-man's compromise with the settled lands, sprawling like an encampment and bounded by an immense palmery planted rather for sentimental reasons (though it produces shade and timber) than for its fruit that does not ripen; a well-watered city where water is lavished with an opulence that only desert people can savour to the full, it accepts and entertains its surroundings. Yussef's Marrakech was, however, originally no more than a fortified camp about which a township grew. In this he followed Idriss II's manner of founding Fes; it was standard Arab practice. Yussef did not use it as an administrative capital. This was in fact his own tent, or anywhere he happened to be between battle-grounds. His was an itinerant court of officials through which he organized the Sanhaja into an established force and set up a civil administration divided into regions each with its own Sanhajan governor.

ALMORAVID DYNASTY (A.D. 1060–1147)

Fes was captured in 1062 also; then lost, and finally regained in 1069. Thirteen years later Yussef held all of the North African coast west of Algiers, less the ports under Spanish Moslem control. The veil the Sanhaja wore is called in Arabic a *litham* and its wearer *el-mulaththamun*, an expression from which the Moroccan Sanhajan dynasty derived the name Almoravid. We can now call Yussef's kingdom by it. Yussef set great store by Fes and the abundant Andalusian talent he found there: he joined the two settlements into one city and greatly improved its amenities.

ALMORAVID CONQUEST OF SPAIN

The collapse of the Ommayed Caliphate of Cordoba had meanwhile caused the disintegration of Moslem Spain into twenty-six states each too small effectively to sustain themselves, let alone the vainglorious pretensions of their rulers. The Christian states in the north of the Iberian peninsula pressed the advantage this offered them and when, in 1085, Alfonso VI captured Toledo, the key to central Spain, he was in a position to dictate to the Moslems. Only Seville, under its poet and soldier emir, el-Muatamid, was active and viable. Both Alfonso and el-Muatamid were the kind of men about whom legends accrue: they are said to have played chess together, the Christian for the table and chessmen, the Moslem — who won — for the safety of Seville. Alfonso is also reliably said to have married a daughter of el-Muatamid's as his last wife, despite the intermittent war between them.* It was el-Muatamid who took the risk — since the Moroccans were thought little better than barbarians by the sophisticated Andalusians — of imploring Yussef's help against the Christians.

Yussef did not hasten to give it. He was seventy years old about this time, a cautious, devout, upright and rugged man compared

---

* Thus bringing Elizabeth II into the family of the Prophet, although, since Alfonso was no sherif, no Moslem would recognize her *baraka*.

with the sophisticated, lax and luxury-loving men of el-Andalus. He began to bargain, first asking for possession of the ports that el-Muatamid held on Moroccan soil (which proves he was not a simple man), then demanding a port on Spanish soil to be his expeditionary base. He was given Algeciras. Eventually, in 1086, he crossed over and won a satisfactory battle against Alfonso with el-Muatamid as his chief ally. He then retired to Morocco, leaving 3,000 troops to help the Andalusians. He probably hoped that he had done enough to check Christian pressure, but such was the disunity and lack of resolve among the Andalusians that they were continually harried from the north.

In 1088 el-Muatimid visited Yussef personally to persuade him to return to Spain. This the old man did the following year. The principal object of the campaign was to retake the castle of Aledo near Murcia, but dissensions between the Andalusian princes so delayed the attack that Christian reinforcements arrived and Yussef was forced to retire, a very disillusioned man. The religious leaders of el-Andalus now petitioned Yussef to rid them of their inept rulers, claiming that their laxity and various taxes imposed in contravention of Islamic law had forfeited them their right to rule. It seems plain that Yussef was not anxious to rule el-Andalus, though he doubtless saw that it would be better if he did. He consulted his own religious leaders and those of the east before, with their permission, he decided to dispose of the Andalusians, returning again to Spain in 1090. El-Muatamid alone offered him serious resistance; he had asked Alfonso's help, but that chivalrous enemy was unable to give it. Yussef became ruler of all Moslem Spain. In exile, the king of Granada wrote a vivid account of his time while, at Aghmat, el-Muatamid mourned his lot in fine verse.

Almoravid distaste for Spain seems illustrated by the way they governed it: through governors supported by garrisons of Sanhajan troops who were sequestered in their quarters like enemy forces. Otherwise the Spaniards were left to live in their own way, at peace for the first time in years. The real losers in the wars were the Christians of el-Andalus — *Mozarabs*, they were called — whose loyalty had become suspect as soon as the Christians seriously attacked the Moslems. This large, highly civilized and prosperous community was disrupted and forced either to emigrate to the north or to Morocco — barbarous lands to their way of thinking — and begin life anew. Almoravid Morocco was the winner all round. Its cities were the new centres of power, patronage and wealth to which skilled Andalusians flocked; the Christian immigrants' talents were welcomed and Yussef constituted an elite regiment drawn from them which was presently based upon Marrakech. An indication of the success of the Almoravid empire is that its coinage was so respected that it was copied in Christian Spain.

Although this guide concentrates upon Morocco — and naturally therefore interests itself in Spain — it should not be forgotten that the Almoravids pressed their conquests into Algeria, the subsequent Almohad dynasty carrying theirs as far as Tunis and Tripoli.

Though Yussef ibn Tashfin died in 1107, over ninety years of age, the dynasty was maintained by his son Ali for another thirty-seven years. Succeeding at twenty-three, Ali began to follow his father's course, capturing Toledo and pushing the Christians back in Portugal. However, he grew increasingly preoccupied with religion and, while apparently coming much under the influence of his religious advisers, devoted himself to his own salvation while caring less and less about his people's welfare. Repeated attempts to recapture Toledo failed and Saragossa was lost to Aragon in 1118. Well before Ali's death in 1144 the notables of his kingdoms had begun to make themselves increasingly independent of the central authority. The realm was crumbling; Spanish laxity and the easy life were sapping Sanhajan vitality. The reign of Ali's son was a losing battle against rebellion; his younger brother Isaac's kingdom extended only as far as the walls of besieged Marrakech, and his life ended when those fell.

ALMOHAD DYNASTY (A.D. 1147–1244)

The Almohads, or 'Unitarians', were yet another reforming Berber sect who trusted less to persuasion than their swords to set the world to rights as they saw them. The sect was founded by Mohammed ibn Tumart, a member of the Masmuda tribe living in the High Atlas and Anti-Atlas regions. A settled people, they detested the desert Almoravids. (It was because of their animosity that Marrakech was founded away from the mountains rather than Aghmat extended by the Almoravids.) A strict puritan, ibn Tumart was also a learned theologian, a sufficiently ambitious, insolent and self-deluding man eventually to claim for himself the title of el-Mahdi, the promised one who is exempt from sin. He went east to study at the great theological schools of Islam at the time of Yussef's death, returning ten years later with but three disciples, 'teaching and reproving what is disapproved and enjoining what is good' — the words are those of the Koran. Ibn Tumart publicly disapproved not only of wine, but of such things as gold laces in men's boots, their wearing garments cut like those of women and their walking with those limbs of the devil during festivals, also of brides riding and, of course, of music. He laid about him to enforce his disapprobation and the police had to restrain him. At Benjaia (ex-Bougie), where this happened, ibn Tumart was joined by Abd el-Mumin, a delegate from a group of students at Tlemcen who invited him to be their teacher. (This encounter, and the other circumstances and events in el-Mumin's life, were soon translated into miracles.) The new disciple was clearly a man of great ability, an outstanding general and administrator whom one suspects of having used ibn Tumart's puritanism as the spearhead of his own secular ambition — though in this one may do injustice to the curiously complex nature of the Moslem desire to reform while seeing that that reform endures; it is at once an excuse and a genuine desire that others shall benefit from the greater chances of heaven a leader believes he can enforce. Certainly Abd el-Mumin was a more cultivated and balanced man than the teacher to whom he attached himself as chief lieutenant and principal disciple.

This pair and their band of followers spent about four years on their journey by Tlemcen, the Rif, Fes, Meknes and Salé to Marrakech, arriving there in 1121. By this time ibn Tumart was a well-known and controversial figure. He had his partisans as well as his enemies. The ostentatious piety of Ali the Sultan could have been an obstacle to his now clearly established plans to lead a revolt, but he successfully insulted the gentle sultan by quoting specious points of law against his habits. Rebuked, Ali forgave him. As so often, the fanatic profited by the saint's forbearance, and when the zealot upbraided Ali's sister for riding unveiled (as all Sanhajan women, like their desert sisters today, commonly went), knocking her from her mount, the saint forbore to execute him and banished him instead.

Ibn Tumart retired to the fastness of Tinmel in the High Atlas where he organized the local Berbers into a closely disciplined religious and military force. The same savagery as that meted out by Abdullah Yasin characterized his rule. Among the mountain tribes those that were not for him were called hypocrites and executed. To teach the Berbers Arabic prayers they were each given as names the words from a prayer and, stood in order, were made to recite these. His teaching so stressed the imminence of the coming of the Mahdi that one day his followers got the point and declared it was he himself. Thus it was a curious mixture of subtlety and sadism that moulded the Almohads.

In eight or nine years' time ibn Tumart's band had gained control of the Atlas and began to attack the plain, unsuccessfully at first. Ibn Tumart died at this time, though his death seems to have been kept secret for a long while during which el-Mumin's succession was ensured — 1129 or 1130. For years the Almohads attacked the Almoravids under el-Mumin's leadership. The Almoravid Christian regiment was largely wiped out in 1144; Ali's son Tashfin ben Ali was killed escaping from Ceuta in 1145, the year Fes was taken; and the end came with the fall of Marrakech in 1147. The Almoravids and their supporters were massacred to a man. Tashfin's boy-son with them, and some of their great key buildings — mosques, palaces and so on — destroyed. This set a sadly wasteful tradition in Morocco where new dynasties tried to blot out the memory of their predecessors and a man, upon inheriting his father's wealth, still often builds his own house and leaves his father's to rot. For a country with so splendid a tradition of building, Morocco is too full of ruins and has too few old buildings maintained as reminders of its proud past. Though to be fair, it must be said that this is not unusual in Moslem lands; for Islam is not really a past-regarding religion since, believing that the truth has been spoken for all time, its aim is not to seek precedent and example but simply to keep that truth pure — which is what Moroccan puritan revivals are about. Moslem saints are Franciscans, never Augustinians or Jesuits, though often mystics.

The twelfth century is one of the greatest moments in the Western world; some synthesis of vitality and, perhaps, of optimism galvanized men's imagination.* It is the peak period in Romanesque art — barbaric vivacity the confident master of old skills — and the greatest period, too, for the older worlds of Byzantium and its Moslem daughter. (The Christian–Moslem conflict was like a tempestuous marriage from which both parties gained.) As in Moslem and Christian Spain, this was a golden age

---

* It was a period of warm and stable weather, which can have been enough to provoke vitality and optimism.

of the mind and spirit in Morocco. It is worth remembering also that it was contemporary with the superb civilization of Norman Sicily to which Arab arts and learning contributed so much. There was no such hybrid style in the Almoravid empire, however. The Arabs had long before evolved their own manner from Syrio–Greek, Byzantine and Sassanian models, and the local Christian contribution was by then absorbed into the Spanish style upon which the Moroccans drew heavily. The Moroccans, however, imposed so marked an austerity on their models that there is a decided difference between building north and south of the Straits: the Giralda at Seville; the Chapel of las Claustrillas at Burgos; Santa Maria la Blanca, formerly the synagogue of Toledo: these against the Koutoubia Mosque and the Bab Aguenau at Marrakech; the shrine of ibn Tumart at Tinmel; the Great Mosque at Tlemcen; the Hassan Tower at Rabat where, too, there are the Bab er-Rouah and the Oudaïa Citadel — you have to see them to understand their temperamental divergence.

This was also the great age of medieval science, medicine and travel in which the Almoravid and Almohad empires led the West.

Abd el-Mumin, now styled Caliph, ruled until his death in 1162. During his later years the empire was threatened by two nomad Arab tribes whom, disorderly and predatory, the Fatimid Caliph of Cairo had deliberately loosed on North Africa. Defeating them in 1152, el-Mumin removed them into Morocco to act as special troops against Berber recidivist movements (for those persisted always upon traditional lines), and primarily to hold the Barghawata down after he had destroyed their state. This had the disastrous result of unsettling the people of the south-west, uprooting them from their prosperous, sedentary existence and laying waste the area. It also had the effect of spreading the Arab language at the expense of Berber, as happened in the former Almoravid deserts when another Arab tribe, the Maaqil, penetrated that area. (This part of what is now 'Mauritania' then became a centre of Arab learning and is still wholly Arabic-speaking.) The Almohads disliked the Jews, many of whom emigrated, while others pretended to accept Islam in order to remain in the empire.

Abd el-Mumin was succeeded by Abu Yaacub Yussef. He reigned until 1184 — twenty-two years — and was succeeded in turn by Yaacub el-Mansur who reigned another nine. Between them they pushed the Almohad empire as far as the Almoravids had in Spain, while, in Africa, they extended their rule as far as Tripoli. El-Mansur's successor, Mohammed en-Nasser, reigned until 1213. Two years before his death he had decided on an all-out attack on Christian Spain. King John of England sent an embassy to him that most probably concluded an agreement by which, should en-Nasser cross the Pyrenees, they would be allies, for John was mounting a campaign to be launched from Aquitaine to recover Normandy, and needed to secure his rear. Other Christian monarchs were prepared at least in principle to defend Europe against en-Nasser. The Caliph was however soundly beaten on the border of el-Andulus, at Las Navas de Tolosa, in 1212, and returned to Marrakech to die. The standard he lost at Las Navas is in the monastery of Huelgas at Burgos, and very fine it is.

Quickly then, Moslem power declined in el-Andalus. Valencia was lost in 1228, Cordoba in 1236 and Seville in 1248. Under succeeding Almohad Caliphs the central authority in Morocco itself grew weaker. The *bled es-siba*, as the unruly, scarcely controlled areas of the country were called, increased at the expense of the *bled el-makhzen*, the areas fully under the control of the Government. The eastern provinces became more and more independent and when the dynasty ended in effect, in 1244, their erstwhile viceroys made themselves independent in fact.

MERINID AND BENI WATTASID DYNASTIES
(A.D. 1244–1554)

The now customary confusion attended the ending of Almohad rule. A saintly leader of the Beni Merin tribes of Berbers founded the movement that raised the new dynasty. Although not a sherif, Abd el-Haqq was revered for the degree of *baraka* with which he was credited, yet this time the impetus towards revolt was not religious. Beginning with el-Mumin himself, the Almohads had increasingly played down the Mahdi's claim to that title because it was an inherently heretical one. Although ibn Tumart's high standards of behaviour had been relaxed. Almohad orthodoxy left little definite for a reformer to attack. The Beni Merin were simply strong and the Almohads weak.

The reign of the first Beni Merin, Abu Yahya,* is usually

---

* Abu Yahya was more a leader and general of the tribe than a sultan of Morocco; some lists of rulers therefore ignore him, counting the dynasty from Abu Yussef Yaacub in 1258.

counted from his capture of Fes in 1248, though sometimes from four years earlier. His long line ruled until 1465, though by that time the hereditary Viziers of the kingdom had held effective power for a generation or more and in that year usurped the throne, which they held until 1554. This dynasty of the Viziers is called the Beni Wattas. There is little difference save in name between them, and the 306 years during which the rule of these native tribes endured was a time of consolidation in Morocco. Attempts to recover lost territory in Spain and to the east failing, the frontiers of the country were stabilized on much the same lines as they occupy today. The Merinids formed the Makhzen or civil stage organization that endured little change until very recent times. It is from this time that the country was described as being divided between the governed *bled el-makhzen* and the lawless *bled es-siba*; an acknowledgment of the perpetually fluctuating, though perennially stable, state of affairs formerly pertaining in Morocco. The Merinids also formed the basis of a regular army largely drawn from Spanish Moslem refugees, Christian converts (or renegades) and frequently supplemented and led by Christian mercenaries. The close involvement with Spain which the Merinids inherited grew ever more intricate, more expedient and less genuinely hostile, although as the Christians increasingly occupied the Iberian peninsula they began to attempt the conquest of Morocco. In this tempestuous marriage neither side seemed willing to let the other go. It was a stormy, failed attempt to find a modus vivendi. At times each side tried to accommodate the other, particularly in matters of religion and trade. They quarrelled over areas of influence and division of property and made alliances across their differences as often as they confronted each other directly. The Christian kings of Portugal, Leon and Castile, Navarre and Aragon were rarely in alliance (they were painfully amalgamating their little states) and the rulers of Morocco, Granada, Tlemcen and Tunis were no better. Strongest among the last group were the Merinids, though they proved subject to inevitable, slow decline.

Granada was lost to the Christians in 1492 and Moslem Spain was finished. The Caliph of Morocco had been unable to do anything to save it; presently the Merinids were to lose all their seaports to the Christians. The bishopric of Fes, with a church and convent at Marrakech, had been established by the Almoravids in 1231 and existed officially until 1639, though the bishops retired to Seville in 1400 and visited Ceuta on African soil only after that port fell into Christian hands in 1415. On the other hand the list of Christian notables and even of royal persons who took service with the Caliphs is too long to enumerate — as is that of Moslems serving Christians. The Knight in Chaucer's *Canterbury Tales* tells how he had been besieged in Algeciras during a Moslem attack and then crossed the Straits to 'ride in Belmarie' — i.e. Beni Merin Morocco. It is a pleasant description of the actual state of affairs around 1400. Nevertheless the act of divorce which the fall of Granada represented altered the relationship; after it the Christians tended more and more to be aggressive and even vindictive, the Moslems increasingly on the defensive. Divorce proved as unhappy as marriage, uneasy mutual attraction persisting despite damaged pride. If it was the Christians who forced the divorce they have regretted it. The French and Spanish ended by raping their old love and Morocco remains in two minds, divided between pleasure and resentment of it, and possibly quite content that the dialogue has been resumed.

One should remember here that the 'expulsion of the Moors' after the fall of Granada had a political meaning only. It was a gesture and, however many Christians then came to Morocco, still in the latter half of the sixteenth century much of southern Spain was farmed by Moslem *fellahin*.

Christian aggression carried the attack scarcely farther than the coastal towns and their surrounding districts. By far the greater part of the country, governed or lawless, now became almost as isolated as it had been before Roman times. Spain and Portugal were returned wholly to the European community, a fact which increased the difficulty of communicating across the Straits. Morocco was further isolated by the advance of the Turks along the North African coast. Although they were Moslems, the Turks were the conquerors of the Arabs and their empire, and were never accepted as anything but enemies by the conquered. Except as mercenaries, however, they never entered Morocco. Establishing themselves in Algiers by 1518, the Turks soon after captured Tlemcen. This erected a more formidable barrier along the frontier than any dynastic rivalries between rulers east and west of it ever had. Morocco's exceptional isolation thenceforward had the happy result of preserving both its Arab-ness and its Berber-ness more intact than elsewhere, but at the same time it caused Moroccan life to become increasingly ingrowing, static and anachronistic, and its people to grow jealous and suspicious of the outside world.

The Beni Merin were a cultured and learned tribe. Under their caliphs, learning was encouraged and most of the beautiful *medrassa* (student hostels or colleges) of Fes and elsewhere were constructed by them, besides Chella (p. 179) which was the burial-ground of their early caliphs, Fes el-Jedid (the palace and administrative quarter of that city) and countless mosques. Their elegant buildings fixed that pattern to which Moroccan building and decoration have adhered closely ever since. Though no Merinid palace has survived, one might almost call the Alhambra at Granada one since it is contemporary and the Merinid style owed more to borrowed Spanish taste than the Spanish owed to Moroccan. During this period the great Arab traveller, ibn Battuta, a native of Tangier, was encouraged by the Caliph Abu Inan to set down his account of his journeys (1355). At the same caliph's court the historian ibn Khaldun resided, an equally great scholar of Sevillan descent. Another learned traveller who bene- fited from Merinid education was (John) Leo Africanus, who was born Hassan ibn Mohammed, in Granada. He studied at Fes before making long journeys in Africa and the Near East. He was returning when he was captured off Djerba by Christian pirates and slavers. Because he was so intelligent and knowledgeable they made a present of him to Pope Leo, who became his patron and, upon his conversion, godfather. It was for this pope that he wrote his famous description of Africa. Around 1552 he returned to Tunis and, it is said, Islam.

The Christian–Arab divorce proved an acrimonious one. The Portuguese and Spaniards carried their attacks across the Straits to the Moroccan ports. As early as 1260 the Spaniards had taken Salé and held it for a fortnight before Abu Yussef Yaacub the Merinid turned them out. In 1400 Tetouan was seized, destroyed, and the inhabitants sold as slaves or killed. The Portuguese capture of Ceuta in 1415 was instigated by the king's half-English sons (their mother was Philippa of Lancaster) who were really to start Portuguese colonial expansion. For a century, raids were constant upon the Atlantic coast towns. In 1427 an attempt on Tangier failed, but the neighbouring port of Ksar es-Seghir went in 1452, Asilah and Tangier itself in 1471. Massa, on the mouth of that river, south of Agadir, was captured by the Portuguese about the end of the century or just after. This was extended to Agadir, where a merchant adventurer had built a fort which he sold to his Government in 1505, by assault in 1513. El-Jadida (called Mazagan by the Portuguese) also began as a fort built in 1502, the town being founded in 1506, the same year as a fortress was built at Essaouira (then called Mogador). Safi, which had enjoyed *ipso facto* independence of the central government under some sort of Portuguese protection since 1486, proved stubborn against direct annexation and held out until 1513 when the inhabitants abandoned the city and all the region round, forcing the Portuguese to supply the port by sea.

THE MARABOUTS

Moroccan national feeling ran high in the face of all these disasters. The Government's powerlessness to prevent or reverse the losses exasperated the people, yet such was the respect the throne commanded that revolution was slow in coming. Instead of rebellion, disaffection took the form of intensified sufism and maraboutism.

Islam has a dry, unadorned clarity about it very different to the sensual and materialistic temperament of many of its adherents. Large areas of the doctrine are open to the intrusion of personal mysticism — this is one of its great strengths — and men who fill out these areas imaginatively find a ready response among others less creative. Sometimes the innovator makes an emotional, colourful, even an orgiastic approach to the deity in an effort to establish a feeling of closer identity with godhead. Mystics of this kind are called sufi. The Shias of Persia proved particularly fertile of sufism but it is in Islam everywhere a potent, stimulating and not altogether orthodox agency. Other teachers, as we have seen, incline to a narrow, ascetic form of piety and self-discipline sometimes amounting to masochism. Discipline of one sort or another is usually a major feature in all these cults. A leader of this kind in fact always creates his cult by disciplining his followers. Some, and there are many of them, reach no wider than a circle of friends in the village or neighbourhood; others attract adherents over a large area, a few nation-wide respect. The cults of some teachers, or marabouts (whether sufis or not), have endured a long while and these, however little the cult may now represent the instigator's teaching, have for long been regarded as saints in terms very similar to the lay Christian conception. Veneration of them, though possibly diffuse, is profound. From the looser or closer societies of followers over whom, in their lifetimes, the founders presided, a few large confraternities have developed. Some marabouts in their lifetimes founded *zouawi* cult centres usually tantamount to monasteries, though sometimes merely places for occasional meetings. Some few have founded movements very roughly corresponding to Christian lay orders.

Morocco is dotted over with the domed tombs (*koubbas*) of marabouts whose names, remembered, legendary or forgotten, are always focuses of holiness, repositories of *baraka*, channels leading more directly to heaven and therefore propitious places by which to pray.

Somewhere between the most widely respected and the very local saint fall those whose attraction is strong in their time, though ephemeral. It was mostly this kind around which the Moroccans gathered during the country's crisis in face of Christian aggression. Under the circumstances it was natural that a strong element of xenophobia should characterize their cults. Leaders were militant from exasperation rather than any desire for reform. Besides satisfying the desire to seek out intermediaries between themselves and God, the Moroccans have found that their religiously based confraternities helped them to a sense of identity and purpose despite a social system designed to exploit the majority and governments which, from the earliest times to most recently, were generally self-seeking and cynical. At this crisis they were almost fanatically drawn to these voluntary organizations which offered the direction and purpose which a weak government failed to inspire. Gradually the various new confraternities took over effective control of the country and formed irregular troops to oust the foreigners from their footholds. In doing so they saved Morocco for themselves, but their intense xenophobia increased still further the country's isolation.

Rise of the Saadi family

In addition to the marabouts there were sherifian families living in the country, any of whose members who showed ability could attract a similar kind of following on account of the inherited *baraka* he possessed. The sherifian family of the Beni Saad (who, tradition claims, had long before been invited to the Sous valley so that the date crop might benefit from their *baraka*), began at this juncture to assume leadership of resistance to the Portuguese in Agadir. Among the plethora of maraboutic leaders no ibn Tashfin nor ibn Tumart emerged, so the active Saadi sherifs were in an ideal position to assume also the headship of the national movement. In the first instance they rose, locally in the Sous, against the rule of the Beni Merin and by 1510 had made themselves a little principality based on Taroudant. Ten years later they captured Marrakech and held all the south. This was the period when, since there were two realms in the country, foreigners spoke of the 'Kingdom of Fes' and the 'Kingdom of Marrakech' — which name became corrupted to 'Morocco' by which the whole country is still known in Europe. At the same time the Saadi kept up a 'holy war' against the Portuguese. It was a dignified title for the constant harassment and ambuscading by which the Moslems sought to deny the Portuguese garrisons all benefit of local produce in order to deplete their numbers. It was not often a savage campaign, prisoners usually being ransomed rather than enslaved, but it was effective. The Portuguese were weakened by the deaths of their ablest general and of their most powerful Moroccan ally. This contributed to the Saadi's success in forcing them to abandon Agadir in 1541. It had been the chief Portuguese base; its loss meant that during the following months Essaouira, Safi and Azemmour were evacuated because untenable. With this notable success behind them, the Saadi were able to push on to the conquest of Fes in 1548. Although in 1553 the Beni Watta caliph did homage to the Turkish sultan and, with Turkish troops, regained Fes for a few months, the Saadi now had nothing more to do than mop up their rivals. This accomplished, they began to fall out among themselves.

SAADI DYNASTY (A.D. 1554–1659)

The conqueror of Fes, Mohammed esh-Sheikh, was the first Saadi sultan. A provincial, the Fasiyin hated him and laughed at his attempts to attain urban graces; this was partly responsible for his decision to make Marrakech his capital, the rebuilding of the ruins of which he began before his death. This occurred while he was on a punitive expedition in the High Atlas in 1557. Turkish mercenaries whom he employed as personal guards murdered him and cut off his head, then smuggled it to Istanbul where it was nailed to the city wall. Hearing of his death, the Caïd of Marrakech ordered the murder of the late sultan's imprisoned uncle and his seven male descendants — this to further the succession of esh-Sheikh's eldest son, Abdullah el-Ghalib. Abdullah's two younger brothers escaped with their mother and took refuge at the Sublime Porte.

Abdullah and his successors had to play a difficult diplomatic game for the independence of the country. The Spaniards and

Portuguese had earlier come to an arrangement that while the Portuguese should have a free hand in Morocco the Spaniards could do as they liked with the rest of North Africa. Both had now been dislodged, the Portuguese by the Saadi and the Spaniards by the Turks (who had responded to appeals from the Algerians and Tunisians, but, once there and in control, intended to stay on as masters). Though anxious to oust the Christians still in Mazagan, Ceuta and Melilla, the Saadi were still more anxious to have an ally against the Turks. Abdullah was thus forced into an alliance with Spain. His position was weak since he could not actively support Spanish enterprises against his co-religionists the Turks, nor, when the Moslems of Granada rose without success against their Spanish masters, could he help them beyond winking at arms smuggling and showing readiness to receive their refugees. (These were of the greatest consequence in Morocco and, again, the arts of the period largely owe their splendour to them.) This enforced inaction when fellow-Moslems were in need brought disrepute to his otherwise almost saintly reputation. However, he died 'still young', writes Deverdun,* 'of an asthmatic crisis having used and abused the pleasures of life' — 'a swinish life,' d'Aubigné goes so far as to say — which ended in 1574. (Islamic piety allows one creature pleasures which Christian piety abhors.)

His son Mohammed el-Masluh was evidently a strange man, cultivated, cowardly and clearly not without attraction if, as a chronicler reports, he was 'greeted with demonstrations of unequivocal joy and enthusiasm'. His refugee uncles returned from Turkey and, armed with troops from Algiers, invested Fes. Unnerved by the defection of his Andalusian troops, which had made the pretenders' advance possible, Mohammed withdrew to Marrakech with scarcely a skirmish. There he was followed by Abd el-Malik, the elder of his uncles, who was able to take the town without opposition. Mohammed bolted for the Sous, Abd el-Malik following. But there Mohammed stopped running, collected a rabble army and, evading his uncle, dodged back to Marrakech to be received warmly by the people. The casbah was, however, closed to him by his aunt, Abd el-Malik's sister, who commanded six hundred infantrymen. (Women wielded unusual influence in the Saadi family, as they generally do among desert Arabs; this was always held against the dynasty by Moroccan

* Gaston Deverdun, *Marrakech dès ses Origines à 1912* (Édit. Techniques Nord-Africaines, Rabat, 1959).

purists.) The Jews of the Mellah (official Jewish quarter) also shut their gates to Mohammed; in revenge he turned his men loose on those Jews inhabiting the other quarters of the city. In a few days' time Abd el-Malik was back and his brother on the road from Fes with reinforcements. Again Mohammed fled to the Sous, and from there presently to Portugal. Inexplicably, the Marrakchi continued to resist after Mohammed had gone and until the notables of one quarter made a breach in the walls to let the besiegers in.

Abd el-Malik was a new kind of sultan for Morocco. Besides Arabic, Turkish and Italian he spoke Spanish (as did many of his subjects; it was then said Spanish was as often heard in the capital as Arabic, the bulk of the people still speaking Berber). His wide-ranging culture included a knowledge of the Bible. His first acts were to dismiss most of his Turkish troops and to improve relations with European powers. Elizabeth of England sent him an embassy in 1577 under Edward Hogan. Hogan has left an interesting account of the city and court — Abd el-Malik employed English musicians and in Hogan's company baited bulls with English dogs. A trade agreement was concluded between the countries, but not the political one the sultan had hoped to reach against Spain. British and Dutch trade was already pretty brisk with Agadir and Safi. With the luxuries of dates and almonds, Moroccan sugar and molasses were much in demand in Europe, Elizabeth's household alone consuming vast quantities. 'Morocco' began to become a generic term in English for a type of dyed sheepskin leather of fine quality. English sailors were held to be the most knowledgeable about the Moroccan coast. In London a Barbary Company was formed in 1585. Montaigne noticed columns being prepared in Italian quarries for the sultan who, like his successors, was a notable builder.

However, his position was soon disputed by his nephew. Taking the only course open to him, treacherous though it may have been, Mohammed did a vassal's homage to King Sebastian of Portugal in return for help in regaining his throne. Success would have meant returning the Atlantic ports; as it was he gave Sebastian Asilah, it being still held by his adherents. Here an immense army, strong in artillery, disembarked in July 1578. Sebastian was young and devout; he regarded this as a crusading campaign. The army was led by Sebastian and Mohammed and accompanied by a papal nuncio and a number of bishops in charge of several hundred priests, very many of the campaigners' wives and children, splendid coaches for the royals and nobles —

> ... two thousand armed horses
> And fourteen thousand men that serve on foot,
> Three hundred pioneers and a thousand coachmen,
> Besides a number almost numberless
> Of drudges, Negro-slaves, and muleteers,
> Horse-boies, laundresses, and courtesans,
> And fifteen hundred wagons full of stuffe
> For noblemen brought up in delicate

— as George Peele, the near-contemporary dramatist, described it in his *Battle of Alcazar.** (His figures are questionable.) Leaving the protection of his fleet at Larache, Sebastian and this sumptuous High Renaissance escort moved inland towards the then important centre of Ksar el-Kebir.

Abd el-Malik was suffering now from a mortal disease. He offered terms which Sebastian refused rather than forgo his crusade. The armies met in the valley of the Makhazen, a tributary of the River Loukkos. Perhaps because they felt themselves to be so strong in faith, artillery and numbers, and thinking that Abd el-Malik's offer declared him uncertain of his strength, the Portuguese elected to fight a defensive battle, forming a square about their baggage, transport, womenfolk and camp-followers. This lost them the day. It was as dramatic a day as any ever fought. Mohammed was drowned in the river; Sebastian killed. Abd el-Malik died of a seizure during the early part of the battle and his brother Ahmed, proclaimed on the field, ended the day with the title el-Mansur — 'the victorious'. It was dubbed the 'Battle of the Three Kings', that is to say, of those who fell during it. The Portuguese lost 26,000 killed or taken prisoner. The victors' loot comprised the entire camp, baggage-train, transport, artillery, women (few of whom were really likely to have been drudges), prelates and valuable noble children — their ransoms were nearly as valuable as the rest of the booty. So, with these riches and his kingdom, Ahmed el-Mansur inherited a great reputation for power, although it was perhaps more the folly of the Portuguese and less his own might which had earned it him.

It was in fact a less glorious victory than it seemed. Sebastian

---

* Marlowe Society Reprint, 1907.

had been childless and his crown presently passed by inheritance to Spain; Portugal, Tangier, El-Jadida (Mazagan) and Portuguese claims to the Moroccan Atlantic ports went with it. The balance of Moroccan diplomacy was therefore altered for the worse. Protestant England and Holland, while they had prayed for a Catholic victory over the Turks at Malta, were ready enough now to brave the displeasure of Catholic Europe by building up trade with Morocco, thereby implying though not actually making a political alliance with her. However, both France and Spain also traded with Morocco, holding their Christian noses the while. Spain in fact had a sizeable colony of merchants in Marrakech.

Sugar, introduced into the Sous as long before as the Almohad dynasty, and saltpetre for gunpowder were Morocco's chief exports. The soft leather of the country was also in luxury demand all over Europe. In return Morocco sought arms, timber and cloth; yet the sultan could not acknowledge the trade any more openly than his partners.

Cultivated and worldly like his brother before him, Ahmed played a role in European politics. When the Spanish threat to England was mounted he proposed to Elizabeth that she should send him a hundred ships to transport an army to attack Spain's rear. He offered 150,000 ducats on their arrival. But Elizabeth could not spare the ships, nor did she want a Moslem invasion of Spain. The defeat of the Armada caused a great riot between the English and Spanish merchants living at Marrakech which Ahmed himself had to subdue.

The Turkish land-threat to Europe had temporarily been halted at Vienna in 1523 and its sea power had, as it turned out, been broken for ever at the battle of Lepanto in 1571. These Christian victories aided Moslem Morocco. Nevertheless the Turks were still the greatest power and influence in the Moslem world. Like his brother, Ahmed had spent seventeen years in Istanbul and affected many Ottoman ways. Since his family had no tribal basis to draw its strength from, his army consisted partly of Turkish mercenaries, partly of Christian renegades, all of them dressed in Turkish uniforms, as were his servants and, often, himself. Neither had the Saadi dynasty any religious foundation beyond sherifian blood. Their fondness for foreign ways and tolerance of foreign relations weakened their position vis-à-vis their xenophobic subjects. For this they had to compensate. Primarily they did this by maintaining peace in the sultanate.

With the exceptions of the civil war and Sebastian's incursion — neither of which involved very many Moroccans or much disrupted life — they succeeded in keeping peace in the country from the reign of Ahmed esh-Sheikh onwards.

El-Mansur also very considerably increased the country's wealth. Possibly out of ambition, possibly out of a desire to gain popular favour, he set out to tap at source the riches which came into the country from the Sahara. A first attempt in 1581 was only partly successful. This was an expedition sent to take the oases of Goura and Tuat in the central desert. These controlled the output of near-by salt-mines and the gold trade. However, the exploiters of the mines merely moved south to other sites and the gold-dealers went with them. Ahmed then attempted to levy a toll on Saharan salt output, but this was rejected by the king of Songhai. In the winter of 1590 Ahmed sent an army of 4,000 men into the desert to enforce his toll. They marched for 135 days until they reached the Niger. Half the force had perished, but the fire-arms of the remainder were so far superior to the weapons of the Songhai warriors that their victory in the spring of 1591 was a complete one. In spite of offers of indemnity and tribute, Ahmed insisted upon the conquest of all the Sudan (North African Arabs call all the country bordering the southern Sahara the Sudan; this can be confusing. We tend to think of this western savannah country as the Sahel.) Probably the territory the Moroccans conquered was a strip north of the Niger, not reaching the sea nor extending so very far eastwards. It was, however, to be one of the major influences in the Islamization of a far larger area in central Africa. The province was ruled from Timbuctou, which was already a centre of Islamic learning. In fact, the Moroccan rule — although the invading force was made up of renegades and Christian mercenaries, its official language Spanish and chief officers eunuchs of Spanish extraction — was chaotic and ruinous to the whole area; cruel, treacherous and rapacious. The object had been to secure the near legendary source of Wangara gold (traded for salt, neither side in the deal — at least not until the eleventh century — seeing or speaking to the other, but setting out their wares and retiring, and only taking them away when satisfied with the silent offer). Though this object was not achieved, the negro gold miners and the Sahalian middlemen kept the location of the mines secret; Moroccan possession of the Saharan salt mines ensured the continuous flow of gold northwards. Thus, with control over immense resources of gold, salt, slaves, ivory, ebony and such high-priced aphrodisiacs (as they were believed to be) as powdered rhinoceros horns. Ahmed acquired another surname: ed-Dhabi, 'the Golden'. For forty-two years the Sudan was ruled from Morocco, after which the Pashas of Timbuctou won varying degrees of independence. Though by then Moroccan claims on the area were little more than honorific, in theory it remained in the sultans' possession until the French occupation of 1893. There may be something in the claim that the spread of Islam in Africa impeded the growth of slavery there — it being illegal for Moslems to enslave Moslems — but since their own consumption of slaves was so high and their command of the trade so complete I think this claim is doubtful.

DECLINE OF THE SAADI

Ahmed died in 1603, leaving no heir strong enough to succeed him without rivalry. Civil war broke out between his sons, the citizenry of Fes and Marrakech adding to its bitterness by each asserting their claims to be the dominant influence in the country. These wars were particularly bloody and ruthless, the inhabitants of both great cities and of the Sous faring the worst and those of flourishing Marrakech worst of all. Already before Ahmed's death, marabouts in various remoter parts had begun to exert a new influence — it was time again for a revival of puritanism — and while the fratricidal wars went on they were scarcely checked at all. In fact they came to be the only powers able to control a large part of the country or to maintain any stability.

Ahmed's son and governor of Marrakech, Abu Faris Abdullah, seized his father's treasure and the casbah while the Fasiyin proclaimed his younger brother Zaydan as sultan. Their elder brother Mamun, who as heir-presumptive had been a notably unpleasant kind of debauchee, was released by Abu Faris from the imprisonment his father had ordered and enabled to raise an army to march on his brother in Fes. This task he left to his own son Abdullah, proclaiming himself sultan in comfort. Abdullah saw his chance and chased Zaydan from Fes and also Abu Faris from Marrakech. He celebrated his victory over the last city by sacking the town. The Marrakchi therefore appealed to Zaydan, a man who appears to have had considerable quality. The citizens let him secretly into the city and rose in his behalf. A three-day street-battle ensued. Finally Abdullah and most of his men tried to escape by a narrow lane under the walls and were there trapped by the people and massacred, Abdullah himself and a few others alone getting away. This 'battle of the Bakkar Garden' took place in February 1607. Others of Abdullah's supporters who held the casbah were induced to surrender, then slaughtered. By that winter Abdullah, who was reconciled to his father and had with him become identified with Fasi claims to the throne, was back at Marrakech. The people had disliked Zaydan's rule and allowed him in. As a reward for their services they were given over to a more thorough spoliation than before. Those of Zaydan's soldiers who had remained in the city were treated no less treacherously than Abdullah's garrison had been, but in a still more horrifying and humiliating manner. Many of the townsfolk fled to the Gueliz, beyond the walls, and there proclaimed one of Ahmed's grandsons, whom they found among themselves, as sultan. Marching back to the city they were able to rid themselves of Abdullah without much difficulty. Their pious sultan proving clement towards Abdullah's soldiers, this so enraged the citizens that they once again sent for Zaydan. They must have been in terrible straits to do so; the Dutch consul reported them to be starving and the city so lawless that he was a virtual prisoner behind the walls of the consulate where he had sheltered many people of various sorts and factions. In 1608 therefore Zaydan was back. He was never able to recapture Fes where he had first been proclaimed. Between his own periodic assaults upon it various of his relatives attacked it on their own behalf and it was reduced to the same anarchy as Marrakech had been. Mamun bribed the Spaniards to his cause by ceding Larache to them in 1610. This was a signal for an uprising in the High Atlas led by a marabout called Abu 'l-Mahalli who quickly occupied the Dra and the Tafilelt. By 1612 he was able to sweep into Marrakech, Zaydan fleeing to Safi with his harem and his goods. (These included a library of Arab books which, being sent by sea to Agadir, were captured by a Spanish ship and held to so high a ransom by Philip II that he was able to keep them. Many were damaged or lost in the great fire at the Escorial, but the survivors of those 4,000 volumes form the core of the superb Arab library still in that palace.)

Meanwhile occupation of the luxurious casbah and palace of Marrakech soon turned Abu 'l-Mahalli's head so far that he forgot his piety which, like Samson's hair, was his only strength. Zaydan sent a rival marabout, Yahya, to dislodge Abu. This Yahya had little difficulty in doing, though Zaydan had to plead with him for more than a year to be allowed back himself. Yahya then betook himself to the Sous where he reigned independently until 1619 when he suddenly returned and took Marrakech again. His misrule very soon delivered the city back to Zaydan, but by then Zaydan was a discredited man. He ruled on over the south until 1627, though as little more than the puppet of the insubordinate and usually religious factions who actually controlled the territory. All the same, Zaydan had a better claim to be the last Saadi sultan than his brothers or either of his three sons and one grandson who, thanks to the fickle support of marabouts and townsmen, sometimes succeeded him. All four of his descendants were assassinated, the last in 1659.

ALAOUITE DYNASTY (A.D. 1659–Present)

Meanwhile the northern principality of Fes had very largely been taken over by the marabouts of Djila, a zawiya near Khenifra. These controlled Meknes, Fes, the plains to the sea towards Rabat, Salé and the slopes of the Middle Atlas, the outlying areas being in the grip of lesser quasi-religious leaders, princelings or chiefs. Accounts left by travellers and merchants suggest that the chaotic conditions of the southern kingdom were equalled by the anarchy of the northern. Only in the south-east were things improving although a curious and briefly successful community of Moriscos — refugees from the old Kingdom of Granada who themselves scarcely knew whether they were Moslems or Christians, Moroccans or Spaniards — had rebuilt Tetouan and also settled in Rabat and Salé. Under the nominal sovereignty of the Sultan the latter group formed the 'Republic of the Bou Regreg' and lived largely by privateering, piracy and slaving. The 'Sallee Rovers', as the English called them, were primarily interested in revenging themselves upon Spain. They made pacts with James I and Charles I between 1627 and 1641, directed against Spanish shipping, but so turbulent were the times that the only maritime law that could be said to run was each man for himself. The Sallee Rovers were active in the Channel and off the south-east of England, selling their prizes to the Dutch, the Portuguese and even the Spanish. The marabouts of Djila finally made away with the Republic of Bou Regreg, but not before the marabout Mohammed el-Ayachi, operating from his base in the Gharb hills, had in 1637 attacked Rabat with the aid of a British squadron.

England's flirtation with Morocco, very much frowned upon by the rest of Europe, culminated in the acquisition of Tangier as part of the rich dowry that Catherine of Braganza brought to Charles II in 1662. The port proved an unprofitable burden, difficult to hold. Parliament used its cost as a weapon against the king while it quarrelled with Charles and refused him reinforcements for its garrison, causing it to be abandoned in 1684. This damped Britain's no doubt predatory interest in Morocco, but did not kill it.

Amid all the confusion, the power that was presently to reunify Morocco was gathering force in the Tafilelt. There, yet another sherifian family had established a zawiya at Sigilmassa (now Rissani). From this base they gradually extended their authority. Moulay Ali esh-Sherif, who had emigrated from Yenbo in Arabia, founded the zawiya, and his son Ali esh-Sherif the dynasty. From 1630 to 1640 this Alaouite family confined itself to establishing its supremacy over the south-east area in which it lived; esh-Sherif styled himself sultan. By 1648 the Alaouites had mastered the desert corridor running north to the sea at Oujda and esh-Sherif's brilliant soldier son Mohammed was powerful enough to take Fes from the marabouts of Djila in 1650. This coup was only temporarily successful and the following year saw the Alaouites forced to withdraw beyond the Atlas again. That year esh-Sherif died, unleashing thereby the intense rivalry existing between Mohammed and his boundlessly ambitious younger brother, Rashid. Four years of bitter fighting between them ended with Mohammed's death. Rashid must have been as good a soldier as his brother. During the following three years he first settled at Oujda, then moved to Taza and from there was able to recapture Fes. Thus in 1666 Fes once again became the capital. It took Rashid only two years wholly to overcome the marabouts of Djila and to destroy their zawiya. All their lands were now under his rule. Slowly Marrakech and the southern kingdom were being encircled. There the tumultuous sects of factious groupings had been more or less under the control of a marabout called Karum el-Haj since 1658. His death led to complete disarray and Rashid was able with little difficulty to enter Marrakech in 1669. His control over the south-west was then fairly easy to establish, though the High Atlas, as ever, remained as *bled es-siba*. Rashid the warrior died horribly in a palace revolution at Marrakech during the celebration of Aîd el-Kebir in 1672, the circumstances being variously recounted.

Trouble was not slow to break out in the Alaouite family. Moulay Ismaîl proclaimed himself sultan at Meknes where he was governor, then marched to Fes and was there acclaimed. A nephew proclaimed himself at Marrakech and a brother did likewise in the Tafilelt. Moulay Ismaîl was tremendously vigorous and a ruthless, able administrator. He was to win himself a bad name abroad as an inordinately cruel man, but since this fame rests on the biased accounts of prisoners and missionaries to whom Moroccan habits were foreign, their portrait of him is probably blacker than he merited. Even so it must be admitted that the ways of Moroccan rulers were more callous even than those of the Europeans of the time. The Moroccans remember Ismaïl as a great ruler who brought peace and prosperity to their troubled country and who was a just man in his ruthless way. He certainly stood no nonsense while establishing himself. Based upon Fes, he had virtually to reconquer the whole country, much of it twice over. After its second defection to his nephew's cause, Marrakech was sacked and its leading citizens executed or blinded as an example. Even so it was fifteen years before he was sole master of the southern kingdom, the High Atlas excepted. He liked Meknes, where he was probably most liked and trusted himself. It was there he had been a young man, for he was twenty-six at his father's death. At all events he decided to create of it a new capital all his own. This he built on a heroic scale — or rather he built the all-important palace complex on vast lines probably designed deliberately to vie with Versailles.

Ismaïl reckoned himself to be the peer of the European kings, rightly. He maintained remarkably friendly relations with them, allowing Spanish and Portuguese priests to operate in the kingdom and to minister to the large number of Christian prisoners who worked on his building programmes. He exhorted Louis XIV to abjure Catholicism for Islam and asked for the hand of the Princesse de Conti, Louis's illegitimate daughter. He tried to convert James II and would have been pleased had that Catholic at least reverted to Protestantism since he thought it less idolatrous than Catholicism. Ismaïl was able to make these contacts despite so closely investing Tangier that he eventually forced the English to abandon it. He recaptured Mehdiya (near Kénitra) from the Spanish in 1681 and went on to take from them Larache in 1689 and Asilah in 1691. The romantic appearance of Ismaïl's embassies to Europe greatly stimulated European imaginations. More friendly towards Europe than the Turks during the late seventeenth century and the early eighteenth, it was the Moroccans who revived that perennial and ardent imaginative *affaire* between 'East' and 'West'.

Ismaïl was black (by no means the first sultan to have been so) and he added a strong Negro force to his family's tribal backing of Oudaïa Arabs to act as his troops. He made an expedition into Mauritania to secure black slaves, was himself always in the market for them and bred them systematically.

The boys were trained in arms on something of the Turkish-janissary lines and the girls with whom they were later to be married brought up to be skilled in domestic arts. It is to this deliberate policy of Ismaïl's — which, like his new capital, was aimed at disassociating the sultanate from the rivalries of the tribes and cities — that the Moroccans owe most of the vigorous black African strain in their blood and their present total 'integration'. Although turbulence was to return again after his death, it is to Ismaïl that Morocco owed the comparatively good ordering of the country, the durability of the Alaouite dynasty and its freedom from the Turks.

Ismaïl died in 1727, having ruled for fifty-five years. A Jew or a woman could walk over the country unmolested, records Ahmed al-Masiri. The country was very prosperous and taxes, if annoying, were neither burdensome nor delayed in the gathering. The old sultan had become a legend — the last to arise in Morocco until Mohammed V should eclipse him. As is usually the case with legendary sovereigns, he is credited with a vast progeny. It may well have equalled that of ibn Saud in our own day (for enormous families born to rich men owning many concubines are not unusual). The evidence — some of it given by the chief queen's English porter, T. Pellew — suggests that his women held great political influence, as is often the case when the master is inclined to uxoriousness.

At all events he left many sons to dispute his throne. One, Mohammed el-Alim, had even so early as 1703 become tired of waiting to rule and had besieged Marrakech. In default of artillery he had used canny generalship to defeat the defence. As usual, the Marrakchi and their goods were delivered up to his troops in recompense for their services. But Ismaïl sent another son to regain the city and Mohammed retired before him to the Sous. Ismaïl has given his disciplined troops too much power; after his death they were able to make and unmake sultans at Meknes much as they pleased until, in 1745, they not only had earlier raised but firmly set Moulay Abdullah on the throne and he proved able to master both them and the country.

Abdullah's son of twenty years, Sidi Mohammed, was made viceroy of Marrakech. He was already known for his fine qualities, his learning and for having at the age of nine escorted his grandmother to Mecca. He rebuilt the wrecked town and the casbah whose el-Badi Palace — the pride of Saadi — Ismaïl had stripped to decorate Meknes. Though he was soon chased from the city by the Rehamna tribe (which had reverted to nomadry during the troubles, and banditry, a way of life it was loath to forsake), Sidi Mohammed proved at Safi what a wise and just ruler he was and the Rehamna themselves asked him to return within a year. Indeed so excellent a ruler was he that the black troops deposed his father in his favour. To the astonishment of all — ourselves included — Sidi Mohammed marched on Meknes and reinstated his father, saying that he would be no undutiful Moslem son.

Long before his father died, Sidi Mohammed was administering the whole kingdom in his name and thus the succession for once passed peacefully to him. He was thirty-eight when in 1757 he ascended the throne, dying at seventy-one in 1790. As his grandfather had favoured Meknes, Sidi Mohammed could not hide his partiality for Marrakech, so much, now, his own creation. His stated policy and to a great extent his practice was, however, to move from place to place, ruling at first and not at second hand. He was able to regain El-Jadida from the Portuguese in 1769 and he re-founded Essaouira. He failed, however, to rescue Ceuta or Melilla, partly because the Spanish intercepted a British arms convoy destined to assist him. At the start of his reign he concluded a trade treaty with Denmark, following this with others with England, Sweden, Venice, France, Spain and Naples. Sidi Mohammed's government was one of the very first to recognize the United States of America and made a trade agreement with her also in 1786. His relations with Britain suffered a set-back during the great siege of Gibraltar whose governor was so tactless as to cause Mohammed to have to retaliate by expelling the British consul and colony from Tangier. As these had been sending Gibraltar useful intelligence this was a disaster for the defence.

For all his wisdom Sidi Mohammed left his kingdom without a capable successor. Though not at first seriously opposed, his son Yazid proved himself so vicious a sultan that civil war was made inevitable. He had shown himself sadistic and vicious before his father's death and as sultan vented a crazed rage on his subjects. Although he was attacking Ceuta — always a respect-worthy pursuit — revolts broke out all over the country. Moulay Abd er-Rahman raised his standard across the Atlas; in the Haouz the Rehamna and Abda tribes proclaimed Moulay Hisham and Marrakech acclaimed him. Returning south from Ceuta, Yazid besieged the city. The townsfolk amused themselves by taunting him from the height of the walls and when, by treachery, he was able to gain entry, they paid dearly for their insults. There were three days of slaughtering and pillaging then. Hisham had been away in the south but now returned. In the engagement that followed he was worsted and lost his treasure, but Yazid died the next day of an untended wound — 1792. The whole country was profoundly relieved. But it was still divided because the Fasiyin and the Meknassi proclaimed Moulay Suleiman, Sidi Mohammed's favourite son. Hisham might have had a chance had he not fallen out with the Rehamna, who promptly proclaimed yet another brother, Hussein, in his stead. The south divided sharply between them and engaged in what was perhaps the bloodiest and most vicious of all the fratricidal wars. Things grew so bad that the Rehamna actually deserted Hussein at one point and made submission to Suleiman at Fes. Marrakech changed hands several times, always to its detriment, and when Suleiman at last arrived there in 1796, judging that the time to intervene between his brothers was propitious to himself, the citizens were very ready to accept him.

Moulay Suleiman was a still more ascetic man than his pious father had been. Both were adherents of the strict Moslem sect of the Wahabi, though where Sidi Mohammed had restored the shrines of sufi and sought to control the religious confraternities in the country by persuasion, Suleiman did what he could to break their hold on his people since he believed sufism to be as good as idolatrous. What with the wars, the plague which had ravaged the people since 1790 and the sultan's zealousness for an arid piety, there was unrest against the Government throughout his reign. However, everyone was perhaps fortunate that four pretender brothers of the sultan, including Hisham (whom he had pardoned) and Hussein, all died of the plague within days of each other in 1799. Nevertheless, the rest of his reign — he died in 1822 — was a continuous campaign against his rebellious subjects and a taxgathering progress over the country.

Two points should be made here. The first is that the brothers who so often fought each other in Morocco were rarely the offspring of the same mother and, among the large numbers of their half-brothers and -sisters, probably very little known to each other and certainly not attached to each other by any fraternal feelings; indeed, they are more likely to have been brought up in their youth to have reflected their mothers' rivalry with one another. The other is to explain what now became the chief occupation of the sultans — the *harka*. As the grip of the central government grew more feeble on the country the sultans devised a simple though arduous method of cowing the *bled es-siba* — and anywhere else for that matter. With his uniformed guards and cavalry, a host of tribesmen whose composition changed as he moved about, and with his ministers and women, a multitude of slaves and campfollowers, the sultan peregrinated over the kingdom. This was the *harka* or 'burning'. This host lived off the land it passed through; it was at once a show of force and a direct as well as an indirect means of collecting taxes. When it was impeded, as often it was, the sultan had to impose his authority. He had the heaviest artillery, some of which was usually operative — cannons were becoming a symbol of the sultanate; people swore by them and claimed sanctuary beside them, even praying to them. The more or less disciplined troops had full licence to despoil anyone who opposed them. In short a burning was a means of pillaging a region on the sound principle that, as it was said, 'an empty sack cannot stand up' — a broken area had not the strength to defy the Government.

Suleiman was even taken prisoner towards the end of his life by Middle Atlas tribes whom he had not bested while on *harka*. However, these differentiated between oppressive ruler and imam; as the latter they treated him with respect and escorted him back to Meknes.

Exterior affairs were dominated by the Napoleonic Wars when Suleiman reversed all previous policies by supporting Spain against France, continuing to do so even when Joseph Bonaparte offered him Ceuta and Melilla if he would only recognize him as king of Spain. The technical superiority which European shipping attained about this time finally forced Moroccan privateers out of business. Even so the sultan of Turkey thought it worth while asking that a Moroccan fleet should be stationed in the Straits to deny Russian ships entry into the Mediterranean in 1806. The Russians did not appear.

Suleiman did not think any of his sons fit to rule and before his death nominated his nephew Abd er-Rahman instead. This created a very favourable impression and a precedent for what is now usual practice — the nomination of successors.

If Eugène Delacroix's three paintings of Abd er-Rahman riding ceremonially to the Friday prayers are not entirely idealized portraits — and there is no reason to suppose they are — he was a majestically handsome man. The country liked him and he ruled well. But Moroccan medievalism was by then not only wholly anachronistic but could be seen to be so — not that that prevented almost all the Moroccans from persisting in it. Since the loss of the Spanish possessions Morocco had been turning in upon itself, not so much stagnating as rotting for lack of stimulus. The Turks in Algeria even cut it off from such movement as there was in the rest of the Moslem world. Relationships with European powers had been of too slight a kind to reach into any real communication with any section of Moroccan thought. At home the administration was slowly breaking down. Perhaps no one could tell when it had cracked. It was a very simple form of government which relied on the loyalty and ability of those to whom the sultan delegated his powers — a delegation of power which the sultan often had to effect in an effort to placate or to win some powerful man's uncertain adherence to the throne. If this failed, force was necessary. It may be that during Sidi Mohammed's long and persuasive reign the machinery for raising loyal troops was allowed to rust while the people grew used to acknowledging justice and a wise diplomacy rather than the mailed fist. The military force which Ismaïl had created disintegrated during the civil wars. Abd er-Rahman had no army and not enough authority in the kingdom to raise the money to recruit one. Like those of his successors, his forces were a rabble of tribesmen drawn from one or more of the tribes in the *bled el-makhzen* who served in return for the remission of taxes. They went home almost at will, particularly for harvesting and holidays, and anyway found it little inducement to give service in lieu of taxes that were neither paid nor collected. Should the sultan play upon tribal rivalries to induce one tribe to help him coerce another, he only made matters worse between them and himself. If Ismaïl had brought Morocco to a point of social development which about equalled that of Elizabeth's England, the falling-off was all the more deplorable for what had been. Abd er-Rahman was once struck in the face by a tribesman with the butt of his rifle.

None the less he was able to hang on by the skin of his teeth for thirty-seven years. Very prudently, he brought up his son and successor to share his authority and learn the intricate diplomacy with which he balanced this and that force into some semblance of harmony.

Mohammed III* reigned from 1859 to 1873, always roving the country on one *harka* or another. He was boating with his son Hassan on the great pool in the Agdal Gardens of Marrakech when their craft sank and the sultan drowned. Hassan lived until 1894, continuing the tradition of precarious and limited rule — right at the start of his reign he had to fight his way to be acclaimed at Fes, spending several months in doing so.

These were three sad reigns spanning the crucial nineteenth century. The only effect which that revolutionary period had upon this westernmost country was that it felt increasingly threatened as its European neighbours nibbled at its weakened edges.

EUROPEAN ENCROACHMENT UPON MOROCCO

In his ignorance of world realities, and despite the ban on the trade which his uncle had been forced to apply, Abd er-Rahman authorized two privateers to operate in 1829. They captured two Austrian ships with the consequence that Austria bombarded Larache and destroyed much shipping. When the French took Algiers from the Turks in 1830 the people of Tlemcen asked for Moroccan protection — the town was as much Moroccan as Algerian and no fixed frontier was defined. Somewhat reluctantly, the sultan agreed and sent irregulars whom he was glad to withdraw when the Tlemceni complained of their behaviour. But when the heroic Algerian leader, Abd el-Kader, did him homage public pressure forced him to help the Algerian resistance. This resulted in an ignoble defeat for the Moroccans near Oujda in 1844. At the same time the French shelled Tangier and Essaouira. The peace then concluded with the French was a humiliating one. It obliged Abd er-Rahman to abandon the Algerians and drew an arbitrary frontier between the countries southwards from the Mediterranean, where it still runs. Six years later there was more trouble when two French wrecks were looted at Salé and the town was bombarded in retaliation.

* The numbering of rulers of the same name is modern and applies only to those of the Alaouite dynasty. (Ismaïl's son Mohammed is credited with a brief reign as No. II).

Mohammed III's reign began with trouble on the Ceuta border which led the Spanish to declare war and capture Tetouan. Being anxious to keep the Spanish from occupying either side of the Straits, the British intervened, but Morocco was obliged to pay a heavy indemnity and to cede to Spain as much ground as it had occupied around a fishing-port it had owned — but later lost — during the fifteenth century (four hundred years earlier — the only historical precedent for acceding to Zionist claims upon Palestine). Settlement of this clause was, however, delayed until 1934 when the French honoured it by the cession to Spain of the Ifni enclave on the Atlantic. This treaty also saw the upgrading of the foreign consulates at Tangier to legations and the Moroccan Government's realization that it had precious little say in its own affairs as far as Europe was concerned.

Hassan, heir of that boating accident which we instinctively visualize in terms of a Persian miniature, was able, energetic and intelligent within the limits of his traditional training. It is small wonder that people were struck by the sadness of expression that never left his handsome face. He saw his mission in life as a conservator's. Living and ruling in the traditional way, he was at pains to buy Morocco's continued isolation by conciliating the foreign powers. He was, however, rather more positive and aware of his predicament than this suggests and did in fact succeed in convening an international conference at Madrid to discuss the abuses of the protection system. By 'abuses' he meant the ethics of a system by which foreign powers claimed the right so to protect their nationals and interests in the country as virtually to have established sovereignty over small areas. This was the position at Tangier where the legations ran the town, and there were similar encroachments made at other ports. Abd er-Rahman had begun it with a treaty signed with Britain in 1856 which was the blueprint for similar agreements with other countries and very soon a world-wide colonial practice. Unfortunately for Hassan all his conference of Madrid did was to regularize the practice and bring it to the attention of still other countries.

Hassan was the last sultan to have to plod over Morocco in search of revenue and authority. In this he was fairly successful. His *harka* even went as far into the *bled es-siba* as Goulimine. He created Tiznit to be the *makhzen*'s capital in the Sous. If ever a man died in the saddle it was he. He made a remarkable *harka* into the Tafilelt in 1893 on which he was joined by Walter B. Harris, one of the brilliant adventurer-journalists of his times and correspondent of the London *Times*. We have Harris's account of the *harka*.* After battling with tribes to cross the pass that leads to the Ziz valley, the sultan's progress was seriously delayed and by the time he came to start back over the rather shorter pass to Marrakech, snow had already fallen in the mountains; it was to be a particularly severe winter. With fever, starvation and the cold, two-thirds of Hassan's escort of over 10,000 men died before the top of the pass was reached, possibly a larger proportion of the animals. Harris describes how the sultan was aged and dirtied by the terrible journey, 'Riding his great white horse with the mockery of green and gold trappings while above his head that was the picture of suffering waved the imperial umbrella of crimson velvet' is how he describes him on his entry into Marrakech after the crossing. So awful were the privations that cannibalism occurred. The Berber tribes whose country the *harka* crossed harried them; men who were wounded were buried alive since otherwise, abandoned, the tribesmen would have cut off their heads. Even so corpses strewed their path and a host of carrion birds flew overhead while jackals and hyenas brought up the rear. Harris's account is quoted at length in Gavin Maxwell's *Lords of the Atlas* (Longmans, London, 1966), a book which all travellers to Morocco should read. Its subject is the Glaoui brothers who were to owe their astonishing fortunes to the succour they extended to Hassan when he reached their eyrie of Telouet, near the top of the pass. With their help, the sultan gained Marrakech, but as soon as winter was past he had to ride against dissidents in the Tadla region (there were others in the Rif whom he also had to attempt to deal with; they were out of his control and had attacked Melilla, involving him in another heavy indemnity). Hassan had been ill all the previous year and worsened during the winter; in the middle of hostile territory near Tadla he died. His freedman and chamberlain, 'bu Achmed, contrived to keep his death a secret while for two days the *harka* made forced marches into the plains and Hassan's thirteen-year-old son Abdul Aziz was proclaimed sultan at Rabat. Soon the sultan's body stank and the secret of his death could no longer be kept; by the time they came to Rabat even the horses drawing the imperial palankeen were made restive by the smell of the week-old corpse decomposing in the heat of the plains.

Hassan's son Abdul Aziz was a nice, bright child, the young

* Walter B. Harris, *Morocco That Was* (Blackwood, London, 1921).

master of a very big nursery. For eight years he had the clever 'bu Achmed to be his regent, and the advice of his Turkish mother. Intelligent and open to ideas, he became fascinated by the products of industrial technology. But he lacked both experience of their application and the education to grasp their significance. Hassan had already taken the rather surprising step of sending a few students abroad, but these had returned at a loss how to apply all that they had learned and experienced back at home; if only Abdul Aziz could have been sent away like them, Morocco's recent history might have been happier. As it was he shopped around with an imperious extravagance. Because there was no way of utilizing his purchases — such as motor-cars, for instance, there being no roads — they could be used only as toys to be thrown away as soon as their unproductive novelty had worn off. With some of these things he imported technicians to operate them and because he enjoyed what seemed to him their exotic company these often stayed on after their charges were abandoned. Harris, who was his friend, lists at one time 'an architect, a conjurer, a watchmaker, an American portrait-painter, two photographers, a German lion-tamer, a French soda-water manufacturer, a chauffeur, a firework expert and a Scottish piper' — and with these and any consul who happened to be at court, the sultan liked to play games of bicycle polo, at which he was adept. It was ludicrous and sad; and ruinously expensive because his agents fleeced him and ordered in his name such things as a gold camera for £2,000 and three times as much worth of photographic paper and other unwanted equipment at a time. A superb state-carriage was ordered from London. When unpacked, Harris and a consul rode inside and the sultan on the box while soldiers and slaves pulled it round a field followed by a medley of the animals from the royal menagerie; next morning rain had ruined it. Yet not all the sultan's projects were quite so pointless. As a start, he proposed a railway to link his palaces at Fes. The Ulema, council of religious elders, forbade it as a misuse of Moslems' lands. This was typical of the opposition he had to deal with. Not altogether ill-advised, he was persuaded on British advice to institute administrative reforms. But there was no one to apply them; they had been too hastily drawn up; there was nobody in the country with the will to enact them. Everything he did seemed to worsen the *makhzen*'s position. Though trade with Europe was increased the customs of most ports were in pawn to foreign powers and thus the *makhzen* lost its one sure source of revenue. Abdul Aziz liked the foreigners living in the country to wear their European clothes so that Moroccans should get used to their presence among them. These increased in numbers in the ports, but the people responded merely by making them the scapegoats for all their ills.

FRENCH AND SPANISH PROTECTORATES (A.D. 1912–56)

In the interior, unrest took its traditional form, culminating in the insurrection of 'bu Hamara who set up a rival government at Taza, a town whose position threatens Fes. Behind the scenes France and Britain (Britain reversing her policy to uphold the Moslem states of North Africa since she saw they were beyond propping up) traded spheres of influence with one another. Thus Britain made no protest at the French annexation of Tunisia and herself began to intervene in Egypt. By 1904 France was given a free hand in Morocco in return for allowing Britain to 'protect' Egypt. However, France was obliged to share Morocco with Spain since that country's interest in Morocco was plain. Posing as the champion of Moroccan independence, the Kaiser Wilhelm visited Tangier in 1905. The Moroccans were delighted, but soon found he was but another predator come on the scene. Two years later, in 1907, attacks made on foreign workers by the people of Casablanca gave the French an excuse to occupy the town and neighbourhood and also to seize Oujda. This was too much. Moulay Abd el-Hafid, the sultan's brother and governor of Marrakech, claiming that Abdul Aziz was allowing the infidel to take the country over while dissipating its wealth, revolted and declared himself the new sultan. For the last of so many times, the armies of rival sultans took the road between Fes and Marrakech and upon meeting fought. Abdul Aziz's army evaporated — it was scarcely a battle at all — and he took refuge with the French, later retiring to a quiet life in Tangier. He had told Harris, tears in his eyes, that he was tired of being sultan. Harris had been scolding him for not paying the soldiers.

Abd el-Hafid became sultan. His reign was a short and tragic one for all that he was able quickly to rid himself of 'bu Hamara. Poor man, he wanted to preserve the past intact. The captured rebel was hung in a cage for the citizens of Fes to gloat upon, then executed. Forty of his men were beheaded and Jews, whose traditional task it was, boiled and salted their heads before affixing them to spikes on the Bab Mahrouk while the crowd laughed when an old one was displayed — because it was that of a rebel scarcely worth the capturing — and applauded those of young men. None the less this traditionalism revealed el-Hafid to be a tyrant of the bad old school and he was disliked for it. There were Spaniards working mines in the Rif under a concession granted by 'bu Hamara. Tribesmen attacked them in 1909 and Spain retaliated by extending the frontiers of Melilla. Abd el-Hafid's grand vizier was Madani el-Glaoui — to whose aid he owed his crown — but Madani had grown dangerously rich and powerful; the sultan hated him for it. El Hafid perpetrated many cruel acts and cannot be absolved of the charge of sadism. When the wife of the governor of Fes was tortured Harris started a campaign in *The Times* and roused both the Foreign Office and French authorities to act. The quarrel with Madani was reaching a climax, leading the vizier to screw still more taxes from the northern tribes in a last effort to placate his master. The tribes had been pushed too far; they revolted and invested Fes. In panic, el-Hafid asked for French help and a column of French soldiers entered Fes on May 11th, 1911. Germany had not been a signatory to the document parcelling up North Africa. She protested at the occupation of Fes and sent a gun-boat to Agadir on the pretext of defending some Germans living there. The Spanish invoked their agreement with France and occupied both Larache and Ksar el-Kebir. Germany was bought off by the cession of territory in the French Congo. Madani had by then been disgraced and all his property and that of his family lying north of the Atlas — that to the south and east being out of el-Hafid's reach — seized. On March 31st, 1912, the sultan signed the Treaty of Fes granting the French the right to protect the country, to represent it abroad and to conquer the *bled es-siba*. El-Hafid had tried to avoid signing, declaring he would abdicate rather than do so. This suited the French book and the last of the negotiations were mere haggling over the price he should be paid to sign and get out. He was a rapacious man and extorted large sums from the protectors; he also tricked the hundreds of royal ladies out of all their jewellery. Within four months of signing the treaty he had abdicated and gone to France, later returning to live at Tangier.

A similar document had also been signed with the Spanish who gladly accepted to protect a section of the country north of a line drawn across the north-west tip from a little to the south of Larache to the Mediterranean at the mouth of the Moulouya River. They made Tetouan their administrative capital. This excepted a small territory south of Tangier which, with that port, now became an International Zone governed by the representatives of the signatory countries to the Treaty of Algeciras (p. 150).

Colonialism is now so discredited and its faults so much decried that it is easy only to see the ugliness it inflicted and to feel horror at the wrongs done in its name. Yet in forty-four years the French wrought a miracle in Morocco for which all but the wilfully obtuse must be grateful. They even withdrew with comparative dignity — enough at all events to preserve some goodwill towards themselves.

The Treaty of Fes was a cynical document which barely concealed the greed which inspired it. Barely civil in tone, it reads like terms dictated to an enemy, humiliatingly. The Fasiyin reacted to its signing by massacring the seventy-odd French then in the city, most of them military men. This revolt was soon put down. On el-Hafid's abdication a third brother, Moulay Yussef, was made sultan — though the post was little more than a symbolic one it was necessary to the fiction of France and Spain's 'protection' of Morocco. Yussef was a man whose personal virtue was sufficiently apparent to preserve respect for his imamate, while he was docile towards the French. He was not a sultan about whom dissidents were likely to rally.

Soon, though, there was a popular figure to attract dissidents in the south: el-Hiba was the son of a respected marabout. He rose against both Yussef and the French and proclaimed himself sultan at Tiznit. Presently he marched to Marrakech, where the French had not yet arrived. He was able to enter the town because the local dignitaries did not know where their allegiance lay and supposed it might well be with el-Hiba since he was evidently powerful and nobody else appeared to be so. However, they did their best to keep in with the French at the same time. There was a handful of Frenchmen in the city and these became pawns in a diplomatic game between el-Hiba and the notables, everybody double-crossing everybody else. The Glaoui brothers won this game and were able to deliver the Frenchmen safe and sound to the commander of the column sent to occupy the city. With mortars and machine-guns against it, el-Hiba's army of tribesmen, armed with long-barrelled flint-locks, were massacred some miles out from the walls. It was a sad day; as those on which we face reality often are sad.

Very soon, of course, the French were desperately engaged in the First World War. They managed not only to maintain themselves in Morocco, putting down the remains of this and another revolt, but also to raise valuable Moroccan regiments which fought in France.

While the Glaoui brothers waxed in wealth and influence by using the French, others attacked both their French and Spanish protectors. Sherif Achmed el-Raisani was an over-large character, courageous, intelligent, arrogantly ruthless. He was credited with a considerable power of *baraka* by his followers in the Jebala area, the hills behind Tangier. His relations with the *makhzen* had varied. Now he was a governor, now prisoner, then an outlaw successful in kidnapping eminent men whom he held to ransom, Harris of *The Times* among them. The Spaniards made him governor, preferring to have him on their side. As such he built himself a palace at Asilah where he had pretensions to be pasha. A staunch traditionalist, his methods appalled the Spanish and he was soon enough in revolt against them. For eight years they fought him in the hills, though he was eventually reduced by Abd el-Krim. The enterprising Rosita Forbes visited el-Raisani and recorded his autobiography — R. Forbes, *El Raisani* (Thornton Butterworth, London, 1924): it is a fascinating document.

Less colourful, though more effective, Mohammed Abd el-Krim el-Khattabi was chief cadi for Melilla and editor of a local paper in Spanish. For a reason which is obscure he fell out with the Spanish and was imprisoned. Released, he took to the hills and with his enormously able brother M'hamid organized resistance on more modern lines than anyone had attempted or thought of before. The Spaniards marched against him from Melilla in ignorance of his ability. In July 1921 his men captured the line of forts the Spanish had advanced, killing or taking prisoner 16,000 officers and men out of a force of some 19,000 and capturing their artillery, arms and supplies. With this resounding success behind him, Abd el-Krim organized the territory he controlled into the more or less modern Republic of the Rif. Very much alarmed, the French moved into adjoining territory which had hitherto not been occupied. As this move threatened Abd el-Krim's food supply he attacked again, inflicting on the French almost as severe a defeat as he had on the Spaniards. For the first and almost the only time, the two protecting powers were driven to collaborate. In 1925 they brought up a combined force of 425,000 men, Pétain leading the larger French contingent and Major (later General) Franco prominent among the Spanish. This was too much for Abd el-Krim; he was overwhelmed and exiled to Réunion in 1926. In a way Abd el-Krim was a founder of modern Morocco. He understood how to combine the virtue of the past — particularly its pride and courage — with modern needs. Neither his contemporaries and fellow-Moroccans nor the protecting powers were ready to value him at his true worth. He has become a legendary figure, but one belonging to the past rather than as a forerunner of the future, which is unjust. While in exile he lost touch with the realities of the growth of Moroccan nationalism and died in Cairo in 1963; having at last weakened in his refusal to return while a single soldier was left on North African soil, he was on the point of returning home.

Resistance did not end there. The French were slow to establish control of the *bled es-siba*, not achieving it in the Middle Atlas until 1932 and then moving to the High Atlas and the pre-Sahara and completing the job in the Anti-Atlas in 1934. Meanwhile the first crop of young men who had benefited by the schooling and example which the French had given them had grown up to a different idea of nationalism and political resistance. They were encouraged by a similar form of nationalism emerging in Egypt. For these men the past counted less by far than did the future. For this the French deserve the credit, although to some extent they earned it inadvertently and, as a colonial power, did not appreciate its effects.

Already before they occupied Morocco the French had experience of governing Moslem lands. This helped them to avoid mistakes they had made elsewhere; for instance, their desecration of the Mosque of Kairouan led to all save Moslems being rigorously banned from entering the mosques and shrines of Morocco. General (later Marshal) Lyautey was appointed first Resident General, a post which he held almost uninterruptedly until 1925 with great distinction. A man who was sympathetic to the Arabs and their achievements, he could not have been a better choice. We owe it to him that the great cities of Morocco are so splendidly preserved, for not only reasons of prudence but also of aesthetics prompted him to set the new towns at a distance from the old, planning them handsomely and connecting the old and new settlements with beautiful avenues which seem to symbolize graciously the journey into the present which the Moroccans have had to make.

It is not possible here to detail all those things which France did for Morocco and yet it is not enough simply to say that out of an antique anarchy she created a modern state capable of prosperous growth and of making a valuable contribution towards that emergent community of nations which needs must be neither eastern nor western, but civilized in a moral as well as an intellectual sense. Where ports were inadequate, roads and railways non-existent, education confined to Koranic schools and *medersa*, cultivation performed by antique and wasteful methods, mineral resources scarcely scratched, the administration corrupt and grossly inefficient, there being no army or police force — all these things were remedied and made to function with that éclat which the French bring to their work when their pride is engaged. In this French pride matched Moroccan and the Moroccans have preserved much that was excellent under the protectorate. It proved mistaken of the French not to teach Arabic in their schools (for one thing this offered a legitimate cause for Moroccan grievance) and mistaken also to discourage Moroccans from renewing close contact with the rest of the Moslem world. It was a mistake, too, to suppose the Berbers could easily be used against the Arab section of the people; they proved staunchly Moroccan and Moslem before all else. Then the French underestimated the quickness and intelligence with which the young Moroccans grasped the significance of the new world they were offered. (This was something which Lyautey saw, but his warnings were not heeded in Paris.)

History was against the French and there was not time for them to gallicize the country as thoroughly as they hoped. Five years after the final 'pacification' of the Anti-Atlas France was again at war; within another nine months France was occupied by the Germans. While suffering the exactions Germany demanded of Vichy France, Morocco stagnated under Pétain's regime. When the Allies landed in 1942 there was little resistance to them and the Moroccan nationalists grew prematurely hopeful under the influence of liberal-minded troops from America and Britain.

STRUGGLE FOR INDEPENDENCE (A.D. 1946–56)

The ten years between 1946 and the granting of independence were troubled ones, the French struggling to hold on in the face of increasing Moroccan nationalism, led by the sultan, and growing increasingly reactionary in the process. Mohammed ben Yussef (Mohammed V) had succeeded to the throne upon his father's death in 1927. Seventeen years old, he was selected by the French for his apparent malleability. Just as they ignored the young men they had themselves trained, they overlooked the fact that he was himself a young Moroccan. By 1934 Mohammed was already a supporter of the nationalist movement. However, it was 1945 before he was in a strong enough position to take over leadership of the movement which in turn was by then massive enough to give him the power he needed to be able to stand up to the French and demand both a democratic form of government and a fundamental revision of the Treaty of Fes. The duel that then took place between Mohammed and the Resident General — Juin, epitome of reactionary French colonialists — makes a splendid story. (Barbour, op. cit., gives an account of it.) In 1952 Juin's more ham-fisted successor, General Guillaume, organized a remarkable and almost openly falsified demonstration against the sultan with the support of T'hami el-Glaoui. The object of this was to justify the forcible removal of the sultan. Mohammed refused to abdicate and was exiled with his family, but no baggage, to Corsica and later to Madagascar.

Although the Spanish did not recognize him, the French set a nephew of the old sultan Hassan on the throne. Mohammed ben Arafa did just as he was told and after two attempts had been made on his life, kept within his palace. As in similar cases, Mohammed V's exile made a nationalist victory certain and his own position unassailable, only members of those governments which order such banishment being unaware of the fact. You can still see displayed charming prints of Mohammed's distinguished face appearing in the moon; these are souvenirs of the popular belief as to how, somehow, in exile he managed still to be with his people. Relations between the French and Moroccans deteriorated and terrorism and counter-terrorism became rife.

Again history showed its hand: in November 1954 the Algerians revolted against the French. After the humiliation at home and the loss of the Far Eastern colonies, and Syria and Tunis, France's own metropolitan province of North Africa was in rebellion. To the advantage of Morocco, Algeria had to come first with that sad, fierce kind of Frenchman (who is perhaps a part of all Frenchmen) who cannot bear it that Napoleon died. It was not many months before French policy in Morocco was reversed; conciliation and liberalism were to be tried. Too late though. The Moroccans wanted more than was offered, and frightened French officials and settlers sabotaged the reforms. A Crown Council was proposed in place of Sultan ben Arafa; all parties were consulted about this and Mohammed V agreed to it, but ben Arafa would not step down. Before he could be persuaded to retire like his cousins to Tangier, Moroccan guerrillas began operations in the Rif. These were not under the control of any party to be represented on the Council or at the conference called to constitute it. Realizing that his own ambitious schemes to succeed ben Arafa had failed, and hoping to save himself and his family, T'hami el-Glaoui (whom the French had allowed to become inordinately powerful) suddenly declared that even the Crown Council would be illegal and that only Mohammed V was rightful sultan. This was a last blow to France's hopes. Mohammed was brought to France; el-Glaoui sought pardon for his past treachery; within a week the French agreed that Mohammed should form a government to make Morocco a democratic state and a constitutional monarchy, while also to negotiate its independence from France. Mohammed returned to Morocco on November 18th, 1955, the twenty-eighth anniversary of his accession to the throne. With the formation of a Moroccan government, native ministers replaced French heads of departments. It is to the honour of French officials that they accepted these changes with a good grace.

INDEPENDENT MOROCCO (A.D. 1956–PRESENT)

On March 2nd, 1956, a formal convention was signed recognizing Moroccan independence. This became the new date for the Fête du Trône. (This was an unofficial national holiday that had been started as a demonstration of nationalist feeling on the anniversary of Mohammed's accession; the French had banned it and so made it the dearer to the people.) Next month a similar convention was signed with Spain and sealed with a symbolic visit of state made by Mohammed to the former Moslem territories of el-Andalus. In October the International Statute of Tangier was abrogated, Ceuta and Melilla, however, remained, as they still do, Spanish possessions. However, Spain's claims upon Gibraltar have had the happy outcome that Ifni was returned to Morocco in 1969.

In 1957 Mohammed V took the style of King. It was an earnest of the changes he desired to make for himself and his heirs from the old absolute sultanate to the new constitutionalism. In 1961 he suddenly died, to the great grief of his people. His son, Hassan II, had already been nominated his father's successor and had been closely associated with the government. Thus he succeeded with out any of the anguish of past accessions.

Short of trained men of all sorts, with immense tasks to perform and adjustments still to make, Morocco has not had an easy passage since independence; but all things considered she has done remarkably well from all points of view. The energy which caused such chaos in the past has now been canalized to the creation of a prosperous and ordered land where more thought is given to the future than to the past.

RELIGION

A good deal has been said (in the historical and other sections) about the Moroccans' attitude towards their religion, Islam. What is not stated there are the tenets and practices of Islam, but a note in a guide-book is no place to attempt a description of one of the world's greatest and most sophisticated religions. However, since this very devout people do not share the Christian's characteristic reticence towards the deity, nor any shyness about religious observances, the visitor will be made constantly aware of what a strong, governing influence Islam is in Morocco. He will want to have some idea of how contact with Moslems may affect him during his stay and will surely want, at the least, to show ordinary respect for the beliefs and customs of his hosts. Perhaps those of us most likely inadvertently to cause offence are we numerous unbelievers who are apt simply not to expect others to have easily outraged religious susceptibilities because we have fallen out of the habit of associating with religious people.

The basis of Islam is a deceptively simple one. God — *Allah*; the word is not a name, but the noun 'god', signifying divinity, the worshipful — embodies the monotheistic conception of deity.* Allah is not so much within the individual (a Christian interpretation) as well as beyond him, as representative of and motive for everything. Of the authors of revelation, whereas Jesus is held by Christians to be God incarnate, Mohammed was merely the Prophet (or Messenger) and mouthpiece of Allah and, although he is vastly revered, he is not worshipped. In effect, any Moslem can at any time approach God directly through prayer.

---

* 'Allah is the one God' – the first article of the Moslem faith – is often read in English to mean 'the true' or 'only' God. The phrase actually implies, rather, a rejection of the Christian Trinity: Allah is one and indivisible. The consonantal, shared roots of words akin in meaning, allow for extensions of underlying import: thus *Ln-illaha-illa-Allah, Mohammed ar-Rasul-Allah* can imply also 'nothing worshipped but the divinity, the praised one, the messenger of the worshipful' (Idries Shah, *The Sufis* 1, Jonathan Cape, London 1969).

Moslems are enjoined to pray wherever they are at dawn, noon, mid-afternoon, dusk and again after dark. For these prayers a man need not go to a mosque, yet many prefer to do so since the act of prayer has always seemed easier in sacrosanct places and corporate prayer is considered to be more effective than private. The Arabic word for mosque, *djemaa*, means simply 'assembly' — the corporate prayers offered there are more holy than the buildings which long ago replaced open spaces furnished only with a niche or other indication of the direction in which Mecca lay, towards which all prayer is directed. Enormous crowds gather in the mosques for the Friday, holy-day, prayer at midday. Here what is parallel to a Christian service is held, with prayers recited in unison, led by an *imam* whose function this is, a sermon preached by a *khatib* and passages of the Koran recited by a *hezzab*.

The Koran is of course the repository of Islamic revelation as delivered by the Prophet speaking God's words — not his own — and also of dogma and law. It is the rough equivalent of the New Testament and about the same length. Each daily prayer is called from every mosque tower or minaret by an officer called a *muezzin*. Women do not attend most Moroccan mosques, but resort instead to a *koubba*, shrine or tomb of a marabout or saintly man. There is no need to be disconcerted by the presence of a man at prayer in the street or shop; he will not be disconcerted by your presence unless you are so unmannerly as to interrupt him. Only the shallowest of people could laugh at the gestures and genuflections of this rite, so dignified and so little perfunctory are they. Since, though, mosques are forbidden to non-Moslems, do not attempt to enter them or to pry within (see p. 35). A Moslem washes himself before praying and all mosques have a fountain for this purpose and often a latrine in association with it. Some older men are sufficiently fanatic as to resent non-Moslems seeing them at their ablutions since these regard them more as a preparation for prayer than as acts of hygiene. This semi-religious attitude is carried over to the *hammam* or 'Turkish' bath, very few of which non-Moslems are allowed to use.

The feast-days of the Islamic year are listed on p. 45. There is also Ramadan, the thirty-day month during the daylight hours of which everyone forgoes all food, drink, smoking and sexual intercourse. This can be particularly trying when it falls in hot weather (which it does now) when daylight can last up to fifteen hours. But the holiday air of release after sunset, persisting long into the nights, is then some compensation to the fasters.

It is incumbent upon all Moslems to support the poor — this is in some ways an extension of the patriarchal structure of Arab society. They must also pay an annual tax, voluntarily, to this end. It is called the *zekkat* and is paid in order to purify the property which the payer retains — or, as the Koran says, 'He who gives his wealth to purify himself and confers no favour on any man for recompense, only seeking the Face of his Lord the Most High; and he shall surely be satisfied.'

The ultimate religious act that all devout Moslems hope to perform is to make the pilgrimage to Mecca. Mecca was a centre of pilgrimage, focal point of the pagan Arab's religious and national unity many ages before Mohammed's revelation and the founding of Islam. The core of its venerability is the Ka'ba, the hollow 'cube' (that is in reality one cube set on another). It is — most probably apocryphally — claimed that Abraham built this as a replica of the house of God. Its almost primeval origin enhances its peculiar sanctity and it is beside this to pray, to touch the *Yemani* stone at its southern corner and to kiss the Black stone at its eastern, that is the principal object of what was formerly a long, arduous and often dangerous journey thither. A pilgrim has many rites to perform during his pilgrimage, not least his duty as emissary of the family and friends who have not been able to accompany him. (Now that the journey is usually made by chartered boat or plane it has lost its dangers, though not the considerable expense, which still puts it out of reach of the majority.) In his capacity as representative of others, the pilgrim is fêted on his return and will ever after bear the honorific title of *hadji* in place of *si'*, or plain 'mister'. The end of the pilgrimage is marked by happy days when small processions of relatives and friends, led by musicians and bearing provender for a feast, perambulate the streets on their way to entertain the newly returned *hadji*.

At other times similar processions, clamorous with tambourines, drums and pipes, denote that a child is celebrating his circumcision, which is not done until he is about seven years old and represents his full adoption or confirmation into Islam. Or, equally, the procession may turn out to be that carrying a new bride to her husband's house. Funeral processions are silent or accompanied by sombre chanting, unceremonious, not marked by a show of grief since to die is to be gathered to Allah. The corpse is wrapped only in shrouds or placed in a temporary bier and carried on a hurdle-like stretcher to the stone-lined grave where more often than not an uninscribed stone will mark its position. Considering that Islam shares with other religions the hopeful belief in after-life it puts little emphasis on death, but is a faith and a discipline for living this life fully and honorably.

If in some ways women seem partly excluded from practising Islam, that is the result of social change as it has developed contrary to Mohammed's teaching. A wonderful saying of his was, 'Old women will not enter Paradise: they will be made young and beautiful first.' Among those who knew the Prophet. Abdullah ibn Harith said he never knew anyone who smiled more; Amas that he had never seen anyone more kind to children; Mu'ad that the last words he had from him were: 'Treat people well, Mu'ad.'

Throughout the Koran, emphasis is laid on charity and justice. 'Glorify your Lord with praise and ask his forgiveness.' There will be a Day of Judgement when 'God, the Merciful, the Compassionate, the Authority on Judgment Day' will show the people individually their deeds and 'he who does a particle of good will see it, and he who does a particle of evil will see it'. 'He who has been obstinate to our revelations, I shall impose on him a fearful doom!' — but at the same time no man will be called to account for involuntary lapses. Above all, Allah is a forgiver. He asks of simple men an uprightness within their capacity and, of complex men, an equal simplicity of probity which it taxes without overstraining their natures to attain. Mohammed eschewed the notion of original sin; a Moslem starts life fair and square and it is up to him to end it with modest honour.

The mystical and intellectual extension of Islam, Sufism, does not claim to be other than a live part of a tradition very much older than Islam itself, though one transmitted to it by Mohammed and his circle of particular disciples. The believing, religious insider — as, I think, the sympathetic outsider also — must be struck by the likeness between many ancient and more recent aspirations towards mystical goals, likenesses which embrace methods of attainment as much as aims. Of course a man who sets out to gain a sainthood can only fail: he is ambitious for *himself*. It is Samuel who best expresses the banishment of the self in service of the unimaginable when, hearing his name called in his sleep, he ran three times to Eli, his master and teacher, saying, 'Here am I; for thou callest me', so that Eli, who had not called for him, realized that the moment had come when the child was ready to communicate with — to know — God directly and told him therefore next time to answer, 'Speak, Lord, for Thy servant heareth.'

A Sufi's aim is so utterly and selflessly to love God that he achieves a degree of understanding of (or perhaps, rather, of possession by) His omnipresence; then to hand on to others what guidance he may towards attaining a like near-identity with God. Some exceptionally gifted Sufi masters have incontestably achieved remarkable powers, though never any beyond what we lesser mortals know in our hearts we are inherently capable of by some vast expansion of our gift for sympathy.

This venerable tradition has found an encouraging spiritual ambience within Islam. Mohammed not only spoke what is collected as the Koran (*not* his own words, but those of God's dictation, he himself acting solely as a passive messenger), but he also left the tradition of his example, his acts and sayings as remembered by his associates and collected in the *Sunna* — his 'teaching' by example and anecdote which is akin to the Christian Gospels (and, it would seem since the discovery of so much Gnostic material, a far truer account than that of the Early Fathers who, so politically engaged as they were, allowed only some of Jesus's teaching to be transmitted into the Christian tradition). Indeed, the Sufis claim now that only in their sternest and most rigorous discipline is this incorrupt eschatalogical tradition preserved. A state of grace comparable to an achieved Sufi's, they own, may be attained by extraordinary personal effort outside Sufism (for God — an impoverished sort of word for the reality — is all-recognizment), but it might be fair to say that Islam as formulated in the Koran should be considered as founding a living context in which 'Sufism' should have the best chance to flourish. Islam is as wide open, as vulnerable, to the entry of grace as it is to abuse.

ISLAMIC ARCHITECTURE IN THE WEST

From the point of view of architecture, 'the west' means Spain, Morocco, Algeria and Tunis — that westernmost or Maghrebi sector of the Moslem world which is isolated from the rest by the Libyan Desert. Although not originally so, Morocco became separated and unique within this area owing to the loss of Spain to the Christians and the Turkish occupation of Algeria and Tunisia.

All Islamic architecture is based upon ideas developed by the Arabs of the seventh-century expansion. These were a people of very limited architectural tradition who came into contact with the sophisticated usage of Hellenistic and Byzantine Syria, Egypt and Sassanian Mesopotamia during the early stages of their wide conquests.

Islam is a religion designed to be lived by in an intense way, the Koran and the Sunna laying down almost all the habits, customs and attitudes that a Moslem must adopt if he is to lead a pious life. One cannot stress too much the extent to which Moslems are aware of God as co-inhabiting their world. Western Christians have not felt that their lives were led in such close company with God since the twelfth century and it seems mysterious to us that people should unaffectedly feel that their very slightest actions and most transient thoughts are partnered with God and therefore can affect the relationship between them for better or worse. Faith of this quality is reflected in all Moslem works; it is responsible for the traditionalism of Islamic architecture, for a man changes what has once been decided to be good in God's sight at his peril, or rather, perhaps, at risk of some estrangement from God. Although the Prophet does not have much to say about the type of buildings his followers should build,* the simplicity of the uses which they were designed to serve were laid down by him and the only other basic influences upon their development have been the hot climate of most of the Moslem world, the wealth it enjoyed and the amplitude of Asian and African spaces. This last consideration encouraged large and horizontal buildings, but it had a deeper significance in that familiarity with great expanses has so worked on the Arab temperament that their buildings are not, as ours are, works in which all the interest is concentrated upon the building itself, this occupying a deliberate volume of space, but rather structures which enclose spaces with walls, domes, roofs, whose form and decoration are designed to enhance the spaces they define rather than themselves. The space defined is always more important than the building defining it. It is no accident that spacious Arab buildings frequently suggest partly opened tents.

What is more surprising is how the Arabs' attitude towards

---

* He is quoted as saying that building was the least profitable of expenditures.

architecture impressed itself upon the many peoples dominated by them or their religious ideals. The key to this is certainly the uniform simplicity of the demands which Islam makes of architecture. Acceptance of the religion meant accepting a way of life asking no more of its temples and dwellings than shelter for the sparest rituals of prayer and, ideally, an ascetic domesticity. One could say that Moslem architecture shelters thought from distraction by the elements.

The forms which Islamic architecture took were evolved under the universal rule of the Ommayed Caliphate — established in 661 and lasting until ousted by the Abbasids in 749. In the subsequent general fragmentation of the empire Spain, however, remained under Ommayed rule until 1056 when, without changing the Ommayed-inspired tradition of building, the Almoravids of Morocco took over. Though elsewhere the general forms were evolved under the Ommayeds, these were further developed under their successors and, along with much Moslem thought, crystallized. Meanwhile in Spain the continuance of Ommayed influence fixed a rather different tradition marked by an easier relationship with God than that developed in the east — a more primitive one perhaps, but a more flexible one. Although Morocco had been more isolated than Spain, yet not beyond its influence or that of the Abbasid east, it too was founding individualistic attitudes which were to persist as tempering agents upon the strong Spanish influences it would soon receive. Despite what was throughout the Middle Ages a close and continuous contact between all parts of the Moslem world which encouraged a unity of artistic expression and the dissemination of innovatory ideas and techniques, nobody would confuse the Maghrebi style with that of Persia, or even with that of Egypt.

MOSQUES

The first demand that Islam made on architecture was for mosques — halls for communal prayer. All that is required of a mosque is that it should shelter a congregation while clearly indicating the direction in which, in relation to itself, the holy city of Mecca lies (so that the faithful know which way to face while addressing their prayers), and that water shall be provided for the performance of ritual ablutions which Moslems are enjoined to make before praying. Before mosques were built the *msalla* was used. This consisted of an open space lying behind a wall built across the line of the direction in which Mecca was situated and having centred in it a niche opening from the cleared space where the worshippers congregated. The feature of the niche was probably derived from the Romano-Byzantine apse set in the centre of the east wall of churches. The niched wall of the *msalla* is called the *quibla* (a word meaning 'the direction' [of Mecca] though extended by inference to the wall marking this) and the niche itself, of course, is called the *mihrab*. The form which mosques took developed naturally and logically from the *msalla*, being merely an extended, roofed shelter erected over the space in front of the *quibla*. As added protection side-walls were added at right-angles to either end of the *quibla* (these may or may not have doorways in them) and further extended to enclose an open court before the sheltered area — walling round, as it were, the rest of the *msalla*'s open space.

An early *msalla* survives at Fes (p. 260). You still see them occasionally in the country places.

The first mosque to be built was that which the Caliph el-Walid made at Damascus from 706 to 714 — the Ommayed Mosque. There the Moslem conquerors had previously shared with the Christians half the great cathedral church of St John. Like Hellenistic Syrian temples, this church was set in a walled, rectangular precinct or temenos and when the Ommayeds converted it to the sole use of Moslems they dismantled the church and built instead an open-sided hall against the southern or *quibla* side* of the precinct. In this they did what first they had done at Jerusalem after the conquest of 637 when they erected a roof over the ruined, three-aisled stoa of Herod that stood along the south side of the temple enclosure. At Damascus too they built their hall of three aisles, carrying their roof on arches upheld by pillars. It left the rest of the old precinct as an open courtyard, around which they built an arcade and in the centre set a fountain for ablutions. This courtyard of a mosque is called the *sahn*. The Byzantine precinct had been orientated on an east-west axis with entrances at each end, that on the east being the larger,

* The *quibla* indicates the *direction* of Mecca and no Moslem says his prayers 'to the east' unless he happens to be west of that city. Mecca lies some 35° east and 11° south of Morocco, but most of its mosques are orientated more to the south than the east, medieval geographers not having had adequate means to calculate direction correctly. Thus, when describing Moroccan mosques, it is more convenient to speak of the *quibla* being on the south side of the building, for to be more precise and say south-south-east would be burdensome.

ceremonial one. The Arabs made another entrance in the north wall beside a tower which they built in its centre, opposite to the *mihrab*, thus creating a new north-south axis. This they further emphasized by making the central aisle between the pillars of the hall — that which led longitudinally from the court to the *mihrab* — wider and higher than the others. They also gave this 'nave' an ornamental front upon the *sahn* and where it intersected with the central of the three lateral or transverse aisles they built a high dome. Although this was an entirely Moslem building its debt to early Byzantine churches is very apparent. Yet the accident of this conversion combined with the natural development of the *msalla* to create the prototypical mosque. All the elements of this building derive from older traditions. It has been plausibly suggested that the hall opening from the court recalled the lay-out of Mohammed's house at Medina where all Moslem tradition began; such a plan is still the commonest for simple houses in that part of the world. Emphasis on a central axis — ornamental entrance, 'nave', dome, niche — all have Graeco-Roman or Byzantine antecedents; so have the arcaded portico and the water basin. According to ibn Hisham, Mohammed ordered Bilal to call the people to prayer from the highest neighbouring rooftop in Medina, in imitation of the horn which the Jews blew for a similar purpose and the clapper which the Christians sounded. There were four short towers at the angles of the precinct of St John at Damascus and these were used by the Arabs as posts for calling prayer-times and even after the building of el-Walid's new tower they continued to be used so. Slender minarets were later raised on the southern pair, and still the prayers are called from them. The idea of the short-angle towers was copied when in 673 the mosque of Amr was enlarged in old Cairo; these were the first minarets deliberately to be built. However, it was el-Walid's tower (for which also there was Syrio-Byzantine precedent) which succeeded to the office when further mosques were built on the Damascene model, the earliest extant being that of Kairouan. Going by different names, among them the calling-towers are called *menara*: 'place of fire', pharos, lighthouse, beacon; from this word we have derived our 'minaret'.

In the Maghreb, first the Zituna Mosque of Tunis, then (727, but later rebuilt) Kairouan, then Cordoba in 785, all were built on the Damascene model. Later additions now blur the purity of Cordoba's original plan.

The earliest Moroccan mosques that we know anything about are the el-Andalus and the Kairouyyin at Fes, both belonging to the later tenth century but subsequently rebuilt so much that nothing is known of their plan. It is not unreasonable to suppose the existence of an early mosque at Tangier. Next certain building is the mosque which Ali ben Yussef is known to have built in connection with his father's casbah at Marrakech, now lost, and his great mosque in the town, now wholly rebuilt though still retaining his name. From our point of view, however, Moroccan architecture begins with the Almohads — mid-twelfth to mid-thirteenth centuries. (But see pp. 213 and 255.)

The general plan of the mosques these rulers built retained most of the features of their Syrian prototype. They tended to have even deeper prayer-halls than their contemporaries built in the east where the three lateral aisles of Damascus had soon been multiplied. They retained, though, that great width which so well expresses the difference in attitude towards prayer that Moslems and Christians hold, the former emphasizing direct contact between the man praying and God, the latter requiring the mediation of priests for whose invocatory rituals churches are designed to form a stage and auditorium. The new extent of the prayer-halls posed a question of where to put a dome over the intersecting aisles so that it should give most formal emphasis. This was solved at Kairouan by widening the lateral aisle alongside the *quibla* and doming its intersection with the 'nave' while also placing another dome over the intersection of 'nave' and the first two lateral aisles, thus making still more of the ornamental entrance into the hall from the *sahn*. With modifications, this T-plan of widened aisles became usual practice in Morocco although the domed entrance is less constant. Also at Kairouan the slightly pointed arch with returns at the base — the 'horse-shoe' arch — was first introduced into the Maghreb. A little-used Syrio-Byzantine device,[*] this had already been employed in the east. Used in a rather more pronounced form at Cordoba, it was later developed to become almost the hall-mark of the Maghrebi style. It is possible that the shape reflected a Visigothic tradition which, if so, would have given its use an added local impetus.

Another Maghrebi idiosyncrasy was the position of the

---

[*] The use of double capitals in the arcading of the *sahn* at Damascus actually suggests this development, and it is explicitly used in Caliph Hisham's palace of Resafa.

minaret. The axial placing of the minaret at Rabat (the 'Hassan Tower') illustrates the exception rather than the rule in Morocco, where minarets are more commonly placed on either of the northern corners of the *sahn*. The square plan of these descends directly from Damascus and earlier Christian towers in Syria, themselves the heirs of a long tradition. Other than those surmounting *koubbiyet* — protective structures built over the tombs of holy or distinguished men — externally visible domes are not a common feature of Moroccan architecture. The Almoravid *koubba* at Marrakech (p. 213) suggests they may once have been, but in general they are covered by a pitched, green-tiled roof. One of these is almost invariably placed over the T-junction of the main aisles of a mosque, however humble a building it is. Under it, a railed or screened enclosure — a *maqsura* — often forms a kind of royal or gubernatorial pew in the great mosques. These were introduced by Muawiya as a protection against assassination — vainly; two subsequent Ommayed caliphs were murdered in mosques. (An adaptation of the practice occurs in the Cappella Palatina at Palermo where a royal pew faces the sanctuary from a position against the west wall. This was built under strong Arab influence just prior to the building of the 'first' Koutoubia at Marrakech.)

A last feature that became traditional — it occurs at Damascus, though as a post-Walidian addition — is the building of a library behind the *mihrab*, a scriptural treasury in a sanctified position.

In the History section (p. 76) we have seen how rural and turbulent Morocco depended on Spain for its models of courtly and urban life, for the skills, techniques and industrial arts that were needed to support such a life, and how refugees from el-Andalus brought these to the cities of the country. Exceedingly rich, Spain had developed an inveterate tendency to luxuriate in its wealth and most of the graces of life in Morocco represented Spanish imports. Moroccan poets wrote in the Andalusian manner; Moroccan sultans wrote Andalusian poetry in the manner of Andalusian sultans. In return, Morocco offered Spain an influence for restraint and a reassertion of Islamic asceticism. Under the influence of cold winters and a lingering Roman tradition for a snugger style of domestic comfort, the open-air virtues of Ommayed architecture soon became modified in Spain. The Romans had also left a more ornate conception of luxury behind them and of all Moslem buildings the Spanish are the least concerned to define space and most preoccupied with the building as an object of intrinsic interest. In this they never succeeded in influencing the Moroccans. Inhabiting the wide spaces of Africa and subject to a constant influx of Arab blood, mixed with Berbers, a people who thoroughly understood space, the Moroccans could not be seduced from their loyalty to this essential and almost unconscious Islamic attitude towards architecture. Almohad mosques lay a firm stress upon the space they define, doing so with a monumental simplicity that seems apposite enough to desert zealots. No amount of surface decoration or intricacy of detail offended this virtue until decadence corrupted all the arts in the seventeenth century. It is a surprisingly marked quality that differentiated Moroccan from Andalusian buildings in a very sure way. It is saddening that a perhaps too keen desire to demonstrate the continued survival of traditional skills induced the (Vietnamese) architect of the new shrine to Mohammed V at Rabat so far to forget it.

Apart from glimpses into the Kairouyyin mosque at Fes, visitors who are interested in Maghrebi buildings will have no chance to study mosques in use. However, they should not miss the opportunity to see the ruined Almohad mosque at Tinmel (p. 331), the uncompleted remains of Yaacub el-Mansur's mosque at Rabat (p. 175) where one may ascend the 'Hassan Tower' minaret, the excavated ruins of the first Koutoubia at Marrakech (p. 206) or the ruins of Chella at Rabat (p. 179). Different in plan and conception, though no less interesting, are the prayer-halls of the *medersa* at Fes, Meknes and Marrakech.

MEDERSA (singular: *medrassa*)

A residential school or college of theology and Moslem law, the *medrassa* was not introduced into Morocco until the twelfth century. The Ayyubids of Cairo had encouraged the idea to reintroduce the study of Sunni orthodoxy as a means to combat the heretical influence of their Shia predecessors. The earliest known use of a house exclusively for this purpose is at Nishabur, eastern Iran, in the ninth century. The earliest remaining in Morocco date from the fourteenth century; Merinid sultans, who generally had a great interest in learning and building, were responsible for most of them.

In plan, the *medersa* descend from the town houses in which theological professors had earlier received their pupils. Each, however, contains a prayer-hall on one side of the central court which itself, with an ablution basin in its midst, becomes more of a *sahn* than a domestic courtyard. This is usually surrounded by ground-floor rooms for teaching, a library, sometimes by masters' rooms; the upper floor being divided into cells where the pupils lived. A sultan expected any work he ordered to be seen to do him honour and these buildings combine a near-palatial opulence with a certain asceticism of design. They are generally very beautiful indeed. The Merinid *medersa* offer opportunities to study wood and stucco carving and mosaic tiling of an excellent period; almost as good is the Saadian *medrassa* at Marrakech, though the Alaouite one at Meknes heralds the decline.

PALACES

If it was the princes who built the mosques and the *medersa*, it was certainly they who built the palaces, even the greatest of their viziers prudently keeping their establishments within the bounds of large houses. All Islamic arts depended upon patronage and, ultimately, upon the standards which the princes set. All kinds of rivalries usually kept these very high, and gentlemanliness was generally synonymous with a degree of cultivation — all the more so since the sultans' sex lives were never for a moment a problem to them and therefore left their leisure time unusually free for intellectual enjoyments. Particularly under the hectic conditions of life endemic to Morocco, a prince liked to see any building he ordered erected as quickly as possible. This was so all over Islam and it probably helped to discourage the building of enormous and elaborate palaces of the European kind. The ascetic nature of Islam encourages its followers to ask comparatively little of their domestic surroundings, be these never so rich and refined. Even very ostentatious sultans lived within traditions that felt no need of a proliferation of rooms designed for special uses. The tradition that each man built his own house was strong, those of his forebears often being cannibalized or abandoned to the weather to destroy; thus there was no tradition of building houses for one's posterity or as deathless memorials to oneself.

Primitive dwellings in the Mediterranean region and the Near East required only a room or two opening from a walled courtyard which might also contain a store or stables besides. Even in antiquity building techniques allowed for the erection of a second storey, though there was little call for these outside the towns. Old as Samaria and Egypt, the courtyard-plan reached its most sophisticated level under the Romans. A small palace like that of the fourth century at Piazza Armerina in Sicily exhibits a high standard of comfort, privacy and style. It lacks, though, something of airiness and real space — very necessary qualities in Asia and Africa where the more open and less sophisticated Pompeian type of house remained the ideal. A link can be seen in the houses of Volubilis — late Roman, but equally early Fasi.

The Ommayed caliphs were richer and more powerful than any of their successors. They were a desert people from what is now central Jordan and while they did not like towns, townsmen hated them. Prudence and temperament inclined them to build desert palaces; they made them wonders of their world. El-Walid's Tamsaft was said to have provoked his assassination. It set a precedent of comfort, magnificence and sophisticated design which, although it remained uncompleted at his death, remains unrivalled. In so imitative and conservative a society as that of Arab dynasts it was natural that others should have followed the style that the Ommayeds adopted, at least in the planning of their palaces. This derived from Syrian models modified by Sassanian and other influences. It incorporated Byzantine traditions inherited from the Graeco-Roman world — Tamsaft and Piazza Armerina have many essentials in common — although the emphasis laid on symmetry is characteristically Arab.

The essential feature of the dwelling was a court, usually rectangular in shape, off which living-rooms opened. In a huge complex like Tamsaft a vast courtyard was central to four main blocks — entrance block, royal buildings facing it, service blocks on either hand — which were themselves subdivided variously, though almost symmetrically, into self-contained sets of rooms each of which was centred upon its own court. It has not often since been possible to achieve the classic symmetry of Tamsaft, but it has been striven for over and over again, and never forgotten. Alone of Moroccan builders, Moulay Ismaïl had some chance to build himself a Tamsaft, but the lie of the land forced many compromises upon him. (Much altered, the main dwelling now houses the Military Academy and all we may see is the ruins of the stabling, and a far from negligible sight it makes (p. 272)). Ahmed el-Mansur's el-Badi Palace at Marrakech — in its day of great wonder — demonstrates better what a 'palace' meant to a Moroccan sultan: a series of rooms round a single court, the whole of a unified and symmetrical design symbolizing the individual builder's personality — i.e. his quarters rather than his palace in our understanding of the word.*

El-Badi, though a classic example of its kind, was actually built as a setting for receptions. Reconstruction shows how utterly delightful it was; the proportions of its ruins, the tantalizing vestiges of its decoration, are enough to suggest its former beauty was equal to its fame — and el-Badi means 'the incomparable'; the impression it made upon European ambassadors is recorded in their dispatches. The court was divided into two by a long watertank having an island carrying a fountain in its midst, and by two sunken garden-plots on its either side, planted with trees as they are today. At the centre of the west end, facing down the length of the pool, a partly open-sided pavilion with two retiring-rooms behind it jutted into the court. It was balanced at the pool's other end by another pavilion which was merely an ornamental gateway leading to a large enclosed garden beyond and below it. Smaller pools were set on either side of both these pavilions. On the north and south sides were rooms so ranged that they had regular, symmetrical entrances on the court and presented balanced façades to it. Of these the central room on either side was larger and higher than the rest, a *liwan* or ceremonial room opening only to the court under a wide and high arch. The northern rooms were the more elaborate and had small suites behind them. The southern side abutted older buildings, differently orientated, with which its rooms were forced to compromise. The main entrance was in the south-east corner; beside it another led into the older buildings. There were many other entrances, and subterranean passages probably enabled the service of banquets to appear almost magically unobtrusive. This was only a part of the palace complex. Since it was built for receptions the sultan's living quarters were elsewhere. It makes no provision for the 'forbidden' harem where the sultan's own women lived,† none for officials' quarters, guests', guards', servants', or stabling; nowhere for the prince's male relatives and their suites of

---

* The palace complex is called the *dar* in Maghrebi and a suite of rooms within it a *bayt*.

† It was the Moroccan habit that the woman visited the man rather than that he stalked the harem 'where hundreds of women might live since it was the convention to own many, while fine women were reckoned suitable presents for sultan since they complimented his virility. A desire for sons was apt to inhibit monogamy, but a comparatively faithful attitude was not unknown; a very large harem might well have conduced to it.

retainers, for the relics of predecessors and the hosts of their concubines, with the upkeep of whom every sultan was saddled. Men of the family were distributed as governors over the country or (as the Alaouite sultans used to do with relatives they distrusted) were rusticated in lonely places like the Tafilelt. All the rest were accommodated elsewhere about the palace quarter, in buildings conceived on much the same lines as el-Badi though perhaps falling into increasing disrepair, in barracks and stables and bagnios — all within the wall of the casbah citadel though behind its second line of defences. If the casbah mosque was used by many of these, there were other royal mosques and oratories deeper within the stronghold where the great could worship away from the hazardous contact with the populace. Necessary features of a palace complex were, too, a judgment-hall and a *mechouar*, a large, open, walled space overlooked by an *iwan* (sometimes a balcony, more often a *liwan* raised above ground-level; a Sassanian invention adopted by the Abbasids) in which the sultan appeared to receive mass audiences of his subjects — tribesmen — come to do him homage.

Any Moroccan sultan's 'palace' was more of a retreat from all this than anything else. Any man might envy el-Mansur his.

The palace of Fes exemplifies both the jumble and, sometimes, the symmetry of detail which characterize these constructions. Its great court — a wonderfully beautiful place — illustrates on the other hand the dogged individuality of successive sultans (p. 245). At Meknes, Moulay Ismaïl was able to start from scratch; he wanted to build a palace to rival Versailles, for his was an age when Morocco was looking outwards, but earthquake ruined his works (p. 270).

To imagine the ruined palaces in their decorated state one has to transpose to their skeletons a memory of contemporary examples from elsewhere, remembering that their exteriors were generally plain and relieved by little else save machicolation, a glimpse of green pantiled roofs and decorated gates. We thus judge Moulay Ismaïl's palace to have verged on the vulgar, this on the strength of the Bab Mansur and the decoration of the Filada *medrassa*, both at Meknes. The el-Badi's decoration can be imagined by thinking of the Saadian Tombs near by — extremely elegant; almost dangerously intricate and lacy — and by remembering the glimpses you will get of the lovely pavilions in the *sahn* of the Kairouyyin Mosque at Fes; they are smaller versions of el-Badi's two and most like that which led into the lower garden. The only example of a palace contemporary with the Merinids is the Alhambra at Granada. Beautifully controlled and framed as the decoration of this building is, I suspect it to have represented a more feminine, elaborate and bijou version of anything then to have been found in Morocco. The Merinid *medrassa* suggest a stronger and more ascetic bent. It may be pertinent to remember the imposing simplicity of overall design to be seen in Mudejar work at Granada. Scant indication of still earlier decorative work, visible to us, survive: Tinmel for the Almohad period; the cupola at Marrakech for the Almoravid – and, of course, for the traditions from which they derive, the mosque at Cordoba and the palace ruins of Medina az-Zahra, also near Cordoba.

There are other traditional buildings that can be visited which are 'palaces' in the Italian sense of the word – great houses: the Badia at Marrakech; Palais Jamaï Hotel and the National Museum at Fes; the National Museum in the Oudaïa Casbah at Rabat; the Dar el-Makhzen at Tangier. These all date from Moulay Ismaïl's reign or later; they are more interesting as domestic houses and it is not reasonable to compare them with their Italian counterparts; those were built as they are for quite other motives than these – for one thing, when a vizier fell from power his servants sacked the house before the sultan's men could arrive to seize all his possessions; death or disgrace, this was the only occasion when the sultan could tax his richest citizen and the future welfare of his dependants thereafter depended on grace-and-favour pensions. No man in this position would build himself a Palazzo Farnese. It is also generally worth while to allow yourself to be lured into tourist-trap places for a few minutes to see the grand town houses they often occupy. These are rarely older than the last century and a certain European influence is often detectable about them; the deep well of the courtyards in many of them is designed for coolness, and is reminiscent of the subterranean summer-rooms at Bulla Regia.

KSOUR (singular: *ksar*)

The impressive *ksour* of the trans-Atlas regions – in the pre-Sahara – built of earthen pisé-blocks, rubble or mud-brick, are mentioned on pp. 336–41. Nothing in the ancient world urged man towards radical innovation. It was not then necessary to rethink problems over again and, among such societies as those of the pre-Sahara, very little has occurred since to provoke a further serious development, particularly as regards the demands people made of their buildings. Yet although the towered form of the mud *ksour* is known from the Atlas to Kano and farther south, and eastwards across the Fezzan to Siwa, it is puzzling that nobody has yet seemed interested in tracing its traditional source. Archaeological research is rendered difficult since neither the *ksour* nor their vestiges have long lives. An old, rare *ksar* such as that at Tiffoultoute contains no fabric older than three hundred years at most, while Talaat n'Yaacub (decorated with what is apparently Almoravid detail) was built in 1875. There exists, however, the marvellous mosaic of the 'Inundation of the Nile Valley' (in the Museo Nazionale at Palestrina), a Graeco-Roman work from the early years of the Roman occupation of Egypt — the first half of the first century A.D. perhaps. Among much other vivid detail, this depicts several country villas, farms and temple enclosures of the Delta region having just such towers as the *ksour*, built of rubble or mud-brick, two and three storeys high, tapering towards their tops, which are decorated with rising angles at the corners, pierced with slit-shaped window-openings and one linked to another by crenellated walls. With the possible exception of megalithic building-techniques, all architectural forms in Morocco appear to have had an eastern provenance and, given that we accept the plausible premiss that building-techniques based upon the use of pisé and palm-trunks developed earlier in Egypt than elsewhere in North Africa, I do not think we have need to look much farther for the source of this tradition.

DECORATIVE ARTS

The prohibition against animate representationalism in the visual arts which has forced Moslem artists to rely so heavily on abstract design had not been imposed at the time of the Ommayeds, Islamic dogma then still being in a state of pending crystallization. It has never been universally observed. Like wine-drinking and dancing, representationalism would creep into favour during periods of lax religious discipline. The Spanish were prone to it. Yet the Moroccans' temperamental bias towards Sunni orthodoxy and ascetic zeal make it extraordinarily rare even among their minor arts. The compromise, universal to Islam, by which stylized flower- and plant-motives were permitted in decoration, was always been a popular one in Morocco. They are rarely handled with anything like the Persian opulence of line and rhythm, however; only the Almoravid cupola shows a rich and baroque taste. Another indulgence which, like their fellows in Islam, Moroccan artists allowed themselves was the use of decorative script. Of this Robert Byron wrote; '. . . Cufic lettering has a functional beauty; regarded as pure design, its extraordinary exphasis seems in itself a form of oratory, a transposition of speech from the audible to the visible.' And '. . . tall, rhythmic ciphers, involved with dancing foliage . . . ' The eye that becomes mazed by the severe abstraction of so much Moroccan decoration lights with joy on the comparative cursiveness of texts and affirmations of the creed incorporated therein — to my mind, most beautifully of all in the dados of the Saadian Tombs.

LANGUAGE

The universal language of Morocco is Arabic, or very nearly so. Classic or literary Arabic — the Arabic of the Koran and the commentaries upon it — is the country's official language though the spoken word language is dialectal and susceptible to regional variations. This overall dialect is not unlike that of Algeria and from Tunis to the Atlantic it is usually called *Maghrebi* Arabic.

Berber is widely spoken, particularly in the countryside, though most Berbers by far are bilingual. Berber is an ancient language of Hamitic stock. (The origins of the Berber race, a 'Caucasian' one, may indeed by the Caucasus itself, but are uncertain. Berbers have inhabited North Africa since before historical times.) The Moroccan Berbers are grouped into three dialectal regions, in each of which there are local variant dialects.

They are:

Rifian, spoken by the mountaineers of the Rif, the eastern sedentary tribes, those of the Middle Atlas and the Figuig oases;

Braber (of Saharan Sanhajan origin) spoken by the transhuman tribes of the Middle Atlas, the eastern High Atlas and the southern valleys of the Ziz, Todrha, Gheris, Dadès and Sargh;

Chleuh, spoken by the sedentary tribes of the High Atlas, the valleys mentioned above, the Sous valley and Anti-Atlas, and the established oases of the still more southerly Jebel Bani.

The first is practically a foreign language to the third, but the second forms a kind of bridge language between them. They themselves call the first and second groups together *tamazight* and the third *tachelhit*. (Place-names with 't's at their either ends are invariably Berber.) Berber is no longer written in Morocco as once it was in Arabic script. It is not known whether it was ever written in its own ancient script here, as it still is among the Saharan Tuareg. It should be noted that though people may remark to you that you are, for instance, going 'among the Chleuh' or that so-and-so is a 'Braber', this does not mean that the people or person so called belong to a certain race or tribe, but to the dialectal group.

An extremely well-born Fasi 'Arab' once told me he had Negro, Jewish, Spanish, Arab and Berber blood — 'for I am a Moroccan'. This heritage cannot help but be reflected in the country's speech.

French is very widely spoken indeed and it is taught even in the remotest village-schools. However, in the old Spanish Zone it can be useful to have a knowledge of that language since French has been generally taught there only since Independence. In Tangier it is usual to find people who speak Arabic, Berber (Rifian), Spanish and French, and quite possibly English besides. English is not otherwise much spoken, though it is now taught in senior classes and is on the increase. Hoteliers of the better categories of course speak English, French, Spanish, German and often Italian too.

MOROCCAN MUSIC

Moroccans are a naturally musical people and making music is to them an important means to self-expression. As a visitor you may very probably be offered *folklorique* musical entertainments which, excellent and interesting as they mostly are, could give you the impression that folk-music is either consciously being preserved or even revived. This is emphatically not so. What you hear on these occasions are excerpts from a living repertoire. I have known what started as an exhibition of this sort for a tourist group to become an impromptu party lasting into daylight next morning — and this stimulated only by glasses of mint tea; for the music that the performers were making took so great a hold over them that it required its own climax and resolution, which no snatch of an excerpt could provide. They were, of course, perfectly oblivious to and uncaring of their audience's early withdrawal.

All the traditional ceremonies and festivals of life require a musical accompaniment, and all Moroccans can sing on note and keep a complex rhythm timed as precisely as a good jazz-combo must. They can always play an instrument, even if it be only a drum. Happy children give vent to their feelings by clapping rhythms that are often complicated or, if they start simply, are soon elaborated, spontaneously invented.

In the old days there was court music and rural music. The first belonged to the Arab school and the second to the predominantly Berber countryside. However, since slaves have been brought up from the black African Sudan since proto-historic times, Berber music, at least, has long been influenced by the very different Negro 'sound'.

Medieval Andalus or court music, Arab-inspired, is still influential upon Moroccan music, particularly so upon that of the northern Jebala area where contact with Andalusia was always easiest and where so many refugees from Moorish Spain were on several occasions settled. There is some purely black-African music to be heard in southern regions, but more often the Negro sound one hears is in fact Berber under strong black influence — as the two racial strains mingle most harmoniously in the flesh, so do their talents for music. The purest Berber music is heard in the Rif mountains, the district which has always been the most successful in rejecting outside influences.

Examples of types of music which you will be most likely to hear are:

Toqtoqa: of the Jebala and the north-west (evidencing Arab influences). The dancing-boys of Tangier and its neighbourhood perform to music of this type.

Gnawa: a wild, drumming music to which troupes of men dance in the Djemaa el-Fna (p. 203) at Marrakech. This is pure black-African music. The Gnawa — members of a religious sect and predominantly Negro — are in great demand for weddings and all other festivals; they ritually exorcize evil spirits (i.e. the mental disorders of medical science) and, with their lively dancing and urgent music, purify houses after a death has occurred in them.

Ahouache: usually sung and danced by women to music made by men (though the division is neither formal nor by any means invariable), this Berber music is often influenced by black-African. It is generally to be heard in the south.

Guedra: danced by women in a kneeling position with much emphasis upon manual gestures. The performers wear the indigo-blue robes of the Sahara, where this dance originates. It is said to have been evolved to be danced under the low roofs of the tents. The professional Guedra women are, or were, prostitutes, and their dance is one of calculated, long-drawn-out seduction. Its undeniable eroticism has often provoked thunderous wrath in zealous, reforming marabouts.

Aïssawa: played by members of the widespread cult of Sidi Aïssa, a seventeenth-century saint from Meknes, where his tomb and cult centre stands. Aïssawa music varies in type considerably over the country and most of North Africa besides. It includes the musical accompaniments to the snake-charmers' performances, for Aïssawa music induces a tranced state in adepts who dance to it (or even only listen to it) during which they can and do lacerate or burn themselves without sensing pain and, similarly, cult membership is believed to protect the charmers from snakebite.

With the exception of Toqtoqa music, the above types (among others almost infinitely varied from tribe to tribe, group to group; regionally differentiated) represent 'trance' music in that they are performed almost or quite continuously over hours of time, so that their effect is cumulative. The emotional release (or, in the Guedra's case, the erotic stimulus) thus engendered in performers and audience alike, slowly rising to a climactic plateau of musical experience, is carried over and beyond into a state of being unlike any inducible by the emotionally direct and simplistic music of the European tradition.

You will be bound to hear also much canned, modern Egyptian music in Morocco. This belongs to quite another school to the native. Sentimental, meretricious and flaccid, it speaks to its auditors in an Occidental idiom wholly at variance with the fundamental purpose of indigenous music, which is to take one out of oneself. As elsewhere in Africa, Morocco has been infected with a passion for reggae, producing a few domestic enthusiasts who compare poorly with the original.

Anyone interested in the subject would be well advised to obtain — as an introduction — the record 'Music of Morocco' in the Ethnic Folkways Library (No. FE4339). It is accompanied by an introduction by the recorder, Christopher Wanklyn, which includes interesting information about the native instruments employed to make Moroccan music.

INTRODUCTION TO ROUTES

The centres and routes described in this book are divided into five sections. The first of these deals largely with the main centres, the following four with routes in the north, west, south and east of Morocco, in that order. (These geographical directions are intended to be only a rough indication of the area covered.) There are separate introductions preceding each of these five sections and a diagram of the routes covered near the beginning of each section. All the regions are shown on the Main Centres diagram (see pp. 140–1). The various route diagrams indicate routes and detours as set out in the text; unbroken lines indicate routes, not whether the roads so marked are in good condition, for example.

Distances given along the routes are in kilometres and one-way. They are marked cumulatively from the starting-point of the single major route described in each of the sections dealing with the north, west and east, and from the starting-point of each of the various routes appearing in the sections dealing with the main centres and the south. These distances do not include detours along the way.

On the Chart of Excursions, pp. 12–13, distances are one-way from each centre appearing in the first column. In some cases, there are shorter routes from the centre to the town or site indicated than those described in the text. When the distance in brackets after the name of a place to be visited differs from that appearing in the text, the reader should consult the end-paper maps where the most direct routes will be obvious. Otherwise, the appropriate route diagrams should be consulted. The number of days allotted to each centre refers to the minimum time for seeing the most important sights within the city and does not include excursions from it.

Our first section, the Main Centres, traces a vaguely oval or diamond-shaped route, all within inner Morocco. However, the ease with which you can now get from Marrakech to Agadir (p. 334) suggests an extension to the latter resort where the sea, the vast sandy beach and the comfortable hotels, are the major attractions. But it would be difficult simply to go there and back, resting up for a few days, if only because, in Morocco, you always want to go on to the next intriguing place — over the next range of hills or mountains. So think about seeing a little of outer Morocco by adding Agadir, Taroudant, and Ouarzazate as a way of looping back to Marrakech.

ROUTES BETWEEN MAIN CENTRES

This section comprises the chief cities of Morocco: Rabat, the capital; Casablanca, the largest city and the most influential commercial centre; Fes, the old capital of the northern area of inner Morocco; Marrakech, the southern counterpart and oft-time rival of Fes; Meknes, Sultan Moulay Ismaïl's capital; Tangier, the most famous tourist resort; Kénitra, an up-and-coming, modern industrial centre; and Tetouan, erstwhile capital of the Spanish Zone.

We have arranged this section to form a round-trip from Tangier — via Kénitra, Rabat, Casablanca, Marrakech, Beni Mella, Khenifra, Fes — with Meknes and neighbouring places of interest as detours from that city — and three alternative routes back to Tangier. The total distances, by the principal roads (less detours) are: 1,431 km. returning from Fes to Tangier via Ouezzane and Chechaouen; 1,399 km. via Sidi Kacem and Souk el-Arba du Rharb; 1,529 km. via Khemisset, Kénitra and Souk el-Arba du Rharb.

The roads throughout are good and fast. For the sake of convenience this very large section is subdivided into the main cities themselves and the roads linking them (see map on pp. 140–1); (for more detailed treatment of these routes, see the appropriate area map). Information about public transport along the roads is given under the appropriate subdivisions, as are any relevant comments on the roads, accommodation along them, etc.

Should you prefer to cut out Casablanca from this itinerary a good plan is to take the P 22 from Rabat, via Rommani and Oued Zem, joining the P 24 to El-Kelaa des Srarhna and Marrakech, although it is 68 km. (or 45 minutes) longer than the route via Casablanca. It is a beautiful and little-frequented road and has the advantage of by-passing the heavy traffic between Rabat and Casablanca.

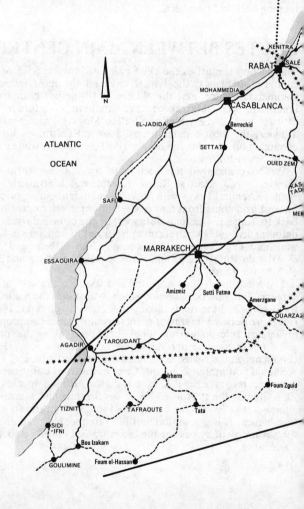

Diagram of Routes linking
Main Centres and Area Maps

N

ATLANTIC

OCEAN

KENITRA
RABAT SALÉ
MOHAMMEDIA
CASABLANCA
EL-JADIDA Berrechid
SETTAT
OUED ZEM
KAS
TAD
SAFI
ME
MARRAKECH
ESSAOUIRA
Amizmiz Setti Fatma Amerzgane
OUARZAZ
AGADIR TAROUDANT
Irherm Foum Zguid
TIZNIT TAFRAOUTE Tata
SIDI
IFNI
Bou Izakarn
GOULIMINE Foum el-Hassan

.... Boundary of Northern Area Map

* * * * * * * Boundary of Western Area Map

— · — · — Boundary of Eastern Area Map

——— Boundary of Southern Area Map

TANGIER

Air, Sea and Rail Air, sea and rail connections are dealt with on p. 21.
Ferry company offices: *Bland Line*, 22 Avenue Mohammed V (tel. 396.33).
Comanav, 149 Avenue Mohammed V (tel. 304.57).
Limadet, Avenue Prince Moulay Abdellah (tel. 336.21).
Transmediterranea, 31 Rue Quévédo (tel. 341.01).
Transtour, 54 Boulevard Pasteur (tel. 340.04).
Airline offices: *Gib-Air*, 83 Rue de la Liberté.
Royal Air Maroc, Place de France (tel. 215.01).
Air France, 20 Boulevard Pasteur (tel. 364.77).
Internal air and rail links are dealt with on p. 23.
Railway information bureau telephone 415.70.
Bus C.T.M. operate twice daily to Rabat, Fes and Meknes; other companies ply the
same routes. There is a frequent service to the nearby towns of Asilah, Larache and
Tetouan (see Routes). The C.T.M. station (see *Map 12*) is adjacent to the rail
terminus at the north end of Avenue d'Espagne; buses also leave from the Gran
Socco.
Taxi If you intend to visit Tetouan or Larache, it may be only slightly more
expensive than the bus and considerably faster and more comfortable to share a
grand taxi from the rank by the bus station. Request *une place* and not *une course*,
which is the whole taxi.

Beware on arrival at the airport of extortionate prices; the correct fare by day is
40DH. (O.N.M.T. have a table of fares in their office for comparison.) There is a
useful taxi rank in Rue de Fes and one at Place de France.
Car Hire *Avis*, 54 Boulevard Pasteur (tel. 389.60).
Europcar, Agence Hispmaroc, Hotel Rembrandt, Avenue Mohammed V (tel. 331.
13).
Hertz, 36 Avenue Mohammed V (tel. 333.22) and at the airport (tel. 341.79).
As elsewhere, car hire is expensive and several small firms discount at up to 40 per
cent. Try along Boulevard Pasteur but do not expect the reliability or service you
would get from a major chain.

Hotels

*****	*Hôtel les Almohades*, Avenue des F.A.R. (tel. 403.30).	
*****	*Hôtel el Minzah*, 85 Rue de la Liberté (tel. 358.85).	
*****	*Hôtel Intercontinental*, Park Brooks (tel. 360.53).	
*****	*Hôtel Rif*, Avenue d'Espagne (tel. 359.08).	
****A	*Hôtel el Oumnia*, Avenue Beethoven (tel. 403.66).	
****A	*Hôtel Solazur*, Avenue des F.A.R. (tel. 401.64).	
****A	*Hôtel Tanjah Flandria*, 6 Boulevard Mohammed V (tel. 330.00).	
****A	*Hôtel Rembrandt*, Avenue Mohammed (tel. 378.70).	
****A	*Hôtel Chellah*, Rue Allâl Ben Abdellah (tel. 383.88).	
****B	*Hôtel Villa de France*, 143 Rue de Hollande (tel. 314.75).	
****B	*Hôtel Pasadena*, Route de Tetouan (tel. 363.15).	
****B	*Africa Hôtel*, 17 Avenue Moussa Ben Noussair (tel. 355.11).	
****B	*Hôtel Velasquez*, 13 Rue Khalid Ibn El Walid (tel. 380.01).	
***A	*Hôtel Tarik*, Route de Malabata (tel. 409.44).	
***A	*Ahlen Village*, Route de Rabat (tel. 430.00).	

***A *Hôtel Atlas*, 50 Rue Moussa Ben Noussair (tel. 364.35).
***A *Hôtel Scheherazade*, 11 Avenue des F.A.R. (tel. 405.00).
***A *Tangier Hôtel*, 29 Rue de la Croix (tel. 355.64).
 **A *Hôtel Djenina*, 8 Rue Grotius (tel. 360.75).
 **A *Hotel Lutetia*, 3 Avenue Moulay Abdellah (tel. 318.66).
 **A *Hôtel Residence Ritz*, 1 Rue Saroya (tel. 380.74).
 **A *Hôtel Mamora*, 19 Rue de la Poste (tel. 341.05).
 **A *Hôtel Anjou*, 3 Rue Ibn Al Banna (tel. 343.44).
 **A *Hôtel Marco Polo*, Avenue d'Espagne (tel. 382.13).
 **A *Hôtel Valencia*, 72 Avenue d'Espagne (tel. 217.14).
 **A *Hôtel Bristol*, 14 Rue El Antakı (tel. 310.70).
 **A *Hôtel Charf*, 25 Rue Dante (tel. 344.93).
 **B *Hôtel Miramar*, Avenue des F.A.R. (tel. 389.48).
 **B *Hôtel Astoria*, 10 Rue Ahmed Chaouki (tel. 372.01).
 **B *Hôtel Panoramic Massilia*, 3 Rue Marco Polo (tel. 350.09).
  *A *Hôtel Andalucia*, 14 Rue Vermeer (tel. 413.34).
  *A *Hôtel de Paris*, 42 Boulevard Pasteur (tel. 381.26).
  *A *Hôtel Biarritz*, 102 Avenue d'Espagne (tel. 324.73).
  *A *Hôtel Al Farabi*, 10 Zankat Essaïdia (tel. 345.66).
  *B *Hôtel Ibn Batouta*, 8 Rue Magellan (tel. 371.70).
  *B *Hôtel Olid*, 12 Rue des Postes (tel. 313.10).
  *B *Hôtel Bretagne*, 92 Avenue d'Espagne (tel. 323.39).
     Hôtel Continental, 36 Dar El Baroud (tel. 310.24).
Camping *Miramonte*, 3 km. west, Avenue Alläl Ben Abdellah (tel. 371.38).
Tingis, 6 km east on the old road to Malabata, lacking in charm but has a swimming pool and tennis court (tel. 401.91).
Sahara, no swimming pool but suitable for caravans.
Information *O.N.M.T. Tourist Office*: 29 Boulevard Pasteur (tel. 382.39).
Syndicat d'Initiative: 11 Rue Velasquez (tel. 354.86).
Consulates British: Trafalgar House, 9 Rue Amerique du Sud (tel. 358.95 & 7).
United States: Rue El Achouak (tel. 359.04).
Banks Concentrated on Boulevards Pasteur and Mohammed V.
Sports and Clubs *Bathing:* famous sandy beach extends south-east of the port and is lined with bathing establishments. The north beach, reached from the medina, lacks these facilities.
Riding: Club Étrier de Tanger, Boubana (tel. 348.84).
Tennis: Emsallah Garden Club, Boulevard de Belgique (tel. 380.26).
Tennis Club Municipal, Rue Raimunde Lulic (tel. 373.24).
Golf: Country Club (18 holes), Boubana (tel. 389.25).
Yachting: Yacht Club de Tanger, port (tel. 385.75).
Flying: Aéro-Club Royal de Tanger.
Restaurants The new town abounds in Spanish-style fish restaurants and modest French establishments. The seafront has a string of cafés offering fixed-price menus without distinction; a short walk towards the medina will find better.
Hammadi's, 2 Rue de la Kasbah (tel. 345.14), has a good Moroccan atmosphere and pleasant *folkloriques* musicians.
Night-life There is plenty about, but whether or not you find it agreeable depends on you. The serious drinking in any number of bars seems in the end the most convivial solution to an evening's entertainment. After hours, drink must be sought in one of the uninspiring discotheques.

Post Office 33 Boulevard Mohammed V (24-hour telephone service).
Emergencies *Hospital Al Kortobi*: Rue Al Kortobi (tel. 342.42).
Police: telephone 19.

Tangier has a population of 266,000 and is the King's summer residence.

This is the least Moroccan of towns and the one most affected by foreign influences. It has a pungent flavour of its own, a life entirely its own and plenty of spirit. It is also the tourist resort so far best-known to foreigners.

Pleasant though Tangier's monuments are, they are of slight importance and need not detain a visitor who is intending to journey farther into the country. Anyone who is visiting Tangier only, though, should not neglect the opportunity they offer for seeing something of the real Morocco that is so different from other places; and the Museum of Moroccan Arts is excellent.

HISTORY

As the Moroccan port best placed for direct contact by sea with southern Spain, Tangier has formed a link between the continents since its foundation by the Phoenicians, more or less contemporaneously with Cadiz, i.e. around, or rather after, 1100 B.C. Originally perhaps no more than a trading-post, it is none the less one of the oldest urban developments in Morocco although in early times Liks was more important. Its fisheries were always prosperous and its chief industry the preparation and export of salt fish and *garum*, a liquid derived from the intestines of fish with which the ancients commonly salted their cooking. The Phoenicians called the town Tingis, or Tingi, and established elaborate arrangements there for storing water for the supply of ships plying between the Mediterranean, the Spanish Atlantic coast and Canary Islands, and the gold-producing states of West Africa. The town's name has endured all its changes of ownership and entered many languages under the guise of 'tangerine', the colour as well as the citrus fruit which, however, is not a native to the area, citrus trees having possibly been imported by the Romans, but more probably by the Arabs.

Greek legend, later in date than the town's actual foundation, ascribes this to Antaeus (the giant son of Poseidon, the sea-god, and Earth) whose home was in 'Libya'. Antaeus successfully wrestled with all comers and killed them until he was himself overpowered and killed by Heracles, whose 'Pillars' the heights either side the Straits were called. The name probably refers to the Rock of Gibraltar and the rather similarly shaped peninsula of Monte Hacho upon which Ceuta stands. These are placed in front of the Mediterranean entrance to the Straits like pillars flanking a doorway. Herculean legends are of comparatively late date, many following the travels of devotees of his very popular hero-cult, though in this case his association with the area most probably derives from the identification which the ancients made between Heracles and the great Phoenician god Melkarth to whom a famous temple was dedicated at Cadiz.

For the history of Tangier as it affected or was affected by that of the country as a whole, see the History section on p. 53. Close to Spain and somewhat detached from the bulk of Morocco by the mountains lying behind it, the position of the port has fostered its individuality and at various times facilitated the formation of separatist Tangerine states even when it has not been in the hands of foreign powers. This, however, has been its most constant condition.

During the Roman civil wars, a local chief called Iphtas made a small, independent state of Tangier. His successor, Ascalis, though supported by Sullan troops, was forced out of the town by a citizens' revolt. The Sullan troops were routed and the revolt put down by Quintus Sertorius, a partisan of Marius' cause, who rather surprisingly reinstated Ascalis in 83 B.C. When this autonomous state collapsed is not known; it must have been absorbed by the Mauritanian kingdom of which Bocchus II and his brother Bogud were from 50 B.C. the co-rulers. Bogud, a supporter of Caesar, espoused Mark Antony's cause on the dictator's death while Bocchus took that of Gaius Octavius (Augustus) at the renewed outbreak of the civil war between him and Antony. Tangier was Bogud's town, but during his absence on campaign in Spain in 34/3 B.C. the citizens rose on behalf of Octavius. After Bocchus' death in 33 B.C. and Octavius' victory, this earned them the privileges and status of a Roman colony. Tangier itself was never again a part of the Mauritanian kingdom. Nor, apparently, did it form a part of Mauritania Tingitana, as the province was called after Rome annexed it in A.D. 45. The Roman Tangerine colony was instead administered as part of the province of Spain. A force of British cavalry then formed part of its garrison. When, however, the province was drastically reduced towards the end of the third century, Diocletian made Tangier its capital. Indeed it was only to secure and supply Tangier and Ceuta, ports vital to

Roman control of the Straits, that the mainland north of a line running from Larache to Tetouan was retained. This territory was a part of the episcopal see of Spain and it has even been suggested that it was the seat of the bishops.

If, as is possible, Genseric the Vandal retained a garrison at Tangier after crossing into North Africa from Spain in 429, Tangier was again separated from the rest of the country. Though Belisarius established a Byzantine garrison at Ceuta in 533, he does not appear to have attempted it at Tangier, which, like the rest of Morocco has no further recorded history until the coming of the Arabs. Belisarius campaigned against a background of appalling natural disasters — earthquakes, volcanic eruptions, floods and pestilence — which may have made him hesitate to extend his forces too far. Morocco may have been affected by catastrophe; it will not have escaped the so-called Plague of Justinian which swept over all the Western world some thirty years later, entirely depopulating very many cities and huge tracts of countryside. It was most probably an epidemic of smallpox. The devastation such a visitation could wreak would be ample to account for Morocco's having no history for the next 150 years.

So far as Tangier is concerned the coming of the Arabs occurred definitively towards 705, when Musa ben Nasser conquered it. Six years later it was used as the spring-board for the conquest of Spain. Heretic Berber malcontents from the Rif, rising against Arab rule, captured the town in either 739 or 740 and appear to have held it for some years. Disputed between the Ommayeds of Spain and the Idrissids of Morocco, Tangier was actually occupied by the Fatimids of Tunis, *circa* 958, until they were ousted from the port, as the Idrissids also were from the surrounding country, by the Ommayeds. The Almoravids captured it in 1075, the Almohads in 1149. During the gradual collapse of that dynasty Tangier elected to come under the rule of the Hafsids of Tunis (1243), but passed to Merinid control in 1274.

By then Tangier was a port of international repute trading with the maritime states of Italy, France and Spain. But now the Christian kings of Spain and Portugal were in a position to attack the Moroccan coasts and this trade fell away. Tangier was unsuccessfully invested by the Portuguese in 1437. It fell to a further assault on August 12th, 1471. Mosques were converted into churches, the chief one becoming the cathedral of the Holy Spirit. When in 1580 Portugal was inherited by Philip II of Spain,

Tangier also came into Spanish hands, but was returned to Portugal as that country regained its independence. Ownership of Tangier changed in 1656, long before all Portugal achieved its independence. Then, at her marriage in 1662, Catherine of Braganza brought Tangier to Charles II of England as a part of her rich dowry. The Saadian dynasty had collapsed and Morocco was divided between various rulers until the Alaouites had finally established themselves. The English in Tangier were at first harassed by Ghailan, a warrior marabout whom they called 'Gayland'. He was master of the Straits area but had himself to contend with the marabouts of a zawiya at Djila near Khenifra who controlled most of the rest of north Morocco, and also with pressure from the rising Alaouites. Gayland accordingly became the ally of the English. The redoubtable sultan Moulay Ismaïl overcame Gayland, but failed to storm Tangier in 1679. Thereafter, however, he kept it tightly blockaded. In 1685 Samuel Pepys, the diarist and Secretary of the Navy, was appointed Treasurer to the Tangier Commission. He spent some miserable months in the beleaguered port while Parliament, as a side-issue in its quarrel with the king, refused to approve reinforcements for the garrison and, that same year, Tangier had to be abandoned. The retiring English blew up the port and most of the town as they went. Short-sighted parsimoniousness on the part of Parliament, the loss of Tangier certainly altered the history of this part of the world, though whether for better or worse is anyone's guess.

Moulay Ismaïl repopulated the town with Rifians. Since neither he nor his successors were able to wrest Ceuta or Melilla from the Spanish, Tangier has been Morocco's principal link with Europe since then − until the French built Casablanca port to supersede it. For all that it was a pretty stagnant place. Ali er-Rif Pasha, governor under Moulay Ismaïl, built the palace in the casbah. His successor and son, Achmed ben Ali, made his province virtually independent after Moulay Ismaïl's death in 1727. By 1810 the population was down to about 5,000. Twenty years later sultan Abd er-Rahman's support for the Algerian leader of resistance against the colonizing French, Abd el-Kader, involved Morocco in a disastrous war with France. During it, in 1844, Tangier was heavily bombarded by the Prince de Joinville, who also demolished its fortifications. By 1860 Morocco was at war with Spain and a Spanish force advanced upon Tangier. However, this was halted by British intervention. The consulates of the various Powers interested in acquiring influence in

ATLANTIC OCEAN

Tangier

1 York House
2 Dar el-Makhzen Museum of
  Moroccan Arts
3 Dar el-Baroud Quarter
4 Socco Chico
5 Great Mosque
6 Yacht Club
7 Railway Station
8 New mosque
9 Hospital
10 Post Office
11 O.N.M.T.
12 Bus Station

A route to
   Cape Spartel
   Grottoes of Hercules
B routes to
   Larache
   Ksar el-Kebir
   Kénitra
   Rabat
   Fes
C route to
   Tetouan
   Fes
   Oujda
D route to
   Cape Malabata
   Ksar es-Seghir

Morocco being raised to legations, the ministers started to meddle in the town's affairs. First they organized an internationally managed lighthouse at Cape Spartel, west of the port, and then, in 1872, formed a sanitary council — both laudable works in themselves, but footholds upon which later international control of the port was to be based.

In 1905 Kaiser Wilhelm II made an impressive visit to Tangier in order to demonstrate German support for Moroccan independence, an act which alarmingly proclaimed to the world that Germany wanted a stake in the country too. Since France and Spain had already peacefully traded the country with Great Britain and Italy (for Egypt and Libya respectively) and settled between them who was to have what, the Kaiser's visit upset the rest of Europe. In the upshot, however, it perhaps helped Morocco in a way the Germans had not foreseen. With the Kaiser's support, the Sultan called a conference at Algeciras at which a treaty was signed which, while it increased French and Spanish control over Moroccan affairs, at least put the Moroccan problem on a firm international footing and an end to any free-for-all. It also was another substantial step towards the internationalization of Tangier. When, by the Treaty of Fes of 1912, the French and Spanish were able to force their 'protection' upon the Moroccans, the Treaty of Algeciras was respected more by semantic trickery than by fact. It left Tangier in a curious position of being not yet under international control although in fact controlled by the resident diplomatic agents. This condition was altered by a Statute of 1923 under which those of the signatories of the Treaty of Algeciras who had not lost the First World War — i.e. France, Spain, the United Kingdom, Portugal, Sweden, Holland, Belgium and Italy — took over complete control of the city and an area of surrounding country. The U.S.A. and Italy would not recognize this for some time, and the Spanish, who found the international enclave in their part of Morocco troublesome, made constant difficulties about it. The Sultan was represented by a legate who was appointed by the French Resident General in his capacity as foreign minister to the Sultan. Each nation had its own post offices, banks, currency, residences and share in policing. The sanitary systems worked admirably, the lighthouse functioned but only smugglers of all sorts and brothel-keepers were really happy with the arrangement.

It ended with the abrogation of the Statute of Tangier on October 29th, 1956, a few months after the independence of the rest of the country. None the less a period of transition in financial matters was allowed since, particularly after the Second World War, Tangier had prospered greatly through the manipulation of currency. Since the expiry of that period of grace the town has languished, though now again prosperity is returning, largely as a result of its vastly increased tourist trade.

PRINCIPAL SIGHTS

Old Tangier is a small part of the present-day town. The casbah rests on a small, cliff-top plateau; the medina slopes steeply from this height, east and south-eastwards to the port. This opens due east and faces Cape Malabata across the wide opening of Tangier Bay which, itself, opens north to the Straits of Gibraltar. West of the medina, old Moslem cemeteries extend over the slope of the hill on whose top lies the grander quarter of the new town, though a small part of this curls south of the cemeteries also. In general, the modern town describes a wide arc following the curving line of the coast, occupying the gentler slopes of the skirts of the hills and overflowing into the valley south of the town.

The spine of the modern town is formed by the Rue de Belgique, the Boulevard Pasteur and the Boulevard Mohammed V. The Pasteur is the heart of the shopping district, as also of the entertainment districts — bars, cabarets, the casino, cinemas, etc. Between the cemeteries and the medina is a wide, irregularly shaped open space known as the Gran Socco or great market-place; this is the real focal point of the town though in practice the insignificant Place de France at the north end of the Boulevard Pasteur makes a more useful map reference from which to orientate yourself in this often perplexingly planned town. If your hotel is not by the beach it will be within a few minutes' walk of this point. From it the Rue de la Liberté leads to the Gran Socco and the medina, where all the sights of interest are concentrated.

LOWER TOWN

Gran Socco

The Gran Socco has recently been disfigured by a local bus station and domesticated with municipal gardening. The *market* for which it was once famous has been banished behind it — half-left across the square from the end of the Rue de la Liberté — and into the side-streets, of which the Rue d'Italie is perhaps the most interesting — straight across the square. Two steps up it and right under the arch leads into the *medina* by the Rue Siaghin, the street of the jewellers. (The Rue d'Italie and Rue de la Kasbah lead on and upward to the *casbah*, following outside the city walls.) The jewellers' street leads to the *Socco Chico* (*Map* 4), no more a market-place though still the centre of the lower town.

Great Mosque
Rue de la Marine (*Map* 5)

The mosque was built by Sultan Moulay Ismaïl in the late seventeenth century, after the English left. It occupies the site on which stood the old mosque that the Portuguese converted into the *Cathedral of the Holy Spirit*. Sultan Moulay Sliman enlarged it in 1815. Opposite is a *medrassa*, probably of Merinid foundation (fourteenth-century).

The *Sea Gate* ends the Rue de la Marine. To its right is a *battery* of 1882 where ornamented guns are still in place.

UPPER TOWN

Casbah

This was the royal and administrative quarter of former times. Occupying the pinnacle of Tangier's hill, it was formerly walled off from the rest of the medina. The walls still exist, but are much breached to facilitate the passage of modern traffic. Its centre is the *Mechouar*, a formal, rectangular open place where the sultans or their governors received mass audiences. The west side is occupied by the *Dar el-Makhzen* (*Map* 2) — the palace (literally 'government house'). It is open every day from 09.30 to 12.00 and 15.00 to 18.00 unless, during Ramadan, the hours are changed. Entrance is free.

Before going inside one may turn into the *Bit el-Mal*, the old treasury, which has three bays across its façade. The interior is rather fine, particularly the *audience-hall* off the courtyard which lies beyond the main hall. A contemporary *treasure-chest* is preserved inside. Like the main palace, the Bit el-Mal was built from 1686 onwards by Moulay Ismaïl and Ali er-Rif. However, the palace was enlarged after their deaths by the semi-independent Achmed ben Ali Pasha, and again by Sultan Moulay el-Hassan in 1889.

Two museums occupy most of the palace, the main rooms

stylishly exhibiting *Moroccan Arts* of earlier times and, in the kitchen quarters, a *Museum of Antiquities*. This includes Paleolithic and Neolithic finds, a charming Roman mosaic from Volubilis and copies of the bronzes in Rabat (p. 178), with an interesting ethnographical collection and another illustrating Tangier's past appearance. In this last are several drawings by Eugène Delacroix. The great French master visited Morocco with an embassy to Sultan Abd er-Rahman in 1832. Lately many rooms have been closed to visitors and, sometimes, the museum itself has been shut for no clear reason.

At the southern end of the Mechouar stands the fine, arch-fronted *Dar ech-Chera*, the old tribunal. Close to it the *Bab el-Assa* leads out of the casbah. Called the 'Lookout Gate', it was the scene of the punishments meted out at the tribunal.

North from the Mechouar another little square opens to the *Rue Riad Sultan*, a walk following the walls along the cliff-top. To the left along it there is a touristically 'typical' café which is often very welcome, and, farther along, through the arched gate, you can see the machicolated front of *York House* (*Map* 1), built to be the residence of the English governors in the seventeenth century.

In the new town, at the corner of the Rue de Belgique and Rue Sidi Mohammed Ben Abdellah (*Map* 8) is a large new mosque in honour of Mohammed V, a gift from Saudi Arabia. It is in traditional Maghrebi style with a finely decorated entrance.

Environs of Tangier

CAPE MALABATA

Route S704 (Route Exit D) 11 km. east to Cape Malabata where the lighthouse stands across the bay. The road follows the seashore fairly closely. Follow the Boulevard Mohammed V to Place Helvetia [See Route Map for Northern Area (pp. 298–9).]

Hotels
*****   *Hotel Malabata*, Baie de Tanger (tel. 401.60).
         Club Méditerranée Malabata (tel. 405.88).

[7 km.] *Villa Harris*: a 'mooresque' nonsense-building built by Walter Harris (p. 106), correspondent of the London *Times* and Arabist.

[10 km.] A turning right which leads to the little port of Ksar es-Seghir, a delightful road. (For Ksar es-Seghir, see p. 293.) The fantasy medieval *Château de Malabata* near this corner, fifty years old, is ruinous.

[11 km.] The *lighthouse*; views over the bay and the Straits.

CAPE SPARTEL AND GROTTOES OF HERCULES

Route S701 (Route Exit A), 11 km. west to the lighthouse and a further 7 km. to the Grottoes [See Route Map for Northern Area (pp. 298–9).]

Hotel
***A   *Hotel les Grottes d'Hercule*, B.P. 228, Tangier (tel. 387.65).

[1 km.] On the 'Mountain' — that hill which you cross for several kilometres as you leave the town; then wild and wooded — the English governor of Tangier, Lord Teviot, and his men were cut down by Rifian resistance-fighters under Gayland, whose base against the town this was.

[5 km.] The *royal residence*, a building from the turn of the century.

[10 km.] A *viewpoint* lies down a side-turning.

[11 km.] Turn right for the *lighthouse*. Cape Spartel was known as *Caput Ampelusium* to the Romans. This was the lighthouse that the diplomats organized in the 1870s.

One or two good beaches can be reached by side-turnings after this point.

[18 km.] *Grottoes 'of Hercules'*. Natural caves of a curious formation, these have nothing to do with the demigod for whom they are now named. But they were inhabited in prehistoric times. They may be visited in the care of one of the guides on the site. Hours are 09.00 until dusk, there is a small charge for admission.

[18·5 km.] On the right are the ruins of a small Roman city identified as *Cotta*. It belonged to the second and third centuries. There are the remains of a little *temple* and a *bath-house* which it is thought was originally part of a factory for the production of *garum*.

The whole of this neighbourhood has been found to have been

dotted over with *Roman farms* of the same period, though one dates from the third or second century B.C. Their oil-presses show that the countryside must have been wooded with olive trees, *Megalithic tombs*, too, are not uncommon in the district. The O.N.M.T. will put you in touch with an appropriate authority should you wish to examine these remains.

Unless you turn round, the inland road will take you back to Tangier.

TANGIER TO RABAT

Route Via Asilah, Larache, Ksar el-Kebir, Kénitra, 277 km. by the P2, an excellent road: leave Tangier by Route Exit B. [See Route Map for Northern Area (pp. 298–9).]

Rail 297 km. by Sidi Kacem; at least four trains daily, some very modern air-conditioned carriages for which a supplement is payable. Connections at Sidi Kacem and Sidi Slimane for Fes and Meknes (tel. Kénitra 50.95 for information).

Bus Two C.T.M. buses go all the way to Rabat daily taking slightly longer than the train. About half a dozen service Larache and Asilah.

Accommodation and food Hotels at Asilah, Larache, Kénitra: for details, see under town entries. Food is obtainable at the same places and the larger villages on the road, the café at Arbaoua being a favourite half-way house and the hotel in the village (right from the main road) having a generally good reputation for food, especially during the season for game.

[46 km.] **Asilah.**

Hotels
***A	*Hôtel Al Khaïma*, Route de Tanger (tel. 72.46).
**A	*Hôtel Oued El Makhazine*, Avenue Mélilia (tel. 70.90).
**B	*Hôtel l'Oasis*, 8 Place des Nations Inies (tel. 70.69).
*A	*Hôtel Sahara*, 9 Rue de Tarfaya (tel. 71.85).
*B	*Hôtel Asilah*, 79 Avenue Hassan II (tel. 72.86).

Camping ranged along the beach of which the *International* is the most favoured followed by the *Ocean* and *Atlas* sites.

This little port was a Carthaginian settlement known as *Zili*. At the time of the Mauritanian Kingdom it struck its own coins and after Augustus had swapped its population — the Asilans had supported Bogud — for that of a Spanish town, it became a colony. In the tenth century it had much trouble repulsing attacks by Normans. It had to be set on its feet again by Hakim II of Cordoba and presently became the last refuge in Morocco for the Idrissids. Trade with Europe increased its importance during the fourteenth century. The Portuguese took it in 1471 and King

Sebastian used it as the disembarkation port of his ill-fated crusading expedition (p. 91). Inherited then by the Spaniards, Ahmed el-Mansur recaptured it in 1589. It was again lost to the Spaniards for a short while before, in 1691, Moulay Ismaïl again retook it and created it capital of the Rif district. The Austrians bombarded it in 1829, as a reprisal for piracy against her shipping; and the Spaniards in 1860. El-Raissoulli's latter-day insurgency — for which he made Asilah his base — is touched upon on p. 111.

The city walls are Portuguese in origin and *el-Raissoulli's palace* is the 'sight' of the town. It is early-twentieth-century in date and rather fun in its way. Friday mornings, particularly during Ramadan, seem to be the worst times for finding anyone to let you in to it. It has recently become a centre for Third World artists as a result of an annual cultural festival.

[62 km.] Junction on the left with the P37, leading to Tetouan. 4 km. along it a left-hand turning leads in 5·5 km. to **Souk et-Tnine de Sidi Yamani**, from which a short walk takes you to a large circle of megalithic stones.

[82 km.] You reach Lixus.

LIXUS

The ruins of this very ancient town are scattered over the hill north of the bay of Larache. There are ramparts and the foundations of temples, a small theatre and houses on the crest and the remains of salt and *garum* factories at the base of the hill beside the road, virtually none of these pre-dating the Roman period, except for the megalithic walls of the oldest structures. It is a pleasant site, but the ruins offer the layman little.

The Phoenicians were anciently credited with having founded *Liks*, as they called it, at the same time as they colonized Gades (now Cadiz), and the date generally accepted for that is *c*. 1100 B.C. Until now it has not been thought that any of the existing buildings on the site antedated the seventh or eighth centuries B.C. Pliny mentions a temple to Melkarth, the Phoenician god, on an island in the River Loukkos, which enters the Atlantic by the bay — a perhaps more probable site for an ancient Phoenician colony than the hill. The site of this has not been found. Historical Lixus (its Latin name) lived by trade with the interior, possibly as a link in, and base depot for, the old sea route to West Africa established by Hanno (p. 60), and on the salt and *garum* it produced. When the Romans withdrew north of here under Diocletian the township declined, though it was still occupied in the fifth century A.D. Salterns still line the shore.

In the era of myth — that indefinable epoch during which the 'Phoenicians' first came here — it was believed that the Garden of the Hesperides lay in these parts, indeed that hereabouts was the country in which the oldest gods were born and that Uranus was its first lord. The Garden, though, was to the Greeks the property of the goddess Hera, and the Hesperides were the daughters of Atlas, who upheld the world on his shoulders; they tended the garden for Hera. Its chief treasure was the tree that bore the golden apples, to steal which was Herakles' eleventh labour. The tree was a wedding-present to Hera from Earth. Herakles tricked the Hesperides and secured the apples. Atlas taught him astronomy (which Herakles taught the Greeks) and got him to hold the world for him a while, then proposed he should carry on with the job, so Herakles said, 'Take it a minute while I put my affairs in order; then I will take it back,' and Atlas did so and Herakles walked off. Herakles had already driven off the flesh-eating flocks of Geryon, the king of Gades, and overpowered and killed Antaeus, the giant son of Earth and Poseidon who had wrestled with, thrown and killed all comers before him. By some accounts, Antaeus was king of Liks; others call him a 'Libyan', which then meant a North African. This remotest west was seen by so few of the inhabitants of the myth-believing and -creating eastern Mediterranean, it is tempting to suppose that its existence was surmised before it was explored — a region apt as the scene of mythic exploits — and that the first pioneers were quick to identify the wonders they found with those they expected to find. Thus Atlas was 'king of Mauritania' until, because it had been foretold he would be slain by a son of Zeus, he refused hospitality to Perseus — who was returning to Greece after killing the Gorgon — and Perseus revenged himself by exhibiting Medusa's head to him, petrifying him into the great mountain range that bears his name and fulfilled the prophecy. The seven Hesperides were known also as the Atlantides, a patronymic derived from their father's name; the ocean is also called for Atlas, and Hermes was surnamed Antlantiades because he was the son of Maia, eldest of the Hesperides. With her sisters Electra, Taygeta, Asterope, Merope, Alcyone and Celaeno, Maia is now a star, their constellation being the Pleiades. Originally a Titan (so a son of Uranus) was set to guard the moon with Phoebe.

It has been suggested they were not those colonizing Phoenicians from the Lebanese coast who rivalled the Greeks of the expansion (and who are best known to us perhaps through their great colony of Carthage) but much earlier peoples from much the same area, though probably including the Nile Delta also. It would be these people — Proto-Phoenicians, as it were — whose exploits are obscurely remembered in the body of the myth sketched above. They could have travelled far earlier than 1100 B.C. — even as much as fifteen hundred or more years earlier still.

The site of Liks has been explored rather than studied, but some of the oldest buildings on the hill have been found and their extent and positioning traced. They are megalithic structures, built of giant stones orientated to the sun. Geographically, a missing link between the oldest civilizations in the inner Mediterranean and those of Mexico and Peru. At Souk et-Tnine de Sidi Yamani stands another megalithic monument. The implications of these facts might be tremendous for prehistory. But as yet so little is known of their builders that it would be a rash archaeologist who dared pronounce on this discovery until the results of several years of excavations here have been published.

The megalith builders were mathematicians and astronomers of notable sophistication and their religious thinking centred on the sun. However, 'megalithic' — or large stone — building techniques varied. Those oddly fitted big stones associated with Phoenician/Carthaginian sites, such as the walk here, do not at all resemble those of western Europe or of Malta, or Sardinia and central Italy.

Although Greek myth does not recall sun worship hereabouts, the old name does — as, remarkably enough, does the local name for the ruins today; Shimish, 'sun' — but Herakles was credited in myth with having learned the art of astronomy from Atlas and then teaching it to the Greeks. Recent and impressive evidence suggests that megalithic mathematics, exact astronomical observation, a sun-orientated religion and megalithic building techniques did not originate, as has been assumed, in the Near East, but in western Europe.

One could wonder whether perhaps there was wider and more intensive, ancient cultural interchange than has yet been supposed — even though the existence of seafaring over the Mediterranean is established as early as the mid fifth millennium — or whether that interchange was more continuous than has been realized, in both directions. Here, our pertinent interest must be what part Maqom Semes/Liks may have played as a centre of dissemination, and in which directions. Did it for a considerable period represent an example of an older culture surviving in that isolation which has so often characterized Morocco?

And how old, anyway, is that most enigmatic figure, Herakles who is Melkarth and who it was believed was buried here?

[87 km.] Larache.

Hotels
**B   *Hôtel Riad*, Rue Mohammed Ben Abdellah (tel. 26.26).
*A   *Hôtel España*, 2 Ave. Hassan II (tel. 31.95).

A nice, if dullish, Spanish colonial town that is the modern heir of Liks. The little fishing-port has charm. The site was undeveloped until the Portuguese of Asilah took an interest in it, from 1479 onwards. The town none the less counts as a Saadi foundation although in 1610 Moulay esh-Sheikh traded it to Philip III of Spain in return for help against the Turks and Zaydan. The Spaniards built the '*Stork Castle*' whose walls you can see overlooking the bay (1618). Moulay Ismaïl rescued it for Morocco in 1689, when it settled to the business of piracy, and Sidi Mohammed ben Abdullah renewed its fortifications and built a *medrassa* and a *market* in it during the latter half of the eighteenth century. It suffered foreign bombardments, like Asilah, and achieved a modest prosperity under the Spanish occupation of 1911–56.

[123 km.] Ksar el-Kebir.

Once a town of major importance in the north-west of the country, it was reduced to a ghost town during the nineteenth century and owes its present prosperous air to the Spanish. It is the market-centre for the fertile Loukkas valley; its weekly Sunday market is a large and lively one.

As a Roman colony it was called Oppidum Novum. It was made a centre of Arab power in the eleventh century and was built up by the Berber dynasties, Yaacub el-Mansur fortifying the city and founding its *Great Mosque*, the *mortuary chamber* of which is built over an early Christian church and the *minaret*, with its paired windows, incorporating antique material. Ksar was the first town to acknowledge Merinid rule in 1223. The Portuguese made several attempts to capture it and it was the first objective of King Sebastian's crusading expedition which ended so disastrously, near by in the valley of the Makhazen River, at the 'Battle of the Three Kings' (p. 91). El-Khider Ghailan (whom the English called 'Gayland') made it his capital in 1666, but was chased away by Moulay er-Rashid, the first Alaouite. It was by then a declining place, though final ruin was postponed until the civil wars between Moulay Sliman and Abd er-Rahman early in the nineteenth century.

If the monuments of the town are not particularly interesting, the *markets* are entertaining and the evidences of its erstwhile provincial importance not without a melancholy charm. The *Bab el-Oued* and *ech-Charia* quarters form the oldest parts. Brick-built and with pitched roofs, these are untypical of Morocco, as are the octagonal minaret of the Saadi *mosque of Sidi esh-Sherif* and the hexagonal one belonging to that of *Sidi bel-Arbi*. There are some old *fondouks* and a Merinid *medrassa* (built by Abu el-Hassan), many *sanctuaries*, *marabouts' tombs* and a number of *zouawi*.

[135 km.] **Arbaoua**.

Hotel
   **A   *Hostellerie Route de France* (tel. 18).

[151 km.] The turning left by the P23, leading to Ouezzane, passes in 11 km. to the right of the ruins of *El-Basra*. Founded in the ninth century by Idriss II, this was a very strong and important town until well into the eleventh century. By the beginning of the sixteenth century the population was reduced to some 2,000 households according to Leo Africanus. All that now remains is the empty, impressive enceinte of towered, ninth-century walls pierced by ten gates.

[160 km.] **Souk el-Arba du Rharb**.

Hotel
   **A   *Hotel Gharb* (tel. 22.03).

A market town where, as the name indicates, Wednesday is market-day. There is a good road from here to Meknes that is described on p. 295.

From Souk el-Arba a side road (S216), right, leads in 44 km. to the coast at **Moulay Bouselham**.

Hotel
   ***A   *Hotel le Lagon* (tel. 28).

This is a centre of pilgrimage where a large moussem is held in June or July. It is also a crowded, sandy bathing-place with summer restaurants.

The road leads first to the lagoon of *Merja el-Lerga*, an inlet of the sea, where you fork right 10 km. for Moulay Bouselham. The Merja el-Lerga was anciently called the Emporic Gulf, according to Ptolemy. It connects by a sanded-up channel with the sea under the hill where the shrine stands upon what was the site of a Phoenician settlement presumed to be that called *Mulelacha*.

Moulay Bouselham (the 'sherif in the burnous' or traditional, hooded men's cloak) was a pantheist sufi, an Egyptian called Abu Saïd who lived early in the tenth century — according to popular belief. At the time of his burial here the *merja* was in use as a port for El-Basra (above); there are the remains of an Arab settlement close by. In a *cave* near the shrine are the tombs of 'Joseph, son of Aristotle', and 'bu el-Korneïn — 'son of the man with a pair of horns' — whom the local Berbers identify with Alexander the Great, the 'son of Ammon'. Both names demonstrate what long memories Berbers have; they can have known Alexander only by his legend and the coins which show him wearing the curled goat-horns of Zeus Ammon; Aristotle of course was his tutor. The pilgrims who come to the moussem (in June or July), having sacrificed bulls and sheep, visit this cave to suck a sacred stalactite which secretes a salty liquid — showing their memory goes back still farther than the third century B.C.

By returning 10 km. to the fork in the road one can continue 79 km. to Kénitra by the coast road 2301 and S206.

[176 km.] **Souk et-Tleta du Rharb**, a Tuesday market.

[178 km.] A turning left crosses the Sebou River where, by turning left and left again (S210), you reach the ruins of *Banasa* in 12 km.

This was one of the Roman colonies established by Augustus within the Mauritanian Kingdom: Julia Valentia Banasa. Almost all of it reduced to its foundations, these are not impressive ruins, though some of the detail is interesting and the site a pleasant one. It goes back to the third century B.C., or earlier perhaps; yet what one can see dates from the last years B.C. or later. Around the *Forum* stand the *Capitol* (with a tribune in front of it), a *Basilica* or judgment-hall and *municipal buildings*. The *Baths of the Frescoes* contain nice pavements as well as wall-paintings. In the town, among houses, shops and markets — of which the porticoed *macellum* is the more interesting — are the small *West Baths*, which belonged to a Dionysiac brotherhood (some decoration remains in them) and the *North Baths* where there is a good pavement.

[223 km.] A track on the right leads in 5 km. to *Thamusida*.

A Roman camp and town, Thamusida appears to have been occupied around B.C./A.D. but abandoned in the forties A.D. at the time of the Roman conquest and rebuilt — after suffering very serious flooding — some time after 161. It was probably not abandoned until the fourth century, having been partly rebuilt after a fire in the third. The square camp was crossed by a street leading from the Pretorian gate and bordered with porticoes. To its west lay the headquarters with a chapel of arms and a third-century basilica. Most of the rest of the area was, as usual, occupied by barracks. In the town, *baths* have been excavated, and a *temple* with three *cellae*.

[229 km.] The P3 branches left to Sidi Kacem and Fes. At 54 km. is **Sidi Slimane**: a small agricultural town near which — 8 km. to its north-west — the ruins of Roman *Babba Campestris* have been excavated. A little place, Augustus created it a colony towards 33 B.C. It remained a Roman town isolated in the Kingdom of Mauritania under both Juba II and Ptolemy. Although it appears to have been founded in the second century B.C., the ruins to be seen date from the third century A.D. They include traces of walls, baths and houses. It is scarcely the sight an amateur would go far to see.

[237 km.] **Kénitra**.

Hotels
> ***B *Hôtel Mamora*, Avenue Hassan II (tel. 50.06).
> **A *Hôtel la Rotonde*, 50 Avenue Mohammed Diouri (tel. 33.43).
> **B *Hôtel Ambassy*, 22 Avenue Hassan II (tel. 29.25).
> *A *Hôtel d'Europe*, 63 Avenue Mohammed Diouri (tel. 35.49).
> *B *Hôtel Astor*, 394 Avenue Mohammed V (tel. 46.87).

With 366,300 inhabitants, a seaport and considerable industrial development, Kénitra is a lively and important place. It was entirely a French foundation of 1913 and holds no interest for the sight-seer. But on the cliff-edged hill at the mouth of the River Sebou, 11 km. beyond the town, stands the *Casbah de Mehdiya*.

Hotel
   ***B   *Hôtel Atlantique.*
Camping
       Mehdia (tel. 48.49).

This splendid site was once that of a small Punic settlement. Abd el-Mumin, the Almohad, planned and began to build a shipbuilding centre on the river, fortifying this height which then had the name of el-Mamora — 'the populous'. But the yards came to nothing. The Portuguese made several attempts to seize and hold the place, and succeeded in doing so in 1515 for a short time. In 1610 the Spanish began a serious attempt to capture it, which they managed in 1614. They then built the present fortress strictly upon the lines laid down by Vauban, Louis XIV's brilliant military engineer, surrounding it with a fosse. However, the redoubtable Moulay Ismaïl chased them out and installed the Caïd Ali er-Rif as governor. To him are due the fine Moroccan *gateway* into the castle and the delightful gubernatorial *palace* inside — both therefore of the last quarter of the seventeenth century, though the gate in particular had to be restored extensively after being damaged during the American landing in 1942. A large American and Moroccan military base perpetuates the military history of Kénitra and lends the place the air of all garrison towns.

Mehdiya Plage is signposted but not worth the bother with better beaches a few kilometres further on.

[259 km.] *Plage des Nations* (Sidi Bouknadel), just before the turning for the village of Bouknadel.

Hotel
  ****A   *Hôtel Firdaous* (tel. 451.86).

[265 km.] On your right the *Jardins Exotiques* make a delightful diversion.

[275·5 km.] A turning right to Salé (p. 181).

[277 km.] Rabat.

RABAT

Population 519,000
Air For Rabat's air links with points abroad, see p. 21. For its internal connections by air, see p. 23.
Airline offices: *Royal Air Maroc*, Avenue Mohammed V (tel. 322.96).

Air France, 281 Avenue Mohammed V (tel. 301.06).

Rail See p. 23. Note that *Gare Rabat-ville* (*Map* **13**) is more convenient for the centre. Railway information bureau 232.40 and 723.85 (*Gare Rabat-Agdal*; Map **18**).

Bus The city is well served by buses from all parts of the country. C.T.M. garage, Boulevard Hassan II; bus station, Place Zerktouni. The Municipal Market (*Map* **10**) is the centre of town bus services.

Taxi Numerous ranks (station, Municipal Market, Place du Mellah), or telephone 205.18. Taxis in Rabat generally use meters.

Car Hire *Avis*, 7 Zankat Abou Faris El Marini (tel. 208.88), and Rabat-Salé Airport (tel. 208.08).

Europcar, Hotel Hilton, Aviation-Souissi (tel. 702.18).

Hertz, 291 Boulevard Mohammed V (tel. 344.66).

Hotels

*****	*Hôtel Rabat-Hilton* Aviation-Souissi (tel. 721.51).
*****	*Hôtel Farah-Sofitel*, Place Sidi Makhlouf (tel. 264.91).
*****	*Hôtel la Tour Hassan*, 34 Avenue Abderrahman Annegai (tel. 214.01).
****A	*Hôtel Chellah*, 2 Rue Ifni (tel. 640.52).
****A	*Hôtel Belere*, 33 Avenue Moulay Youssef (tel. 238.63).
****B	*Hôtel les Oudayas*, 4 Rue Tobrouk (tel. 261.13).
***A	*Hôtel Scheherazade*, 21 Rue de Tunis (tel. 222.26).
***A	*Hôtel Terminus*, 388 Avenue Mohammed V (tel. 608.95).
***B	*Hôtel Balima*, Rue Jakarta (tel. 216.71).
***B	*Hôtel d'Orsay*, 11 Avenue Moulay Youssef (tel. 613.19).
**A	*Hôtel Royal*, 1 Rue Amman (tel. 211.71).
**A	*Hôtel Bou Regreg*, 1 Rue Nador (tel. 241.10)
**A	*Hôtel Capitol*, 34 Avenue Allal Ben Abdellah (tel. 312.36).
**A	*Grand Hôtel*, 19 Rue Patrice Lumumba (tel. 272.85).
**A	*Hôtel de la Paix*, 2 Rue Ghazza (tel. 229.64).
**A	*Hôtel Luxeor*, 2/4 Rue Abdelmoumen (tel. 229.64).
**A	*Hôtel Dahir*, Avenue Hassan II (tel. 330.24).
**B	*Hôtel Darna*, 24 Boulevard El Alou (tel. 224.56).
**B	*Hôtel Velleda*, 106 Avenue Allal Ben Abdellah (tel. 228.25).
**B	*Hôtel Splendid*, 2 Rue Ghazza (tel. 232.83).
**B	*Hôtel Gaulois*, 1 Zankat Hims (tel. 230.22).
*A	*Hôtel Central*, 2 Rue Al Basra (tel. 221.31).

Restaurants

The very good hotels provide good food, of which the *Tour Hassan* has the nicest ambience. Almost every national cuisine represented in the new town.

Information

O.N.M.T. Tourist Office: 22 Avenue d'Alger (tel. 212.52), also an information desk at the central railway station (*Map* **13**).

Syndicat d'Initiative: Rue Patrice Lumumba and Rue Van Vollenhoven (tel. 232.72).

Consulates

British: 17 Boulevard Tour Hassan (tel. 209.05 and 314.03).

Canadian: (for Australian citizens too) 13 Zankat Toafar Essadik (tel. 713.75).

United Arab Emirates: (for Algerian visas) 8 Zankat Azrou.

United States: 2 Avenue de Marrakech (tel. 626.65).

Banks
Many along Avenue Allal Ben Abdellah in the new town.

Shopping
Co-opartim, Rue Renard and Rue Jabarti, offers craft-ware whose prices are controlled by the government and which are of guaranteed quality. Rabat is an excellent source of western goods which you may need for adventures in remoter country. As befits a capital, Rabat has fine jewellers and antique shops for the rich. The *American Bookstore* in Rue Tanja stocks English books.

Sports and Clubs
Watersport: Fath Union Sport, Quai de la Tour Hassan, Port de Rabat (tel. 336.79).
Cercle de la Voile et de l'Aviron de Rabat (tel. 235.87).
Olympic Marocain, Quai de la Tour Hassan (tel. 251.23).
Rabat Yacht Club, Quai de la Tour Hassan (tel. 202.64).
Apart from beaches on both banks of the Oued Regreg (*Map* 2) below the Casbah, better bathing is to be had at the Plage des Nations (see p. 163) and Temara Plage (see p. 185).
Tennis: Stadium, Avenue Haroun Rachid (tel. 237.41).
Olympic Marocain, 2 Avenue Ibn Khaldoun (tel. 223.51).
Club El Wifak, Route des Zaërs (tel. 545.33).
Golf: Royal Golf Club Dar Es-Salam, Route des Zaërs (10 km).
Golf Club du Souissi (tel. 503.59).
Riding: Club Équestre, Route des Zaërs (3·5 km).
Flying: Aero Club Royal (tel. 513.35).
Climbing: Club Alpin, Librairie des Belles Images, Avenue Mohammed V.

Night-life
Again, the best hotels offer the best amenities. Modern Rabat is still too new, too earnest, to have developed its raffish potentialities much. There are a number of discotheques around Place de Melilla and cafés and bars in the vicinity of Avenue Mohammed V; the terrace of the Hotel Balima is a popular gathering point for young Moroccans and a pleasant spot to while away the early evening.

Post Office
The central P.T.T. is adjacent to the central railway station, the telephone section opposite operates night and day (*Map* 21).

Emergencies
Police: telephone 15.
Ambulance: telephone 19.

Rabat had been becoming increasingly important during the last decades of the old sultanate and the French made it capital of their protectorate. Since Independence it has been capital of the reunited kingdom. It is a growing, modern city attached to an old one whose fortunes were most varied. The medina and casbah crown cliffs over the Atlantic and the mouth of the Bou Regreg River, on the southern bank. Rabat's sister-city, Salé, stands on the heights overlooking the river-mouth from the north — a traditional, whitewashed town facing its odd, hybrid, delightful fellow which is wholly forward-looking and alive with hopes for the future.

The centre of the new quarters of Rabat lies mostly in the valley behind the cliffs, between the medina and a crest of hill lying within the circuit of twelfth-century walls built to protect a projected city and only now for the first time fully occupied, though even now part filled with large gardens, parks, wide avenues, a leafy, flower-filled diplomatic quarter and the vast extent of the royal palace and its private gardens. The city has, though, spread far beyond the Almohad walls, in suburbs and in estates for light industries, but the real Rabat consists of the double personality of the crowded, though not very picturesque medina, the valley of officialdom (built in an altogether idiosyncratic style that perhaps owes most to Californian Spanish — though it is at once less pretentious and more domestic than Beverly Hills — and which its French inventors improbably called 'coquette') and the garden city of *résidences du mission*.

The life of the city is both active and earnest. It has its nightspots, its diversions and frivolities, but it appears to go to bed betimes and to have scant time for dawdling or dalliance. It is very active indeed by day, and purposeful. The very air of the streets makes one hopeful for the future of Morocco.

Among all this present-day living there remain the splendid and diverse evidences of Rabat's past: the beautiful Casbah des Oudaïa where the Museum of Moroccan Arts is housed, the dreamy, peaceful Necropolis of Chella, the ruin of Abd el-Mumin's vast Mosque of Hassan; the extraordinary girdle of the walls with their gates and, not to be missed, the beautiful bronzes from Volubilis in the Museum of Antiquities.

HISTORY

The neighbourhood of Rabat has been inhabited since Paleolithic times. As an urban settlement, its history goes back to the Phoenicians. At least during the latter Phoenician period the town appears to have been sited on the spur of the hills now occupied by Chella. This was the site of the Mauritanian town of Sala. It is thought Sala was still at the time a largely Punic centre and it may have enjoyed a partial independence from the Kingdom — of the fate of Punic colonial communities after the fall of Carthage little is known; here where the Romans did not exert their influence until much later there would be no alternative but to merge gradually with the local population, though one can imagine the various colonies in the west continuing to trade among themselves much as the Jewish ones were later to do, the stronger colonies being the slowest to become absorbed into the populations harbouring them. Sala struck its own money. It is thought, too, that Sala became a Roman municipality towards the end of the first century A.D., under Trajan. Previously, however, it would have been occupied by the legions. In the second century it became the colony of Salacolonia. A dedicatory inscription to Constantine found in the forum of Chella and Byzantine references to the town suggest that it may have remained as an isolated Roman post after Diocletian's withdrawal northwards.

During the eighth century the Barghawata Berber tribes to the south of the site established their heretical, independent Salihian state (p. 69), challenging the orthodoxy of the rest of Inner Morocco. At some time during the tenth century this challenge was taken up by either the Ommayeds of Spain or the nomad Arab Zénéte tribe who had entered Morocco. By whichever power it was, a *ribat* was built on the headland site of the present Casbah des Oudaïa. (Hence the present city's name.) A *ribat* is a monastic stronghold serving as base for a confraternity of militant zealots, usually belonging to an individual sect; this *ribat* was to be a base for military operations against the Barghawata. In the eleventh century the Beni Ifren tribe, also full of zeal against the heretics, set up an independent state on the north of the river and built Salé as its capital. As the Almoravids established their rule over the country they occupied both Salé and the *ribat*. Tashfin ben Ali built a fortress on the river around 1140. This was probably a reconstruction of the *ribat*. However, Salé had become the important place locally. In 1146 it submitted to Abd el-Mumin (the Almohad) without opposition, but during the repeated campaigns the sultan was forced to make in order to reduce the Barghawata, Salé revolted, was stormed by the Almohads and had its walls dismantled. Abd el-Mumin undertook extensive works at the *ribat*, building himself a palace there to which he was partial. He made this fortress the rallying-place of the tribes coming to assist his expeditions into Spain — the *moujehaddin* who made a holy war of repulsing the Christians and establishing the Almohad Spanish Empire.

It was Yaacub el-Mansur, however, who decided to make a city on the site, still calling it after the fortress *ribat* and entitling it el-Fath, the Ribat of Victory. Evidently building upon its usage as the rendezvous of expeditions to Spain, Yaacub seems to have planned his city as an imperial capital. His plans for it were immense. It is known to have received its victorious name by 1191 and the 5,250 metres of towered walls from the Casbah des Oudaïa to the escarpment over the river were completed by 1198. The enormous mosque of el-Hassan was perhaps nearing completion when, in the following year, Yaacub died and all his plans were abandoned. Without his support and, more importantly, as soon was the case, without a Spanish Empire to be ruled, Rabat dwindled to a small settlement in the shelter of the fortress. It first fell to the Merinids in 1249 though the later Almohads disputed its possession until 1261. Meanwhile it continued to act as the traditional assembly-point for Spanish expeditions and it may have been because of this association that the early Merinids elected to fortify the site covering that of the Roman forum — Chella — to be their necropolis and place of religious retreat. When Leo Africanus visited Rabat around 1500, he found only a hundred houses there.

Next comes the extraordinary story of the Republic of the Bou Regreg, set up by refugees from Spain. First to arrive were the Hornacheros from the town of Hornachos near Badajoz. They were settled here by Sultan Zaydan who employed them as mercenaries in the civil wars. Presently they were joined by other groups of Moriscos — as the Christian Spaniards called the unfortunates among them who appeared to them to be Moslems but whom the Moroccans thought more probably Christians since their ways were so thoroughly Europeanized (and whom they called Andalusians). These later groups came from other Spanish provinces and never satisfactorily settled down together. But there was one thing on which all could agree: the harassment, if not the reconquest, of Spain and Portugal. Together, sometimes, and as often in rivalry, Hornacheros and the other Andalusians built fleets of ships to harry Iberian shipping. In this they were joined by the people of Salé. The Hornacheros had been settled in the old *ribat*-palace or casbah; the other Andalusians colonized the area now occupied by the medina, building its southern wall to make a suitable subdivision of the Almohad enceinte which was much too large for them to occupy or defend. The revived town thus created came to be known as New Salé and the older settlement over the river as Old Salé. The joint efforts of their citizens on the seas very soon degenerated into outright piracy and no shipping was safe from them. They ranged far and wide and were known to British waters where they took prizes. The

English called them the 'Sallee Rovers'. Besides Iberian and English shipping, French and Dutch were the main sufferers. The Sallee Rovers so far forgot their original aims as to sell prizes from other nations to Spain and Portugal.

In 1627 they set up an independent republic under a caïd whom they elected annually, presiding over an elected council of sixteen. Theirs was a wild existence. The Republic of the Bou Regreg controlled a certain amount of land in the river valley but was almost wholly dependent upon piracy for its living. At sea it was at war with the world and on land with the sultan and the redoubtable marabouts of Djila. Betweenwhiles there was violent dissension between Hornacheros, Andalusians and the population of Old Salé. This free-booting life none the less attracted recruits, Christian renegades and some very tough traders who acted as intermediaries for the release of ransomed prisoners who were their co-nationals. They also did a brisk trade in arms. The Sallee Rovers not only penetrated to the Channel but to the Caribbean also. They were the world's outcasts with nothing but their lives to lose, a desperate condition that rendered them almost invincible. The mouth of the Bou Regreg was not navigable to European shipping for the sand-bar across it could be crossed only by craft of shallow draught. The casbah was both well-armed with cannon and all but impregnable. Numerous punitive expeditions against the two Salés proved ineffectual, though not always so. As early as 1629 the Chevalier de Razily forced a truce and the release of French prisoners. Admiral Blake was able to release British ones in 1655 when he blockaded the river-mouth. When Mohammed el-Ayachi besieged Rabat by land in 1637/8 the Duke of Medina-Sidonia sold arms and food to the Rovers while Charles I of England supplied the attackers. During a period of intense civil war within the Republic, the British and Spanish were rivals for peaceful possession of the cities; England came near to succeeding. England had in fact negotiated an alliance against Spain with the Salés, but English skippers would not recognize it and King Charles I, while approving it, would not sign a treaty with an unrecognized power. In 1641 el-Ayachi took the towns; it was the end of the Republic, but not of piracy.

When in 1666 Moulay Ismaïl put an end to the independence of el-Ayachi's state, the sultans merely became the ultimate bene-ficiaries of the Rovers' gains. The piracy practised out of all the northern Moroccan ports — by those 'Barbary pirates', 'Corsairs', 'Moors' or 'Saracens' whose legend dies so hard in Europe — was kept in business by the Moroccan Government until the nineteenth century. The last ship to be seized by them was an Austrian taken in 1829, which brought a heavy reprisal. Meanwhile the victim nations continued with varying success to take action against the twin cities and other ports. As naval armament increased its power and range, the reprisals became steadily more effective. After the death of Sultan Moulay Ismaïl in 1727 Rabat sided with Abdullah and Salé with a brother of the dead sultan; Rabat was unsuccessfully besieged during fourteen months. The French were able to bombard both cities for two days in 1765 and as a result forced uneasy terms upon Morocco; they succeeded in placing a consul in Rabat. The sultan who granted this concession was the wise Sidi Mohammed ben Abdullah; it was he who also built the beginnings of the modern royal palace and vainly attempted to encourage the reputable growth of the town during the 1780s.

In 1912 Rabat was selected as capital of the French colonial administration and remains the capital city of Morocco.

PRINCIPAL SIGHTS: MEDINA AND CASBAH

Casbah des Oudaïa

The history of Rabat, above, tells how this casbah citadel came to be built and how it was used. The Oudaïa after whom it is called were an Arab tribe who entered southern Morocco in the thirteenth century. Moulay Ismaïl enlisted them among the *guich* tribes, those who served the throne as regular mercenary forces — to some extent they formed the Alaouite family's main backing. However, they proved insubordinate and riotous and had to be split up, a section of them being installed here with the special responsibility of controlling the neighbouring Zaër tribe, a task which kept them very busy and frequently on the defensive. The casbah walls still contain much Almohad masonry dating from the reign of Abd el-Mumin and from Yaacub Yussef el-Mansur's ambitious building of the city.

Of this work, the late twelfth-century Oudaïa Gate is one of the most remarkable examples of Maghrebi architecture extant.

Oudaïa Gate

This was a ceremonial gateway leading to staterooms. Built of a rosy, deep-ochre-coloured stone and decorated with bold, sharp-

Rabat

1. Museum of Moroccan Arts
2. Quai Tarik el-Marsa
3. Borg Lalla Qadia
4. Bab el-Alou
5. Hammam el-Jedid
6. Great Mosque (Medina)
7. Merinid Fountain
8. Maristan
9. Hassan Mosque and Tower
10. Municipal Market
11. Mausoleum of Mohammed V
12. Bab el-Had
13. Railway Station, ville
14. Archaeological Museum
15. Great Mosque (Jemaa el-Souna)
16. Bab er-Rouah

17. Necropolis of Chella
18. Railway Station, Agdal
19. Dar el-Makhzen
20. Cité Universitaire
21. Post Office
22. O.N.M.T.

A route to
   Salé
   Tangier
B route to
   Casablanca via P 36
C route to
   Casablanca via P 1 and motorway
D route to
   Meknes, Fes

cut relief, it glows between the two protruding quoins flanking it. Its design is based upon a square in the centre of which a circle is placed whose diameter is half the square's width. Yet with extraordinary subtlety the circumference of the circle is indicated rather than traced, the strongest accents in the design disguise it and it appears to hover in front of the eye chimerically, while the magnificent, heavy decoration flares upwards and outwards from no firmer base than one's instinctive knowledge of this circle's centre and presence. Yet the square — which is partly concealed also, its upper edge being drawn by the second cornice and also carried across the quoins — paradoxically counterpoises the lightness of the airy circle and one hardly knows whether or not this is a massive four-square and trenchant gate set uncompromisingly on its eminence or a floating, evanescent thing. The two shell-like palmettes (so often repeated in Almoravid, Almohad and Merinid art that they take on an almost emblematic significance) seem small and mean in themselves, yet they carry the full stress of the flaring movement of this extraordinary design, so extremely intellectual yet so full of controlled passion. The interior face (actually set at right-angles and through two interior halls) is also an exercise in loading an optical illusion. The stonework is rather better preserved than on the outer gateway and to make a detailed comparison of the two can be instructive to anyone who desires to understand the art of design.

Inside the Oudaïa Gate you find yourself in a delightful village, mostly the creation of the Hornacheros. The houses looking over the river have become the most desirable in Rabat though the more modest elsewhere in the casbah are generally those of poor and traditional people. The *casbah mosque* — el-Atiq — though first built by Abd el-Mumin in 1150, was reconstructed by Achmed el-Inglis, the English renegade, for Mohammed ben Abdullah, the *minaret* perhaps being rather older — around 1700. Over the high point dominating the mouth of the river there are various comparatively modern *defence-works* and a splendid view from the *semaphore*, beside which is a carpet-weaving factory in a later-eighteenth-century *storehouse* built by the mad el-Yazid.

However, the principal sight of the casbah is the Museum of Moroccan Arts.

Museum of Moroccan Arts

Open Daily, except Tuesdays, from 08.00 to 12.00 and from 16.00 to 18.00. Admission is free.
Map 1.

This is housed in palatial quarters built by Moulay Ismaïl around 1680 or so and lying in the lower part of the casbah which can be entered through the gate in Moulay er-Rashid's walls, below the Oudaïa Gate, leading from the Place Souq el-Ghezel (the old wool-market where also the corsairs' captives were traditionally sold).

Moulay Ismaïl's 'palace' is built into the walls of an older building which also enclose its delightful garden, off which opens a small *mosque* (where carpets are now displayed) and several other galleries. No museum could be more pleasant in itself, while the superb quality and variety of articles displayed here entrance one. There are some cases of clothing of great splendour and several rooms decorated and furnished in the styles of eighteenth- and nineteenth-century fashions prevalent in latter-day corsair society which will astonish. There are local differences between the fashions of Salé and Rabat, while these differ again from those of the Jewish community. This is the best of the Moroccan museums of the kind.

There is a *café maure* on the ramparts overlooking the river which, if it is not really in the least Moresque, is most pleasant and welcome.

Medina

Since of the buildings here few date from before the seventeenth century, when the Andalusians settled among the ruins of Rabat's earlier habitations, this quarter has a more Spanish and less 'eastern' flavour than the medinas of the interior of Morocco. The recent prosperity and importance of Rabat has also very much encouraged its rebuilding. It is a lively part and still often picturesque in the side-streets, but it has few monuments of interest. A Merinid *fountain* built by Abu Faris around 1370; the *Hammam el-Jedid* (*Map* **5**) is also fourteenth-century (its takings supported the upkeep of the tomb of Abu el-Hassan at Chella); the *Great Mosque* (*Map* **6**) was perhaps also a Merinid foundation though Moulay Hassan rebuilt it in 1822; the *Maristan el-Azzizi* (*Map* **8**) once a hospital and now office of religious charities, was also built by Abu Faris.

The *Rue des Consuls* is perhaps the most interesting of the main streets. Its lower end begins at the *Port Gate*, near the *Borg Lalla Qadiya* (*Map* **3**), a strong-point named for the near-by sanctuary where, traditionally, pilgrims returned from Mecca sleep the first night on Moroccan soil. Foreign consuls were obliged to live on this street as Jews were obliged to live in the Mellah to the left of its continuation, Rue Ouqqasa. Some of the bigger buildings in it are old consulates.

The chief interest in descending to the little *port* — erstwhile nesting-place of the Sallee Rovers — is its views of the casbah and Salé from below.

WALLS

The Almohad walls which Yussef built during the 1190s ring the high ground west of the Casbah des Oudaïa and thread through the city in a southerly direction along the Boulevarde Amnar Ibn Yassir and the Avenue Al-Mourabitine — and magnificent they are.

Bab er-Rouah
Map 16.

The finest of the five city-gates, it stands, set between two great bastions, near the Place Maréchal Leclerc — the 'gate of the winds'. Here the relief decoration is shallow-cut and intricate — scarcely more emphatic than is enough to lend it a rich texture — while concentric engaged arches surround the doorway like ripples widening on the surface of water; an astonishing, delicate and linear design on a structure of massive simplicity. The Almohads contrived a great variety of treatment within the strict limitations of the puritan conventions they elected to work within; compare this with the Oudaïa Gate and the opulent breadth of the Bab Aguenau at Marrakech (p. 226). The interior, eastern face of the gate repays looking at though it is more modest and even more chaste than the exterior. The passage through it, *en baïonnette*, is classic. Its cupolas are extremely fine, as are the rooms, gallery and terrace which the building contains. Unfortunately they are usually to be seen only when exhibitions are held here.

The other main section of the walls of Rabat runs across the south side of the Medina, facing the boulevards Hassan II and Joffre. These are the *Andalusian walls* built by the Spanish refugees in the early part of the seventeenth century. At their western end lies the Bab el-Had.

Bab el-Had
Map 12.

The 'first-gate' or the 'gate of the Sunday market', this too is an

Almohad gate, though it has been much altered during reconstructions of 1814 and under the French. It contains three vaulted rooms with a fourth great one above.

Bab ez-Zaër
At the southern end of the avenues Yaqoub el-Mansour and Mermoz (close to Chella), this is also Almohad, though restored in the eighteenth century. Very simple and distinguished, it contains rooms like the other four.

Bab El-Alou
Map 4.
This, the fourth gate, opens on the Place des Martyrs; it is the least remarkable of all.

OTHER PRINCIPAL SIGHTS

Hassan Mosque and Tower
Map 9.
Magnificently placed on the escarpment above the river and overlooking Salé, this ruined mosque's rosy-ochre minaret symbolizes Rabat as the Eiffel Tower does Paris. It is extraordinarily noble and a little sad in its incomplete state and bereft of the huge, low-lying building which would have given it purpose. Built between the years 1195 and 1199 (the year Yaacub Yussef el-Mansur died, when work at Rabat appears abruptly to have ceased) and for an unknown number of years previous to that recorded period — perhaps as many as three or four — this enormous mosque was never finished although it was most probably in a usable state when the sultan died. The *tower*, which claims one's interest first and foremost, was designed as axial to the mosque's plan, standing on the north. The floor-level of the mosque is higher than the surrounding terrain here and the tower therefore measures 44·22 metres on the south and 50·55 metres to the north. It is higher than the Giralda of Seville and shorter than the completed minaret of the Koutoubia of Marrakech; it might well have been the finest of the three. Instead of rising in expanding triumph as both the Giralda's and the Koutoubia's does, the Hassan's decoration has a pendant, icy grace which gives the soaring tower in a soaring position a markedly reflective air. The only concession to the Almohad habit of weighting the

upper parts of buildings is the close interlacing of arches in high relief on all four upper faces, but here this is treated with such delicacy, hanging as it were fringed above three blind arches — a motif echoed on the lower stages of each face — that it has almost the lightening effect of a lace collar on a dress. Probably it would have been finished with faience tiles, small columns and perhaps with plaster coating — but we cannot help but be pleased with the warm, weathered colour of its Rabat stone.

You may climb this tower, entering by the door to the internal *ramp* in the south face. The ramp was designed to allow animals to carry up the stone as the tower was raised. There are six rooms one above the other in the core of the tower, vaulted or domed and visible through keyholes and cracks in their doors. These get the richer in treatment the higher they are. The view from the top is glorious. You are on a level with kestrels hovering and swooping. Late afternoon is the moment to climb here.

From this vantage-point you can best make out the plan of the ruined mosque below where ranges of broken round columns stand. By far the biggest mosque to have been built in the Maghreb (the second largest in all Islam), its very extent imposed eccentricities upon its design. It measured 183·14 metres by 139·32 metres. This rectangle was divided by twenty-one longitudinal aisles and twenty-eight lateral ones. Those against the outside walls were wider than all the rest save the long central nave-aisle leading to the *mihrab* (which has largely disappeared). The *quibla*-aisle is fractionally wider than those against the other walls; however, in so big a prayer-hall as this the widening of the *quibla*-aisle was insufficient to emphasize the sanctuary and a symbolic screen of heavy, transversally spanned arches was set two lateral aisles in front of the *quibla*-aisle. Two longitudinal aisles inwards, on the east and west and starting from this 'screen', three aisles in width and eleven in depth, two courts were opened to the sky to allow air and light into the prayer-hall. These were arcaded like the 'screen' with which, on their south sides, their arcading was incorporated. The *sahn* was also set two aisles in from the north wall. It stood over immense cisterns and was eleven aisles in width, five in depth — small in comparison with the whole building, yet large in itself. It was surrounded by a massive arcade. There were four doors in the north wall and six in either side-wall; none in the *quibla*. There were 312 marble columns formed of drums and 112 pillars to support the heavier arching. Even now, walking among the stumps of the columns, you can get an idea of how impressive the arched vistas must have been; how the three courts must have lent them variety and modified the light inside; how the mathematical precision of the plan — a seemingly simple proposition yet resolvable in innumerable ways — would have lent it a sense of firm and supple control.

Fire and earthquake,* doubtless assisted by subsequent despoliation, added to the fact that Rabat never until now had the population to warrant such a vast building, account for the ruin of what must have once been one of the architectural triumphs of Islam. At the beginning of the sixteenth century Leo Africanus wrote that he 'was marvellously moved to pity' by the bramble-covered ruins of Rabat; it seems to me that we can be glad this is the only one left desolate, while still deploring that it is so.

Mausoleum of Mohammed V
Map 11.
Standing to the east of the Hassan Mosque this modern mausoleum and mosque constitutes the nation's tribute to the late king whose successful leadership of Moroccan resistance to French and Spanish colonial rule made him a national hero such as few, if any, of his predecessors can have been; the first sultan to put his people before himself and the first to step from the past towards the future. Predictably, this shrine will acquire a major national importance. I wish I could praise the building half as much as its purpose, but to me it seems unfortunately 'coquette' in style. While it is neither downright unsuitable nor displeasing, it lacks the characteristic virtues of Moroccan architecture.

Archaeological Museum
Rue Pierre Parent (*Map* 14).
Open Daily, except Tuesdays, from 8.30 to 18.00 and 09.00 to 17.00 during Ramadan; closed for lunch from midday to 14.30.
Entrance: Free.

This collection comprises articles belonging to the pre-Roman and Roman periods in Morocco, including finds made at Volubilis dating from its later period of lingering Roman influence. It is excellently set out and labelled to serve as an introduction to the Paleolithic, Neolithic, Punic Bronze and Iron Ages with the Roman era in the country, not excluding the Jewish and Christian

---

* The terrible one of 1755 which struck Lisbon to the ground.

communities of Mauritania Tingitana or imported goods from Greece and elsewhere.

The splendours of the museum are, however, the *bronzes* displayed in the *Salle des Bronzes*. These you should be sure to ask to see if, as sometimes happens, you find yourself alone in the galleries because they are kept locked up when there is no reason to station a custodian in their oval gallery. The collection is a small, though superb one. The figures come from Volubilis, Banasa and Thamusida (pp. 276 and 162). The magnificent *guard-dog* is believed to be a Roman work of the beginning of the second century. The *ephebus* — called the *Lustral Dionysus* — is a Roman copy of a Greek work attributed to Praxiteles. The *fisherman* is Alexandrine, first-century; the *rider* is a Roman copy of an archaistic Greek work; the provenance of the *bed ornaments* is not known. All these belong to much the same period — first and second centuries.

The extraordinary *head of a young man with his hair bound by a fillet*, a Hellenistic work of the first century, is believed to have been of local workmanship. It has been called a portrait of Juba II (p. 62) and Sir Mortimer Wheeler* seriously accepts it as such. If it is a trifle idealized, it is none the less certainly a portrait and the portrait of a Berber youth by an artist who was much moved by his subject. It is one of the finest works of its period to have been preserved — as, indeed, in its different manner, is the *head of Cato the Younger* — or 'of Utica' — where he defied Augustus in the name of the Old Republic and, failing, committed suicide. This at first sight seems a typically Roman bust, but may be local if, as Wheeler suggests, the slight flatness of form and smoothness derives from a death-mask model. Cato was the friend and ally of Juba I, which would account for this having been found at Volubilis and, indeed, for its having been made — if it was — after his death. One should try not to be too much biased by the attractiveness of the one characterful subject and the lack of it in the other still more characterful one. Both men were ornaments to their age; they were lucky to have been recorded with such superb skill and talent, and we are still luckier to have those records. All Rome is evoked in this curtain-hung room: its ferocity and self-discipline; its cosmopolitanism; its learning and sensitivity; its *luxe*; its humanism; its robust humour and brilliant

---

* Roger Wood and Mortimer Wheeler, *Roman Africa in Colour* (Thames and Hudson, London, 1966).

energy. It is both rather odd and most appropriate to find these things assembled in this corner of the old empire, treasured by a society which at first seems alien to them and which yet, in fact, shares to an extraordinary degree the qualities they display.

Great Mosque
Place de la Grande Mosquée (*Map* 15)
Also called the Jemaa el-Souna, this was built by Sidi Mohammed ben Abdullah in the eighteenth century.

Dar el-Makhzen (Royal Palace)
Map 19.
Though begun in the eighteenth century by Sidi Mohammed ben Abdullah and built again by Abd er-Rahman in 1864, the present building is largely modern and post-French-occupation. It comprises, beside the King's quarters, the *Supreme Court* and the *offices* of the President of the Council, a *cathedral-mosque* and an *oratory*, all set in or around extensive *gardens*. It is here that the traditional ceremony of the royal progress to the Friday service takes place, the King riding to the mosque in a carriage and returning on horseback, robed as imam, shaded by his state parasol and attended by his ministers and guards on foot. The ceremony takes place only when the King is in residence at Rabat and then not necessarily every Friday. It is announced in the press, not always before the day itself unless held in connection with one of the great feasts of the Moslem year. You should by all means take the opportunity to attend if one arises. King Hassan II is a modern monarch who allows himself few concessions to traditionalism save in his capacity as imam but, when he does so, makes a stirring sight of the occasion.

Necropolis of Chella
Map 17.
This area, the site of the ancient town of *Sala*, had been a cemetery since Almohad times when in the 1320s the Merinid Abu Saïd Uthman began to wall it around. Further building was carried out by Abu el-Hassan and Abu Inan. The enceinte encloses a copious spring — adequate reason for siting the ancient town here and doubtless why also the Merinids chose the spot. However, there is no doubt that it was Rabat's role as assembly-point for the expeditionary forces into Spain which caused the Merinids to choose to have their burial-ground here. The dynasty

had no religious or reforming backing, but committed leadership of the holy cause of rescuing el-Andalus from the Christians served the earlier Merinids almost as well — and for a time they had a certain success in the enterprise.

Architecturally speaking, Chella has small importance. The walls and the gateway are attenuated and curiously feeble-looking; for all the quality and delicacy of much of the decorative detail, nowhere is it carried upon a sufficiently firm architectonic foundation. Yet this is one of the most memorable places in all Morocco. It is a walled enclave of perfect serenity, sun-baked yet green and watered, shaded in places by great trees. The weathered ruins of the sanctuary buildings have a magical quality and one is not surprised to learn that local folk-lore has it that 'Moulay Yaacub' (the first of the dynasty), King of the Djinni, set a large number of them to guard the place and the treasure he deposited here.

Once through the gate — en baïonnette — there is a restaurant-café on the left in ruined buildings which were either a hospice or perhaps royal quarters. The ground slopes steeply down to the sanctuary contained in a smaller, rectangular enclosure. You enter directly into the sahn of the mosque — of Abu el-Hassan. The prayer-hall opens opposite; it has four longitudinal aisles, three transversal ones and two flanking areas. You may pass through beside the right of the mihrab where you will find a recess (hard back on your right) in which Abu el-Hassan's grave lies. This faces the koubba raised over the tomb of Abu Yussef Yaacub, 'King of the Djinni'. Turning back towards the minaret, in a recess or chapel to the right of the pathway lies Abu el-Hassan's slave, Chams ed-Douha, who was the mother of Abu Inan. She may have been a Christian at one time; the legend on the stele records the pomp with which her son buried her here in 1349. Beyond lies the sahn of the tiny zawiya or monastic place of retreat which was a special feature of the sanctuary. The pleasant minaret crowned by a stork's nest is at the left and the small prayer-hall on the right. Somehow the belief grew up that the Prophet had prayed here and a visit to this shrine, walking seven times around its mihrab, conferred the title of hadj or 'pilgrim' upon visitors who would otherwise have had to journey to Mecca to earn it. For this reason a narrow passage circles round the large and typically deep Merinid mihrab. Apart from the cells of the zawiya, the functions of some of the other parts of the sanctuary are not understood. Leo Africanus counted thirty-

two Merinid graves here at the beginning of the sixteenth
century.

There are several marabouts' tombs outside the sanctuary, and
the spring with, alongside it, the remains of the *hammam*
attached to the sanctuary. Beyond lie the current diggings on the
Roman forum site; they are not open to the public. Finally there
are the small gardens, terraced plots under trees that are cooled
by the spring-water − 'I shall forgive your sins and admit you to
gardens watered by running streams': the Koranic promise is
already fulfilled in this beautiful place.

Environs of Rabat: Salé

Festivals Mouloud (Sidi Abdullah): August moussem of Sidi Moussa ed-Doukkali.

Besides being a highly traditional town, Salé is typically Moroccan in a way that Rabat cannot have been since the Merinid
period. The contrast between the two places today is a remarkable one although the distance between them across the bridge
over the Bou Regreg River is less than 2 km. by an excellent road,
frequently served by buses. It is much of a size with the medina of
Rabat.

HISTORY

There is little to add to what has been said of Salé's history
together with that of Rabat. Its walls, demolished by Abd
el-Mumin, were rebuilt after Alfonso X of Castille had seized the
town with ease during the Feast of the Aïd es-Seghir in 1260,
plundered it and captured a large part of the population before
retiring a few days later. Salé was the principal port of Morocco
during the later Middle Ages and consequently a most prosperous
place. The Merinids showed it favour and did a good deal of
building in it − founding a medical school among other works.
Leo Africanus found it to have an old-fashioned appearance in
the early years of the sixteenth century, but also to be rich and
having 'all the ornaments, qualities and conditions necessary to
make a city civil and this in such perfection that it was frequented
by several generations of Christian merchants, like Genovese,
Venetians, Englishmen and Flemmings'. He was most struck by
the sumptuousness of the mosques. It was ceded to the Saadi by

the Wattasids as ransom for Achmed el-Wattasi and received Andalusian refugees after 1609 who, presumably, led its citizens into the uneasy partnership with those of Rabat which became the Republic of Bou Regreg. After its reversion to Moroccan government, it began to lose ground to Rabat, particularly so in the eighteenth and nineteenth centuries.

PRINCIPAL SIGHTS

The most interesting of the gates, the *Bab Mrisa*, is very early Merinid and was completed before 1270 by Yaacub el-Mansur. It was in fact a water-gate admitting into the town the passage of boats sailing and being drawn up from the river along a woodlined canal. This accounts for its height and lightness of design, though not for the comparative feebleness of its decoration. (In this respect none of the other town-gates compares well with those of Rabat or even the rather later Merinid gate of Chella.)

Inside the Bab Mrisa there was formerly a *water basin* for shipping and an important *arsenal*. When the area was drained, it became the *Jewish quarter* or *old Mellah*, but in 1700 Moulay Ismaïl built quarters for his garrison of black troops over the part lying to the left of the road leading from the gate. The *new Mellah*, then created, lies on the right hand and the gate is still often called the '*Bab el-Mellah*'.

Near the town centre stands the *Fondouk Askour*, a four-teenth-century hospice built by Abu Inan, with a lovely gateway. Hereabouts are the principal markets which can still be good places to find first-class goods.

The *Great Mosque* lies to the north-west. It is thought to have been founded by Abu Yaacub Yussef and its simple doorways have that authentic Almohad elegance and inventiveness of design.

The small *Medrassa el-Hassan* stands opposite the Great Mosque. It was built in 1341 by Abu el-Hassan. This is a delightful little building very finely decorated. However, you may not approve the eccentricity of its columns decorated with faience mosaic. The views from the roof are charming.

Near by is the *Zawiya of Sidi Abdullah ben Hassoun*, patron of Salé and its boatmen and a personage somewhat analogous to St Christopher. His tomb is visited by intending travellers. They lay coloured sticks on it in a certain order, on the eve of their departure, and if the sticks are found in the morning to have been disturbed it is taken to be a good augury for their journey. The saint came from the far south, removing to Salé because he found he took an unseemly pride in the victories of his tribe over its rivals. When his reputation grew, a delegation of his own folk came to urge him to return home, but he filled a jar with sea-water and asked them why what had been so agitated in the sea was now stilled; when they said it was because it had been withdrawn from the sea he agreed that exile was calm and purifying, a parable which they understood and left him in peace. He died in 1604 — having been teacher to el-Ayachi, it is, most probably apocryphally, said.

It is in Sidi Abdullah's honour that on the eve of Mouloud (p. 45) the people move in procession round the town bearing extraordinarily complicated wax constructions that are really a kind of fantasy candle. These are attended by the boatmen wearing splendid costumes of a Turkish sort, the saint's own descendants and a host of torch-bearers who lay their burdens up in the tomb until they are taken back to the master-maker's workshop after Achoura, the 'New Year', to be restored for the next procession.

This tribute of wax creations is also paid to Sidi Achmed Hadji whose *sanctuary* too is in the town, near the Great Mosque.

Across the large cemetery occupying the north-west of the town is the *Sanctuary of Sidi Achmed ben Achir*: an Andalusian marabout and a learned contemplative who died in 1362. He is often called the *tabib* or 'doctor' as his principal services to the living are the cure of ills, particularly for the blind, paralytics and the mad. Among his many and various miraculous powers are the ability to attract ships to be wrecked on near-by rocks — last reported used in 1844 on a Danish vessel — and the quietening of storms to allow the Saletans to bring home their booty and slaves in safety. A pirates' saint. In 1846 Moulay Abd er-Rahman built around the *koubba* a series of rooms for the afflicted to lodge in while soliciting cures.

Tomb of Sidi Moussa

This lies some 3 km. north of Salé; take the road closest to the sea. The mausoleum itself is largely a rebuilding made by Moulay Ismaïl. Sidi Moussa ed-Doukkali was a sixteenth-century ascetic who lived on wild onions, gathered and sold drift-wood and flotsam to buy bread for the poor and a man who could translate himself magically over distances — annually to Mecca and back, it was believed; a country, seaside saint. Each August a tremendous moussem is held at the tomb.

Casbah des Gnaoua
(beyond Sidi Moussa)
A fortress of pisé, now in ruin, built by Moulay Ismaïl to house his black troops. It is of small interest, but on the walls graffiti can be seen — ships, arms, etc. — drawn by renegades or captives and the soldiers themselves. They seem to bridge time more effectively and vividly than does writing.

RABAT TO CASABLANCA

Route (1) Autoroute RP36, 90 km.
    (2) P1, 93 km.
    (3) Coast road P36 and S222, 96 km.
These three roads are becoming intertwined as the Autoroute, branching from the P1 taking a largely middle course between the two other parallel roads, for a while usurps the coast road and cuts back across the P1 close to Casablanca.

Leave the walled area of Rabat by the Boulevard Hassan II. Bear left after the Bab el-Had with the very adequate signposts along the Avenue de Temara for P1 and the Autoroute (Route Exit C) which branches right 5 km. from the gate. For the P36 turn right out of the Bab el-Had and left at the Place des Martyrs where there is a signpost (Route Exit B). [See Route Map for Western Area (pp. 314–15).]

The Autoroute is an excellent one although increasing traffic makes one wonder how long it will be adequately wide. However, the P1 is really a pleasanter road, and where the traffic from the Autoroute is not diverted to it, by far less busy. The P36 is embroiled with the Autoroute and is of little use except as a way of getting to bathing-places south-west of Rabat or others, like Mohammedia, north-east of Casablanca. If you want to bathe along the road, either start along the P36 and then join the Autoroute or, starting by that road, leave it by the lead road for Mohammedia to continue into Casablanca on the S111.

Rail 89 km.: eight trains a day, taking about 1 hour.
Bus A dozen or more a day by the C.T.M., about 1½ hours.
Accommodation and food Hotels at Mohammedia, Temara Plage, Ech-Chiahna, Skhirat Plage and, if pressed, lodging at Bouznika. Restaurants and bars are very numerous along the P1 or off the Autoroute, but they are more concentrated towards Casablanca.

Route 1

When fully opened you will have to turn off this Autoroute by the signposted lead roads for any place that interests you among those described under Route 2 below.

Route 2

[14 km.] **Temara**, a village near a ruined casbah and the *Koubba of Sidi Lachen*, where there is an August moussem. Turn right for **Temara Plage**, a lively resort however synthetic.

Hotel ***A *Hotel la Felouque* (tel. 443.88).
Camping *La Palmeraie.*

[20 km.] **Aïn Attig**, where a road on the left leads 2 km. to the source (*aïn*) of Gheboula whence an aqueduct was built to carry its waters to Rabat. To defend this water-supply Abd el-Mumin, who engineered it in the twelfth century, built a massive castle there. This is now completely ruinous, but interesting to students of military architecture.

[23 km.] Turn right for **Ech-Chiahna**, a beach resort like Temara.

Hotel ****B *Hotel la Kasbah*, Rose-Marie Plage (tel. 416.33).
Camping *Rose-Marie*, (tel. 423.07).

[27 km.] **Skhirat**, where there is a Sunday market and a students' moussem in September. The turning to the right leads to the sea at *Skhirat Plage*.

Hotels (at Skhirat Plage)
   ***A *Hôtel Amphitrite* (tel. 422.36).

[41 km.] **Bouznika**.

[59 km.] A turning left leads in 22 km. to **Ben Sliman**, deep in the forest of *Ziada* where there is a September moussem — and a camping site near by.

[59 km.] **Louizia**. Road on the right to **Mohammedia** (8 km.).

Hotels (at Mohammedia)
*****   *Hôtel Meridien Miramar*, Rue de Fes (tel. 20.21).
   ****A *Hôtel Samir*, 34 Boulevard Moulay Youssef (tel. 20.05).
Residence la Sablette, (tel. 31.15).
Camping
Camping International Loran (tel. 29.57).
Sports A golf-course of international standard; a racecourse; yachting and sandy bathing.

This sandy seaside resort serves Rabat and Casablanca. Besides the luxurious *Miramar* there are many places to stay. It is also a commercial port and an industrial centre of great importance in petrochemicals, supporting a population of over 50,000. All this is due to the French. Previously it had been a place of small account, though in the seventeenth century the Portuguese thought it worth while to seize, but they could not hold it. It was of rather greater importance as a port handling foreign ships under the Merinids. Its old and large *casbah* surrounds a *Portuguese fort*; Mohammed ben Abdullah built the old *mosque* in the eighteenth century — but it is not for these things that one comes to Mohammedia, rather for the jolly summer-life among the holidaymakers who throng it.

[75.5 km.] Road on the right to Mohammedia, on the left another to **Tit Mellil** and **Mediouna**, 9 km. from Mohammed V airport — the only way to avoid Casablanca's traffic if you are making for Marrakech.

[93 km.] Casablanca.

CASABLANCA

Population 2,140,000.

Air *Mohammed V* at Nouasseur serves both Rabat and Casablanca. It lies 27 km south on the P7. For internal air links, see p. 23.

Rail For rail links, see p. 23. Note that *Gare du Port* (*Map* 2) is in the centre of the city and *Gare des Voyageurs* an expensive 3 km taxi ride east. Railway information bureau telephone 22.30.11.

Bus Casablanca is as well supplied with buses from all over the country as the capital. The C.T.M. station is at 23 Rue Léon l'Africain. Local services mostly pass through Place Mohammed V.

Taxi Numerous ranks, of which the one at Place Mohammed V seems most productive; alternatively telephone 203.93. Casablanca taxi drivers are jackals who cannot be shamed into using their meters.

Car Hire *Avis*, 19 Avenue des F.A.R. (tel. 31.44.51).

Europcar, 144 Avenue des F.A.R. (tel. 36.79.73).

InterRent Maroc, 44 Avenue des F.A.R. (tel. 31.37.37).

Hertz, 25 Rue de Foucauld (tel. 31.22.23) and at Mohammed V Airport (tel. 33.91.81).

Leasing Cars, 100 Boulevard Zerktouni (tel. 26.14.18).

Hotels

*****	*Hôtel Hyatt Regency*, Place Mohammed V (tel. 22.41.67).	
*****	*Hôtel El Mansour*, 27 Avenue des F.A.R. (tel. 31.30.11).	
*****	*Riad Salam*, Boulevard de la Corniche (tel. 36.35.35).	
*****	*Hôtel Safir*, 100 Avenue des F.A.R. (tel. 31.12.12).	
****A	*Hôtel Suisse*, Boulevard de la Corniche (tel. 36.02.02).	
****A	*Hôtel les Almohades*, Avenue Moulay Hassan I (tel. 22.05.05).	
****A	*Hôtel Marhaba*, 63 Avenue des F.A.R. (tel. 31.31.99).	
****A	*Hôtel El Mounia*, 50 Boulevard de Paris (tel. 27.27.07).	

****B   *Hôtel la Corniche*, Boulevard de la Corniche (tel. 36.27.82).
****B   *Hôtel Transatlantique*, 79 Rue Colbert (tel. 22.07.64).
****B   *Hôtel Tropicana*, Boulevard de la Corniche (tel. 36.72.67).
****B   *Hôtel Anfa Plage*, Boulevard de la Corniche (tel. 36.36.45).
****B   *Hôtel Toubkal*, 9 Rue Sidi Belyout (tel. 31.04.50).
****B   *Hôtel Karam*, Boulevard de la Corniche (tel. 36.73.14).
****B   *Hôtel Tarik*, Boulevard de la Corniche (tel. 36.78.41).
***A   *Hôtel Washington*, 107 Boulevard Rahal El Meskini (tel. 27.97.17).
***A   *Hôtel Metropole*, 89 Rue Mohammed Smiha (tel. 30.12.13).
***A   *Hôtel Astoria*, 63 Rue d'Azilal (tel. 30.74.17).
***A   *Hôtel Noailles*, 22 Boulevard du 11 Janvier (tel. 26.05.80).
***A   *Hôtel Plaza*, 18 Boulevard Mohammed El Hansali (tel. 22.02.26).
***A   *Hôtel Bellerive*, 38 Boulevard de la Corniche (tel. 36.71.92).
***B   *Hôtel de Cernay*, 8 Rue de Cernay (tel. 31.45.61).
***B   *Hôtel Windsor*, 93 Place Oued El Makhazine (tel. 27.88.74).
**A   *Hôtel Trocadero*, 88 Boulevard Lahcen Ou Ider (tel. 30.47.02).
**A   *Hôtel Excelsior*, 2 Rue Nolly (tel. 26.22.81).
**A   *Hôtel Triomphe*, 11 Passage Sumica (tel. 26.15.32).
**A   *Hôtel Georges V*, 1 Rue Sidi Belyout (tel. 31.24.48).
**A   *Hôtel Astrid*, 12 Rue Ledru Rollin (tel. 27.78.03).
**A   *Hôtel Sully*, 284 Boulevard Rahal El Meskini (tel. 30.95.35).
**A   *Hôtel Balmoral*, 9 Rue Reitzer (tel. 26.01.15).
**B   *Hôtel Guynemer*, 2 Rue Pégoud (tel. 27.57.64).
**B   *Hôtel d'Orsay*, 17 Rue Mohammed Diouri (tel. 30.18.03).
**B   *Hôtel de Paris*, 2 Rue Branly (tel. 23.38.71).
*A   *Hôtel Majestic*, 57 Boulevard Lalla Yacout (tel. 31.09.51).
*A   *Hôtel Lausanne*, 24 Rue Poincarré (tel. 26.86.90).
*A   *Hôtel Rialto*, 9 Rue Claude (tel. 27.51.22).
*A   *Hôtel de Louvre*, 36 Rue Nationale (tel. 27.37.47).
*A   *Hôtel Colbert*, 30 Rue Colbert (tel. 31.42.41).
*A   *Hôtel Lincoln*, 1 Rue Ibn Batouta (tel. 22.24.08).
*A   *Hôtel Touring*, 87 Rue Allal Ben Abdellah (tel. 31.02.16).
*A   *Hôtel de Foucauld*, 52 Rue de Foucauld (tel. 22.26.66).
*A   *Hôtel Olympia*, 31 Cours des Sports (tel. 25.33.43).
Residence Atlantis, 2 Boulevard de Biarritz (tel. 36.04.04).
Camping *Oasis* 10 km on the road to El-Jadida (tel. 25.33.67).
Information *O.N.M.T. Tourist Office*: 55 Rue Omar Slaoui (tel. 27.11.77)
Syndicat d'Initiative: 98 Boulevard Mohammed V (tel. 22.15.24).
Touring Club du Maroc: 3 Avenue des F.A.R. (tel. 27.13.04).
Royal Automobile Club: 3 Rue Lemercier (tel. 24.17.93).
Consulates British: (commercial representation) 60 Boulevard Anfa (tel. 22.16.53).
United States: 8 Boulevard Moulay Youssef (tel. 22.41.49).
Banks Offices of all Moroccan and many foreign banks.
Shopping *La Maison d'Artisan*, 57/59 Avenue Hassan Seghir and *Co-opartim*, Avenue de l'Armée Royale are state controlled as to quality and prices.
Sports and Clubs *Bathing*: the best beaches — or rather bathing establishments — line the coast of Aïn Diab and Anfa, west of the main centre.
Riding: Club Bayard, Anfa (tel. 27.25.81).
Club de l'Étrier, Quartier des Stades (tel. 25.37.71).
Tennis: USM Tennis Club, Arab League Park (tel. 27.54.29).

Golf: Royal Anfa Golf Club, (tel. 25.10.26). Note also the impressive complex at Mohammedia (see p. 185).

Racing: Hippodrome, Anfa.

Watersport and yachting: STE Nautique de Casablanca, Delure Jetty, Port (tel. 22.57.21).

RUC Rowing Club, Moulay Youssef Jetty, Port (tel. 27.79.81).

Night-life Somebody has tried to build Casablanca a wicked image in the public mind, but 'Casa' has done little to support it in fact. Sailors find it a dull port of call; tourists find it hard even to find sailors there. Since fashions in night-spots are anyway fickle and transitory, we suggest talking to your hotel porter about it. At least no Casablancan porter will be surprised by any outlandish hopes you may entertain, though whether he can realize them for you is another matter.

Post Office Place des Nations.

Emergencies *Ambulance*: telephone 15.

Police: telephone 19.

The largest city in Morocco, Casablanca is also the chief industrial centre, the largest port and commercial 'capital' of the country. It is a wholly modern city, owing its importance almost all to the French and, more specifically, to the port they constructed there.

Since its name means 'white house' (in Arabic *Dar el-Baïda*), you would expect Casablanca to be the whitest of cities. And, true enough, it is far whiter than most cities are, though less white than some other of the Atlantic towns. Often its buildings are washed ochre or pink, or are just a dusty, concrete colour. Few parts of Casablanca have been there long enough to wear an established air; much of it has been run up too fast and often too cheaply — nearly always without enough consideration — and yet it has a vigorous individuality that lends quite a heady and stimulating air to its streets. You can eat well, sleep in luxury and amuse yourself how you please in this cosmopolitan city; but its romance is modern as a TV commercial's and its aesthetic pleasure nil. After spending weeks elsewhere in the country I have, though, been glad to return to the restaurants and shops — Rabat has the best bookshops, but Casablanca's are good also — pleased to return to that general air there is about Casa (as it is generally called) of its being a place which a European can understand without conscious effort. That air is superficial; Casa is probably the most complex place in Morocco and the hardest really to know. Seemingly the least Moroccan city, it is not less so than any other and certainly it is the one whose citizens are feeling most the stresses imposed by rapid 'westernization' and the local industrial revolution.

HISTORY

Anfa, now one of the western suburbs of Casablanca, is the older inhabited area. It was the capital of the heretical, Salihian Berber state set up by the Barghawata tribes (p. 69). It may have been the chief town of their territory long before the arrival in the seventh and eighth century of Arabs and Islam. Abdullah Yassin died during the Almoravids' attempt to subdue the Barghawata, who were not reduced until mid twelfth century, by the Almohad Abd el-Mumin. Yaacub el-Mansur moved nomad Arab tribes into the territory in 1188, a great mistake as it turned out since they uprooted the sedentary farmers who made the plains highly productive of wheat and barley which had been exported in quantity through Anfa. Abu Yussef the Merinid took Anfa in 1259, but when the dynasty became enfeebled the town and district asserted its independence and as such dealt with Portugal and England, although its chief activity was piracy. By 1468 the Anfa pirates were such a nuisance to Lisbon that the Infanta Ferdinand sailed with 10,000 men in fifty ships to attack the port and, after sacking it, abandoned the ruin he had made. This punishment was repeated in 1515 and sixty years later the Portuguese returned to stay. They fortified the port and named it Casa Branca. The tribes of the interior harried the little colony and when in 1755 the same earthquake that destroyed Lisbon seriously damaged Casa Branca, the Portuguese abandoned it. Sidi Mohammed ben Abdullah then repeopled it, built a fort and a mosque with its annexes, and named it Dar el-Baïda — which the Spanish correctly translated as Casablanca; they shipped grain from it in large quantities. Sultan Moulay Sliman closed the port in punishment of a local revolt and it was not reopened until 1830, under Abd er-Rahman — but it was by then only a village of some 600 inhabitants. Anfa port was not obstructed with a sand-bar, as Rabat and El-Jadida were, and this led to its growth. The European industrial revolution was, however, the prime factor in this, for France and England had a new need to import grain and — more — wool. From 1854 foreign factors were installed at Anfa; from 1857 consuls, the British being the first. By 1866 the population had risen to an estimated 80,000 including 100 foreigners. Regular French shipping-services began to serve the port from 1862 and in 1906 work was begun to improve the port facilities. It was particularly here at Casablanca that the foreign colonies, hoping to safeguard themselves against the xenophobic Moroccans who resented their increasing influence, and indeed their very presence, insisted upon making protective, extra-territorial claims which only increased Moroccan animosity towards them. The murder of nine French port-workers and the destruction of the French consulate's block-house provoked a not unwilling France into occupying the town (and also Oujda), thus leading to the downfall of Abdul Aziz and his replacement by the disastrous sultan Abd el-Hafid whose conduct provoked in 1912, the French occupation of the whole country as a 'protectorate'. General Lyautey, the first Resident General, decided at once greatly to enlarge the port and by doing so created the present prosperous city.

PRINCIPAL SIGHTS

The sights of Casablanca must include the remarkable 'Moorish' *official buildings* erected by the French in the 1920s, the *cathedral of the Sacré Coeur* of 1930 (*Map* 5) and, by far the most intriguing, the *Aquarium* (*Map* 1). The *Medina* is a sad-looking place dating from Sidi Mohammed's rebuilding of the town, but it is quite lively by day.

Many people are really fond of Casablanca and it doesn't do just to exclaim that it has no apparent centre or social nucleus. The publishers of this guide find it hard to believe it has no 'sights' (not even a *zoo*?). There *is* the Aquarium, but the whole spreading city is a sight in itself, just because the life led there is so intense and different. You have to follow your nose, walking it about to test the scents. It is full of bars where, as everywhere, contact with people can readily be made. It has eerie suburbs and a riotous sea-coast — if there is nothing obvious awaiting your curiosity, there is a great deal that is the more interesting for being both the more subtle and the more dependent on your own effort to seek it out. The population may at first sight seem a sophisticated and urban lot, but in fact most of it has newly arrived from the provinces. Perhaps you should not expect everyone you meet to be as urbane as they look and it could be wise to avoid solitary rambles in the shanty-towns, but otherwise there is no need at all to feel timorous about following this advice.

ATLANTIC
OCEAN

PCRT

Casablanca

1 Aquarium
2 Station (Gare du Port)
3 Municipal Market
4 Central Post Office
5 Cathedral of Sacré Coeur
6 Town Station (Gare des Voyageurs)
7 Parc de la Ligue Arabe
8 Marcel Cerdan Stadium

A route to
  Azemmour
  El-Jadida
  Safi
  Essaouira
  Agadir
B route to
  Marrakech
C route to
  Rabat
  Tangier
D route to
  Rabat via
  Mohammedia

0   500   1 km

metres

CASABLANCA TO MARRAKECH

Route Take the P7, an excellent road (241 km.). Leave the centre of the city from the Central Post Office (*Map 4*), going south-east along the Boulevard de Paris and its continuation Avenue Lalla Yaqoute to the Place de la Victoire, where you bear half-right by the Rue de Strasbourg, keeping straight on up the Route de Mediouna (Route Exit B). The journey should not take more than 2¼ hours. [See Route Map for Western Area (pp. 314–15).]

Rail Three trains a day, taking 3 hours 45 minutes or 7 hours by the night train. Day trains have a buffet on board.

Bus Three services daily, taking about 4 hours.

Accommodation and food It is possible to lodge at Settat 1 km. after Berrechid there is an *auberge*. Several wayside bars, well spaced along the road, offer rather more welcome refreshment.

[42 km.] **Berrechid** (Monday market). The *shrine of Sidi Ameur ben Lahcen* attracts a large moussem at Aïd el-Kebir.

From here the P13 runs left, 74 km. to **Khouribga**, the most important mining centre in Morocco.

Hotel
****A *Hôtel Sofitel*, Corner R.P. 13 and 13a (tel. 20.13).

It leads in a further 33 km. to **Oued Zem** (p. 334) and in another 47 km. to **Kasba Tadla** (p. 232).

[72 km.] **Settat**.

Hotel
**A *Hôtel M'Zamza*, 1 km. on the Casablanca road (tel. 23.66).

A town of 50,000 people founded by Moulay Ismaïl in the late seventeenth century, to which date belongs its *casbah*.

From here you can make a diversion to *Casbah de Boulaouane*, right, 64 km. by the S105. This lies by the head of the lowest of the three lakes formed by damming the great Oum er-Rbia River. **Boulaouane** itself is a small village, but the casbah built in 1710 by Moulay Ismaïl above the river is a fine, seven-towered affair enclosing a ruined palace and a mosque.

You can rejoin the P7 by the S128 which in 49 km. passes over the *dam of Imftout* forming the middle lake on the Oum er-Rbia.

[120 km.] **Mechra Benabbou**, close to the head of the Imftout lake.

[142 km.] **Skhour des Rehamna** (Wednesday market).
Administrative centre for the great Rehamna tribe's lands.

[171 km.] **Benguerir** (Tuesday market).

[206 km.] **Sidi bou Othman** (Monday market).

It was here that the French fought a battle with el-Hiba in 1912 (p. 110). This village lay on the intersection of the main caravan routes Fes–Marrakech, Marrakech–El-Jadida and Safi–Fes. The remains of a *dam* and of great, covered *cisterns*, built by the later Almohads, have been found near by — works designed to ensure the water-supply of this once important staging-post.

Over the last 20 km. of the way the road rises to cross the Jebilet hills by a *pass* 650 metres high. At the bottom of the descent, as you enter the great palmery of Marrakech, you cross the Tensift River by a *bridge* which dates from 1170, having been built by Abu Yaacub Yussef, the Almohad sultan.

[241 km] Marrakech.

MARRAKECH

Air For external and internal flights, see pp. 21 and 23. Taxis to the airport, 6 km. away, are quite exorbitant.

Royal Air Maroc, 197 Avenue Mohammed V (tel. 309.39).

Rail Five trains daily to Casablanca with connections through and including two trains direct to Rabat. The night train is not recommended for solitary travellers. The day trains average four hours to Casablanca. Railway information bureau telephone 311.07.

Bus Three C.T.M. services daily to Casablanca and at least daily services to Rabat, Fes, Tangier, Essaouira, Safi, El-Jadida, Ouarzazate, Agadir, Taroudant; many other destinations possible. The bus garages are at Bab Doukkala (*Map* 5).

Taxi Drivers are as rapacious as those of Casablanca. Horse-drawn cabs ply for hire and expect as much as a *petit taxi*. Several ranks (Djemaa el-Fna, Bab Doukkala, Municipal Market, Mellah, Sidi Bel Abbes, *Hotel Mamounia*, Avenue Mohammed V, etc.).

Car Hire *Avis*, 137 Avenue Mohammed V (tel. 337.27) and airport.

Budget, 159 Avenue Mohammed V (tel. 321.04).

Europcar, 59 Boulevard Mansour Eddahbi (tel. 331.84).

Hertz, 154 Avenue Mohammed V (tel. 344.75) and airport.

Hotels

***** *Hôtel Mamounia*, Avenue Bab Jdid (tel. 323.81). The *Mamounia* is considered one of the finest hotels in Morocco with the *Gazelle d'Or* in Taroudant and the *Palais Jamai* in Fes. Prices are three times higher than the maximum for ****A category but the comparison stops there. For the gardens and cooking alone the *Mamounia* is worth the money and the accommodation, whatever the criticisms of those who remember the original building which was favoured by Churchill, is luxurious.

*****   *Hôtel Palais El Badia*, Avenue de la Menara (tel. 330.77).

*****   *Hôtel Es-Saadi*, Avenue Quadissia (tel. 320.11).

*****   *Hôtel Sofitel*, Avenue Kennedy (tel. 346.26).

****A   *Hôtel Club N'Fis*, Avenue de France (tel. 347.72).

****A   *Hôtel le Marrakech*, Place de la Liberté (tel. 343.51).

****A   *Hôtel Toubkal*, Place Haroun Errachid (tel. 329.72).

****A   *Hôtel Siaha*, Avenue Kennedy (tel. 342.52).

****A   *Hôtel la Tafilalet*, Route de Casablanca (tel. 345.18).

****A   *Hôtel Semiramis*, Route de Casablanca (tel. 313.77).

****A   *Hôtel Kenza*, Avenue Yacoub El Mansour (tel. 305.50).

****A   *Hôtel Tichka*, Route de Casablanca (tel. 31.13.16).

****A   *Hôtel El Andalouss* (tel. 300.26).

****B   *Hôtel de la Menara*, Avenue des Ramparts (tel. 329.77).

****B   *Hôtel Sahara Inn*, Route de Casablanca (tel. 343.88).

****B   *Hôtel Agdal*, 1 Avenue Mohammed Zerktouni (tel. 336.70).

****B   *Hôtel Chems*, Avenue Houmane El Fetouaki (tel. 348.13).

****B   *Hôtel Amine*, Route de Casablanca (tel. 349.53).

***A   *Hôtel les Almoravides*, Arset Djenan Lakhdar (tel. 251.42).

***A   *Hôtel Ibn Batouta*, Avenue Yacoub El Marini (tel. 341.45).

***A   *Hôtel Imilchil*, Avenue Echouhada (tel. 314.53).

***A   *Hôtel Tachfine*, 18 Boulevard Zerktouni (tel. 343.08).

***A   *Hôtel Smara*, Boulevard Mohammed Zerktouni (tel. 841.50).

***B   *Hôtel Sun*, 25 Rue Moulay Ali (tel. 311.39).

***B   *Hôtel du Pacha*, Boulevard de la Liberté (tel. 313.26).

***B   *Hôtel la Rennaissance*, 89 Avenue Mohammed V (tel. 312.31).

***B   *Hôtel Les Ambassadeurs*, 2 Avenue Mohammed V (tel. 300.07).

**A   *Hôtel Mouatamid*, 94 Avenue Mohammed V (tel. 315.82).

**A   *Hôtel Koutoubia*, 51 Avenue El Mansour Eddahbi (tel. 309.21).

**A   *Grand Hôtel Tazi*, Cnr. Avenue El Mouahidine and Rue Bab Aguenau (tel. 221.51).

**A   *Hôtel Excelsior*, Cnr. Tarik Ibn Ziad (tel. 317. 33).

**A   *Hôtel El Maghreb*, Avenue des Ramparts (tel. 309.99).

**B   *Hôtel Foucauld*, Rue El Mouahidine (tel. 254.99).

**B   *Hôtel Gallia*, Rue de la Recette (tel. 259.13).

*A   *Hôtel la Palmeraie*, 8 Rue Souraya (tel. 310.07).

*A   *Hôtel C.T.M.*, Place Djemaa el-Fna (tel. 223.25).

*A   *Hôtel Oasis*, Avenue Mohammed V (tel. 311.35).

*B   *Hôtel des Voyageurs*, 40 Boulevard Zerktouni (tel. 312.35).

*B   *Hôtel Franco-Belge*, 62 Boulevard Zerktouni (tel. 303.72).

Club Méditerranée, which has a casino (tel. 257.75).

Residence El Hamra, 26 Avenue Mohammed V (tel. 306.30).

Camping *Municipal*, 400 m. south of Place de l'Empereur Haïlé Sélassié on Avenue de France. Has the quality of an army parade ground with few trees but a useful swimming pool. Telephone 317.07. Another campsite is planned.

Information *O.N.M.T. Tourist Office*: Cnr. Avenue Mohammed V and Place Abdelmoumen Ben Ali (tel. 302.58).

Syndicat d'Initiative: 176 Boulevard Mohammed V.

Banks Most are represented on Avenue Mohammed V and Boulevard Mohammed Zerktouni and duplicated in the medina on Rue Bab Aguenau.

Sports and Clubs Two public swimming-pools, one very large, on Rue Abou El Abbes Sebti, the first right turn off Avenue Mohammed V as you enter the medina. Many hotels will allow you to use their facilities, according to whim and season, for a fee.

Night-life Two *casinos*, one at the *Hotel Es-Saadi* apart from the one at *Club Méditerranée* already mentioned. Night clubs in the *Mamounia*, the *Marrakech* and the *Palais El Badia*, also two, *la Fantasia* and *le Flash*, on Avenue Mohammed V.

Festival Folklore Festival of music and dancing is held in early June, in the spectacular ruins of the el-Badi Palace (*Map* 14). If the regional contributions are but snippets, the sight is none the less a stimulating one, the production good and the music gripping.

Post Office Place 16 Novembre in the Gueliz and, like the banks, duplicated in the medina on Rue Zitoun El Jdid, between the Djemaa and the Mellah.

Emergencies *Ambulance*: telephone 15.

Police: telephone 19, or visit the handily sited French colonial blockhouse in the medina at Avenue Houmane El Fetouaki. Every barred keyhole window bespeaks Beau Geste.

With a population rising to 400,000, Marrakech — so often the capital of Morocco and equally often a derelict town — is now a thriving city. It is still very much as Deverdun[*] describes it, 'an immense market without bourgeoisie', though its growth of suburbs is based on a prospering industrialization and consequently an enlarging bourgeoisie. This contributes to the medina's random air of being an encampment that has become permanent, stone and pisé having replaced canvas and hair-tenting. It is not a beautiful city, although there are beautiful things about it and it contains things of beauty. It is marvellously placed against its background of the High Atlas mountains. These stand at a sufficient distance to be seen to their full height — and they are so improbably high as to create an illusion by tricking one's sense of the familiar; you expect a rise of this sort, seeming close at hand, to belong to a nearer and lower mass of hills; but the lights on the Atlas, the sharp and often snow-clad peaks seem to tear at the clouds; the way its bulk recedes behind the haze of heat — these denote the mountains' distance and excessive altitude. They are like a curtain drawn against the sky; it is easy to see how such a barrier shields inner Morocco from the aridity of the Sahara.

The dusty medina of Marrakech is surrounded by gardens and a great palmery whose fronds shade ground-crops; this lushness stands in a dry, pastoral plain which, seasonal pasturage, is more

[*] Gaston Deverdun, *Marrakech dès ses Origines à 1912* (Édit. Techniques Nord-Africaines, Rabat, 1959).

desert than sown. Thus Marrakech is a true oasis and has the charm peculiar to places which contrast with their surroundings. It is a city of positive attraction. There is a feeling of unreserve about it; the Marrakchi are vital and ever-active; it smells of stables and spices, charcoal and its own dry dust. All day long it is filled with countrymen. It is full of marvels. It is metropolitan in a way all its own. The new town, known as Gueliz, is spacious and agreeable, a garden city which, if it is a little seedy these days, is nevertheless a place where there are pleasant lodgings, good food and animated cafés.

The famous winter climate of this part — so much relished by Sir Winston Churchill, who loved to paint the neighbouring countryside — has been a major attraction ever since the area was opened to travel. It is still the most easily accessible of warm winter resorts for Western Europeans and it is very well provided with opportunities for relaxation. However, it is built principally to be habitable during its long and very hot summer and this is the season when it is most itself, the time when the Marrakchi are the most extended; winter is the season of their rest, the short spring their cheerful morning and the shorter autumn their idle evening. For all the heat (40°C and over is not unusual in July/August, though the nights are pleasant) summer is now the height of the tourist season and spring only slightly less busy.

As little as forty-five years ago it was quite an adventure to go to Marrakech; previous to that it was a journey of exploration. It could be dangerous. The half-legendary fame which it enjoyed, combined with the exoticism of the actuality which the French opened up in 1912, has lent Marrakech the special appeal of a place which haunts the imagination. It is therefore surprising nowadays to find it so easy to reach and so comfortably civilized when you arrive. It is the more surprising, too, to find that accessibility has not dimmed one's excitement to be there, nor made it any the less stirring and exotic in fact.

The alleyways of Marrakech are notoriously bewildering. You will need a guide — they are available at the O.N.M.T. office — for your first visits to the sights of the town but soon you will get the hang of the place and be able to explore on your own.

A hurried sight-seer in Marrakech might do worst than to walk about the exterior of the Koutoubia Mosque, onwards through the markets to the Medrassa Ben Yussef and the all-important Koubba el-Baroudiyin near by; and then to the marvellous Saad Necropolis and the el-Badi Palace ruins. Do not neglect to look at the Bab Aguenau in passing, and spare a moment for the minaret of the Casbah Mosque inside it — a full morning's tramp during which you will get quite a good idea of the city. In the afternoon drive round the Agdal and Menara gardens — you will see the splendid walls that way. End up in the Djemaa el-Fna towards evening.

HISTORY

Marrakech was founded by the Almoravids. If this was done as early as 1062, as some think, Abu Bekr was the founder; if as late as 1070, then by Yussef. It was in any case Yussef and his successor who developed the settlement. As a new foundation it was itself the successor of Nifs and Aghmat, the old towns sited higher in the foothills of the Atlas, to the south-east of the town.

Each of these towns had been the principal centre for the region, owing its importance to the fertility of the foothills and valleys, the usefulness of the plains for pasturage and the fact that the south-western passes over the mountains open towards this point — the most western of which, crossing from Taroudant, being the least obviously of service to the region, yet most probably the one the Sanhaja and Saadi used the most. The Haouz plain is also in relatively easy communication with Fes to the north, and with the Atlantic seaports of Safi, old Anfa, El-Jadida and Essaouira (though this was, of course, not active until a comparatively recent date). The region had been inhabited by Neoliths and has doubtless been populous ever since. The site of Aghmat is known (see p. 227), that of Nifs has not yet been found; it may have lain towards Amizmiz.

Quite apart from the ingrained Moroccan habit of starting afresh whenever possible, the Almoravids needed a new settlement of their own. They never came to really satisfactory terms with the Masmuda tribes of the foothills and higher slopes. These were traditionally hostile to the sedentary tribes of the plains and naturally so towards intrusive desertmen who, in the case of Sanhaja, added insult to injury by showing a marked readiness themselves to settle to a sedentary existence. Nifs and Aghmat were too much controlled by the Masmuda and this made them unsuitably insecure bases for further Almoravid conquests northwards.

The original 'city' consisted of a stone-built casbah or *ksar* and a collection of tented encampments protected by a stockade of jujube thorns. According to some chroniclers, the area was then lightly wooded with these trees. Such a camp would naturally attract a large market about itself, but it is sensibly suggested that, this being neutral ground between the territories of various tribes, a weekly market may already have been held on the site and that if so Abu Bekr perhaps bought out any claims to its use or ownership. At any rate the site was clear of Masmuda lands and could not easily be surprised by them or any other tribe.

The word *ksar* (the plural of which is *ksour*) has nowadays a fairly wide meaning. It has been defined as 'a Saharan village encircled by walls', but this sense has probably been extended — as the villages south of the Atlas have themselves been — from a strong-point or castle. Such a growth exactly parallels that of European townships where a castle (itself housing a complex society) attracted a suburb or 'borg' to the protection of its walls, this in time being also walled around to make a defensible whole with the castle whose innermost and strongest core was the original keep or *ksar*. So the simplest Moroccan *ksour* are mere keeps, others are like castles with outer ring-walls and some are defensible villages. The development of urban centres in Morocco simply extends this: the casbah is the strong-point or citadel surrounded by walls and housing royal or gubernatorial complexes; the medina represents the borg, and to this the new 'French towns' are attached.

Thus the thorny stockade around the camp of Marrakech became a wall of pisé, the tents were replaced by houses and the old *ksar* grew to be a strong casbah. Yussef also built a mosque which most probably lay within the casbah defences. All his conquests in the north, particularly those in Spain, tended to draw the centre of Almoravid power away from Marrakech to Fes. Much is made of Marrakech as being the Almoravids' own dear capital, but rather it was Ali ben Yussef's capital; his father was too much a nomad to need such a home-base and did not much mind where he was so long as it was on the African side of the Straits, for he felt distaste for the Andalusians. Thus Marrakech was originally founded to be the Sanhaja's southern base and regional capital, Fes being accepted as the northern, but presently becoming the natural centre of the empire. The two capitals are somewhat cut off from each other during winter and neither is really well placed to control all Morocco, though both together can easily enough hold at least inner Morocco. Individual rulers and sometimes whole dynasties of them have personally favoured one or other capital city, but all have needed both and most have striven to maintain both with equal state and pomp. Since neither city liked the other to be favoured the sultans played them against each other; they had only to build some splendid work in the one they did not choose to reside in, to bring the favoured one to heel by implying they might move. None the less, for Ali ben Yussef certainly, as for his father quite probably, Marrakech was the Almoravids' preferred city; it was their own creation and had no traditions save those they themselves established. Their conquests went enormously to enrich and beautify it.

Ali, son of a Christian slave and the redoubtable Yussef, was the real creator of the city. He succeeded his father in 1106 and proved a warrior king who was also a pious and most cultivated man. To him are due the tremendous underground systems of irrigation which enabled the planting of the palmery and gardens besides supplying the city with adequate water. The city could not have grown so great without these *khettara*. Based on the water thus provided, Ali undertook extensive building-works, both public and private.

Beside the casbah his father had built, Ali added a palace. If this was not large by later standards, it was built on traditional lines of many rooms around courts. Ali also built the largest mosque in the Maghreb, set in the very centre of the city. It is still called after him. Beside it he erected a fountain which survived until the last century and became the pattern for all subsequent ones. The city walls that Yussef and Ali built still stand in part and those sections that have been replaced follow the same trace as theirs, only two small additions having been made to their circuit, apart, that is, from the extended royal gardens to the south.

For the fortunes of the city and the dynasties that ruled it reference should be made to the History section on p. 53. But there are some details to be added to what is said there.

When the Almohads became strong enough seriously to challenge the declining Almoravids in 1147, dissatisfied Christian mercenaries or enslaved soldiers opened the Bab Aghmat to them. The town was given over to three days of sackage and murder during which, allegedly to honour instructions left by ibn Tumart for its purification, the Almoravid buildings were largely destroyed. The mosque in the casbah and Ali's palace were the principal losses; Ali's great town-mosque was, it is thought, shut and despoiled rather than destroyed, while the city walls, Ali's fountain and wash-house (which still survives — see p. 212) and the great gate of Ali's palace were spared.

Abd el-Mumin built the Koutoubia Mosque, in two stages. Under his successor, Abu Yaacub Yussef, there was a terrible outbreak of the plague in 1176, the sultan himself being infected, though surviving it. None the less the town prospered and twelve years later an extension was made to the city walls on the west, creating a small new quarter into which perhaps el-Mumin invited Sanhaja and Haksoura tribesmen since it was adjacent to the new casbah. This was built by his successor, for el-Mumin died the following year. It is possible that Yussef had been a coloured man; Yaacub el-Mansur certainly was — sufficiently so to be nicknamed the 'Black Caliph' (for the Almohads abrogated this greatest of Moslem titles to themselves). He was very much the Arab prince and little of the fiery Almohad tradition survived in his way of life. Within the protection of his new casbah he built a dozen palaces whose names still suggest their legendary luxury. 'Palace' here most probably means a set of apartments — a *dar* — each centred on its own court and largely self-contained. In the casbah also he built a mosque (p. 213) and a market. He provided a cavalry exercise-ground and a hospital. The great Arab doctors Abu Marwan Abd el-Malik ibn Zohr and Moham-med ibn Rashid — known respectively in Europe as Avenzoar and Averroes — both served at his court.

The decline of the dynasty brought much trouble to the city. The casbah was despoiled in 1224; 1227, 1230 and 1232 all saw pillage and disaster wrought during the fratricidal wars between rival claimants to the throne. These wretched times persisted until the Merinid conquest of 1269. Soon after, Fes became the capital. Marrakech was occasionally used as a base for revolts, notably (and successfully) by 'bu Inan, and from 1374 to 1386 it was the capital of a Merinid kingdom separate from that of Fes. The Mosque of Sidi Mohammed ben Salih (p. 217) and that of el-Ksour were built during this period, also the *medrassa* in the casbah which has disappeared.

The Portuguese established in the coastal towns made a vain attempt on the city in 1515. A severe famine between 1519 and 1521 halted all activity in the city and the south, where the two Saadi brothers Achmed el-Araj and Mohammed esh-Sheikh shared their father's growing kingdom, the former the outer lands and the latter the Saadi homeland of the Sous. This family had been leading the resistance to Portuguese infiltration and slowly making a state for itself. In 1521 Achmed was able to occupy the city without resistance, though not the casbah. This was peacefully taken over after its Wattasid occupier, 'bu Santuf, had been poisoned during a hunting party in 1524. Marrakech was then but half alive, the population having been fearfully reduced by the famine. Abu 'l-Abbes Achmed, the new Wattasid ruler of Fes, besieged the city until a revolt at home forced him to desist. Further battles with the Fasi Wattasids eventually left the Saadi the victors in 1536 and the state was formally recognized by Fes, Tadla being the understood frontier between the two kingdoms.

The year 1541 saw Mohammed's prestigious success in driving the Portuguese from Agadir; because of this, the Christians abandoned the other seaports, retaining only El-Jadida. Mohammed then attacked Achmed, his brother, taking him prisoner. A family council reconciled them, but they fell out again almost at once. This time Achmed and his family were sent to the Tafilelt as prisoners while Mohammed used Marrakech as base for an attack on Fes. That city he captured in 1549 — removing the Wattasid sultan and his family for poisoning at Marrakech. Another Wattasid, with Turkish support, chased Mohammed from Fes in 1554; but soon he recaptured it. The Fasiyin, however, disliked him, and he them. He gave up the attempt to make Fes his capital and returned to Marrakech. A pressing need of money caused him to dispossess mosques, other religious institutions and regional officers, provoking revolts over all the country. While repressing one such he was murdered in 1557 by Turks of his personal guard. Achmed and seven cadets of the family were then also murdered, this to secure the succession for Abdullah el-Ghalib, governor of Fes and one of Mohammed's sons. Mohammed had at least started the work of reconstruction and rebuilding necessary at Marrakech. It was he who instituted a customs house for the Christian colony established there and in general regulated their position in the kingdom. He had done this as early as 1547.

Abdullah was strong enough to maintain a prosperous peace in the country and became a great builder on the proceeds. The battered city was to be made a fitting capital again. But plague beset the place during 1558/9, causing a new recession. Otherwise Abdullah's fourteen-year reign was a fortunate one. The casbah was refurbished and a palace built. The ghetto or *mellah* was created — not in those days as a concentration of Jews for easier persecution but largely for their protection and to minimize friction between the adherents of mutually exclusive religions. The Great Mosque el-Mouassine (p. 218) was built on a large scale, with its annexes; the Mosque Ben Yussef was rebuilt and the fine *medrassa* added (p. 212). The Maristan, a new hospital, was founded, and, for political reasons, an elegant *koubba* built over the remains of the not very remarkable marabout Sidi Yussef ben Ali.

The civil wars which broke out after Abdullah's death are recounted in some detail on pp. 90–2. When eventually the intellectual Achmed el-Mansur reigned with so much success and prosperity, great works were put in hand at Marrakech. It is true these were mostly confined to the casbah and included above all the building of the 'peerless' el-Badi Palace (p. 223). The techniques and skills of latter-day Moslem Spain, in some ways superior, certainly rather different, to those of elsewhere in the Moslem world, were brought to their climax in this building. Though probably begun by Abdullah, the Saadi tombs to be seen today (p. 216) are largely Achmed's work. They give us some idea of the richness and grace of his palace. His mother built the Mosque of Bab Doukkala (p. 219) in the town, while libraries, baths, *khans*, many private houses and other amenities were built during this reign. It was a golden era for the city and a most prosperous one for all the country — only to lapse into prolonged anarchy during which Marrakech again became ruinous.

Among the Alaouite sultans, Moulay Ismail now has a bad name for having dismantled the el-Badi Palace, although it was in a poor condition by then and its marbles most precious. He did, however, order some religious buildings in the city. It was the wise Sidi Mohammed ben Abdullah who rebuilt the terribly shattered city in the second half of the eighteenth century. He had almost everything to do over again, the walls to repair, the casbah to reconstruct, new palaces to build and gardens to make. He built a state prison, a palace and mosques in the casbah, *mechouars*, more gardens and pleasances, and repaired many of the mosques and other buildings in the town. Moulay Suleiman, the pious, rebuilt the Ben Yussef mosque very early in the nineteenth century and did other works also. But apart from the creation of still more gardens (the Menara among them), repairs to various buildings, gates, etc., the nineteenth century saw only the renewed decline of the city. The most interesting monuments to the period are the vizier's palaces, themselves testaments to the decline of the arts in Morocco (pp. 224–5).

The houses shrank back from the walls and the area given over to gardens and cultivation became larger — you can see today something of how it must have looked, around the Koutoubia Mosque and the Hôtel Mamounia, though infilling buildings begin to mask this now. Since French days, however, there has been a great revival. Not only has the new town of Gueliz been built, but the life of the medina has greatly revived and expanded. The major French innovation in the medina was the resettlement of the area between Koutoubia and the old mellah and the creation of the Place Foucauld with the chain of gardens leading towards Gueliz. A part of the resettlement area comprised the brothel quarter. Prostitutes are by no means unknown in Morocco, but the very idea of officially established brothels is anathema to Moslems and everywhere one of the first acts of the independent Government was to abolish them. Within living memory the gates which divide one quarter of the town from another were closed each night.

PRINCIPAL SIGHTS

All the sights described below lie in the medina except the Agdal Gardens which are attached to the casbah on the south, and the Menara Gardens which lie to the west of the medina.

DJEMAA EL-FNA

Although it does not now seem to be so, this large and irregularly shaped *place* lies very close to the centre of the medina, a little to its south. Apart from the exterior of the Koutoubia Mosque (*Map* **10**), visible at a distance, the Djemaa el-Fna exhibits nothing of architectural distinction. Rather the reverse in fact. It is simply an open space which probably lay between the earliest casbah and palace and the market area – a general assembly-point, secular forum, place for communal celebrations, fairs, executions and riots. Except for executions, it still fulfils these offices although it is now many centuries since the sultans prudently removed themselves from its near proximity.

The name 'Djemaa el-Fna' is a corruption of 'the ... something ... mosque'. What does 'Fna' mean? Discussion, fancy and legend attach to its meaning, but the devoted Dr Deverdun most probably has it right when, citing both good etymological reasons and old references, he argues that it means, roughly, 'the ruined'

Marrakech

1 Zawiya of Sidi bel-Abbes
2 Zawiya of Sidi ben Sliman el-Jazouli
3 Mosque of Ali ben Yussef
4 Medrassa ben Yussef
5 Mosque of Bab Doukkala
6 Koubba el-Baroudiyin
7 Mosque of ben Salih
8 Great Mosque el-Mouassine
9 El-Ksour Mosque
10 Koutoubia Mosque
11 Dar Si'Saïd (Museum of Moroccan Arts)
12 'La Bahia' Palace
13 Mamounia Gardens
14 El-Badi Palace
15 Casbah Mosque
16 Saadi Necropolis
17 Dar el-Makhzen
18 Dar el-Baïda
19 Agdal Gardens
20 O.N.M.T.
21 Post Office
22 Railway Station

A route to Beni Mellal, Fes, Oued Zem and Rabat
B route to Casablanca
C route to Essaouira
D route to Amizmiz, Tinmel, Taroudant, Agadir
E route to Ourika, Oukaimeden
F route to Ouarzazate

or 'the tumble-down mosque', or even 'the mosque that came to nothing', since the only explanation known for the presence of the ruins of a mosque shown standing to its westwards on some old sketch-maps of the town is that given by a seventeenth-century Sudanese historian who states that the Saadi sultan Ahmed started to build a mosque which he was prevented from completing because of the disturbed times and that it had come to be known as 'the mosque that came to nought' because it had fallen into ruin before it was built.

In the cool of the later afternoons the Djemaa el-Fna comes into its own. Then all the stalls open (among much else, you can buy the ingredients for any magic spell, talisman or potion) and the entertainers for which it is famous — trick cyclists as well as acrobats, story-tellers, snake-charmers, lottery-men; itinerants for the most part, few among them staying many weeks at a time, though always returning – draw circles of bystanders around themselves. These last are more the country visitors than the blasé townsmen who have seen it all before. Then there are the tourists whose every click of a camera costs them 1 DH or more to the watchful collectors (snake-poses 5 DH), fees which there is no good reason to begrudge.

The Djemaa el-Fna is always attractive because of the vividness of the life led there. At midday, when it is at its most empty, it has the excitement of a stage under preparation for the performance. In the summer weather it will be lively all night. Neither the barbers nor the tiny cafés, ever seem to shut. Dawn, when flocks of women pass through on their way to work, is its most beautiful moment of all. For anyone who wants to soak himself in this atmosphere, the little *Hôtel C.T.M.* — with its rooms round a flowered courtyard bang on top of the bus station — might be an attractive proposition.

RELIGIOUS BUILDINGS

The section on p. 116 gives the necessary background to the following descriptions of the mosques and other monuments in the city. The annexes any mosque may have are described with it.

Koutoubia Mosque
Avenue Mohammed V (Map 10).
Visible from far off over the plains, the tall and sturdy *minaret* of this venerable mosque is always the first indication of the city.

It belongs to the third cathedral mosque to have been built in succession close to this site. The existing building was erected in the twelfth century under the Almohad sultan Abd el-Mumin.

Ali ben Yussef, the Almoravid who did the most to make Marrakech a fine city, built the first mosque — or it is thought he did; his father may have begun it, or even completed it. This was probably within the confines of his father's casbah which occupied an area to the north of the present building. Ali built himself a palace adjacent to the casbah's southern wall — over the area occupied by the present mosque. Both palace and mosque were destroyed during the Almohad 'purification' of the city after their conquest of it (p. 80).

Presumably starting work at once — in 1147 therefore — Abd el-Mumin built the second mosque over part at least of the razed remains of Ali's palace, setting it against the south wall of the casbah just as the palace had been. Through this wall he built the main, axial gateway leading directly into the *sahn* of his mosque. The building was placed immediately to the west of what had been the ceremonial entrance into Ali's palace, a monument known as the *Qaws el-Hajar* or 'Stone Arch', and a minaret for the new mosque was built upon the western pier of this massive gate which now led from the town into the old casbah. This tower was a much slighter construction than the present minaret and, probably often renovated, seems to have existed as late as 1803. The mosque to which it was attached was, however, rather mysteriously dismantled almost as soon as built and a new one erected to replace it, attached to its south. Indeed, the southern *quibla*-wall of the earlier was used (much as the casbah wall had been before) to serve as the northern wall of the later. Nowadays, to the north of the present building, beside the road to Gueliz (Avenue Mohammed V), the *foundations* of el-Mumin's 'First' Koutoubia lie exposed in an excavated area bounded on the north by the remains of a section of Yussef's casbah wall. Scraps of the foundations of Ali's palace have been uncovered at a lower level than the pavement of the *sahn* of this building.

The first Koutoubia was begun in 1147; it is known that the Second (or existing) Koutoubia was inaugurated with special prayers during the autumn of 1158 although it may not have been fully completed at the time. The First Koutoubia did not form a perfect rectangle in plan; its irregularity suggests a slight miscalculation rather than a structural weakness. The existing one is built to a deliberately mis-shapen plan, the object of which is clearly to alter the alignment of the *quibla* while either respecting the older *quibla* or simply utilizing it — probably the former since there is no central gate through it which, had one been made, would have destroyed the old *mihrab*; indeed, the curious contiguity of these two buildings suggests that Ali's old mosque may have lain immediately inside the casbah and that each successive building was so placed as to derive a certain sanctity from its shrine and *quibla*. The new orientation of the Second Koutoubia's *quibla* is in fact rather farther out of the true direction of Mecca than the old, yet the most plausible explanation for there ever having been a new building was a desire to alter this. In 1157 Abd el-Mumin was able to blackmail the religious authorities of Cordoba into giving up to him a very precious and holy copy of the Koran. This had belonged to the third caliph, Uthman ibn Affan (644–56), associate, blood-relative and son-in-law of the Prophet. Interleaved with it were four prayers written in Uthman's own handwriting.* El-Mumin built a special shrine for it in the new mosque and it is just possible that the mosque was built upon a 'corrected' orientation to house it.†

The fame of the Cordoban Koran too may have influenced the naming of the mosque. The word 'Koutoubia' (the stress is on the 'i') is a Europeanization of the Marrakchi word *Kotbiye* which is itself a corruption of *kutubiyyin* meaning 'of the books' or 'libraries'. Leo Africanus describes a market of 'a hundred bookshops' on either side the mosque. These were one of the glories of the intellectual centre the city had been earlier and was again to be. Excavation has indeed disclosed the foundations of a street of copyists' and booksellers' shops beside the building and it seems most probable that the name derives from these.

First Koutoubia

From the north-east corner of the excavations you can easily follow the plan of this building. At hand is the crumbled block which is all that is left of the pier of *Ali's Stone Arch* on which the

---

* This was carried on all important expeditions made by the sultans until it was lost at sea during a storm that overtook Abu el-Hassan while retreating from Tunis in the middle of the fourteenth century.

† Caliph Uthman ordered that the oral tradition of Mohammed's Koranic pronouncements be collated, authenticated and written down. Four copies of this authorized version were made and sent to the four far-flung areas of the empire. It seems likely that this was the 'Western' copy, probably sent in the first instance to Kairouan, but later coming into Moroccan hands, perhaps through Spain. If this was the case, its special sanctity would be amply accounted for.

first minaret stood. This could be climbed either from the inside of the mosque or from the casbah. Its position on the outside of the mosque set a precedent sometimes to be followed later, while the modification made in the second building — whereby the minaret stands within the same north-east corner of the building — was frequently copied. Although the paving of the *sahn* had been dug through to disclose the remnants of Ali's palace and the long trench-reservoirs below it, it is not hard to discern the shape of the court since this is free of the column bases regularly spaced over the rest of the diggings. The *sahn* itself is bounded by massive bases designed to carry a monumental arcading. There was no portico along the casbah wall, but the arches of the rest were reflected by similar arcading engaged with it. On either side the *sahn* four longitudinal aisles of the *prayer-hall* extend to the north wall to create a pair of annexes whose separateness from the prayer-hall proper is indicated by a symbolic screen formed by the continuation of the heavy arches marking the southern side of the *sahn*, carried across their width. The two areas thus defined were used for the instruction of students of Koranic law and theology. Such an arrangement was not altogether unusual; it was prefigured as early as 722 at Raqqa on the Euphrates and rather similar additions were made to Kairouan during the restoration of 1054. (The practice was discontinued in mosques of the Merinid period, when *medersa* were substituted for such teaching areas.) Over the rest of the area seventeen aisles, arched longitudinally, run towards the *quibla* — which forms the exterior wall of the existing building and still shows traces of what was once its interior decoration. The central aisle, running directly to the *mihrab*, is wider than the rest, as is the transverse one beside the *quibla* — thus following the model of Damascus as modified to a T-plan at Kairouan and adapted by el-Mumin's architects at Taza some nine years before. The *quibla*-aisle is also marked by transverse arching, again to form a symbolic screen between it and the prayer-hall. Although the regular longitudinal arching stops at this last, lateral range of columns, further spans are engaged with the *quibla* from the first, fourth, fifth, seventh and eighth ranges, counting from either hand, the increasing density of spans marking the presence of the shrine before the *mihrab*. In the existing building these arches have finely scalloped (foiled) edges to their span while those in the rest of the hall are plain horse-shoes. There were high windows in the *quibla* and the *mihrab* was a shallow niche. There were four entrance-doors in the east wall of the mosque and although the western wall has disappeared, it too doubtless had four.

SECOND KOUTOUBIA

In effect this duplicates the plan of the first. It is fractionally wider. Because the old *quibla* was retained while the orientation of the new was altered, the rectangular plan of the main part of the building is based upon a wedge-shaped arcade set against the north wall; on the east this is as wide as the base of the minaret and it tapers to nothing on the west. It was probably this space which prompted the architect to place the minaret within the building. Not only is the central aisle wider than the others but so, also, are those on each side of it, all three transversely as well as longitudinally arched. Surmounted by a semi-dome, the *mihrab* is a tall and shallow niche which so closely resembles that of Tinmel (p. 331) that it is virtually certain both are the work of the same artists. (Tinmel was built in the interval between the two Koutoubias.) The roofing of the T-aisles is among the earliest examples of Hispano-Moresque *artesonados* work. The *mimber* — a lofty throne at the head of a flight of narrow steps approximating to a Christian pulpit — is believed by Deverdun to have been brought from Ali's other mosque in the town — the Ben Yussef; it is said to be a superb example of Cordoban workmanship and is certainly Almoravid rather than Almohad in date. A dome rises over the T-crossing and four others, each decorated internally with stalactitic forms, are spaced along the *quibla*-aisle. These five domes are visible on the exterior. Each square pillar in the prayer-hall is decorated by two engaged columns whose capitals are carved, in a strong and almost barbaric manner like that of Berber jewellery, with forms reminiscent of Romanesque versions of Corinthian foliage. Upon these are set the returns of the horse-shoe arches, springing in slightly pointed spans. A severe simplicity reigns over the whitewashed interior. In almost the only moment of lyricism he allows himself, Deverdun says, 'at the end of the long perspectives the decoration of the *mihrab* shrines in the shadow and the *sahn* in the light'. Between these counterpoints there extends a reflective coolness of superb architectural grace equally strong, in a notably masculine way, as it is delicate. Apart from the minaret, the whitewashed, green-tiled exterior is not greatly impressive. The doorways have often been remodelled and there now remains nothing to suggest that its walls were probably decorated with arched recesses set in rectangular panels beneath an elaborate entablature — as we know the First Koutoubia to have been since a small section survived to be photographed early in the century. From this it is possible to see that it has been imitated to decorate the arcade on the north-east of the mosque of Bab Doukkala (p. 219). Today only a trace or two of this decoration survives.

MINARET

From the non-Moslem tourist's point of view everything must depend on the minaret. It is nearly 70 metres high and 12 metres square, a perfect monument to the art of that wonderful twelfth century which saw a peak of creative achievement over so much of the world. The tower is slightly younger than its peers, the Giralda of Seville and the Hassan Tower at Rabat, but it has been preserved almost as built where they are, respectively, re-topped in the sixteenth century and unfinished. The Second Koutoubia built, the First does not seem at once to have been dismantled. One contemporary account speaks of a double mosque with minaret standing between the two halves. The new tower seems to have been begun rather after 1152 but not finished until the 1190s, under Yaacub el-Mansur, who perhaps did not do more than add the *doomed lantern* that crowns it. This conforms in proportion to the scale of one to five on which the harmony of the whole is based, but one cannot always avoid a feeling that it is too slender for its height — or rather, perhaps, that the arches piercing it have the effect of weakening its impact, so that the solid, oblique views are the more satisfactory.

The *main tower* is built of an outer and inner wall between which a ramp climbs by left-hand turns. This allowed animals carrying materials to be driven up as the work proceeded. The stones of which it is built become the smaller the higher for the same practical reason and if this now lends the tower a slightly shoddy appearance it should be remembered that it was originally faced with a coat of mortar or plaster. The interior contains *six chambers*, the one upon the other, vaulted or domed and richly decorated, the topmost being the finest. Each exterior face is different although all conform to the same scheme by which the ornamentation of bold, rich carving in relief widens as it rises, the lancets of the windows multiplying. Of the faience band around the top, little now remains. All four faces of the lantern are alike; it contains two rooms and in fact stands quite low down behind the machicolated top of the base tower. The two *golden balls* and *pear-shaped drop* which surmount it share with those over the minaret of the Casbah Mosque the legend that Yaacub's wife gave her jewels to make them, or at least the topmost of them. Even the tall wooden gibbet upon which a flag is broken during the hours of prayer is of a great age.

I can think of no other tower with so compelling a presence as this.

Mosque of Ali ben Yussef
Map 3.
Open Daily, except Monday and Friday, from 08.00 to 12.00 and from 14.30 to 18.30.

Built by Ali ben Yussef in the third decade of the twelfth century, this is the oldest mosque to have survived in Marrakech although its actual fabric is of recent date. When first built it was the largest mosque in the West and fully twice as big as it is now. The nearly rectangular path of the alleys surrounding it (a rectangle now interrupted by a corner of the *medrassa* and partly filled with other buildings) probably indicates its original extent. A part of the original walls, built of very thick pisé, exists on the north and Deverdun found the base of the minaret close to the Derb Baroudiyin on the west. The first building was probably very much influenced by Cordoba. A *marble basin* from this building is preserved in the Medrassa ben Yussef, described below. The Marrakchi have shown themselves very attached to this mosque. It was probably shut rather than destroyed by the Almohads, and el-Mutarda, the next but last of that dynasty, and a very cultivated man, restored it and enriched its library some time during his reign from 1248 to 1266. Under the Saadi, it appears to have been even more popular than the Koutoubia — after el-Ghalib had once again restored it; both he and his successors made important gifts to its library, some of which survive there. By the beginning of the nineteenth century, however, there was nothing for it but to rebuild it — perhaps largely in response to popular demand Moulay Suleiman raised a completely new building between 1806 and 1820, based on the Merinid style with a wide *prayer-hall* of only three lateral aisles, a double arcading either side the *sahn* and a single one opposite the *mihrab*. This otherwise austere building is noted for the magnificence of its ceilings. The *minaret* is a beauty, though its decoration is now once again in need of repair.

In Marrakech, *medersa* were all built as annexes to mosques, either at the same time or as additions to existing ones. The only one of interest to survive is that built for this mosque.

Medrassa ben Yussef
Map 4.

When Ali built the mosque and el-Mutarda restored it there were no such things as *medersa*. That it should have been built in a way that seems to impinge on the plan of Ali's mosque shows perhaps the extent to which that had fallen into ruin by Saadi times, when the mosque was again restored and this, the largest *medrassa* in the Maghreb, built by Abdullah el-Ghalib in 1565. A very beautiful building, in some ways it obviously derives from the earlier Merinid colleges, though in others it differs. The circuitous entrance was probably designed to give extra privacy and quiet to the interior while the paucity of upper windows upon the court would also exclude from it noise from the living-quarters. This scarcity of windows, I feel, does not sufficiently break up the high walls of the court, so that their highly decorated surfaces and heavy wooden entablatures can seem rather oppressive. Yet there is a really monumental grandeur to the court and its details are exquisite.

In the lovely *prayer-hall* stands the *marble basin* that came from Ali's mosque. It was already more than a hundred years old when it was installed there. An inscription among the heraldic beasts and vegetation with which it is carved says it was ordered to be made by an Ommayed chamberlain known to have been living at the end of the tenth century. It was probably brought by Ali from Fes. Its decoration exhibits the Ommayed fondness for representationalism in art and it is perhaps odd that Ali should so far have shared the taste as to have transported it here, admirer though he was of Andalusian arts.

Upstairs in the *medrassa* there are more than a hundred cells for students and masters. The rules were that students had to be over twenty years of age and to be diligent in their studies; even if they were not, they could not be expelled before six years were up, by which time it was considered their want of application reflected unfavourably on their masters' reputations.

FOUNTAIN

The fountain associated with Ali ben Yussef's mosque — also built by Ali — disappeared during the last century when the Fasi *kissaria* or 'covered market' was built. It had been the model for most subsequent public fountains and probably escaped Almohad destruction as much from religious as practical considerations. The Prophet himself laid down that to give water to man or beast was a paramount form of charity, the virtue upon which Islam lays so very much stress. Thus when a mosque was built some of the water diverted to serve its washing-places was generally played into a public fountain. This lost one set the pattern: a basin for human use set beside two troughs for watering animals and the whole enclosed in a decorated frame. The expense of all this was gladly borne, as inscriptions often indicate, from a mixture of generosity, humility and vainglory, but always, also, out of that instinct that Moslems have who undertake religious and quasi-religious works — a thoroughness stemming from a determination that what they build shall be beautiful enough to set beside God's own works. This is something understood by all Moslems without discussion or the necessity of speech; it is a very different attitude to ours towards similar works. The making of a beautiful thing is all-important; since beauty is axiomatically necessary to its existence, it is not held to be a quality of intrinsic worth or merit. If the object should be preserved it will be for other considerations than its intrinsic beauty, though these reasons for preserving it will sustain satisfaction in its beauty. The decline of a beautiful thing will be mourned because of the circumstances that cause its decline; hence things were restored in good times, but left to disintegrate in bad ones. It is not true to say that if a tile falls from a roof it does so at the will of God, but it may well be that it is His will which prevents a man from being able to replace it. Which digression does not explain why Ali's venerable fountain was done away with.

Koubba el-Baroudiyin
Map 6.
This sturdy, two-storeyed and domed kiosk is all that survives of the annexes to Ali's mosque, with which it was contemporary. It is arguably the most important building in Morocco. It shelters a *water-basin* for ablutions and formerly stood in the *mida* courtyard surrounded by cubicles and lavatories. Possibly the work of Spanish builders, its appearance is deceptively simple. Large arches at ground-level — twin horse-shoes in either longer side and scalloped ones in the ends — are set in plain, recessed rectangular panels; these are multiplied on the second storey to

small horse-shoe arches alternating with ones of a curious keyhole-shape and others with scalloped edges — all of them set in broken rectangular recesses; stepped machicolations, again more numerous than the upper arches, crown the façades while behind them rises a dome decorated with a strong relief of interlaced arches topped with the zigzag pattern of a seven-pointed star. This is a design in which complexity increases with height upon an almost coldly mathematical progression made brilliant by the way its own rules are broken; the same principle is seen again in the decoration of the Koutoubia minaret. The interior decoration of the dome, based upon two levels of intersecting arches, is again exceedingly complicated, while a most luxuriantly carved *relief* of foliage and 'shell' motives (these look like rococo shells but are really palmettes — fan-like forms based on the spreading fronds of palms) lends it a baroque voluptuousness quite unlike the taste one might expect of Saharan zealots, yet one in which strength is so apparent that it seems, too, an unexpected offspring, as it undoubtedly was, of the style of el-Andalus. Only discovered in 1947, this small building is one of the finest examples of Maghrebi work in existence; with justification, Deverdun claims it is unsurpassed in Moslem art.

Casbah Mosque
Inside the Bab Aguenau (Map 15).
The second-oldest Almohad foundation, this mosque was built by Yaacub el-Mansur between 1185 and 1190, when he built the present casbah to replace the Almoravid one. The disastrous explosion of a gunpowder magazine in 1569 severely damaged it and the Saadi Moulay Abdullah restored it. Along with almost everything else in the city, Sidi Mohammed ben Abdullah had again extensively to restore it in the eighteenth century. None the less this beautiful and rather eccentric building conserves its original form and much Almohad fabric. In plan it derives from the Fatimid mosque at el-Mahdiya in Tunisia, though no reason is known why it should have departed so much from local tradition. If it had any special and local significance, this too is unfathomable. It set no precedent later to be followed; yet it has always been much admired and equally highly esteemed by the Marrakchi as the Koutoubia itself.

Occupying a square, the plan has a central axis running from the great *north gate* to the *mihrab*. The *prayer-hall* is, like

Damascus, only three aisles deep, those of the *quibla* and the short stem of the T being wider than the others. There are eleven longitudinal aisles ranged across the width of the building. The five central aisles open to the *sahn* proper; the two flanking them on either side open to rectangular spaces surrounded by arched arcades open to the sky. These have the width of the two aisles and a depth of three. These spaces are matched by two more occupying the northern corners of the court, the two pairs being separated from one another by roofed structures of an aisle's width. The first and eleventh aisles are carried along the whole length of the building and roofed. Another roofed arcade runs along the north wall; it occupies the eleventh lateral subdivision of the mosque's total area. A *dome* over the sanctuary is balanced by another over the north gate and by two on either southern corner. The *minaret* stands off the north-west corner. The plan incorporates a large number of chambers in the outer walls, north, west and east, opening outwards only. Four doors now give access where originally there were seven, while another beside the *mihrab* led through the *royal cemetery* to the palace. The cemetery contains the *Saadian tombs* (see below). The *mihrab* is a deep, polygonal one; its rounded arch is decorated with scalloped relief supported by four jasper columns ending in Ommayed capitals. The doors flanking this niche have similar columns. Though these features may have been to some extent remade, their general likeness to those at Tinmel causes one chagrin that they should be invisible.

The exterior, with its heavy and elaborate brick entablature and exceptionally fine *minaret* with green-tiled band and trenchant lantern, is well worth careful looking at. The minaret at least set a precedent with its beautiful *relief-decoration* of interlaced figures that has a texture almost as rich as damask.* The gilded *bronze balls* surmounting it share the legends with those on the Koutoubia minaret. Thomas Pellew of Falmouth who was for

---

* Recent restoration has dimmed this damascene effect. The minaret looks brand-new. In fact we now see it as it was built; it no longer looks old. The same treatment has been given the minaret of the Ben Salih mosque but after strong protests the Koutoubia minaret was 'spared' from such drastic restoration. But what is it that we want to see, a patina of decay that we recognize as old or the building which the builders built? These are scrupulous restorations made in a traditional manner – fresh weathering will give them back that patina which, emotionally rather than rationally, we cherish – and after the first shock of seeing these towers so very renewed I think one must be glad of them.

some years a slave here early in the eighteenth century had hopes to steal them.

A Merinid *medrassa* attached to this mosque and once famous for its size and beauty has disappeared.

Saadi Necropolis
Map **16**.

Lying at the back of the Casbah Mosque, this royal graveyard was discovered in 1917 and we owe it to Marshal Lyautey's curiosity that we may see it, an entrance that does not pass through the mosque having been made for him. For this reason we follow a path round the main construction, between it and the high wall built to surround the cemetery by the Saadi themselves.

The site had previously been used for interment and after the death of his father, Mohammed esh-Sheikh (1557), Abdullah el-Ghalib built a small, square *koubba* over his grave. Between 1591 and 1598, el-Ghalib having died, as also his brother and successor Abd el-Malik, the third brother, Ahmed el-Mansur, built a *pavilion* around the *koubba* that principally consisted of a larger chamber set in front of it, though linked to the wall of the mosque by two very beautiful, arched side-entrances. This is the farther away of the two buildings as you enter the graveyard. Mohammed's grave lies in the centre of what is now the inner chamber. The outer chamber is named after Ahmed's mother, Lalla Masuda, who, dying in 1591, was buried there.

Ahmed may have intended his own grave to have been there also, but since its decoration is incomplete, he seems to have changed his mind and to have built the larger *mausoleum* instead. This is on the left as you emerge into the enclosure. It has two entrances, the nearest at hand giving into a small *prayer-hall* with a *mihrab* on the left and a *lantern* supported by four pillars in the centre. This was probably not originally intended to contain graves as now it does. Leading from it is the '*Chamber of the Twelve Columns*' — those which uphold the dome that roofs the room — into which we can see from the garden by what was originally a window and not the entrance it appears to be. Beyond this again is a smaller chamber containing three niches. At the centre of the colonnade lies Ahmed (he died of the plague at Fes and was brought back here). Beside him are two of his sons and successors — Abdullah and Mohammed esh-Sheikh II — and the third, Zaydan, lies between the colonnade and the inner chamber. Sixty-six of the Saadi are buried under these two shelters and over

a hundred more lie outside them. Yet this sunny corner shaded by
a few trees and dignified by the two restrained buildings suggests
content and happiness rather than sorrow. The Moresque sense
of balance between plain surfaces and decorated, an almost
saccharine richness of texture contrasted with flatness — exuberance sternly disciplined; a masterly restraint bending to a deep
joy in colour — can be seen here at its most refined.

I think more space is needed to allow these contrasts to be seen
at their most pleasurable; here the delight is in intricacy and fine
balance. We are not used to this attitude towards the use of
colour. If we are to enjoy it we must make the effort to forget our
own terms of definite, chosen colour stated by wash and contrast,
and instead let the pointilliste effect of the seemingly busy,
polychromatic designs merge into their sum, which is an un-
mixable tint — a mood almost more than a colour — extremely
sensitive to the effect of light. The decoration of the square
Chamber of the Twelve Columns, combined with this glaze of
mood and light, renders it seemingly a rotunda. This is not a
theatrical effect, but an extreme refinement of the use of decoration to induce an emotional response.

If Ahmed el-Mansur's el-Badi Palace was half so beautiful as
this mausoleum it must have fully deserved its legendary fame.
There is far too much detail to extol and describe, but see as far as
you can into the dome over old Mohammed's tomb, look at the
lettering on walls, plaques and chiselled gravestones; remark the
ivoried patina on the marble.

When found, the place had been neglected since some time
after the mad sultan Moulay el-Yazid was buried in the balus-
traded tomb in the prayer-hall in 1792; semi-ruinous, it has
been restored with a skill that does credit to modern Moroccan
craftsmen.

Mosque of ben Salih
Off the Derb de Bashi, on the north (Map 7).
This mosque was built by the Merinid sultan Abu Saïd Uthman
between 1318 and 1321 in association with the tomb of a saintly
butcher called Sidi Mohammed ben Salih. Nothing factual is
known of ben Salih though it was said of him that he could lead 'a
double life', presumably in the sense of being in two places at
once.

From the outside, the mosque's chief attraction is the delightful
minaret (now restored; see note on p. 215) which combines the

interlaced relief of the Casbah minaret with windows reminiscent of that of the Koutoubia. Brilliant green faience, inset as a background to the relief, lightens the whole effect. Its roofs and the white doorway leading to a passageway off which the main, axial gateway opens make a charming effect.

Beside the minaret, an unengaged roof belongs to a *funerary hall* next to the saint's tomb which, itself, is incorporated in the north-west angle of the arcaded *sahn*. The shallow *prayer-hall* of the Casbah mosque reappears here (though not the divided *sahn*). The arch over the white gate mirrors the form of the internal arches, a light, elegant variation of the Almohad theme, and the only decoration inside is that which frames the *mihrab*. This resembles those in the contemporary *medersa* at Fes: the el-Attarine and the one in the Dar el-Makhzen.

Great Mosque el-Mouassine
Derb el-Mouassine — beyond the dyers' market (Map 8).
Visiting Marrakech twice between 1511 and 1515, Leo Africanus described the ruin into which it had fallen: two-thirds uninhabited, cultivation only within the walls because outside the nomads pillaged everything, birds nesting on library shelves, a half-dozen students only in all the town and one ignorant teacher, part only of the palace 'still habitable'. Twelve years later the city came into Saadi hands and they were presently able to rebuild it to be their capital. None the less it was sixty years before they could do any great works there. It was Abdullah el-Ghalib who did the most, spending so much on his buildings that people believed he had discovered how to transmute base metal into gold. A new dynasty ruling a reunified country reaping great harvests of peace, the Saadi thought they had come to stay; they felt they had succeeded where others had failed and were filled with a desire to start things over anew. Abdullah's mosque was built to epitomize this. It was to rival the huge Mameluk mosque complexes in Cairo — mosque, *medrassa*, bath, Koranic school, lodgings for the officers of the mosque, lavatorial *mida* and fountain. The building was performed during the decade following the early 1560s; the story is that a Jewish area that included a cemetery was cleared to make room for all this, and thus the mosque was of doubtful sanctity. The name el-Mouassine is enigmatic: local lore claims it to be the name of a sherifian family formerly resident near by; Daverdun suggests it may be a corruption of 'cutlers', the occupation of the ousted Jews; it used

to be known as 'the sherifs' mosque', but these could be the Saadi themselves. A slight stigma of public disfavour has always clung to it.

The mosque is a very large one with a great *sahn* and a deep *prayer-hall* built on the T-plan. For a symbol of a new era it is curiously full of derivative and archaistic features. The way the *sahn* is enclosed by arcades extending the side-aisles and the mathematics of the axial plan somewhat recall the Casbah mosque. Three domes over the arcade on the north of the *sahn*, counter-pointing those over the central aisle, represent the only Saadian innovation. The *mihrab* copies that of the Casbah, as does the *mimber*. The glories of the building are the *ceilings* of carved cedarwood held aloft by high and noble arches. The three *doorways* are genuinely beautiful and unostentatious. The plain *minaret* is oddly short; the story being that had it been taller it would have overlooked the women's quarters of the vizier's house.

The *fountain* has three bays, two for animals and an elaborate and beautiful one for human use. The *bath* exists; you can see its octagonal dome but may not use it. The very dull *medrassa* may be of a later date. The *mida* has a very pretty kiosk obviously modelled on the Almoravid Koubba el-Baroudiyin.

Mosque of Bab Doukkala
Inside the gate of the same name (Map 5).
That Ahmed el-Mansur was fond of his mother is plain from the tomb he built for her (see above). It is pleasant to realize that she was a lady of so strong a character that she emerges from the obscurity both of the harem and the past. Her two passions were travellers and the city of Marrakech, and she built lodgings for travellers in the city, paved streets, made bridges and, beginning in 1558, built this rather smaller version of the el-Mouassine complex.* The mosque acknowledges its model's debt to older traditions but creates something very much more typically Saadi out of them. It also makes an interesting and successful innovation: by widening the first lateral aisle (the nearest to the *sahn*) to equal the *quibla*- and central aisles, the usual T-plan is converted to an H set on its side. This arrangement makes the first lateral aisle into a kind of vestibule between the prayer-hall and the *sahn*. This looks well on the plan and is said greatly to enhance

---

* She had accompanied her sons during their educative exile at Istanbul.

what is a notably beautiful interior rich in the intricate decoration of its main arches, cupolas and sumptuous *mihrab*. The slender *minaret* shows its obvious debt to the Koutoubia, the Casbah and the ben Salih. It is of perhaps rather later construction than the rest of the building. The north-east wall of the mosque between the minaret and the main door has had to be buttressed and an *arcade* has been built between the piers of the buttresses. The arches of this arcade have been decorated in imitation of the decoration of the First Koutoubia's exterior (see p. 207).

The *medrassa* is a ruin; a *Koranic school* exists still; the *mida* is charming and the *fountain*, which is based on that of the el-Mouassine and perhaps built rather later than the mosque, is even more beautifully made.

Zawiya of Sidi bel-Abbes and Zawiya of Sidi ben Sliman el-Jazouli
In the northern tip of the walls and south-west of Sidi bel-Abbes, respectively (Map 1 and 2).

Among the many tombs of saints, oratories and sacred institutions in the city these two great centres are the most important. A *zawiya* is a cult centre. Its precedent is the Prophet's own house at Medina — the place where the teacher lived and his followers congregated, where his disciples who accepted his discipline also lodged and where the whole group prayed together. The influence of a *zawiya* exactly matches that of the master who founds it, and this depends on his ability to capture the public's imagination. There are hundreds of *zouawi* over the country, very few having more than a local influence and a score or so only whose appeal has persisted very long after the founder's death, on a national scale at any rate. If the founder's reputation is such that his cult persists to become an enduring one, the *zawiya* may come to resemble a Christian monastery. These two have become institutions of this kind.

Undoubtedly the troublous conditions into which Morocco has lapsed almost as often as it has been well governed and stable have encouraged the establishment of *zouawi* and enhanced their importance, cult discipline very often providing the social order which feeble government failed to ensure. This is true of orthodox, reformatory cults like the Almoravid and Almohad equally as of sufistic, mystic and heretical ones. But the cults have always intimated a challenge to established government. However a dynasty might arrive at power, it soon became strictly orthodox since orthodoxy upholds the sultan's throne by regarding him as imam and the very existence of a cult implies criticism of the sultan as effectual imam — or used to.

Sidi bel-Abbes was born a potter's son in Ceuta, in 1145. Apprenticed to a weaver, he proved instead a religious zealot and scholar. When he was twenty years old he moved to Gueliz and established there a kind of hermitage. Forty years later Yaacub el-Mansur invited him into the city and provided him with facilities for teaching and lodgings for his vast family, probably in the old casbah. He appears to have belonged to that tiresome kind of holy man who for ever berates everyone else, but he was a passionate extorter of charity, particularly on behalf of the blind — so much so that his ghost is still believed nightly to haunt the terrace of the Koutoubia minaret until every blind person in the city has been fed. A distribution of food is made every evening at the *zawiya* and the blind beggars congregated there make a Breughelian sight. El-Mansur's act in bringing Sidi bel-Abbes into the city was doubtless a move to control him and the movement he inspired. The saint was by then prophesying with success and working miracles and presently the sultan himself was forced at least to pay him lip service; yet when he died his cult does not seem to have prospered. Even his tomb to the north of the city, in the cemetery of Sidi Marwan, was lost. However, his legend persisted, the cult revived and so considerable a sanctuary and *zawiya* spread over the cemetery that some time in the second half of the eighteenth century Sidi Mohammed extended the circuit of the walls to enclose it in the city. To Sidi Moham- med, too, are due the present buildings — *mosque, medrassa* and other appurtenances grouped round the *mausoleum* of the saint which Moulay Ismaïl built over the hypothetical tomb. Both the mosque and the *medrassa* had originally been built by Abu Faris, Ahmed-el-Mansur's son, in 1605, though even then they must have replaced earlier buildings.

Marrakech has seven patron saints. The most influential period for the *zouawi* was the decline of the Saadi dynasty, and when Moulay Ismaïl tackled the pacification of the country he realized that he must placate the sentiment behind the maraboutic movement. He also wished considerably to diminish the popular appeal of the Seven Saints of the Regraga — 'Companions of the Prophet' they were called — whose month-long festival drew many thousands of potential dissidents from all over the country. Groups of seven saints were common over the country; their origin is obscure but they may stem from the seven Christian Sleepers of Ephesus. According to popular belief the Marrakchi group, laid together under small tombstones, were septuplets. Upon the basis of their legend Ismaïl created a pilgrimage to the sanctuaries of seven among the multitude of Marrakchi saints whom he nominated Patrons. Although the festival has fallen much into disuse now, it was immediately successful and that it was so throws an odd light on the pious of the times: what the sultan ordained was in itself sufficiently holy to mask the political contrivance involved, while the honour done to the chosen saints and the town (and the commercial opportunities a pilgrimage offered) were immediately acceptable. A circuit of the sanctuaries, rather like that of the Basilicas in Rome, was made the foundation of the pilgrimage.

During a week, the faithful visited the sanctuaries or *zouawi* of Sidi Yussef ben Ali, Caïd Iyad, Sidi bel-Abbes, Sidi ben Sliman, Sidi Abd el-Aziz, Sidi el-Ghazwani and Sidi es-Suhayli. Sidi bel-Abbes was the chief patron.

Sultan Moulay Suleiman, a convert to the Wahabi sect, denounced the cult of the Seven Patrons because, though they had served Ismaïl well, they presently became the objects of an unorthodox idolatry. The honour in which they are still held perhaps owes a good deal to the pilgrimage, but it is far less extreme than formerly. Ismaïl's choice of saints was a careful one related to the current political situation. All were Arabs and in this unlike the Berbers of the Regraga. Three were scholars famous over all Islam. He ignored Yussef ibn Tashfin, the founder of the city who, it is true, was a Berber. (His popularity continues, however, to be such that although his tomb has been lost for centuries the Marrakchi have appropriated another by which to do him homage, not far from the Koutoubia.)

Sidi Mohammed ben Sliman el-Jazouli posed a different problem to Sidi bel-Abbes. He came from the far south where he had been born towards the end of the fourteenth century. He was a scholar and may well have been a sherif, as he claimed. He became one of the great maraboutic leaders against the Portuguese and his cult was spread over the country through very many *zouawi* founded in his name. He died in 1465, perhaps of poison since he was a thorn in the flesh of the sultans, and in death caused quarrels over the possession of his remains until at last Achmed el-Araj brought them to Marrakech and built a fine *mausoleum* for them. Achmed hoped to attach some of the saint's glory to the

Saadi dynasty and when he and his seven sons were murdered to secure the succession for his brother Abdullah they were all buried in the sheltering lee of el-Jazouli's tomb, a daughter who survived building a *koubba* over their graves. El-Jazouli had not shown them protection in life and the later Saadi seem to have abandoned any claim to his patronage. The *zawiya* that grew up round the tomb soon became a nest of maraboutic influence, largely directed against the established government. Though Ismaïl did not make el Jazouli a patron of the city, he tried to harness the cult to the throne by putting the sanctuary in good repair, while Sidi Mohammed ben Abdullah rebuilt the *zawiya*, as he did that of Sidi bel-Abbes also. The two patrons Sidi Abd el-Aziz and Sidi el-Ghazwani were both followers of el-Jazouli.

PALACES

El-Badi Palace
Eastern casbah (Map 14).
This was built by Ahmed el-Mansur from 1578 and was still in course of final beautification in 1602, the year before his death. Its name means 'the incomparable' and in its day it appears to have merited such a description. Now it is a stately brick ruin, its parterres replanted with trees and very many storks' nests crowning its walls. The plan is described on p. 129, where other remarks are made about it also. Moulay Ismaïl began to dismantle it in 1696, most probably more because its marbles and other valuable materials (the marbles from Italy and other things from as far away as India) were useful for the decoration of his new palace at Meknes than from any spite for his predecessor. The ruin now forms a fine setting for the exciting annual Festival of Folk-lore, generally held in June.

In order to raise the level of the five pools in the courtyard so that their waters might irrigate the parterres and garden, the whole of this building is raised upon a substructure of vaults; the trees do not grow in sunken plots, it is the pools and pavements that are raised above ground-level. The court is 135 metres long by 110 metres across. The pools were lined with coloured tiles; a fountain formed by an upper and lower basin played on the island in the centre of the great pool. Columns were the main theme of the building: galleries of them were ranged over the faces of the pavilions at either end of the long pool and by the entrance to the three main rooms or pavilions facing its either side. There were possibly towers at each corner; that on the north-east alone seems to have contained an airy belvedere reached by a staircase. Both pavilions and either *liwan* facing the centre of the pool had names: that leading to the garden was called 'the crystal', as was the garden below, or 'the golden'; the pavilion to the west, where the sultan positioned himself on ceremonial occasions, was called 'the fifty' after the columns surrounding it; the northern *liwan* was called 'the green' — the colour of Islam — and the southern 'the Hayzouran' after the sultan's favourite, a Negress who was the mother of the two sons who succeeded him.

All descriptions of the splendour that was once here fall into amazed superlatives at its richness in jasper, gold and marble. Ahmed asked Elizabeth of England to prospect for granite columns in Ireland, but no monoliths large enough to satisfy his ambitions could be found. Another feature constantly repeated in the decorative scheme was secular poetry, verses being inscribed on many surfaces. As an indication of what el-Badi meant to its creator, we have an account of the house-warming party he gave for it. All the great of the kingdom were called upon to attend and were served food on gold plate and porcelain from China; each man was given a present big as a bribe. Ahmed asked his jester what he thought of the palace; the jester replied that it would make a fine ruin. It does.

Among the rooms on the north is one with an original *painted ceiling* where some salvaged antiquities of merit are housed. These include a fine early *mimber*.

'La Bahia' Palace
North of the old Mellah (Map 12).
Open Daily, except Tuesday, from 09.30 to 12.00 and from 14.30 to 17.30.

Begun by the Grand Vizier Si' Musa, who served Sidi Mohammed II, and enormously extended by his son Abu Ahmed who was vizier to Hassan and Abd el-Aziz, this is mostly a late-nineteenth-century creation. Properly called el-Bahia, its name means 'the brilliant'. This overstates its claim to fame, for it is shoddily built, tastelessly designed, hideously decorated for the most part and lacking any plan. Only Si' Musa's great *court* and the *garden-rooms* beside it have any distinction. These remind one of contemporary Turkish miniatures in their delicacy and frivolity; the court is really pretty. Ba-Hmed* turned the whole

---

* Ba-Hmed = Abu Achmed in Marrakci dialect; otherwise known as 'bu Ahmed.

quarter upside down as he acquired neighbouring properties to incorporate into this rambling house, building across streets and making many of them into culs-de-sac. Short, fat and shorter than normal in the leg, he found stairs a difficulty to him — so he eschewed upper floors. When he died in 1900, the sultan, returning from his grand funeral, pillaged the palace. And that was that.

If there is not much aesthetic pleasure to be got out of visiting 'la Bahia', it is nevertheless an oddity that has a twisted kind of charm.

Dar Si'Saïd (Museum of Moroccan Arts)
Map 11.
Open Daily, except Tuesday, from 09.30 to 12.00 and from 14.30 to 17.30.

This large and sometimes pleasant house was built towards the end of the nineteenth century by Sidi Saïd, brother of Ba-Hmed who enlarged the more pretentious 'la Bahia' Palace. Though wanting in intelligence, Saïd was also a vizier, to Moulay Hassan.

The collection forming the museum is of real interest. Many of the objects it contains are of a considerable age and fine quality — often startlingly so when they are compared to that of the workmanship displayed in the design and decoration of their setting.

Dar el-Makhzen (Royal Palace)
Map 17.
Although one may not visit this or see much of it over the high walls encircling it, curiosity is aroused about it. It was built by the wise Sidi Mohammed ben Abdullah who began it in 1747, while he was still his father's viceroy, starting at its northern end lying immediately south of el-Badi Palace. Sidi Mohammed was a great builder and, as is typical of his kind, died while still in the midst of further projects and uncompleted works. This is the only example remaining in Morocco of a classic Arab palace in plan — symmetrical, balanced, harmonious and based upon a great central garden, the *Arsat en-Nil*. Rather surprisingly, Deverdun suggests its architect was either the renegade Englishman el-Inglis, or Idriss, a great court official who is believed to have been Austrian born. By all accounts it is still a very beautiful building despite later and tactless additions and alterations.

WALLS

These were built to replace the thorn stockade originally surrounding the settlement by the Almoravid sultan Ali ben Yussef, between 1126 and 1127. Though much repaired and rebuilt, the line they follow has hardly changed since. Additions to the enceinte have been small save where the palace quarter has been extended to include the vast Agdal Gardens to the south. The long line of ramparts on the west that borders the Avenue el-Yarmouk is almost all of original workmanship. The drive round the city is an agreeable one and impressive, particularly on the eastern side. If you make it you should stop to look at the inner faces of the gates as well as the exteriors. *Bab* means door, gate or gateway.

Bab Doukkala

This imposing gate with heavy, unequal *towers* is now only Almoravid, but preserves its original plan even to the cornered defensive passage through it *en baïonnette*.

Bab el-Makhzen

This gate led into the Almoravid casbah and may have been that reserved for the sultans' use. It was once very strong but was dismantled under the Merinids. The present structure is more recent still.

Bab er-Rob

The angle of the walls here comprises an Almohad extension of the town. The plan of the gate dates it as a contemporary with the extension, 1185. It is named for raisin juice which, extracted under pressure, was made into a syrup used as a wine substitute. This gate leads into both the medina and the casbah, through inner gates, and is one of the few points at which the one could be reached from the other.

Bab Aguenau

Most beautiful of the gates, it lies behind the above and now gives access to the town though formerly it was the ceremonial gate into the Almohad casbah. It was built at the end of the twelfth century by Yaacub el-Mansur, of blue Gueliz stone carved in low relief. It was upon this gate that the heads of rebels were usually exposed, though sometimes they were mounted on the Bab er-Rob. The gate has recently been restored.

Bab el-Ksiba
Not an original gate, this leads to a small casbah lying south-west of the site of the *ksar* or casbah that Yaacub el-Mansur built in the twelth century.

Bab Igli
This comparatively modern gate leads to the *mechouars* beside the palace. Should you be making a tour of the walls this is the place to enter the Agdal Gardens before going farther.

Bab Ahmar
This remarkably well-fortified gate was built under Sidi Mohammed and was perhaps designed by a renegade known as el-Inglis — the Englishman. It now leads into the courts and *mechouars* of the palace though formerly into the compound or quarter where the black troops were housed. A sacred jujube tree grew within the gate and the little houses of the soldiers were clustered around it.

Bab Aghmat
This gate has been much rebuilt since the Almoravids first erected it and the disaffected Christian regiment opened it to the Almohad besiegers in 1147. Unlike any other of the gates, the passage does not lie between the twin bastions, but through one itself.

Bab Aylen
This is thought to retain its Almoravid plan and is probably also the one whose appearance has changed the least. When they attempted the city in 1130, the Almohads suffered a bloody defeat before it. Inside it stands the *mausoleum of Ali esh-Sheikh*, ancestor of the Alaouite dynasty, and other tombs of the same family — Moulay Suleiman and Sidi Mohammed II (ben Abd er-Rahman) among them.

Bab ed-Debbagh
The tanners' gate; Almoravid, though much rebuilt. Its present shape is not that of the original.

The *Tanneries* inside it are of equally ancient origin. Like those of Fes, they form a curiously beautiful sight, smeared with various colours and peopled by lithe and furiously active men. Their trade is practised exactly as it has always been, the many small establishments being co-operatives. The smell of the neighbourhood is nauseous, but after the first moment of horror surprisingly easy to ignore.

Bab el-Khemis ('Gate of the Thursday market'; formerly Fes Gate)

Built by the Almoravids, it has been remade; its twisting passage is now straight.

Bab Taghzout

This now lies within the northern tip of the city but marks the position of the Almoravid wall. The small quarter north of it was walled around in the eighteenth century so as to enclose the Zawiya of Sidi bel-Abbes (p. 220). The gate has been much reconstructed.

GARDENS

Marrakech has always been a city of gardens. The shallow basin in which it lies is irrigated by *khettara*, remarkable underground conduits, into which wells are sunk, bringing water from a considerable distance. They were built by Ali ben Yussef early in the twelfth century, on the model of some Saharan oasis irrigation works. These allow the palmery and surrounding cultivation to exist and still to some extent water the town, though supplementary supplies were later brought by pipe or aqueduct from the streams flowing down from the mountains. All this meant there was always water to spare for the gardens, which are a chief delight to desert people like the founders of the city. Gardens may be a status symbol to Arab plainsmen and tentmen but most of all they are a source of sheer, unaffected pleasure. In the Koran, after asking the Faithful to attend to their prayers and pay the alms tax, God (in a practical mood) says, 'If you believe in my Apostles and assist them and give Allah a generous loan, I shall forgive your sins and admit you to gardens watered by running streams' — which is to say, into Paradise.

The Marrakech gardens have often enough been abandoned left to run wild or to dry up as the tribes outside the walls stole the water. They have been built over or been made in areas where a quarter has been abandoned through lack of population; some have been several times remade. None of the important ones existing at present date from before the middle of the eighteenth century although some are replantings of older ones. Only those that one can visit are described here.

Agdal Gardens
Map **19**.

These were planted by Abd er-Rahman after he had reasserted the royal claim to the waters of the Ourika that had for long been traditionally stolen by the tribes. The largest of the two great *pools* is, however, probably of Almohad construction and last repaired some time after 1844 when the smaller pool was also built. Nowadays it is an immense walled olive-yard and orchard rather than a pleasance or garden in our flowery sense, a wonderfully big, shady, peaceful place where the huge sheets of water have a magical stillness and the terrace of the pavilion of the water-side *Dar el-Hana*, once a pyrotechnics factory, over-looks a liberating view. This is a strange and lovely place to find tacked on to a bustling city.

The *Dar el-Baïda*, to the north-west of the Agdal enclosure (*Map* **18**), has been renovated. It had been a summerhouse built by Mohammed II which Moulay Hassan very much enlarged for the use of his womenfolk in the late nineteenth century. It has since served as a hospital.

Outside the walls of the Agdal, themselves defensible, on the west stands a low artillery fort. This is the *Sqallet el-Mrabit* which Mohammed II built to defend the gardens against the tribesmen.

Mamounia Gardens
Map **13**.

These (among which the renowned Hôtel Mamounia is built) were possibly laid out in late Saadian times although their name is that of a prince who died about 1785 and who was an Alaouite. The charming *pavilion* at the crossing of the main paths dates from the reign of Sidi Mohammed ben Abdullah in the second half of the eighteenth century.

Menara Gardens
Map **20**.

The enormous and much-photographed *reservoir* that is the chief feature of this olive-garden was originally built by the Almohads. It is known that there was a Saadi pavilion beside it, but it was Sidi Mohammed II who reconstructed the pool and built a new pavilion there. The building bears the date 1869/70 (by our calendar). It is not a distinguished building, yet its effect in that setting is tranquil and happy. The ground floor is for service and the upper for pleasure — everything is just as it should be for a delightful and comfortable picnic. Deverdun says of it, 'The Menara restates in classic terms the imperial Moroccan garden where the prince's pleasure is intermixed with utility, royal luxury with rustic freedom.'

Excursions from Marrakech

AMIZMIZ AND TAMESLOCHT

These are described on p. 333 in connection with the S501 road across the Tizi n'Test pass from Taroudant. This is the road which continues to Tinmel to which, if rather distant perhaps, it is still very worth while making a day's excursion to see the ruined Almohad mosque there. It is described on p. 331.

OURIKA VALLEY AND OUKAÏMEDEN

Route (Route Exit E) 67 km. to Setti Fatma at the head of the Ourika Valley. Oukaïmeden is reached by branching right from the road to Setti Fatma at 43.5 km on to the 6035. The S513 and 6035 roads are subject to flooding and landslips in stormy weather, though road gangs clear them very quickly. [See Route Map for Western Area (pp. 314–15).]
Bus Infrequent buses from the Djemaa el-Fna.

It is very well worth while to make the excursion up the Ourika Valley. It provides a delightfully sylvan contrast with the comparative barren-ness of the Haouz Plain and the town, the greenness of the landscape and the river trickling along the valley making this an ideal spot for a picnic afternoon away from Marrakech.

Oukaïmeden provides winter sports; this ski-ing resort has been developing in recent years.

[33 km.] **Dar Caïd Ouriki**.

Overlooked by an old *ksar* and under the shade of pepper trees, a delightful Monday market is held here — left of the road. The site of ancient **Aghmat** lies to the north of here; there is scarcely anything to be seen. Mention of the city is made on p. 77

[43.5 km.] The second right-hand turn leads to **Oukaïmeden**. The road climbs with many a twist, giving marvellous views over the mountains and plain to this ski resort, which is reached 28.5 km. after you branch off the Ourika Valley road.

Hotels
***B *Hôtel Imlil* (tel. 03).
  **B *Auberge Chez Juju* (tel. 05).
Skis can be hired at the shops by *Chez Juju*.

The easiest to see of all the interesting Moroccan prehistoric rock carvings are here: close to the Refuge du Service de la Jeunesse et des Sports, the Refuge du Club Alpin and near the base of the tele-ski.

[50 km.] Back on the Ourika Valley road, *Irhef* village lies on the right. 2 km. from the village there is a *refuge* at 1,300 metres.

[52 km.]

Hotels
****B *Hôtel Ourika* (tel. Arhbalou 04).
   **B *Auberge Ramuntcho* (tel. Arhbalou 118).

4 km. higher and across the stream there is a mule-path which, with a number of scrambles, some of a mile or more, leads to a wealth of prehistoric *rock carvings*. To see them you will need a guide and a two-day excursion with food and bedding-roll, returning by the Ouarzazate road — more of an archaeologist's than an ordinary tourist's expedition. J. Malhomme, *Corpus des gravures rupestres du Grand Atlas* (Publications du Service des antiquités du Maroc, Rabat, 1959 and 1961) gives the information an amateur will want.

[67 km.] *A *Hôtel La Chaumière*.

[67 km.] **Setti Fatma** — village and *zawiya* lying at 1,500 metres.
From here it is quite possible to climb onwards across the *National Park of Jebel Toubkal*, rising to 3,200 metres, to **Timichi** and **Tacheddirt** villages (10 and 20 km.) and another 10 km. to **Tamatert** and **Imlil**, which is 17 km. from **Asni** on the Taroudant road. There is a *refuge* near Tacheddirt. Across the valley from **Setti Fatma**, the female marabout of the same name is commemorated by an August moussem. Hiking is very popular in the *National Park* and the ascent of Mt Toubkal itself not problema-

tic or terribly exacting physically. However, go prepared, well clad and shod, equip yourself with a 1:50,000 survey sheet and local knowledge from Imlil, where guides and mules can be hired and through which other hikers generally pass. The approach by road is described on page 333. Serious climbing should be undertaken with up to date information from the British Mountaineering Council and reference should be made to Roger Collomb's 'Atlas Mountains Guide'.

ESSAOUIRA

The easiest place from Marrakech to get sea-bathing is Essaouira. The 171 km. journey can be made in 2 hours by car. See p. 322.

AGADIR

A new road (259 km.) allows fast travel to this seaside resort and, at about 2½ hours' driving time, it might now be considered as an excursion from Marrakech: see p. 334.

MARRAKECH TO FES

Route (via Beni Mellal) 485 km. by the P 24, a good road. You can make the journey in one not too strenous day. Leave Marrakech by the Avenue Mohammed V. At the Café Renaissance corner turn east along the Boulevard Mohammed Zerktouni and follow the signposts thereafter (Route Exit A).

An alternative route from Marrakech to Fes may be taken by travelling from Marrakech to Ouarzazate (see pp. 336–41), thence to Er Rachidia (see pp. 346–8) and from Er Rachidia to Fes via Midelt (see pp. 365–7). [See Route Map for Western Area (pp. 314–5) and Route Map for Eastern Area (pp. 362–3).]

Bus A dawn start is recommended if you intend to complete the eleven-hour journey in one stage; otherwise break your journey at Beni Mellal or Kasba Tadla. There are usually at least three buses daily on this route but they are often full.

Accommodation and food Hotels and restaurants at Beni Mellal, Kasba Tadla (simple lodging in three unclassified pensions), El-Ksiba, Zawiya des Aït-Sheikh, Khenifra, Azrou, Ifrane and Imouzzer du Kandar.

[55 km.] **Tamelelt** (Tuesday market).

[60 km.] A turning right for (59 km.) **Demnate**, a fine walled town of 10,000 inhabitants lying in a high, fertile valley. There is a Sunday market here worth seeing. The highly picturesque S508 leads on by Tannant and Azilal to the dam of Bine el-Ouidane (see below), whence the S508 A continues to Ouaouizarht.

[85 km.] **El-Kelaa des Srarhna** (Friday market) — partly walled village.

[123 km.] A turning right goes in 10 km. to **Bzou**, an oasis-like collection of villages about the valley of the Oued el-Abid. It stands in ancient olive-yards and orchards — there is a spring waterfall where women burn candles in small caves as fertility offerings and a sixteenth-century *zawiya* at **Aghbalou** village.

[176 km.] A turning on the right leads to **Afourer** and the Barrage of Bine el-Ouidane (see below). If you follow the S508 A north of the lake you can reach Ouaouizarht and so get back to the P24 12 km. before Beni Mellal.

[184 km.] A road on the right by Ouaouizarht to the *Barrage of Bine-el-Ouidane* (300 metres long and 130 metres high; producing 500 million kilowatts annually from two power-plants) and the great and beautiful lake which it has created on which ferry-boats ply daily except Saturday afternoons.

Hotel
  *A   *Auberge du Lac.*

A very bad track circles the east end of the lake to the marketplace of **Et-Tnine Aït Mazirth** (Mondays) and 68 km. more up the mountains to the '*Cathedral Rocks*' and the *Zawiya d'Ahnsal* — a dramatic road.

[196 km.] **Beni Mellal.**

Hotels
****B   *Hôtel Ouzoud*, Route de Marrakech (tel. 37.52).
****B   *Hôtel Chems*, 2 km. on the Route de Marrakech (tel. 34.60).
  **B   *Hôtel Gharnata*, Boulevard Mohammed V (tel. 34.82).
   *A   *Hôtel de Paris*, Nouvelle Medina (tel. 22.45).
   *A   *Hôtel du Vieux Moulin*, Route de Kasba Tadla (tel. 27.88).

Restaurants There are good restaurants here and it has become the traditional lunching-place between Marrakech and Fes.

The *casbah* dates from Ismaïl's reign, having been built in 1688, though often restored since. Now a growing town of at least 25,000 people, Beni Mellal's prosperity is modern and due to the fertility of the region made possible by the great dam of Bine el-Ouyidane (see above) and extensive irrigation-works. It is above all the centre of an increasingly prosperous agricultural district, a country market town, Friday being market day.

Near by, among gardens, stands the old *Zawiya of Sidi Achmed bel Kacem* whose minaret was built — according to local tradition — by Yussef ben Tashfin, the Almoravid; an indication rather of its venerability than of its architectural interest.

[226 km.] **Kasba Tadla**.

With 10,000 inhabitants, Kasba Tadla is a sizeable town. It stands sentinel over the approach from the plains to the upper valley of the Oum er-Rbia and owes its importance to Moulay Ismaïl who made his son Achmed ed-Dehbi governor in 1700. Ed-Dehbi was instructed to enlarge an old casbah here in which to house the 3,000 black troops he was given, but instead he built a new citadel — that noble, double-walled, many towered *castle* of almost orange stone that stands over the river. It encloses two *mosques* (the *minaret* of the eastern one of which is finely decorated with arabesques) and the *governor's palace*. Moulay Ismaïl used Kasba Tadla to overawe the tribes of the mountains, but his successors — lesser men — found it turned into a strong point against them. Moulay Sliman was defeated by the tribesmen here in 1818 and Moulay Hassan could not use this road from Fes to Marrakech, having to go round by the plains instead. You can visit the casbah and palace. The old *bridge* across the river also dates from Ismaïl's reign.

[248 km.] A turning right leads in 7 km. to **El-Ksiba**, an agreeable place with a Sunday market.

Hotel
**B *Hostelerie Henri IV* (tel. 2).
Camping *Taghbalout*

You can continue to Midelt, over what is a poor track from **Arhbala**, through wonderful country; or drive 104 km. to **Imilchil** where in September a moussem is held that is a famous marriage-market. Do not attempt the still farther 109 km. to Tinerhir (p. 347) through the High Atlas passes. If you are adequately supplied, this would make a glorious walk, however.

[264 km.] **Zawiya esh-Sheikh** (Wednesday and Saturday markets).

[290 km.] A road on the left goes in 3 km. to **Zawiya des Aït Isehak**. The Aït Isehak people claim direct descent from Moulay Ismaïl's black troops. The *zawiya* itself was an important centre of learning at which Moulay er-Rashid studied in his youth, tutored under the aegis of the marabouts of Djila whom, as sultan, he had to vanquish.

Hotel
***A   *Hôtel Transatlas* (tel. 30 via Khenifra).

[296 km.] The P33 — a good road with staggering views of the High Atlas — leads 121 km. right to Midelt.

[299 km.] **Maamar** (on the right), near which lie the ruins of the *zawiya* of the redoubtable marabouts of Djila (p. 96) whose power was broken and the *zawiya* destroyed by Moulay er-Rashid in 1668. *Sidi 'bu Beker's tomb* stands in the ruins of the *mosque*.

[302 km.] **Es-Sebt** (Saturday market-place).

[325 km.]. **Khenifra**.

Hotel
****A   *Hôtel Hamou* (tel. 60.20).

A town of 15,000 inhabitants in the valley of the Oum er-Rbia created by Moulay Ismaïl, who built a *bridge* defended by a *casbah* to make it an important link in the communications system of the interior. Moulay el-Hassan made the mistake of appointing Moha ou Hammou to be governor here towards the end of his reign. Moha built up the town, giving it a *mosque* and other amenities and attracting merchants to it, but he turned against the sultan's government, enrolled deserters in his private army and, under Abdul Aziz, preyed upon trading caravans over a wide area and raided even as far afield as Meknes. He refused to accept the French who, once they had captured the town in 1914, were extremely hard put to hold it. Until 1921 the garrison could be supplied only by strong and heavily armed columns, Khenifra has to this day a rather eccentric, gloomy air that is not unattractive.

From Khenifra it is possible to reach the Springs of Oum er-Rbia (see below).

[356 km.] **Mrirt** — a big Friday market. To the right, a road leads in 11 km. to **El-Hammam**, the centre of the Aït Segougou tribe noted for their carpets. The *casbah* is of the latter half of the nineteenth century. Tribal migrations are celebrated with fairs in the neighbourhood — ask the authorities for information about these.

[388 km.] **Assak n'Tatsa** (Sunday market).

The women wear distinctive white garments here.

[390 km.] A turning right for **Aîn Leuh**, 12 km. away, the picturesque village centre for the Beni Mguild with market-days on Mondays and Thursdays. By a track which should be avoided in bad weather you can go on to the beautiful *Springs of the Oum er-Rhia* cascading from a cliff.

[407 km.] **Azrou**.

Hotels
***B   *Hôtel Panorama* (tel. 20.10).
  *A   *Hôtel des Cèdres*, Place Mohammed V (tel. 23.26).
  *A   *Azrou Hôtel*, Route de Khenifra (tel. 21.16).

A summer and ski resort, but more of a town than neighbouring Ifrane, having 10,000 inhabitants. It is also an attractive place where green tiles are commonly used. The old and now dilapidated *casbah* was built in 1684 by Moulay Ismaïl. There is a good cooperative for carpet-weaving, the local designs being those of the Beni Mguild tribe, Friday is market-day and a sheep-fair is held in spring.

From Azrou you can make a detour of 43 km. to Ifrane by **Mischliffen** — a beautiful drive among the cedar forests of the region. There is a *refuge* at Mischliffen and a tele-ski up the *Jebel Hebri*.

From Azrou the P21 goes to Midelt and the Tafilelt (see p. 365).

The P21 also connects Azrou with Meknes. This is a pleasant drive of 69 km. of which the first 20 or more pass through very fine mountain-country. 38 km. along this route is **El-Hajeb**.

[424 km.] **Ifrane**.

Hotels
*****   *Hôtel Michlifen* (tel. 62.57).
  ***A   *Grand Hôtel*, Boulevard de la Poste (tel. 64.07).
  ***B   *Hôtel Perce Neige*, Rue des Asphodelles (tel. 63.50).
Camping *International*.

This is both a summer resort and a centre for ski-ing in winter. It lies in fine, forested country and is a modern, Frenchified place of bogus chalets. It is very pleasant, civilized and fashionable in summer, when the mountain air is cool and the sunshine hot. It makes a good centre for exploring all the Middle Atlas.

The vast château across the valley from the centre is the royal *Summer Palace* to which the court moves in high summer.

A scenically splendid 'circuit of the lakes' may be made either from here or from Imouzzer du Kandar (below). This is an excursion of 60 km. for which, unless you have a very good map, it will be best either to ask your hotel for a guide or to collect yourself a bright lad to act as one.

[441 km.] Right turn for **Dayet Aoua**, a series of picturesque lakes where trout may be fished.

Hotel
**A   *Hôtel Chalet du Lac* (tel. 0).

[449 km.] **Imouzzer du Kandar**. A summer resort at 1,345 metres.

Hotels
***B   *Hôtel Royal*, Avenue Mohammed V (tel. 630.80).

[485 km.] Fes.

FES

Population 449,000
Air Internal and external connections with Fes are dealt with on pp. 21 and 23. *Fes Saïss Airport* lies 10 km. south on the P24, about 30 DH by taxi. The offices of Air Maroc are at 54 Avenue Hassan II (tel. 204.56).
Rail For rail connections, see p. 23. The station is situated in the new town off Avenue des Almohades and convenient for the centre. Railway information bureau telephone 250.01.
Bus Fes is very well served by long distance buses. C.T.M. bus station, Boulevard Mohammed V; other carriers at Bab Ftouh and Place el-Baghdadi in Fes el-Bali, Place des Alaouites in Fes el-Jedid. Local bus services connect the new town, Avenue Hassan II, with the old.
Taxi Ranks at Avenue Hassan II, Boulevard Mohammed V, Bab Boujeloud, Bab Ftouh etc. Unusually, Fasi taxis having working meters.
Car Hire *Avis*, 50 Boulevard Chefchaouni (tel. 209.67) and at the airport.
Hertz, Hotel des Fes, Avenue des F.A.R. (tel. 228.12) and at the airport.

Hotels
*****   *Hôtel Palais Jamai*, Baba Guissa (tel. 343.31).
*****   *Hôtel de Fes*, Avenue des F.A.R. (tel. 250.02).

*****   *Hôtel Merinides*, Borg Nord (tel. 452.25).
****A   *Hôtel Sofia*, 3 Rue de Pakistan (tel. 242.66).
****A   *Hôtel Volubilis*, Rue Allal Ben Abdellah (tel. 211.25).
****B   *Hôtel Salam-Zalagh*, Rue Mohammed Diouri (tel. 228.10).
***A   *Grand Hôtel*, Boulevard Chefchaouni (tel. 255.11).
***B   *Hôtel Splendid*, Avenue Mohammed V (tel. 221.48).
**A   *Hôtel Amor*, 31 Rue Pologne (tel. 233.04).
**A   *Hôtel Olympic*, Avenue Mohammed V (tel. 224.03).
**A   *Hôtel de la Paix*, 44 Avenue Hassan II (tel. 250.72).
**B   *Hôtel Lamdaghri*, 10 Avenue Hassan II (tel. 203.10).
**B   *Hôtel Royal*, 36 Rue d'Espagne (tel. 246.56).
*A   *Hôtel C.T.M.*, Rue Ksar El Kebir (tel. 228.11).
*A   *Hôtel Kairouan*, 84 Rue d'Espagne (tel. 235.90).
*A   *Hôtel Excelsior*, Boulevard Mohammed V (tel. 256.02).
*B   *Hôtel Central*, Rue Mohammed El Jai (tel. 223.33).

Camping *Moulay Slimane*, well appointed and popular on Rue Moulay Slimane in the new town and quite close to the centre (tel. 224.38).

Information *O.N.M.T. Tourist Office*: Place de Résistance (tel. 234.60).

Syndicat d'Initiative: Place Mohammed V (tel. 247.69).

Banks Almost all the major banks are found on Boulevard Mohammed V.

Shopping As every guide will tell you more than once, Fes is the 'capital of handicraft'. It is also the capital of high pressure selling. If you want to buy carpets here (and there are some fine examples), always compare the price with official maxima, set in dirhams per square metre. Visit the *Centre Artisanal* on Boulevard Allal Ben Abdellah in the new town for guidance and see classic examples in the Dar Bartha Museum (see p. 249).

Sports and Clubs *Riding*: Club Équestre de Fes, Moulay El Kamel (tel. 234.38).

Tennis: Club Fassi, Boulevard Essaoudia (tel. 242.72).

Flying: Royal Aeronautical Club, 4 km. on the road to Sefrou (tel. 120.55).

Skiing: Ski Club, c/o Delegation de Jeunesse, Boulevard Chefchaouni (tel. 236.61).

Post Office Corner of Boulevard Mohammed V and Avenue Hassan II.

Emergencies *Hospital Al Khassani*: Quartier Dhar El Mehraz (tel. 227.76).

Police: telephone 19.

Unique and, surely, uniquely beautiful, Fes is a city that we may consider ourselves privileged to visit before the modern world overtakes it. Though it is to be physically preserved from spoliation by being brought under the protection of the UNESCO Department of International Cultural Heritage, it cannot now be very long before its late-medieval life begins to alter and what now is a living and functioning survival from the past becomes a museum harbouring a different society. There is nowhere left in the Arab world (except Mecca and Medina, where we cannot go) to compare with Fes as a survival illustrative of that brilliant past for which we revere the Arabs and base our hopes for their future.

The city lies in a bowl between the Middle Atlas, to the south, and the Jebel Zalagh, which is really a last peak of the mountains, a sentinel over the high plains connecting the Atlas with the Rif. In shape, the town is a diamond with blurred points and the oval of Fes el-Jedid ('new Fes', the palace quarter) appended on its south-west point. Fes el-Jedid stands high and represents the defensible casbah of other towns. It contains the ghetto also. It is separated by the Boujeloud Gardens from the older quarters which are collectively known as Fes el-Bali ('old Fes'), that part which fills the bowl in the hills. The western and northern parts are the highest, the Andalus quarter to the east the lowest. Because the summers grow oppressively hot in the hollow of the bowl, the grandest houses are the highest, many being built to overtop the walls which enclose the whole city. Because there are cemeteries outside the walls, but more particularly because Marshal Lyautey was a man of taste and vision and took care to set the new town well away from the old, there has been no outflow of building beyond the walls. Woods and pasturage, the ragged lands where headstones stand awry, run clear up against the marvellous old masonry of the city walls. Clusters of *koub-biyet* (tombs of marabouts) ornament the slopes beyond the walls, but apart from them there is scarcely a cottage or a shed to mark a compromise between the country and the town. One such cluster of tombs, very noble ruins, stands to the north high over the city. These are the tombs of the Merinid sultans. Near by is a new tall hotel, the Hôtel des Mérinides. This is less of an aesthetic error than was feared and it has the best of situations; it is from here that you get the most entrancing view of the town, looking steeply down into the houses and across the great mosques at the high houses on the farther side.

There are a surprising number of places in Fes where you can see something of the interiors — or at least the courtyards — of private houses and this may be a good place to say a few words about the life led in them.

The women's quarters are of course segregated from those of the bachelors of the household, but among ordinary people family life is conducted much like ours, with none of the rigidity of the harem into which the great lord penetrated only for purposes of pleasure and propagation of the species, the male children being taken from their mothers at an early age. It is even remarkable to what an extent mothers rule their families in this ostensibly patriarchal society. If — a man — you go into a house, the women will cover their faces and keep out of the way while you are there, but intimates will know the women of the family as easily as they know the menfolk. Reception rooms, however, are for the receiving of male visitors only unless, in grander houses, the women have such rooms of their own, where of course they entertain their women friends. But, these days, the grand houses are the most westernized in their ways and there the younger women at least live on an equal footing with the men, unveiled and wearing French clothes. But these families are more and more away from Fes these days; the activities of Rabat and Casablanca claim their time. Indeed in this country of capital cities, Fes now wears a somewhat provincial air.

It is now a town that takes tourists very seriously. This is nice in some ways, less so in others. The famous Hôtel Palais Jamaï at the lip of the bowl to the north of Fes el-Bali is a converted late-nineteenth-century vizier's palace, exceedingly attractive though rather wanting in finish and finesse as a super hotel. One should certainly have a drink there as an excuse to see inside, and stay there if you have the means. The new hotels are comfortable and have delightful swimming-pools. Food for the tourist is not remarkable in Fes; the Tour d'Argent still attracts French residents; it always pays to look out for where these eat. The Palais de Fes in the Andalus quarter, a renowned, not too touristy Moroccan establishment, is not half as good as the Maison Arabe in Marrakech. This is a pity since the Fasi is really one of the world's great schools of cooking.

Perhaps because the Fasi is the most reserved of Moroccans, making few concessions to visitors, one is inclined to 'go native' there, to stay in cheap hotels, frequent the cafés of the Place Boujeloud or the Grande Rue de Fes el-Jedid, to eat in the jolly — and excellent — restaurants in the *souk*. Fes does not really want you and the implication of impending change you carry with you, so, contrarily, you want the more to get under its skin. If you make this small effort it is immediately welcomed. The Fasi does not make the overtures — nor does he like to be a spectacle for you — but his reserve does not preclude friendliness. Also he expects you to see the sights of the city in a day and then be gone elsewhere, so that if you stay some days he becomes the readier to accept you.

You will certainly need a guide in Fes el-Bali (see p. 249). There are trunk alleys among the maze and it is not difficult to learn them after a couple of visits, but the first visit is rather bewildering. The old city itself is the main thing to see. If your time is very short get a guide to lead you from the Bab Boujeloud, by the Medersa 'bu Inania and the Kairouyyin Mosque, over the river and out again by the Bab Ftouh, then take a taxi round the outside of the town by the north. This is a pitiful idea but better than nothing. You could dawdle a bit over it and still do it in 3½ hours. Guides can be booked at the O.N.M.T. office in Place de la Résistance, or at the Place Boujeloud where they have a station in the wall on the right, or outside first-class hotels. With a distinguished intellectual history, a genuine student can generally be found who is willing to show you the domestic aspect and underside of Fes. (Try for one of the specially trained ones.)

A guide is not strictly necessary in Fes el-Jedid, nor for helping you to find the Dar el-Baïda and Dar Batha, but one is still a great help on a first visit, for the topography of all old Fes takes some understanding. We give the sights of the town in two groups: those in Fes el-Jedid and those in Fes el-Bali; the Dar el-Baïda and the Dar Batha Museum of Moroccan Arts head the latter group since these lie outside the bowl of the city and the normal approach to them is away from that for the rest.

The Dar el-Makhzen, the old palace in Fes el-Jedid, is enormously worth while seeing, but it has been closed for repairs. One had to apply at the Tourist Office (O.N.M.T.) for permission to visit it and an appointment was arranged, not necessarily for the same day, though not later than the following morning. It is necessary to have this permission to see the Makina. This is a noble, Italianate arms foundry, pleasant to see, though an extra rather than a must.

HISTORY

The history of Fes is so bound up with that of the country that we will not repeat here what has been said in the History section on p. 53.

However, — as a reminder — the town was perhaps founded as a small settlement by Idriss I, though it was his son, Idriss II, who decided upon the site as his capital city. The older village lay on the east bank of the Oued Fes, a perpetual stream that is a tributary of the River Sebou, and the new town arose on the west bank. The early influx of refugees from Cordoba and Kairouan was decisive in the creation of the city since the immigrants came from well-established, urban centres of Arab civilization bringing more advanced techniques, skills and learning with them than any hitherto to have been found in Morocco. Of these the Andalusians from Spain occupied the east bank district and the Kairouani the west. The two great mosques and the names of their respective quarters still commemorate this division.

The city's first hundred years were troublous since the rival houses of the Cordoban Ommayeds and the Aghlabids of Tunis (or Ifriqiya) fought for the disintegrating Idrissi kingdom. It was then, nevertheless, that a much larger circuit of walls was built and bridges thrown over the Oued Fes. That the walls then followed much the same course on the north, east and south as now is indicated by the fact that both the Bab Ftouh and the Bab Guissa were constructed at the time. These improvements were carried out by various rulers belonging to various camps, the city several times changing hands between them.

It was taken by the Almoravids in 1069 and greatly developed after the conquest of Spain, when its position caused it to become a more important town than Marrakech. Walls which separated the two halves of the town, lying along the stream-bed, were then dismantled.

Fes

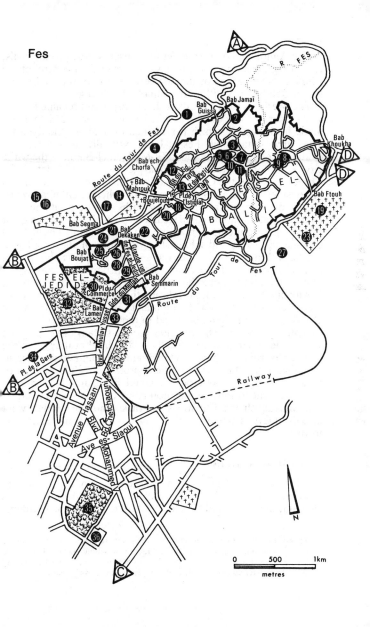

Fes

The Almohads conquered Fes in 1146 and destroyed the walls, rebuilding them only when they were sure of their control of the whole country. Much of the northern section of the wall round Fes el-Bali belongs still to this Almohad building.

The Merinids took the city in 1248, lost it and regained it two years later. Abu Yussef Yaacub, reigning from 1258 to 1286, made it his capital, which it remained throughout the dynasty. The same sultan built Fes el-Jedid, virtually as a new, self-contained city. Officially called El-Medinat el-Baïda — the white city — its formal foundation took place on March 21st, 1276. Three years later the Great Mosque of the place was consecrated — considering the ambitiousness of the scheme, entailing walls, palace, mosque, markets, barracks, baths and the great houses of court officials, building could clearly be pushed forward at a great rate when absolute masters decreed it should. Thus Fes el-Jedid became the royal and administrative centre of the country, a capital within a capital. Here was stationed the garrison; Syrian archers occupying the citadel, and Christian mercenaries the town. (A mutiny among these had been instrumental in winning Fes for the Merinids.) Later, during the first quarter of the fourteenth century, the Jewish community was removed from Fes el-Bali and Fes el-Jedid enlarged to the south to provide a new Mellah* or 'ghetto'. The advantage to the sultans of keeping the Jews under their wing is cynically said to be that they were the handier for robbing, but in fact this valuable commercial community always stood in need of official protection while, like garrisons of foreign mercenaries, it could be counted upon to a certain extent to rally to the protectors' defence when needed. (At Marrakech the Christians' barracks and the Mellah were actually interposed between the casbah, or palace quarter and the town.)

PRINCIPAL SIGHTS

Gardens separate the new from all the old parts of Fes, as they do el-Jadid from el-Bali. Those walled ones south-west of Fes el-Jedid, the Agdal and the more elaborate Lalla Mina Gardens,

* The word derives from this locality and does not translate 'ghetto'. It means literally 'salt' and originates from the practice of salting the heads of those executed, a task required of the Jews. The heads were then displayed on the city walls. It was later adopted in other cities to denote the Jewish quarter.

belong to the palace. Those on the right of the approach road —
Boulevard Moulay Yussef — are the Biarnay Gardens. A more
delightful approach could hardly be imagined. At the summit of
the hill the Bab Lamer gateway (Bab means 'gate') gives into the
Place du Commerce. To the left of this lies Fes el-Jedid.

FES EL-JEDID

Mellah

Few Jews now remain in this quarter. The houses lining the
Grande Rue du Mellah remind one a little of Istanbul in their
partly Western manner. They must mostly belong to the early
nineteenth century although some are clearly rather earlier.
There is an old *Hebrew cemetery* (Map **31**) south-east of the outer
wall of the Mellah, crowded with white gravestones. Two of the
larger synagogues can be visited: the *Serfati* and that of the
Fasiyin.

The Grande Rue du Mellah leads through the Bas Semmarin
and continues as the *Grande Rue de Fes el-Jedid* leading to the
palace. The town is comparatively orderly in plan.

El-Azhar Mosque
Map **29**.
Built by Sultan Abu Inan in 1357, it has a good *minaret* and the
carved stone *doorway* was brought, according to tradition, from
Andalusia. Two other Merinid mosques, the '*Red*' and the
'*White*', open to the Grande Rue on the way to the large, walled
mechouar in which it ends.

Dar el-Makhzen ('Palace of the Sultans')
Map **28**; *entry is by permission: see p. 241*.
The great Bab Dekaken by which the palace is entered lies across
the *mechouar* to your left hand.

You pass through many, generally very plain courts and
mechouars, showing your pass to a grave, most handsomely
dressed official and being passed on from one of these to another.
Many of these men — or at any rate the older among them — were
formerly slaves. You will not easily see their like elsewhere,
proud of their royal service and secure under the paternalist care
of sovereigns whose households are to an extraordinary extent
their families — much in the sense that a seventeenth-century
English gentleman spoke of his 'family'. These men show what is

an unusually high proportion of Negro blood for Fasiyin. If most of the Negroes of Morocco were originally brought in as slaves, not so many of their descendants remained in that class. Among the Arabs a child takes the status of his father, who may marry whom he pleases and support concubines at his pleasure. The fact that a woman bears his child almost automatically means that he will support her for the sake of her child, if from no other consideration, and the child itself will be on an equal footing with all his other offspring. Obviously it was the richer who were apt to produce large families of this sort, and it is now these who incline to take a less feudal attitude towards matrimony.

Finally you reach the great *court*. Most beautifully kept, it is now very silent. It is many acres in size and of a beauty to take the breath away. It seems to frame all the sky. Flocks of white doves inhabit it. Sultans since Abu Yussef Yaacub have built themselves pavilions and audience-halls around this glorious space, none liking to occupy the quarters of his predecessors. Though asymmetrical, the result is harmonious, partly because the great basins of water reflect and balance the buildings. The more recent buildings must have replaced those of the earlier sultans. All are very richly decorated though not all are as finely done as others. The older are the best. In these the plaster-work is very deeply carved. A guide — student son of one of the erstwhile slaves — remarked of this work, 'In those days there was no time or all time. The little workmen came every day with the sun, bringing their tools and their bread and worked, smoking their little pipes of kif and having a sleep at noon — just working all their lives. You can see it was like this'. You can indeed. The very precision of the workmanship, its depth, has an intensity which seems a concentrate of patience, a perfection and a startling kind of introversion that suggests the heightened concentration the drug can lend the smoker. But the overall designs have a lucid, geometric simplicity which carries the intricate detail beautifully. This tended to become blurred later and inferior workmanship could not compensate for over-elaboration of design.

There is also a fine *medrassa* of 1320; small and, surely most exclusive. It was built by Sultan Abu Saïd Uthman. Its *minaret* is late-nineteenth-century. The palace also contains an old *menagerie* and a *mosque*.

The *Dar Ayad el-Kebira* (*Map* **26**), where you are finally led, belongs to the latter half of the eighteenth century though some of the work is later still. This too is set about an enormous *courtyard*. In parts of it a collection of clothes, pottery, arms and furniture has been set out. Many of these objects are quite worthy of their splendid setting.

Basically the design of palaces of this sort stems from ancient Mesopotamia. It is a plan that very well suits the climate of the Arab world and lends itself specially well to these great spaces of Africa and Asia. If the detail here is rather different from that in the east there is none the less a very great affinity between all Arab art and architecture and if you can sometimes feel irked that there has been so heavy a tradition upon it that a natural development has been blighted, here that tradition seems to acquire great virtue from its continuity. Walking back through the Great Court you feel as though you might reach eighth-century Baghdad at the farther end. (See also p. 128.)

In all, the palace occupies some 80 hectares; there is a great deal that one does not see. Even so, I believe this to be the finest single sight Morocco has to offer; one of the wonders of the world.

Here is a poem, 'The Andalusian Fountains', to read in this setting. It is by the medieval Maghrebi poet, ibn Hamdis. If there were ever, as is likely, lion fountains here (like that at Granada) this poem would be perfectly apposite. It will in any case have often been recited before in these courts.

> And lions people this official wood
>> encompass the pools with thunder
> and profuse over aureate-banded
>> bodies their skulls gush glass
> Lions like stillness stirred
>> questing mobility there
> and trophies of carnivores
>> proper those deployed haunches
> Sun is tinder to the stirred
>> colours, is light to long tongues,
> is a hand to unsheath the lunging
>> blades that shiver out in a splash
> By a zephyr damp and thread
>> are woven and corsleted
> on a branch sits sorcery netted
>> like incandescent birds from space
> That lest they fall to freedom
>> are forcibly propped, lest their songs

start a whistling on the ponds
and warbling in the mercurial trees
And they dipped in cascades
of chrysolite and tossed pearl
and they chatter an astral
mischief; while expert armourers
Garnish with gilt hoods
the gates: and an invert
terrace of stalactites
glows in a submarine recess.
This specialist brocade
is a mere hallucination
its azure and sun and plantation
ephemeral as fine skies
Some with beasts in the wood
some with the fowl in disaster
are the antique lineal masters
hunting their sperm down ornate galleries.*

Bab es-Siba
In the same mechouar from which the palace is entered.
It is Merinid in date. That savagery which was never far beneath
the surface of Moroccan life is here recalled by thought of the
Infanta Ferdinand of Portugal, a hostage whose life was forfeit in
1437 and whose naked body was suspended upside down for four
years from this gate before being cut down and its stuffed skin
exposed a further twenty-nine years in a coffin.

Through the Bab es-Siba lies the ten-hectare *Old Mechouar*
(*Map* 24) where in the late afternoons entertainers used to come
and the townsmen gather to watch and to listen to them. Fes grew
sophisticated and this pleasing habit declined; everyone goes to
the cinema instead. Here, too, is the *Makina* (*Map* 21), easily
recognized by its Italianate, baroque *doorway* which rather sur-
prises in this setting. Built in 1886 by an Italian mission, the enormous building was an arms factory. Part now houses a carpet-
weaving business. The Makina can be visited with a special
permit, for obtaining which see p. 241.

Other sights in Fes el-Jedid
Beyond the Makina, north of the Old Mechouar, stands the *Bab*

* Translated by Herbart Howarth and Ibrahim Shukrallah: *Images of the Arab
World* (Pilot Press, London, 1944).

Segma. A Merinid building, it was a ceremonial gate in the outer wall. It now stands beside a modern *gateway*. It was built in 1315 and of its original two octagonal *towers* now only one remains.

The *Moulay Abdullah Quarter* (*Map* 25) lies in the north-west angle of Fes el-Jedid. It can be reached from the *mechouar* in front of the palace, through the *gateway in its western wall*.

This is a pleasant part containing the *Great Mosque of Fes el-Jedid*. This was built by Abu Yussef in 1276; Abu Inan is buried in the *sepulchre* annexed to it. The mid-eighteenth-century mosque of Moulay Abdullah has a tall, traditional *minaret*. Besides Moulay Abdullah himself and Moulay Yussef (1912–27), many of the members of the Alaouite family are buried here. The westerly *Bab Boujat* gives out to yet another enormous *mechouar* built by an ex-engineer of the French army, a convert who served the sultan as Abd er-Rahman Desaulty. He built this in 1870 and his other works, besides bridges, include constructing the Fes-to-Meknes road. His grave lies outside the Bab Segma.

Isolated from the town by this cemetery lying outside the Bab Segma stands the very large walled enclosure known as the *Casbah Cherarda* (p. 261; *Map* 14) which is closed to the public.

FES EL-BALI

Fes el-Jedid was linked to Fes el-Bali by an extension of the walls running on either side the saddle of land which connects the lip of the bowl and the small plateau on which the former stands. This saddle of land is by no means so densely populated as either settlement proper. Apart from the Boujeloud Gardens in which the Oued Fes has been dammed to make a lake lying under the walls of Fes el-Jedid, the area on its southern, sloping side is filled with gardens, all its streets being avenues. It is rather like a rich suburb.

Dar Batha Museum of Moroccan Arts
Map 18.

Open The museum is open from 09.00 to 18.00 except on Tuesdays; shut from 12.15 to 15.00. Admission is free but it is courteous to tip.

This is scarcely a hundred years old. It was built, as a palace, by Moulay el-Hassan and Moulay Abd el-Aziz. It has a much more domestic air, despite its scale, than anything we have described before.

The collections it houses are perhaps the best of their kind, certainly the widest in range, for here there are many details rescued from decayed *medersa*, mosques and other old buildings, some things among them being really early. The section of clothes is of an extraordinary sumptuousness — in fact the person who could be bored here defies description. If you are interested in buying carpets this is an excellent place to form an opinion about the possibilities of Moroccan ones, for those on display include fine peasant-works beside the sophisticated products of the towns.

Dar el-Baïda
Map 20.
This perhaps was originally a pleasure-garden built in the late eighteenth and early nineteenth centuries. *Pavilions* from that date remain, though the main building has been very much added to during the last century and even in this. For a time during the early years of the French Protectorate it was used as the Résidence Générale. One cannot go into it, but it is worth stopping to look through the doorway if it happens to be open. The elegant pavilions you can then see all belong to the middle of the last century.

Bab Boujeloud
Place Boujeloud.
Fes el-Bali proper, so to speak, though perfectly enterable through streets leading from the neighbourhood of the above houses — particularly if you cut through the Rue du Petit Tala — is most conveniently entered from the Bab Boujeloud. This is set at what was clearly the weakest point of the enceinte before the building of Fes el-Jedid, and it is heavily fortified with gates within gates, series of walls and two casbahs, very few of which defences have been used as such for a very long while. New gates and open arches have been opened since the defence-works became of no vital importance and spaces between them have become squares. Unless they are very intricate, maps do not help one to understand this part, and since you will need a guide on your first expedition into the town in any case, we will not attempt directions how to reach this or that place.

The Bab Boujeloud is nowadays in fact two gates: the older is on the left, the brilliantly tiled one, built in 1913, on the right. The *Mosque of Boujeloud* stands to one side with the *casbah* of the same name behind it. This is now a residential quarter but the walls retain some of their original masonry. An Almoravid castle stood here; it was destroyed by Abd el-Mumin in the mid twelfth century. The Almohad Mohammed en-Nasser rebuilt the casbah at the beginning of the thirteenth century and it was here that the Merinids lived while Fes el-Jedid was building.

Casbah el-Filala
Map **12**.

Also called the *casbah en-nour* — of flowers. It was also built by Mohammed en-Nasser though the walls now date from the reign of the Alaouite sultan Moulay Suleiman, at the end of the eighteenth century. The *Bab ech-Chorfa* is rather fine with its flanking bastions. It has its own *mosque* inside.

Bab Mahrouk
Built in 1214, again by Mohammed en-Nasser or his son el-Mustansir. Its name means 'the burned' and there are rival claims as to whose *auto-da-fé* the name commemorates: that of El-Obeïdi, a rebellious chieftain, or ibn el-Khatib, a fourteenth-century literary figure of distinction who suffered the same fate and whose tomb is still to be seen in a cemetery near by.

Inevitably, from this corner of the town, you will descend into the bowl of the city by the *Rue du Grand Tala*; it is the nearest Fes goes to a main street. After passing the *Sidi Lezzaz Mosque* with its charming green-tiled *minaret*, you come to the small complex of buildings belonging to the Medrassa 'bu Inania.

MEDERSA*

Medrassa 'bu Inania
Map **13**.

Open Daily from 08.00 to 18.00 (17.00 in summer) except on Friday mornings.

This is the only kind of building in religious use into which a non-Moslem may enter, and even then one must not attempt to go into the prayer-hall across the courtyard from the gateway; this is in use.

---

* Not all the *medersa* are currently open to the public since they are being restored in rotation.

    Tip the custodians of those you do visit.

As you come down the lane you see an elaborately carved *bridge-building* over it. Before reaching this, on the left is the entry to the *washing-place* attached to the *medrassa* and, fairly high up, facing the street, the ruins of what is called the '*clock*'. The whole thing forms an ensemble in brick and carved cedarwood, with the bridge and the front of the *medrassa* on your right. It is not known exactly what the 'clock' was, but it is thought most likely to have been a mechanical carillon. Its date is 1357. Both clock and bridge are being repaired, though it is not expected the clock can be restored.

Sultan 'bu Inan built this last and largest of the Merinid theological colleges of Fes in 1350 to 1357. There is little question but it is the finest of them all. Everywhere the work is superb, the proportions perfect. It is also in very good condition. There is a moving austerity in the use of cedar-wood, plaster and stone, the colour coming only from the dado of tiles, some of which is obscured by the magnificent wooden grilles between the columns. It is not really a thing to describe in detail — any fool can see what it is made of, piece by piece — but it is a sight on no account to be missed. It is the sacerdotal counterpart of the Alhambra of Granada. Upstairs are the nice little rooms of the students divided by balconies, screens and niches so that each, though sharing, had some privacy of his own. Persevere to the roof for the sake of the view over the town. And go through to the smaller entrance on the Rue du Petit Tala to see that doorway also. Overcome your good manners somewhat and peer into the *prayer-hall*; its furnishings, its old glass and indeed its construction are as rich and fine as all the rest. Look for the especially elegant *minaret*. Told the price of this building, 'bu Inan is said to have commented that what is beautiful cannot be expensive at any price; what is enthralling is never too costly.

Men may use the *mida* or wash-house. I have in fact never found that one cannot use those appertaining to mosques, but you do not feel very at ease doing so, nor are they generally very salubrious.

This one, however, should be seen. It is of the same date as the *medrassa* — mid-fourteenth-century — and is beautifully designed round a *court* with a large *marble basin* in its centre. The carved wood-work is magnificent, the flow of water prodigal.

Medrassa el-Attarine
Rue du Souq el-Attarine (*Map* 3).

Open Daily from 09.00 to 12.00 and from 14.00 to 17.00 except on Fridays.

Built in 1325 by Sultan Abu Saïd, this is smaller than the above, equally fine, if not even finer in its finish and, in its effect certainly prettier and more delicate. The *bronze doors* are splendid, as is the contemporary *candelabrum* in the *prayer-hall* where for once, since it is disused, you may walk and admire the meditative simplicity of an Islamic prayer-hall.

From the roof-top there is a quite extensive view into the great courtyard of the Kairouyyin Mosque (p. 255). Its roofs give a good indication of its plan. And from here you see more of the monumental simplicity of its decorated parts than any glimpse through its doors can allow. The mosque received this definitive form in 1135, though various decorative details have been added, repaired, replaced or altered since. The two kiosks in the *sahn* are Saadi additions.

Medrassa el-Misbahiya
A few doors right of the above (Map 3).
Sultan Abu el-Hassan caused this *medrassa* to be built in 1346. It is named for its first and famous head-teacher, Mesbah ben Abdullah. Marble has to be imported into Morocco, mostly from Italy, and is regarded as the very pinnacle of luxury. The *marble basin* at the centre of the *court* here has earned the college the nickname er-Rokham, 'the marbled'. It was brought from Algeciras. Rather less satisfactory than either of the above, this has some excellent details for all that − the *portière* over the entrance, the *ceiling* of the vestibule and the *entrance* to the prayer-hall, for instance. Lately, this medrassa has been open only infrequently.

Medrassa es-Seffarin
Close to the river (Map 11).
This is the earliest of the Merinid *medersa*, being built by Abu Yussef in 1280. It was the first college of the sort to be founded in Morocco and was in fact a foundation-stone for the great reputation which Fes was to acquire as a centre of Islamic learning. Its plan is quite different from that of the other *medersa* and its construction is very simple. The other *medersa* are based on the type of house in which well-to-do Cairenes lived (although the Moroccans adopted rather the Syrian variant from the Egyptian, based on Cairene houses). They were the sort of house teachers who attracted students could afford and those therefore upon which the Ayyubids based their *medersa*. They thus represent an imported tradition; but the interest of this particular building lies

in the fact that it reflects the type of house in which, earlier, a Fasi teacher lived — there are still many houses in Fes with a great arch over a balcony to a courtyard and which share the general plan of this *medrassa*. (A grand example can be seen from the roof-top they take you to at the *Tanneries*.) There is a lovely ablutions pool here and a straggling vine. Abu Yussef gave it a rich library, but this was long ago moved to that of the Kairouyyin University (*Map* 7). (Near by is the *Gzam ben Zeklam bridge* over the Oued Fes; in fact there is a nice view of the river quarters from here. A walk through the *dyers' street* brings you to the shop-lined *Sidi el-Awad bridge*.)

Medrassa ech-Cherratin

In the street of the same name (Map 10).

This is the latest of the *medersa* to be built, in 1670, by the Alaouite sultan Moulay er-Rashid. Though built round a *court*, it is rather different and not nearly so distinguished as the Merinid ones. But the plan is interesting with three '*houses*' in three of the corners of the courtyard, the fourth being occupied by a most capacious *latrine*. Its bronze *entrance-doors* are far simpler in design than any of the earlier ones in the city, but really fine all the same. Not so much building survives from this period and that alone makes it interesting to see this example, which is still used to accommodate students.

Medrassa es-Sebbayin

Close to the el-Andalus Mosque (Map 9).

This Merinid college was devoted to the teaching of the seven formal manners in which the Koran can be recited, hence its name which means 'of the seven'. The courtyard has an eccentric charm and it is hoped it will soon be restored. Also in current use.

Medrassa es-Sahrij

Also close to the el-Andalus Mosque (Map 9).

This simply conceived building with extremely rich decoration is in a ruinous condition, though undergoing restoration, and it may be some while before it can be opened to the public. It was built in 1321 or so, by the then heir to the throne, Prince Abu el-Hassan Ali. It was the parent establishment of the Medrassa es-Sebbayin and is on rather a grander scale; indeed, its very fine basin of water in the court gives it its name.

MOSQUES

El-Kairouyyin Mosque
Map 7.

This is the largest mosque in Morocco. It began, however, in a small way during the ninth century — 859–62 to be exact — when a pious lady refugee from Kairouan built it for her fellow-refugees, all of whom had settled in the quarter. Her name was Fatma bint Mohammed ben Feheri. It was a Fatimid governor who raised it to the status of cathedral mosque, enlarging it at the same time, 933. In his turn, Abd er-Rahman III of Cordoba embellished the building with the existing plain *minaret* (though this was restored by the Merinids). This was in 956. In 1135 the Almoravid Ali ben Yussef much enlarged the mosque to its present dimensions.

Built on a T-plan, it has sixteen longitudinal aisles each of twenty-one spans, and fourteen doors, one of which is axial. Of these only two are still covered with their bronze lining, and one partly. The one almost opposite the Palais du Fes is of exquisite, Almoravid workmanship, dating from 1136. Through others of the doors one may see into the *courtyard* with its two elegant Saadian *kiosks* and the handsome central, Almohad *basin* placed there in 1202. One cannot get any chance to see either the *mimber*, which is very beautiful and dates from the twelfth century, or the enormous bronze candelabrum of 1203; these are in the sanctuary or shrine before the *mihrab* (an Almoravid one) but you can sometimes see the elaborate *anazah*, a carved screen of wood which partly closes the entrance from the *sahn* to the axial aisle. One cannot help but be struck by the simplicity of the interior, the unity of the design and furnishing, particularly the fresh matting with a light, bright-red design woven into it which lines the walls. This gives a very beautiful colour to the light within. It is standard mosque matting. The round-topped arches have a great spaciousness. These are Almoravid. Twenty thousand people, it is said, can worship here at the same time, but one of the things that catches the eye as one passes the doors is the classic grace of single figures or small groups isolated in these spacious aisles, praying or in contemplation.

We are denied sight of the glories of this mosque's interior, for they are concentrated upon the axial, 'nave' aisle leading to the *mihrab*. With the *mihrab* itself this ensemble constitutes the most important example of Maghrebi art of the first half of the twelfth century. Even more than the Koubba el-Baroudiyin (p. 213), it forms a highly significant link between Cordoba and the Medina az-Zahra, even Kairouan, with the Almohad style and all that grew from it.

Except for one or two comparatively unimportant remakings, the whole dates from Ali ben Yussef's rebuilding of the mosque between 1135 and 1143. Piety, most probably, induced the architects to preserve something of the *nave* of the older building which they planned to replace on the same site. The older had extended from the second to the seventh Almoravid transverse aisle; its position being marked by piers conserved and re-used in the new building. This aisle was lower than the Almoravids wanted the new to be, a circumstance which led them to invent a magnificent progression of ascending arches and rising domes approaching the culmination over the junction of the nave and *quibla*-aisle off which the *mihrab* niche opens. Along the length of this nave lobed, scalloped lambrequin and serpentine arches span both longitudinally and transversely, becoming more elaborate as they approach the sanctuary. Cupolas roof these intersections save where, between the eighth and ninth transverse aisles, an arch is left out, the rectangular space above being roofed with a remarkable vault of stalactitic or *muqarnas* decoration. Four of the other crossings are roofed with *muqarnas* cupolas, two others being of ribbed domes. Purely decorative and quite unstructural, these are among the earliest-known examples of *muqarnas* — they are also perfectly designed and rendered. A feature of all the ensemble is carved plaster, floral motives, Cufic and cursive script being rendered in relief upon variously coloured grounds. The manner of much of this carving — like that in the Koubba el-Baroudiyin, yet more delicate — is extremely opulent. Some of it represents a last flowering of the classic motif of the acanthus leaf, while the potentialities of the palm are also variously and luxuriously explored. Almohad taste — ascetic, puritan, or however it should be described — disapproved this rich Andalusian work and it was plastered over, two years after being finished, and thus preserved to be discovered during restoration in the 1950s. The glorious face of the *mihrab* — somewhat damaged and more or less clumsily restored over the lower part, intact and wholly original in the upper — set the pattern for subsequent ones (all those you see in the Merinid *medersa*) but in a unique way its design is one with the *muqarnas* dome over the *quibla* crossing into which it rises. The *mimber* standing beside it is also Almoravid and of Cordoban work-manship — an incredibly fine thing of inlaid ivory and woods, intricately carved.

All the nave cupolas are hidden from outside view under a high, ridged roof. Nor can one manage to see from outside the windows in its southern gable end which open, inside into the *mihrab*'s facing and the cupola over the *quibla* crossing. On the exterior these are embraced in a frame of mouldings enclosing interlaced, engaged arches which prefigure Almohad designs, especially those of the windows in the Koutoubia minaret.

The mosque is also the seat of the *Kairouyyin University of Fes*, one of the oldest foundations of the kind in the world. Across the lane that runs around the mosque is the very handsome front of the administrative centre of this university and library. There are still some 300 students normally attending the courses in Islamic law, the Koran itself, the *sunna* and the vast body of commentaries upon them. The *library* has weathered the tempestuous history of the city and is one of the richest in Islam. There is a story that Gebert d'Auvergne (from 999 to 1003 Pope Sylvester II), in his day the towering intellect of Christendom, learned Arab numeration and the use of the zero at the Kairouyyin University. He is credited with a leading role in the introduction of Arab mathematics into Europe, but he is not known certainly to have studied here although he did so in Moslem Spain. Fes would then have been under Andalusian Ommayed control and this would have been an academy he would have wished to attend.

El-Andalus Mosque
Map 8.
This too was built for refugees (this time for those coming from Cordoba) in the ninth century by a pious lady called Meriem. Fes was still in Idrissid hands at the time, Yahya ben Mohammed ben Idriss being then on the throne. The *minaret* was added in 956 and remade when the original building was thoroughly reconstructed by Mohammed en-Nasser in the first decade of the thirteenth century. The Merinids gave it a *fountain* (restored by Moulay Ismaïl in the eighteenth century) and *library* in 1415. The *mimber*, although much restored since, dates back to the eleventh century. ('Pulpit' is not exactly the right translation of *mimber*, for this is a high throne or seat set under a canopy at the summit of a long, narrow flight of steps. There are one or two in museums.)

However, all one can really see of this venerable building is its sober exterior ennobled by the *north doorway* which dates from en-Nasser's reconstruction.

OTHER SIGHTS IN FES EL-BALI

Fondouk en-Nejjarine
Place en-Nejjarine (Map 5).
There are many *fondouks* in Fes — caravanserais or stables with stores for goods and lodgings above — but few of them have any architectural interest. The exception is the Fondouk en-Nejjarine which belongs to the eighteenth century. A tall building of several storeys, it is remarkably grand and elaborately decorated. Its *façade* and *entrance-gate* is aptly described as monumental, its *courtyard*, if somewhat well-like, most splendid. It was used as a hostel for poor students.

Close by, in the Place en-Nejjarine, there is the much-photographed *fountain of en-Nejjarine* (Map 5), decorated with tiles and having a carved wooden canopy. Its design, as you will notice as compared with others you will have passed, is unusual.

Zawiya Moulay Idriss
Map 6.
This is the principal shrine of Fes. Moulay Idriss II is buried in the sanctuary upon which the *zawiya* really depends. It was he who founded Fes as a capital city in 809 or a little earlier. It would not be too much to say that although Idriss II made a kingdom of his father's little principality (p. 69) nothing about him has come down to us to suggest he was personally of such saintly stature that he merits quasi-deification, but that his cult is rather that of the Arabism and Moslemism of Morocco, which is to say that this is essentially the national shrine of the kingdom. In fact the *zawiya* lapsed into ruinous disuse between the ending of the Idrissid dynasty and the rise of the Merinids, who re-established it, and it was not until the rediscovery of the tomb of Idriss II in 1437 that the Wattasids revived the cult of this founder sultan. It is not unnatural that the Berber dynasties should have allowed the cult to fall into oblivion and equally natural that the Merinids, devoted as they were to Arab culture, and the Wattasids, who needed to ground their rule on firm Arab foundations, should have been at pains to revive the memory of the Idrissids, the first creators of a Moroccan and Arab Moslem state. None the less

Idriss II has subsequently become something very much more personal to the simple citizens of Fes, something that corresponds to the patron saint of Italian towns. Before Moulay Hafid had them removed in this century, the sanctuary was hung with documents, like pennants, upon which the tribes and townships of the country set out the terms upon which they accepted the suzerainty of each new sultan — a typically independent, Moroccan arrangement very indicative of the place this shrine has in the nation. The *zawiya*, too, has the right of sanctuary (*horm*) which is still occasionally invoked. The guilds of the many trades of the city process here annually on different days during August to make offerings and propitiatory prayers before they hold their festivals.

The building largely dates from 1437 though the sanctuary was reconstructed during the eighteenth century. As one sees it through the doors, usually those two that are reserved for the use of women, the interior is rich and curiously reminiscent of Catholic shrines whose altars are sometimes the repositories of offerings, flowers, candles and burned incense.

The exterior of the tomb/sanctuary has a slightly baroque air. Facing the lane there is a *copper plaque* let into the wall with a hole in it into which passers-by place their hand for a minute to gain contact with the saint and receive his blessing. It is pleasant to glimpse even so little of the active life of such a shrine, particularly so one which is served by women who, elsewhere in Morocco, seem to have so small a place in the rituals of national life. (It is not uncommon to see women kissing the door-jambs of mosques where entry is denied their sex.)

Trade quarters

In your walks from one sight to another you will inevitably have passed through many of the districts where trades of different kinds are practised or shops are grouped which all sell a similar type of goods. Some of these form themselves into markets under one roof or round an arcaded courtyard. One which you should perhaps make a point of seeing is the *Kissaria*, the smart shopping area, though so many of the goods are in fact imported and therefore less intrinsically interesting than the locally produced — but since a covered Kissaria was in the first place usually built to accommodate shops selling imported goods, this upholds an old tradition. The *Souq el-Attarine*, the grocery-market, I find entrancing; and the *spice-market* is a heady place.

One of the more curious sights of the town is the *Tannery Quarter*. It lies to the north-east of the Kairouyyin Quarter, by the Oued Fes. There is a moment of acute nausea as you turn down the alley leading to the *tanneries*. If you can overcome this it is extraordinary how the sickly smell no longer bothers you, how soon, in fact, it seems quite agreeable. Return visits produce no problems of the kind, and you may well want to make them because with their very many pits of dye in the varying tints, covering wide areas, and the supple, active figures of scantily clad tanners and dyers always on the move in an altogether curious and rather beautiful setting of old buildings and hillsides beyond the town — the whole bathed by a great range of brilliant light — this is one of the most attractive subjects for photography imaginable. The guilds involved work closely together and the many establishments grouped in the quarter are co-operatively owned by the master-craftsmen occupying them. Masters, craftsmen and apprentices all work furiously all morning, but in the afternoon the pace falls off. Men like these, working in almost exactly similar conditions, have made Moroccan leather justifiably famous throughout Europe for a thousand years.

When in the *Andalus Quarter* you may find a visit to both the *potteries* and the *silk weavers* interesting. The green pantiles of Fes, used principally for roofing mosques, palaces and other official buildings, are of the finest quality, though not the only ones, for Safi makes them also. The silk is first class. Both industries are carried on quite close to the *Bab Ftouh*.

ROUTE DU TOUR DE FES

A few things beside the entrancing spectacle of the town from above remain to be seen on or outside the walled edges of Fes el-Bali. One can start from outside the Bab Segma (p. 249) and work round clockwise by the Route du Tour de Fes.

Msalla es-Sultan
Beyond the large cemetery which lies across the junction of the Route du Tour de Fes and the Meknes road (Map 16).
A *msalla* is a spacious open-air prayer-place with a section of wall to the south-east with the *mihrab* niche set in it and so orientated it indicates the direction of Mecca. The sultan who set up this *msalla* at the beginning of the twelfth century was Abu Abdullah en-Nasser. Enormous crowds can be accommodated at a *msalla*

and they come here particularly on the morning of the Aïd el-Kebir and the Aïd es-Seghir.

Sidi ben Kacem
Beyond the *msalla* stands the *koubba* of Sidi ben Kacem (*Map* **15**).

Casbah Cherarda
Outside the north wall of Fes el-Jedid and opposite the Bab Segma (*Map* **14**).
This very large, isolated casbah was erected by the Sultan Moulay er-Rashid in 1670 to defend the camp of the *makhzen* tribes — those upon whom the Government could prevail to serve as semi-regular militia. Various tribes served in this capacity, the Cherarda being the last, in the nineteenth century. The best of the gates is in the western wall and can be seen from the road circling the town. The casbah is also known as the 'Thursday casbah' on account of the animal-market held beside it on that day of the week. Between the casbah and the walls of the city there is a *sanctuary* to Sidi 'bu Beker el-Arabi, a saintly lawyer from Spain who died here in 1150. The casbah is closed to the public.

Borg Nord
Map **4**.
This is a defensive castle which, like its southern counterpart, the Borg Sud, was built by the Saadi Ahmed el-Mansur in the last quarter of the sixteenth century. Both may in fact have been designed as much to overawe the Fasiyin as to defend them. Both were built by Christian slaves, it is said. This fort has been turned into an Armoury Museum (*Musée d'Armes*) and houses an interesting collection, well displayed in its handsome setting.

Ksar el-Beni Meri
A turning left climbs a hill with a fine view. The scattered foundations of the first Merinid settlement here — a ksar which contained the usual buildings of a palace complex — lie round about.
The *ksar* was built in the second half of the thirteenth century. It is called the Ksar el-Beni Meri (the name of the Merinid tribe) and its existence, like that of Fes el-Jedid, emphasizes the distrust existing between rulers and ruled.

The road passes a *table d'orientation* on which the direction of the sights of the town are marked to help one identify them, for from here the view over the city is an excellent one.

Merinid Tombs
Map 1; *for these you have to branch right on a short side-road past the Hôtel des Merenides.* This was the later of the two necropolises, established after Chella (p. 179) was forsaken. The tombs are now but the elegant ruins of the *koubbiyet* which protected them, only scraps of decoration adhering to their interiors like swallows' nests to suggest the richness which Leo Africanus describes. Evening is the best time to come here to watch, and to hear, the town subsiding into rest.

The walls below this hill — *el-Kolla*, it is called — are the oldest remaining workmanship, twelfth-century Almohad. The nearest point, a bastion called the *Borg Kaoukeb*, is especially imposing.

Walk behind the tombs, eastwards, to look at the countryside over which the *Jebel Zalagh* dominates, a deeply moving view beyond a foreground of ruined *koubbiyet*.

The road veers away round a valley and, returning near the city wall, a right-hand branch leads to the Bab Guissa.

Bab Guissa
Build by the Almohads in 1204 and restored and improved by Abd el-Haqq. Through this gate the road, turning left and right again, leads to the Hôtel Palais Jamaï (p. 237) or you can reach this from the next lead road right, passing through the modern breach in the walls. Below the Bab Guissa, the quarter is still called the *Fondouk el-Ihoudi (Map* 2) — 'the Jews' *fondouk'* — a name which recalls the time before the Jews were moved to the Mellah of Fes el-Jedid.

The road again circles away from the town into the verdant valley of the Oued Fes, returning to the town close to the *Bab Khoukha* and rounding the wall to the Bab Ftouh.

Bab Ftouh
This not unimposing gate belongs to the eighteenth century, built by Sidi Mohammed ben Abdullah. Close to it stands the *Koubba of Sidi ben Ali Harazem*, a sufistic pantheist within the range of Islamic orthodoxy who died about 1164. He perhaps epitomizes the reputation of the Kairouyyin University in that it was said that his eloquence was such that djinns, invisible, attended his dis-

courses 'and recognized the authority of his science' — an ambiguous statement made by H. Gaillard.* He also cast out devils, to put it in medieval Christian terms. The actual building probably dates from 1554. The body of Moulay er-Rashid, founder of the Alaouite dynasty, was brought from Marrakech to be enshrouded here — Moslems should properly be buried within forty-eight hours of death, preferably in twenty-four, and are laid in the earth wrapped only in seven shrouds. The biggest Fasi festival is that of the students who come here each spring on the first Friday of the reign of their 'sultan', whom they elect to a year's office as a kind of prefect, to make their homage to their patron sufi — though in part the homage may be to er-Rashid who in his day was their great benefactor. This ceremony is preparatory to their two weeks' camping holiday in the Oued Fes during which traditional rites are performed and a great deal of fun is had, even today.

Through the Bab Ftouh, to the left, lies an extensive *cemetery* (*Map 19*). It is the only one within the circuit of the walls. Its northern section contains the *mausoleum of Sidi Ali bou Ghaleb*, a saint from Spain who studied at Fes at the beginning of the twelfth century. A moussem is held here in October, for Sidi Ali is much venerated as a worker of healing miracles — an Aesculapian figure beside whose grave the sick sleep on Tuesday and Wednesday night or every night until they are cured. Cures are said to be certain should the sleeper see the saint in his dreams. Though perhaps fewer come now than once, it is touching to see the ailing brought here at nightfall. It is easy to feel a little superior to such a superstition, yet the first major discovery in medicine was certainly the isolation — and often the cure — of psychosomatic diseases by this means, one discovered by the Greeks and probably brought to Fes, if not by Phoenician agency, then by the Romans. The cemetery of Bab Ftouh is in fact very much a scholars' graveyard, others of whose tombs are cult centres — particularly that of the seven anonymous holy men, the Sebatou Rijal, whose protection is most valuable. Again evening is the best time to come here, for then, as everywhere in the Arab world, the women and small children frequent the cemeteries to combine the pleasure of the cooler air with that of performing their devotions, exiled from the mosques, beside the tombs of saints whom they believe will intercede for them in some way.

* H. Gaillard, *Une Ville d'Islam: Fès* (Paris, 1905).

In this connection (and remembering that to be a Sufi is to detach from preconceptions; and not to try to avoid what is your lot),* the following is told:

A Sufi sheikh was asked by a visitor:

'Is there any value in saint-worship?'

He at once said: 'It is illogical, and it is forbidden by Islam.' The inquirer went away, satisfied.

A disciple who had been present said: 'But your answer did not cover the implications of the question.'

The sheikh told him: 'The questioner was at the stage of *Shariat* (conventionalist religion). The way in which he put the question showed that there was a certain reassurance which he wanted, and he sought it from me, of whom he had heard as a reliable source of opinion. There is, however, another kind of relationship with saints, one other than worship. Visiting their tombs has a virtue. But this virtue is operative only for those who can perceive it. This man was not one of them, so this other aspect of the question was void in his case.

'A man last month asked for verification of the fact that "cures wrought by shrine-meditation were entirely due to the aspiration, not the saint". I agreed with him. He had no capacity for more complex ideas: that, in other words, this may be partly true on some occasion, wholly on others, and so on.

'It is characteristic of the blind that they can see only certain questions. Saints were men, visiting a shrine to some is bound to be "saint-worship", saint-worship is ignorant. Therefore there can be no advantage in saint-worship.

'One in a thousand, perhaps, who visits a shrine will know inwardly why he is there and what is the nature of the virtue which he may derive from it. It is but natural that all pilgrims will imagine that they are "devout" and hence that they are all doing or experiencing exactly the same thing. Of course they are not. Have you ever tried to show a misguided man that his vision is narrow? He may listen to you in appearance. But for the sake of his own self-esteem he will reject what you *mean*, if not that you say.'†

---

* See Abu Said, son of Abi-Khair in Idries Shah, *The Way of the Sufi* (Cape, London, 1968).

† 'Saint-Worship' in Idries Shah, op. cit. Copyright © by Idries Shah. Reproduced by permission.

There is another *msalla*, that of the 'pasha' (*Map* **23**), on the hill-top opposite, and the near-by southern *Borg Sud* (*Map* **27**) overlooking the lowest point of the amphitheatre of Fes el-Bali.

Casbah dar Debibagh
Map **36**.

In the new town in this 'casbah of the tanner', beside the Parc de Chambrun, an early-eighteenth-century palace built by Moulay Abdullah during his siege of the city in 1729. It came in handy since, though he succeeded in taking the city, he had several times to retreat here for his safety and in the end died here. It was between this palace and the Dar el-Makhzen that Abdul Aziz wanted to build his railway (p. 107).

Environs of Fes

SIDI HARAZEM

Route 15 km. from Fes — take the P1 eastwards towards Taza (Route Exit D) and turn right at 14 km.

A thermal spa newly developed for leisure seekers who abound in summer. A moussem is held in honour of Sidi Harazem in April. Formerly known as Hammam Khaoulan, an old *dome* covers an old *thermal bath*. Near the spring there is a prehistoric *stone circle* of twenty-five monoliths with another in its centre.

Hotel
****B   *Hôtel Sidi Harazem* (tel. 455.22).

Excursion from Fes to Meknes

It might be thought rather insulting to Meknes, a prosperous agricultural centre these days, to suggest it is worthy of mention only as an excursion from Fes, but a visitor may enjoy more bustle about him in the evening than Meknes provides and, if he is touring a country, is glad of an excuse to unpack suit-cases and stay in one place long enough to get his laundry done. Since Meknes is only 60 km. distant from Fes, and Volubilis and

Moulay Idriss much the same distance, we describe them here as one excursion from that city. It is an excursion of a day's duration (152 km.), unless you are a really serious sight-seer. However, we give more detail and describe a wider area than could be comprised in a day's outing from Fes made by car. One day for visiting Meknes, another for Moulay Idriss and Volubilis and a shorter exploration of the Jebel Zerhoun would be ample to give you a good idea of the neighbourhood. And, of course, if you want to be thorough about it, there are hotels — an especially good one among them — and attractive restaurants in Meknes to induce you to stay there. It is, after all, a highly individual town which you could well find has that kind of attraction which prompts you to want to get to know it more intimately than excursioning allows.

Route The P1 road from Fes to Meknes is an excellent one. Leave by Route Exit B. [See Route Map for Northern Area (pp. 298–9).]

Rail and bus You can, of course, travel by train or bus between Fes and Meknes: nine trains a day, either way, and frequent buses; both means of travel take about an hour.

[5 km.] A turning right 15 km. to **Moulay Yakoub**, a thermal spa whose springs may have been the Roman *Aquae Dacicae*, for the remains of *antique baths*, rebuilt in the early Moslem era, have been found near the modern town which has gathered around new baths and the Koubba of Sidi Moulay Yaacub. It lies in a rather lovely situation. (If you want to bathe, bring your own towels as none are provided.)

[14 km.] A turning left towards **Ras el-Ma** (3 km.), a village close to the sources of the Oued Fes, by one of which stands a *casbah* to which the sultans called the tribes making up their armies or *mehallas* rather than allow them into Fes. Tradition says that it was here that Moulay Idriss II contemplated building a new capital, though Fes was chosen instead.

[21 km.] On the right can be seen a decorated, disused *bridge* which was built, like the original road over which you are passing, in 1870 by the French engineer Desaulty who became a Moslem and entered the sultan's service.

[42 km.] A turning 3.5 km. right for **Sebaa Aïoun**. Across the Oued Jedida from this village there stands a remarkable pre-Roman Berber *mausoleum*. It was built in the last period before the advent of the Romans — around and probably before the turn of B.C./A.D. It is called the *Bazinh of Souk el-Gour* (a Friday market near by). A *stone circle* 40 metres in diameter holds up a stepped, conical *mound* enclosing the *funerary chamber*. An *altar* is placed to the east of it, as is usual with similar burial mounds. This possibly indicates that sun-worship was involved with the Berbers' attitude towards death.

[60 km.] Meknes.

MEKNES

Population 319,783

Bus C.T.M. station at the corner of Ave. des F.A.R. and Ave. Mohammed V. Daily departures for Rabat, Marrakech and Midelt.

Taxi Ranks for *grands taxis* in Place el-Hedim; Place de France; station (*Map* 4).

Car Hire Meknes is served by Fes with the exception of a few purely local operations.

Hotels

*****	*Hôtel Transatlantique*, Rue el Meriniyine (tel. 200.02).
****A	*Hôtel Rif*, Zankat Accra (tel. 225.91).
***B	*Hôtel de Nice*, 10 Zankat Accra (tel. 203.18).
**A	*Hôtel Palace*, Rue de Ghana (tel. 223.88).
**A	*Hôtel Majestic*, 19 Ave. Mohammed V (tel. 220.35).
**A	*Hôtel Panorama*, 9 Ave. des F.A.R. (tel. 227.37).
**B	*Hôtel Continental*, 92 Ave. des F.A.R. (tel. 202.00).
*A	*Hôtel Volubilis*, 45 Ave. des F.A.R. (tel. 201.02).
*A	*Hôtel Touring*, 34 Ave. Allal ben Abdellah (tel. 223.51).
*A	*Hôtel Excelsior*, 57 Ave. des F.A.R. (tel. 219.00).

Camping *Agdal*, two kilometres from the centre, opposite the Heri as-Souani (see *Map* 19).

Information

O.N.M.T. Tourist Office: Bab Bou Ameur (tel. 212.86).

Syndicat d'Initiative: Esplanade de la Foire (tel. 201.91).

Consulate French: Boulevard Ferhat Rachad (tel. 222.27).

Banks Ave. Mohammed V.

Shopping Some excellent carpets offered at the *Souk Joutiya as-Zerabi*, near the Mosque en-Nejjarine (*Map* 7).

Sports and clubs

Tennis and swimming: Lahboul (tel. 204.15).

Royal Golf Club: Ave. Mohammed V (tel. 211.81).

Racing: (tel. 307.51).

Festivals

Moussems: Sidi Bouzekin in September; Moulay Idriss in September (see pp. 285–7) — you will have to stay in Meknes for it; Aïssawa at Mouloud; Hamdcha des Dghoughia (in the Jebel Zerhoun) a week after Mouloud.

Post Office Main P.T.T. by the Place de France.

Emergencies
Police: tel. 19
Ambulance: tel. 15 or 211.34 (Mohammed V Hospital).

This was Moulay Ismaïl's capital — but before him it was always a considerable place since a very fertile region surrounds it. Modern farming techniques have greatly enhanced that fertility and the new quarters of the city present something of the aspect of a go-ahead, up-to-date market-town, very prosperous indeed. In contrast, the medina wears a rather outworn air. Ismaïl's palace (the Dar el-Kebira) makes a remarkable ruin, easiest seen by car; its external, defensive wall had a perimeter of twenty-five kilometres. It makes a pretty long walk — if you are not driving, you could take a taxi or carriage, and a guide from the O.N.M.T. office would simplify things for you.

HISTORY

Meknes takes its name from the great Meknassa tribe which was divided into two main parts in early Arab days in Morocco, one section commanding the Taza region and the other this around Meknes, which was probably no more than a concentration of *ksour* when the Almoravids took it in 1069. It may than have acquired the nucleus of a township. In 1145 or 1146 Abd el-Mumin the Almohad occupied it and apparently for some time treated it harshly, so that the population diminished, but presently the Almohads began to build it up; its mosque was restored, the water supply increased.

During the Merinids' long battle for power against the later Almohads, Meknes suffered greatly. The Beni Merin were for a long time content not to occupy it but instead, effectively commanding the countryside, to isolate it, extorting capital levies from it in return for permission to buy food. This probably began in 1217 and continued until the Almohads relieved it in 1244, Sultan es-Saïd defeating Abd el-Haqq, the real founder of Merinid strength, who died soon after. His son, Abu Yahya Abu Bekr, returning the next year, this time took the town, though he soon abandoned it at the advance of es-Saïd with a large army. After es-Saïd's death in 1248 Abu Bekr again returned and took possession of it. His son again, Abu Yussef Yaacub, rebuilt the town, casbah and Great Mosque around 1276. Towards the end of his reign, Abu el-Hassan built a *zawiya* in the town and began the *medrassa* which it was left to his Abu Inan to finish in the mid fourteenth century. In the fifteenth century Meknes was from 1417 to 1437 the base of el-Lihiani, a Merinid prince claiming the throne. Town and neighbourhood had suffered in 1415 during the revolt of the rebel es-Saïd and were to suffer again when el-Hayaïni also raised a revolt in 1480. It more or less belonged to the Wattasids, and even for a time prospered again just before the Saadi captured Fes in 1547, in which year they also gained Meknes.

As a young man, Moulay Ismaïl was governor of the town for his father er-Rashid, the first Alaouite sultan, and after he had fought for and won the succession − 1672 − he made Meknes his new capital of the country. As a centre of government it is really better placed than Fes although its position is less easily defended, and while Ismaïl distrusted both the Fasiyin and the Marrakchi, he was strong enough never seriously to have to defend the capital of his choice. It is not possible, on the evidence, to acquit Ismaïl of the charge of megalomania. A great administrator and general, a ruthless autocrat, he made Morocco work and prosper as a country − a sufficient accomplishment to give a man a good opinion of himself. He knew that Morocco could become a considerable power in European affairs if only its government would let it be so, just as he was anxious for its own sake that it should be. He was evidently an able self-publicist − a useful talent in an autocrat − but he did go that much too far which suggests imbalance of character. His dealings with European powers were at once productive and foolish in a way that exhibits ignorance and a manic kind of self-confidence. His enormous palace complex here, built at a tearing pace by armies of slaves and workmen sometimes whipped on by Ismaïl in person, is often enough compared to Louis XIV's Versailles. He may have modelled it to some extent on accounts of that extraordinary building, but I think the resemblance is closest in the purpose behind both palaces: to make a fresh base for government, a purpose entailing the need to house enormous numbers of people which offered both monarchs an opportunity to collect these under their surveillance in a way that had not been previously possible but which was an admirable safeguard against insurrection in countries become habituated to civil war. Versailles was more obviously successful in every way, but Meknes too served its purpose.

After Ismaïl's death in 1727 the traditional balance between Fes and Marrakech was slowly reasserted under Moulay

Abdullah and his son Sidi Mohammed, who was to restore Marrakech as his capital. The terrible earthquake which destroyed Lisbon in 1755 severely damaged Meknes; the real ruination of the palace dates from that disaster.

PRINCIPAL SIGHTS

The medina and Dar el-Kebira palace quarter lie on the west bank of the Oued Boufekrane, the former to the north and the palace south-eastwards of it. The new town is confined to the east bank of the river. Traffic for the old quarters almost inevitably ends up in the *Place el-Hedim* (*Map* 11) which faces the great wall into which opens the *Bab Mansur el-Aleuj* — the great ceremonial entrance to Moulay Ismaïl's imperial palace, the Dar el-Kebira. This gate is named for Mansur, the convert from Christianity, who was its architect.

Amongst ever-growing new quarters of the city, to the southeast, there now rises a really splendid, huge new mosque. Its exterior proportions are beautiful. Approaching Meknes from Fes, it is impossible to miss it.

DAR EL-KEBIRA

Map 9.

A general date for the palace as a whole is 1697 although the entire complex was not completed until five years after Ismaïl's death, under Abdullah. This gate probably belongs to the early years. Its great size and brilliant colour compensate for the lack of elegance of which — in comparison, say, with the Almohad gates of Rabat — it is possible to complain. In fact it is not at all bad; one's only real criticism is that the traditional means of lightening the effect of so massive a structure by a subtle and, as it were, internal, hidden design has not been well enough understood by the architect, so that the emphasis upon it is too slight and the whole therefore too ponderous. It is, though, interesting to see the traditional gate, flanked by two defensive towers, rendered in this purely decorative and ceremonial way. El-Aleuj has been inventive, carrying the flanking piers upon columns — probably taken from Volubilis, which was much cannibalized to decorate this palace.

On the right of this gate stands the less impressive *Bab Jemaa en-Nour*, built at the beginning of the eighteenth century to give

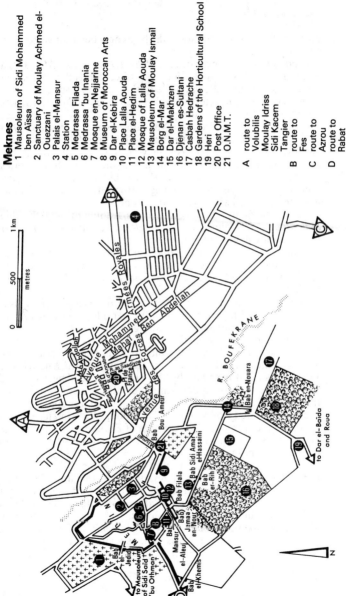

Meknes

1 Mausoleum of Sidi Mohammed ben Aïssa
2 Sanctuary of Moulay Achmed el-Ouezzani
3 Palais el-Mansur
4 Station
5 Medrassa Filada
6 Medrassa 'bu Inania
7 Mosque en-Nejjarine
8 Museum of Moroccan Arts
9 Dar el-Kebira
10 Place Lalla Aouda
11 Place el-Hedim
12 Mosque of Lalla Aouda
13 Mausoleum of Moulay Ismaïl
14 Borg el-Mar
15 Dar el-Makhzen
16 Djenan es-Sultani
17 Casbah Hedrache
18 Gardens of the Horticultural School
19 Heri
20 Post Office
21 O.N.M.T.

A route to
  Volubilis
  Moulay Idriss
  Sidi Kacem
  Tangier
B route to
  Fes
C route to
  Azrou
D route to
  Rabat

access to the Mosque en-Nour which has now been converted to a school.

Inside the Bab Mansur lies the *Place Lalla Aouda* (*Map* **10**), a great *mechouar*. On the far left, opposite, stands the *Mosque of Lalla Aouda* (*Map* **12**), once one of the palace mosques.

Immediately opposite the *Bab Filala* opens. Through it lies your way to the rest of the palace, along a corridor of a road. Around the left-hand bend, on the left, opens the *Mausoleum of Moulay Ismaïl* (*Map* **13**). It is open daily from 09.00 to midday and from 15.00 to 18.00. You may go into the *courtyards*, the mosaic-decorated great court and the smaller which has galleries decorated with carved plaster-work also, but not into the *mosque*, though you can see the *sarcophagus* from the doorway. All this has been restored and is really quite fine.

Beside the mausoleum there is a lane leading through the *Bab Sidi Amar el-Hassaini* into the *Dar el-Kebira Quarter* — a rather nice, oldish village among the ruined splendours.

Your way leads under the *Bab er-Rih* after which the wall on your right is that of the more recent, present royal palace or *Dar el-Makhzen* (*Map* **15**). It was built from the end of the eighteenth century.

Where the lane turns right there is the *Borg el-Mar* (*Map* **14**), the 'water bastion', after which you enter a large *mechouar*. On its right is a late-nineteenth-century *gateway* into the palace; the *Bab en-Nouara* leads from the left side into the *Casbah Hedrache* (*Map* **17**) — an old barracks; while, straight ahead, another *gate* gives into the delightful *Gardens of the Horticultural School* (*Map* **18**). You should continue by the lane, now leading along the western side of these gardens until it divides at a point formed by the *Heri* (*Map* **19**), or 'granary', containing large underground silos with vaulted stores above. This belonged to Ismaïl's palace. In one of the stores are two tricycles of European make — relics of one of Abdul Aziz's enthusiasms? Beyond this granary stand the ruins of another.

Beyond this lies an artificial *reservoir* covering four hectares. These serve what are still the palace gardens west of the present palace — the walled *Djenan es-Sultani* (*Map* **16**). The left-hand fork of the lane from the Heri leads to the *Dar el-Baïda*, Sidi Mohammed ben Abdullah's very large palace of the second half of the eighteenth century. It is used as a military academy. One can see at least into the large *garden-court* where there are *capitals* to be seen, most probably originally coming from the el-Badi Palace of Marrakech. Like the Dar el-Makhzen of Marrakech, this appears to have been planned as a traditionally symmetrical palace.

Beyond this building lies what is called the *Jbabra Quarter* where you can visit the *Roua* or 'stables' — the sight you have come these 4 or 5 km. to see. It consists, now, of a walled enclosure divided by a great number of high, arched aisles of massive pisé, pock-marked by weathering, the forms of both pillars and arches transformed by erosion. Acacias grow among them. The place is empty of everything save a goat or two grazing. It is mysteriously beautiful and impressive. The light is extraordinary; the violet-tinged, pinkish earth tamped into this dry *tabia* is a wonderful colour. These stables were reputed to have housed 12,000 horses in Ismaïl's time. Over them, on the great platform they formed, stood the el-Mansur palace, a building said to have consisted of not less than twenty-four pavilions. The entire Dar el-Kebira, according to the chronicler ez-Zayyani, comprised something like the same number of separate and isolated buildings, besides two mosques, barracks and gardens and *mechouars*.

In this Jbabra Quarter there is a *mosque* of the same name, built by Sidi Mohammed, where more columns, capitals and marbles salvaged from the ruin of his grandfather's palace were employed. Some of these things are of Saadi workmanship and must have belonged to the el-Badi Palace.

You can leave the palace by the *Bab el-Bettioui* and get back to the town by taking the road left.

MEDINA

There is less here worth your attention, yet it is a typical and lively enough place with a quite interesting *market* and artisans' streets.

Medrassa 'bu Inania
Map 6.
This is a Merinid building begun by Abu el-Hassan and completed by, and named for, 'bu Inan in the early 1350s. It is a fairly small *medrassa* with a tall *court* and a high-roofed *prayer-hall*. It does not make an impression upon one comparable with that of its contemporary at Fes, though it should be seen.

Museum of Moroccan Arts (Dar Jamaï)
Map **8.**
Open Daily except Tuesdays 09.00–12.00 and 16.00–18.00.
Entrance: Free.

The same vizier to Moulay el-Hassan as built the palace at Fes
(now the hotel of the same name) built this. It is a not very interesting late-nineteenth-century house, but it now shelters an
excellent collection of local artefacts particularly strong in things
of a Middle Atlas provenance.

Medrassa Filada
Map **5.**
This small *medrassa* was built by Moulay Ismaïl in the late seventeenth century. It follows the pattern of its predecessors, but the
decoration and detail is comparatively clumsy. Its effect is rather
gay, however; there was a decided exuberance about the Ismaïlite
peace which shows itself in buildings like this and some of the
ksour built to overawe the countryside.

Mosque en-Nejjarine
Map **7.**
This was the Almohad foundation, but what one sees belongs to
Sidi Mohammed ben Abdullah's rebuilding in the eighteenth
century.

Palais el-Mansur
Map **3.**
A grand nineteenth-century house, now a souvenir-market.

Bab el-Khemis
The best of the town gates; built by Ismaïl in the late seventeenth
century. Inside it, to the north, lies the old Mellah, the new to the
south.

Sanctuary of Moulay Achmed el-Ouezzani
Map **2.**
Moulay Achmed el-Ouezzani − whose sanctuary, built in 1917, is
in the town − was one of the most recent Moroccan saints. An
extreme ascetic who would not touch money, he died in 1933.

Mausoleum of Sidi Mohammed ben Aïssa
Map 1.
This lies outside the Bab el-Jedid, on the west of the medina, in a large cemetery. Non-Moslems may not even enter the cemetery. The sanctuary and mausoleum were built by Sidi Mohammed ben Abdullah; late-eighteenth-century. Ben Aïssa died in 1523, yet legend has him live under Moulay Ismaïl. The Aïssawa cult has adherents all over North Africa. It is hard to say in what lies its attraction, though the legends hint that Sidi Aïssa rewarded his hearers with leafy branches which turned into silver and gold after his sermons — 'Ismaïl's builders' readily forsaking their work for this bonus given with edification. Ben Aïssa is also said to have recommended a destitute person to eat anything as long as it was poison from which, upon his eating it, he received no harm. The Aïssawi used until recently to eat scorpions, spiny cacti, snakes and lizards at their gatherings. Perhaps the saint's real message is that there is good in all things, everything having proceeded from God. A large moussem is held in ben Aïssa's honour at Mouloud.

For Aïssa music, see p. 135. Almost every Friday you can see a group of Aïssawa in the cemetery, some of whom will be tranced. Rather less emphasis is put upon wounds self-inflicted under trance in this cult than among the Hamadchi, but the practice persists. In both cults these orgiastic rites are officially banned and carried on now only in secret. Yet those traditions to which the people are devoted die hard in Morocco. In many small ways the Moroccan penchant for anarchy seems to be reasserting itself, one being the now more open practice of both these cults' rituals, barely restrained from going their whole gory hog.

Another *sanctuary* is built about the tomb of Sidi Saïd 'bu Othman, father from the town on the Rabat road. This saint was Ben Aïssa's teacher; the mausoleum was erected by Abdullah ben Ismaïl in the mid eighteenth century.

Excursion from Meknes to Volubilis and Moulay Idriss

Route From Meknes and back this is an excursion of about 64 km or, continuing back to Fes by the P32, 92 km. Take the P6 towards Sidi Kacem (Route Exit A). [See Route Map for Northern Area (pp. 298–9).]
Bus Buses to Moulay Idriss help you to come within walking distance of the ruins of

Volubilis, which are open from dawn to sunset. *Grands taxis* ply the route, departing from Bab Mansour.

The ruined provincial monuments of Imperial Rome have a specially poignant flavour about them and Volubilis is no exception. The site is a beautiful one and there are fine mosaics to be seen *in situ* in a number of its houses. Moulay Idriss is a very attractive town; its *raison d'être* is the national shrine of Morocco's first Arab king of that name, though of course you cannot enter the building where he lies buried.

[10 km.] A turning right on the P28 to Moulay Idriss, or, alternatively,

[15 km.] **Aïn el-Kerma,** near which lie the ruins of the *Tocolosida* camp, one of four Roman camps built to defend Volubilis, and from there turn right for Moulay Idriss.

Either way it is about 15 km. to another turning before the ascent to Moulay Idriss. For Volubilis, continue on the P28 for Col du Zeggota.

VOLUBILIS

Open Daily from dawn to sunset; entrance charge. There is a bar on the site.

History
There are reasons to think that this city was an important one before the Roman occupation of Morocco, that indeed it was the capital of the Berber Kingdom of Mauritania. However, there is as yet no archaeological proof that this was so. That this fertile and well-watered neighbourhood was populous and that its inhabitants lived in circumstances of considerable, Punic-influenced civilization is incontestable, but as to whether there was an actual city housing an urban society is uncertain. One is reminded of those places in southern Morocco today where the population is grouped into concentrations of *ksour*: early Volubilis could have been a centre of that sort, and it could still have been the kingdom's capital. Tangier was at that period undoubtedly a great city in the sense accepted over the Mediterranean basin and Near East — but it is hard to think that Juba II should have contented himself with a palace of pisé. If capital this

was, then from 25 B.C. to A.D. 23 or 24 it was the learned Juba's western capital — his eastern being the very Romanized Caesarea (see p. 61). And from A.D. 45, when the Romans annexed the kingdom to direct rule, Volubilis was quite certainly a true city and seat of the procurators governing the province of Mauritania Tingitana. It was also for a long time a forward base against the recalcitrant Berbers of the mountains who objected to becoming Roman subjects. The greatest revolt was the first, when Aedemon — who had perhaps been the murdered Ptolemy's minister — resisted the Romans with the backing of the greater part of the country. Things did not really settle down until the next century, and during most of the third also — the good period for all Roman North Africa.

The walls were built in 168, and later enlarged. Four camps were set about the city to provide defence in depth, three of them being at Tocolosida, Aïn Chkour and Bled el-Gadaa.

By the end of the third century the province and the city were declining. The Romans themselves withdrew about Tangier, abandoning Volubilis before the end of the century. The city, however, remained an urban centre, a market for the oil trade and an enclave of very Latin and Romanized culture. It appears also to have become largely Christian though it had a Jewish colony and citizens who were pagan, as so much of the country then still was. It was never overrun by 'barbarians' as was the rest of the old western empire. Like Britain and Farther Gaul, its people were, from a Roman's point of view, though, already barbarian and only superficially latinized; from their own point of view they were civilized in the Roman's sense of the word and since they were spared invasion by more primitive peoples — as Britain and Gaul were not — they were able to keep something of their civilization alive until the Arabs brought a different and stronger — more internationally based — one to the city in the seventh century

It was to Volubilis that Moulay Idriss came about 787. He was accepted as leader of the Aouraba tribe, but since he removed from Volubilis into the hills near by within so few years — he was poisoned in 791 or 792 — it looks as though he did not get on particularly well with the townsmen. But his new town, now called Moulay Idriss, and Fes, which his son founded as his capital, drew the population away. Volubilis was abandoned for these new centres. (It is convenient to refer to the city as Volubilis, but after the Romans left it became known either as Oualila or Oulili.)

We have a brief description of the then existing monuments of the city left by John Windus, who visited the site in 1721. If we can see more detail than he since the excavations, seriously begun by French archaeologists in 1915, Windus saw a good deal more still standing; the earthquake of 1755, which destroyed Lisbon and so much damaged Ismaïl's palace of Meknes, severely shook Volubilis also.

Principal sights

From the point of view of the visitor who is not an archaeologist, the Volubilis site is just about perfect. The town was quite small — the walls encircling it measure 2,350 metres — and those ruined buildings which still stand to a fair height make a fine showing, while you can see all that really matters by making a short and easy walk in most attractive surroundings.

The entrance is through the *south-east gate* in the walls. It has been partially rebuilt.

Opposite the *guardians' lodge* is a *garden* where architectural fragments and carved inscriptions are displayed, also a good *head of Medusa* in mosaic.

You cross the *Oued Fertassa*, which flowed through the town to join the *Oued Khouman* which provided some defence upon the south — where now the walls are most fragmentary.

Climbing from the *bridge* over the Fertassa, the path passes the remains of an *oil-press* on the left before turning right up a paved lane. Industry and habitation were much intermixed at Volubilis, oil-presses being common — as might be expected in a centre of oil production.

Turn left around the angle of a house — the '*House of Orpheus*' (*Map* 1) — which is the largest in this otherwise humble quarter. Round the corner, the first entrance into this house gives into the domestic part of it — the *boiler-house* for the heating, *kitchen* and *baths* around a little *courtyard*. There is a *dolphin mosaic* in one room. The second entrance leads to the main *living-quarters* set about a larger court where there is a *mosaic of Amphitrite* in a car drawn by a sea-horse and surrounded by sea-creatures. In the *southern room* is the *mosaic of the Orphic myth* for which the house is named and on the right is another *mosaic-paved room*; on the west an *oil-press*.

Where the path turns right again the building on the left was the *Baths of Gallienus* (*Map* 2), that emperor having restored these public baths. No decorative features now remain in them.

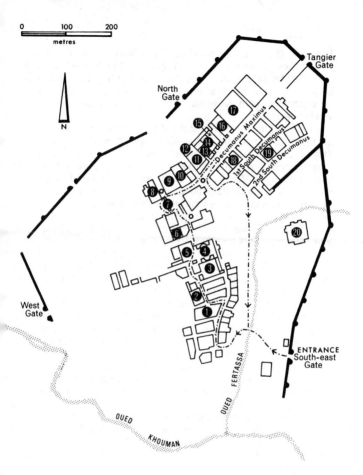

Volubilis

1 House of Orpheus
2 Baths of Gallienus
3 Capitol
4 Basilica
5 Forum
6 House of the Jumper
7 Triumphal Arch
8 House of the Ephebos
9 House of the Columns
10 Knight's House
11 House of the Labours of Hercules

12 Bath-house
13 House of T. Flavius Germanus
14 House of Dionysus and the Four
    Seasons
15 House of the Nymphs Bathing
16 House of the Wild Beasts
17 Gordien Palace
18 House of the Nereïds
19 House of the Cortege of Venus
20 Temple B

Beyond, the path approaches the official buildings, coming beside them in what was a small *square* with a *market* on the left side and the *Forum Baths* on the right abutting the Capitol and Basilica, a group of ruins which makes an impressive ensemble, very picturesque in the romantic manner and crowned by several storks' nests.

The first part is the *Capitol* (*Map* **3**), **a** *court* surrounded by *porticoes* in which stood a small temple preceded by an altar. Steps led up to the temple which, comprising a single *cella*, had four columns across the front to support the pediment. This, and also the Forum Baths, were built upon older buildings, first a forum dating from the second century and below that an unidentified building dating from the reign of Juba II. The Capitol was dated, by an inscription to the Emperor Macrinus, as 217. It was of course the temple of the state cult of Capitoline Jove, Juno and Minerva. This temple is unusual in not opening to the east, but this can be explained by the position which it occupies. Instead of being housed in an ante-chamber behind the *cella*, the cult objects and state records generally laid up in a Capitol must have been kept in the side-rooms off the portico.

The larger, adjoining building is the *Basilica* (*Map* **4**) or judgment-hall. At its either end are large *apses*. Five aisles ran the length of the building, the central, wider one linking the apses, across both of which stood a screen of two columns. It was built in the early third century.

The point at which you can enter the side of this building formed part of the *Forum* (*Map* **5**). Much of it is still paved with large blocks. There is a small *market* round a *court* on its west. This forum was built under the Severi at the beginning of the third century and replaced earlier buildings among which was one that may have been a temple of the earlier Roman period which itself had replaced what appears to have been two small temples and an open, forum-like area belonging to the Mauritanian period.

The path crosses the Forum and passes on the right a *monument* to the family of Septimus Severus with several plinths for statues, one of which was of Marcus Valerius Severus, Aedemon's vanquisher. It then passes between two buildings. That on the left is the *House of the Jumper* (*desultor*) (*Map* **6**) where there is a *mosaic* of an athlete holding the cup he has won by vaulting the horse on which he rides. Behind this house and the next-door shops beyond it, are the remains of the house in which the bronze *guard-dog* (now in the Archaeological Museum at Rabat) was found.

Beyond this group of buildings again, the *Triumphal Arch* (*Map* 7) stands. This is now perhaps the single most considerable monument in Volubilis although the Basilica may well have been a nobler building in its day. The Arch is merely a decoration for the town — it leads nowhere particularly and is ornamented to any extent only on the easterly face which looks across a wide open space and up the length of the *decumanus maximus*, or principal street, towards the *Tangier Gate*. Its purpose was in part to beautify the town and to do it honour, but also to remind the citizens that the emperor, Caracalla, was great and beneficent and, as it were, watching them. It also reminded all comers that the Severi were Africans, that they favoured Africa and expected its loyalty in return. This is not really a distinguished building — though the attic or upper section has so far disappeared that one cannot now tell whether anything happened there to redeem the whole design. The masonry is of pleasant-coloured ashlar (like all of it here; from quarries in the Jebel Zerhoun) and well cut; the Corinthian columns are of imported marble. In the *niche* on either side the arch stood statues of nymphs or water-gods from between whose feet sprang water-jets falling into basins below. The *inscription* over the arch records that it was built by the procurator Marcus Aurelius Sebastenus in 217 in honour of Caracalla and his mother Julia Domna — whose heads were probably those on the *medallions* above the niches — and that a six-horse chariot (driven by the emperor or a god most likely having the emperor's likeness) surmounted the arch. This was presumably of bronze; it would add much to the effect of the whole. Fragments of the *relief* of trophies and arms which flanked the inscription are now propped against the low wall to the right of the arch. They are quite boldly carved and evidently of local workmanship.

The first house on the right through the Triumphal Arch is called the '*House of the Ephebos*' (*Map* 8). It is a classic example of the better-class Volubilis house, such as those occupying the north-eastern quarter on either side of the *decumanus maximus*. In it was found the bronze *Ephebos* now in Rabat Museum. The open courtyard of a Roman house was once — at Rome — the central living-room or *atrium*. Rome suffers quite hard winters and in so far as it really can be postulated that the *atrium* evolved into the courtyard, this was a development made in warmer parts.

Hellenistic Greek houses were, however, planned round courts and it was rather this fashion that entered Rome by way of the Greek cities of southern Italy where, at Pompeii for instance, many houses have both an *atrium* off which open rooms and behind it a garden-court surrounded by more rooms. Delos represents the best-preserved collection of Hellenistic dwelling-houses remaining to us and it is plain that the 'Roman' houses of Volubilis have a closer affinity with these than with those really Roman ones at Ostia Antica. In particular the Delian habit of grouping 'public' and 'private' rooms separately is very marked here. The front court, in which there is an ornamental pool, is surrounded by the public rooms — the *tablinum* where papers were kept (in this house it is the room with the *mosaic* of interlocked circles, ovals and octagonal shapes with a nymph astride a sea-beast set in one of them), the *cenacula* for entertaining (there is a *pavement* showing Bacchus riding his triumphal chariot drawn by panthers in one of these here) and rooms which acted as offices. The private or domestic rooms are grouped round a second, back courtyard, also having a pool in its midst. These include the domestic offices, sleeping-rooms and — often the case here — an olive-press. An oddity in this particular case is the *cellar room* made out of part of the base of an older mausoleum which seems to have been dismantled to make room for the narrow street between this house and the *House of the Columns* (*Map* 9) next door. This leads to the open place in front of the Arch. This house is easily identified by the row of standing columns facing the street. It has been dated as belonging to the short reign of Gordien III (238–44). It is, as it were, No. 1 Decumanus Maximus.

Next door is the *Knight's House* (*Map* 10), rather ruinous, though with a *mosaic* of Dionysus discovering Ariadne asleep on the Naxian shore in it.

Opposite are the ruins of the *North Baths* and one of two *fountains* fed by the *aqueduct* supplying these baths. It runs behind the houses lining the left side of *decumanus maximus*.

The next house on the left (entered from the side-turning) is called the *House of the Labours of Hercules* (*Map* 11) after the *mosaic* in its *triclinium* or banqueting-hall where *benches* for reclining feasters line three walls. The mosaic, with two blank spaces among twelve frames, is in fact really one of 'scenes from the life of' Hercules since, besides the labours of killing the birds of Stymphalus, the kidnap of Cerberus and that of the Cretan bull, the slaughter of the Nemean lion, the hydra of Lerna and the boar of Erymanthus, with the cleansing of the Augean stables, his infantile exploit of strangling the serpents in his cradle, his mysterious association with Hippolyta the Amazon and his triumph over Antaeus are also illustrated. The back part of this house is occupied by a *bath-house* (*Map* 12). Behind it lay a cemetery.

You will have noticed that behind the colonnades of the houses lining this street, giving shelter and shade to pedestrians, are small rooms opening only to the street. These were shops let off by the owners of the houses. This was a Roman habit — a common practice in Italy up to the nineteenth century — and confined the outward show of a man's house to a noble front door or, as here, to the splendour of its colonnade. The practice combined economy with quiet, the shops acting as an insulation against the noise of the wider streets clamorous with people, hawkers, chariots and carts (whose wheel-marks you can see on the paving-stones), barrows and animals and servants shouting to make way for their masters' litters.

The next five houses on the right of the *decumanus maximus* are rather smaller. The first was that of *T. Flavius Germanus* (*Map* 13), as an inscribed *altar* to the household-gods found in one room tells us. The second is called the *House of Dionysus and the Four Seasons* (*Map* 14) for a *mosaic* of this subject — which is very well preserved. Next door is the *House of the Nymphs Bathing* (*Map* 15) where a *mosaic* of this scene lies in a room off the inner courtyard. The fourth is the *House of the Wild Beasts* (*Map* 16), but the mosaic has been removed, and the fifth is very ruinous and unnamed.

Next comes the very large *Gordien Palace* (*Map* 17) with an imposing colonnade across its front. This was the residence of the procurators of the province and has been called Gordien's because an inscription found in it dated it as having been built during the reign of young Gordien III. Its building seems to have followed upon the reorganization of the Forum area under Caracalla and Macrinus which may have made away with the earlier official 'government house'. There is not now much to see in it except the fine pools in its courts and, up a few steps, three small rooms that could be warmed in cold weather, and a large *bath-house*. The surviving pavements are mostly quite ordinary geometric marble inlays, very much damaged.

Between the palace and the Tangier Gate there is little to be

seen and the houses on the left-hand side of the street are in a con-
fused and very ruinous condition. However, that directly opposite the Nymphs Bathing and Dionysus and the Four Seasons —
the *House of the Nereïds* (*Map* 18) — has *mosaics* in the courtyard
and around the pool which are pleasant.

Go down behind the rubble of this house's lower neighbours,
beside the fountain and aqueduct mentioned above, to the first
south *decumanus*, which runs parallel to the *maximus*. Turn left
along this street; the third house on the right is the *House of the
Cortège of Venus* (*Map* 19). This is a spendid house with many
mosaic pavements in which were found the wonderful *bronze
heads* of Cato and Juba II now in the Rabat Museum (p. 177).
You enter down steps into a first and then a second *vestibule*
leading to a square *court* in which there is an I-shaped pool. In the
room facing this entrance across the court is a damaged *mosaic* of
bird-drawn chariots racing in a hippodrome, its *spina* decorated
with three columns upholding the two eggs by which Leda bore
the Dioscuri and Helen. The large *triclinium* off the right-hand
portico was decorated with the *mosaic* of Venus 'navigating',
which is in the Tangier museum — how often here are the rooms
of these dwellers in the interior of the country decorated with
marine subjects! In the room to the left of the *triclinium* is
Bacchus — again with the seasons — the god being damaged. In
the far right-hand corner are two *rooms* with *mosaics*, 'Hylas captured by nymphs' being in the first of them and 'Diana with two
nymphs surprised while bathing by a woodland god' in the
second. These last two rooms are believed to be rather later than
the others, which are dated as of the end of the second century.

You go back down the street and follow the path left for the
way out. As the path bends slightly right, you can see on your left
the line of a *wall* protecting the south-east flank of the quarter you
have just quitted. This dates from the Mauritanian period and
marks out with the other walls around the quarter a nearly symmetrical, polygonal area — which leads one to speculate whether
this uppermost part was not the nucleus of the town, a kind of
urbanized *ksar* built in the sophisticated Roman way suitable to
house a Juba II. At the near end of this wall are the remains of a
quite elaborate *tumulus tomb* and the foundations of a small
temple-shrine. Across the valley of the stream you can see the
remains of *Temple B* (*Map* 20), a large structure in a *court* surrounded by *peristyles*, which is called 'of Saturn' but may have
been that of a local pre-Roman deity later Latinized.

You return to the Moulay Idriss turning the way you came and climb up the 1 km. to the town. Or, upon leaving the ruins, you can turn left and left again to return to the ascent road, a way which passes below the ruins so that you can better see the defensible situation of the old town.

MOULAY IDRISS

This is a delightful town, picturesquely set on spurs of the hills; a busy country town with a Saturday market and the site of the tomb and *zawiya* of Moulay Idriss — called el-Akhbar, to distinguish him from his son Idriss II who is patron of Fes.

One should add to what is said of Moulay Idriss on p. 69 that his full name was Idriss ibn Abdullah ben el-Hassan ben Ali, a name which proclaims his descent from the Prophet's daughter Fatima by her marriage to Ali. Ali was the Prophet's cousin, brought up by him and one of the first, if not the very first, of his followers. Ayesha, Mohammed's widow, hated him and was instrumental in barring him from the caliphate while first Abu Bekr, Omar and then Uthman ruled. Ali was thus the fourth caliph, his short reign being a time of civil war with Muawiya and Amr. Ali died of a wound made by a poisoned weapon, and his son by Fatima, el-Hassan, succeeded him to the caliphate of part at least of Islam. The division of Islam between those who acknowledged Ali's right to succeed the Prophet and those who adhered to his rivals became more serious than anything a mere struggle for power could provoke. It caused a schism, each side claiming the other to be heretical; the Shias* for Ali and the Sunnites against him. The first Alids lost their battles. It was their defeat in 786 at the battle of Fekhkh near Mecca, by the Abbasid el-Mansur, that drove Idriss to look for a refuge in the far Maghreb, where he arrived the following year soon to create a principality based first on Volubilis and then upon his own town built here. It was this deep and very general division in Islam that

---

* The several Shia sects of today, however, represent a somewhat Gnostic elaboration of this original schism. Believing Ali to have been the only true Caliph in the succession of the Prophet they believe he never died but will one day reappear as temporal and spiritual head of Islam. Ali's death is explained as a 'passion' in the sense of Jesus's death (or that of Osiris or Adonis); Fatima takes on something of the character of the Virgin Mary; Ali's return parallels that of the 'promised' return of Jesus. In none of these aspects of later Shiism would Idriss have himself believed save in the genuineness of his claim upon the caliphate.

enabled one man and his servant, never so able as both Idriss and
his Rashid might have been, to build an Arab state out of the
respect of a few Berber tribes; for as an able Alid Idriss attracted
a flow of Arab adherents from the East. It was for this reason too
that Harun er-Rashid was so fearful of Idriss's influence that he
had him poisoned in 791 or 792 by stealth and treachery. (Later
generations would have called Idriss a Fatimid rather than an
Alid, members of the family of Ali and Fatima coming to make
this distinction between themselves and the descendants of Ali's
other wives.) One cannot help the feeling that Ali had a raw deal
— or that, as the Shiites claim, he was too good and simple a man
to counter the political manoeuvres of Ayesha and the others —
and that he was unlikely to have retained the Prophet's high
favour had he been, as the Sunni claimed, a mere place- and
power-seeker. Islam has always been the poorer for the quarrel.
It remains so today although, for upwards of a generation, Shias
have been formally accepted as 'within Islam'. It none the less
provided Idriss with a strong background for the attractive
gallantry of his exploits here.

For the infidel visitor to Moulay Idriss there is little to see save
the entrance to the *zawiya* and *mausoleum*, rebuilt by Moulay
Ismaïl in the late seventeenth century, or to climb the town to a
terrace with a splendid view across a valley to the Tasga Quarter
of the town with the green roofs of the sanctuary in the foreground. However, the walk through the town is well worth while
and the view a notable one. The moussem of Moulay Idriss
attracts great crowds in September.

From Moulay Idriss a beautiful drive of 17 km. on the S306 leads
in a north-easterly direction to join the Fes-to-Sidi Kacem road,
where Fes is a another 50 km. The P28 leads 10 km. to Col du
Zeggota and the P3 to Sidi Kacem.

There is also a track from Moulay Idriss which brings you close to
the summit of *Jebel Zerhoun* and to a lookout peak south of
Volubilis which is spectacular. This mountain harbours several
zouawi of the formally banned, allied Hamadcha and Dghoughia
sects. These used to have an enormous following over the country
and perhaps their underground influence is still considerable
since they practised the mysticism of song and dance very much
like that of the Eastern dervishes, inducing that strange state of
being under which heavy blows, wounding with knives or axes

and the application of fire does not at the time appear to harm one — a state which seems to have a universal attraction for certain types, while the intoxicating preliminaries of rhythmic music and unending dancing captivate many more, and Berbers particularly so. However, the sects are now undercover and their ceremonies certainly not public; the mountain's moussem, held seven days after Mouloud, is no longer what it once was. It is held near the village of **Beni Rachid** at the *tomb of Sidi Ali ben Hamdouch* — who died in the early 1660s having been in the habit of furiously beating his followers into a trance-like state of spiritual ecstasy.

FES TO TANGIER:
Route 1 (via Chechaouen)

Route 335 km. by the P 26 road to Ouezzane, the P 28 to near Tetouan and the P 38 to Tangier — a good enough road at the worst and an excellent one over much of the always attractive drive. Leave Fes either from the south-western end of the Avenue Hassan II or via the Route du Tour de Fes (Route Exit A). [See Route Map for Northern Area (pp. 298–9).] (For a journey 23 kms. shorter, by a quicker though less interesting route, leave Fes by the P 1, as for Meknes, and fork right on the P 3 at 11 km. and right on to the P 28 at 46 km., joining the foregoing route at Ouezzane.)
Bus Changes of bus will be needed if you want to stop off at the main towns on this route, but the journey can be made in a day.
Accommodation and food At Chechaouen, Tetouan.

[15 km.] To the left of the road there rises, dramatically enough, the *shrine of Sidi Achmed el-Bernoussi*, one of the patrons of Fes. The present tomb dates from the reign of Moulay el-Hassan, its dependencies from that of his son Abdul Aziz — none of the ensemble is older, therefore, than ninety years. But the saint lived, and was buried, here in the twelfth century. He was a pupil of Sidi Ali ben Harazem (p. 262) and later the associate of Sidi 'bu Medine el-Ghouts of Tlemcen, with whom he founded a hermitage hereabouts. 'Bu Medine retiring home, el-Bernoussi stayed on here to die. In May a very popular moussem is held here, patronized not only by sober Fasiyin but also by country-folk. Remnants of orgiastic cults marked this festival.

[64 km.] A turning left leads in 7 km. to **Karia Ba Mohammed**, a tribal administrative centre where there is a Thursday market.

[80 km.] 1 km. to the left, close by the village of **Moulay Bouchta**, is the *tomb* and small *zawiya* of the saint of the same name and his daughter. Bouchta means, roughly, 'rain-maker'. The saint lived in the sixteenth century and was one of those mildly deranged or alienated people whom simpler Moslems believe to be holy. They called him El-Khammar — the 'drunk' (though drunk with God) — until he was one day asked to intercede for rain and his prayers were answered. As if this were not a nice enough country-tale, Moulay Bouchta is the local patron of music and dance, a fact which adds zest to the moussem held here in October.

[83 km.] The peak on the left of the road is crowned by the ruins of eleventh-century Almoravid fortifications called, after the hill, the *Casbah d'Amergou*. The exterior walls are still quite substantial and interrupted by towers and four gates, that on the west being vaulted. Inside are the remains of three courtyards with cisterns and, it is believed, stores below them. Rare though Almoravid remains are, it is rather for the view that one climbs here.

[88 km.] A road on the right leads to Ouartzarhr and Aïn Aïcha (see p. 300).

[90 km.] **Fes el-Bali**.

This village was an Almoravid foundation like the Casbah d'Amergou. It was designed to overawe the difficult local tribes, but these revolted and massacred the garrison during Abd el-Mumin's reign, in 1163. The vestigial ruins of what was probably an Almoravid *fountain*, called the 'hammam', are virtually all that now remains of a town that seems to have existed into the seventeenth century, albeit probably in a small way only. This is the beginning of the Abd el-Krim country (see p. 111).

[115 km.] **Souk et-Tleta** (Tuesday market-place).

[159 km.] **Ouezzane**.

This town of 35,000 inhabitants was the creation of Moulay Abdullah, a descendant of Idriss II, who founded a religiou confederation called the Taïbia in 1727. He chose the village or this delightful hillside site in which to build his *zawiya*; it was ther called the village of the hill of myrtles — Dechra Jebel er-Rihan The *zawiya* prospered enormously, the Taïbia brotherhood extended over all North Africa and many subsidiary *zouawi* wer founded. The sheikhs of Ouezzane became extremely importan people, not least because Ouezzane was sited upon the borders o the *bled-el-makhzen* and the *bled es-siba* of the Rif, into which th sheikhs' authority penetrated while that of the sultans could no

Walter Harris was a friend of the sheikh of the time and would come here early in this century to enjoy the peace, order and princely sophistication which this court enjoyed in marked contrast to that of the sultans. The sheikh's gardens were a wonder.

The *zawiya* continues to function today. The *mosque of Moulay Ali Sherif* stands beside it and it is itself dominated by its own large *mosque* with a fine octagonal *minaret* decorated with faience and interlaced arches. Many of the grand houses are also decorated with tiles and charming balconies; at the top of the town there is a *weavers' quarter*. This is a delightful place with a great air of well-being about it. It is one of the few towns not to have expanded greatly in recent years.

Most of the further 68 km. to Chechaouen are through superb mountain-country, though there is nothing along the road to delay you. 8 km. before reaching Chechaouen you cross the junction with the P 39 to reach the town by a lead road.

[227 km.] Chechaouen

Hotels
  ***A   *Hôtel Asma*, the unlovely lines of this hotel are visible from almost every point in the town below the hill (tel. 60.02).
  ***B   *Hôtel de Chaouen*, off Place de Makhzen (tel. 61.36).
  **A   *Hôtel Magou*, 23 Rue Moulay Idriss (tel. 62.75).
  *A   *Hôtel Rif*, 29 Rue Tarik Ibn Ziad (tel. 62.07).
  *A   *Hôtel Hibiza* (tel. 63.23).
  *B   *Hôtel Salam*, 39 Rue Tarik Ibn Ziad (tel. 62.39).
Information *Syndicat d'Initiative*: Place Mohammed V.

The most extravagantly picturesque town in Morocco. White, coral-red, astonishing blue, amber-stone and umber tiles — the citizens do not rest content with these basic colours for their buildings, but flaunt many others besides growing flowering trees and gardens filled with flowers. The town perches over a valley and under a crest of a hill; the air is mountain air, clear, the sun hot and the nights cool. The architecture of Chechaouen is an amalgam of Spanish and Moroccan into which much local invention seems to have been injected. It was something of a holy city — Walter Harris was desperately adventurous to penetrate it in disguise and by night around the turn of the century — and it is full of sanctuaries and tombs. Yet it has a pre-eminently domestic air, so much so that it is something of a surprise to learn that the Spanish did not enter it until 1920, so staunch was the independent spirit of its people. The town was founded by Spanish refugees — Moriscos — in1471, primarily as a base against the Christians in the northern parts. It was never taken by those intruders until the arrival of the Spanish colonial forces seven years after the zone was annexed. When the twentieth-century Spaniards arrived here they found the Jews in their quarter speaking tenth-century Spanish and even writing it in its contemporary Castillian script. Leather was tanned and ornamental as it had been at Moslem Cordoba. The *casbah*, in ruins, was built by Moulay Ismaïl in the seventeenth-century. Adjacent to the *casbah* and also on Place Outa El Hammam are the prison cells in which Abd el-Krim (see p. 111) was confined after his defeat by the Spanish. There is a *carpet factory* and *weaving school* — the carpets here are of good designs. But the real joys of this enchanting town are to be found simply by walking, waiting, watching, sitting in cafés. The quality of the light here is extraordinary — it must be this that has made such colourists of the people; it makes their colours endlessly engrossing to see.

Leave Chechaouen by the north lead road to rejoin the P 28 5 km. off.

[247 km.] A road on the left 2 km. to **Souk el-Arba des Beni Hassan** (Wednesday market). The road rejoins the P 28 7 km. beyond the village — a pretty road.

[262 km.] On the right **Zinat**, birthplace of el-Raisani (p. 111) who built its *ksar*. Another road leads 38 km. left from here to the *sanctuary of Moulay Abd es-Salam ben Mchich*, site of a nationwide pilgrimage in May/June (or December). Moulay Abd es-Salam is patron of the Djebala religion and one of the great saints of Islam. He died in 1188. Islamic orthodoxy embraces four rites or schools, the legacy of early teachers, one of whom was Abd es-Salam ben Mchich. He is thus one of the four 'poles' or 'pillars' of orthodoxy, the rite he preached being the Malekite. This is adhered to throughout the Maghreb, as it formerly was also in Spain.

[282 km.] The junction of the P 28 with the P 38. You go right 4 km. to Tetouan. The site of ancient Tamuda (see under Tetouan) lies close to this fork.

TETOUAN

Hotels
  ****A *Hôtel Safir*, Avenue Kennedy (tel. 70.44).

**A   *Hôtel Dersa*, 8 Rue Général Franco (tel. 42.15).
**A   *Paris Hôtel*, 11 Rue Chakib Arsalane (tel. 67.50).
**B   *Hôtel Régina*, 5 Rue Sidi El Mandri (tel. 21.13).
 *A   *Hôtel National*, 8 Rue Mohammed Torrès (tel. 32.90).
 *A   *Hôtel Principe*, 20 Avenue de la Résistance (tel. 27.95).
 *A   *Hôtel Trebol*, 3 Rue Yacoub El Mansour (tel. 20.93).
Information 30 Boulevard Mohammed V.

Provincial capital of 317,600 inhabitants. Erstwhile capital of the
Spanish zone, most of Tetouan is a quite handsome modern
town, the old quarters of which occupy a plateau overlooking the
valley of the Martil River.

History
Tamuda, a Mauritanian city, was founded in the third or second
century B.C. and destroyed in the first half of the first century A.D.,
perhaps in connection with the revolt of King Ptolemy's minister,
Aedemon, against Roman annexation of Mauritania. The
Romans built a camp on the site in the second century which was
improved towards the end of the third, though abandoned in the
early years of the fifth century under Honorius. The site was not
reoccupied until 1306 or 1307 when the Merinid Sultan Abu
Thabit founded a town to be a base against Ceuta, then in the
hands of a rival Merinid claimant to the sultanate from Spain. The
place became very prosperous, but was destroyed in 1399 by
Henry III of Castille, who carried off what population he did not
massacre. Again the site was abandoned until at the beginning of
the sixteenth century the town was refounded by Moriscos and
Jews coming as refugees from Spain. These practised piracy
among other occupations and brought on themselves the wrath of
Philip II of Spain who, in 1565, forcibly closed their port at the
mouth of the Martil. More refugees arrived at the beginning of
the seventeenth century, when Tetouan was a more or less
independent city allied to the surrounding country, though more
stable and better based upon it than their fellows settled at Rabat.
Under Moulay Ismaïl the city prospered once more, handling
foreign trade. A French consul was posted in 1712. In 1859 a
Spanish force captured the city and held it until 1862, after which
it was constantly threatened by the Spanish until their arrival
under treaty in 1913 to establish the colonization of their zone.

Principal Sights
There are mosques, *zouawi* and markets behind the fine old walls
of Tetouan, a mellah and a casbah too; but the real interest of the

town lies in its sophisticated domestic architecture and the delightful colours everywhere to be seen in the old quarters. There is nothing quite like it anywhere else, neither in Morocco nor in Spain; yet it belongs to both and perhaps in some ways constitutes a clearer memory of old el-Andalus than any other persisting today. It is a town to walk about in at random.

The impressive *Palace of the Khalifa* in the Place Hassan II represents a rebuilding of 1948, though the palace was originally built in the seventeenth century.

There is an interesting collection in the *Museum of Moroccan Arts* near the *Bab Oqla*. The objects displayed are mostly of the Rif and Pays Jebala regions and different to those in other museums of the kind therefore. It is open daily from 09.00 to midday and from 14.30 to 17.30 except Tuesdays and Saturdays.

The *Archaeological Museum*, in the *Place Al Jala*, also houses an excellent small collection. It keeps the same hours as the Museum of Moroccan Arts. The pleasant *garden* contains exhibits, the *vestibule* a large *mosaic* from Lixus of the three Graces with the Seasons in medallions. Other mosaic pavements, bronzes, pottery and other domestic objects are displayed in the different rooms, all of good, and some of excellent quality; all highly illustrative of the Romano–Punic world of ancient North Africa. Altogether this is a museum well worth visiting.

Excursion to Ceuta

From Tetouan the P28 leads 37 km. north to Ceuta. A branch road, the S607, leads to the sea at **Martil** (11 km.) and another south-east, the S608, along the coast 45 km. to **Et-Tleta de Oued Laou**, the first being the principal bathing-resort for Tetouan where a big moussem is held in July.

15 km. along the P28 is **M'diq** where a yachting- and fishing-resort is being developed. Facilities for all sorts of sea-fishing are available.

Hotels
****A   *Hôtel Golden Beach*, M'diq village (tel. 85.51).
****B   *Hôtel Kabila*, 4 km. beyond M'diq (tel. 85.17).
  *A   *Hôtel Playa*, M'diq village (tel. 85.10).
Holiday Club, B.P. 25 Tetouan (tel. 85.45).
Park Hôtel Méditerranée (tel. 85.24).

A turning right from M'diq leads in 2 km. to **Taifor**, on *Capo Negro* headland, which is also rapidly becoming a modern holiday resort.

Hotels
***A   *Hôtel Petit Merou* (tel. 81.05).
Club Méditerranée Yasmina (tel. 81.98).

20 km. from Tetouan is the new resort of **Restinga-Smir** lying
by the wonderful beaches that line this Mediterranean coast. Smir
is being developed enormously. With all its amenities this
planned holiday area has become attractive and lively.

Hotels
***A   *Hôtel Carabo* (tel. 87.07).
***A   *Hôtel Boustane* (tel. 87.07).
Club Méditerranée (tel. 87.07).
Village de Vacance Maroc Tourist, B.P. 431 (tel. Maroc Tourist Rabat 639.15).
Camping
El Fraja (tel. 77.22).

At 37 km. you reach **Ceuta** (or, in Arabic, **Sebta**). It occupies
the promontory of *Monte Hacho*, the southern of the two Pillars
of Hercules, Gibraltar being the northern. Considering that it has
been a Portuguese or Spanish possession since 1415 it has little to
show of merit or interest. The *cathedral* has a certain gloomy,
death-adoring charm. The fortifications are massive and therefore impressive. The church of *Our Lady of Africa* is the most
interesting building and the views from the summit of the promontory are the pleasantest sight that Ceuta affords. You will need
your passport, car and money-changing documents to visit the
colony.

[282 km.] Having returned from Tetouan to the junction of the
P28 and P38, you keep straight on for Tangier.

[285 km.] The S601 turns right 44 km. to **Ksar es-Seghir** (close by
Cape Malabata), a small port on the Straits of Gibraltar and
opposite Tarifa. As an embarkation-point for the crossing to
Spain — whether peaceful or not — the port was fortified by
Yaacub el-Mansur in 1192. The Portuguese held it between 1458
and 1550. The enceinte of their walls and the keep they built
remain. One can reach Tangier from here direct (see p. 153), as,
equally, the P28 5 km. from the Ceuta border by a road branching
from the S601 which circles north of the *Jebel Moussa* to **Fnideq**,
close to Ceuta. It is a pretty road.

[308 km.] The P38 joins with the P37 from the Tangier-to-Rabat
road.

[324 km.] On the right *El-Benian*, site of a nine-towered Roman camp.

[332·5 km.] On the right is a rocky crest called *Er-Rorba* where a Roman fort stood.

[335 km.] Tangier (p. 142).

FES TO TANGIER:
Route 2 (via Sidi Kacem)

Route Leave Fes from the top of Avenue Hassan II by the P1 towards Meknes (Route Exit B). Take the P3 to Sidi Kacem and the P6 onwards to Souk el-Arba du Rharb, after which continue along the P2 to Tangier. [See Route Map for Northern Area (pp. 298–9).]
Rail (via Meknes) Change at Sidi Kacem or Sidi Slimane for Tangier.
Bus Two a day direct.
Accommodation and food At Sidi Kacem, Ksar el-Kebir, Larache, Asilah.

[10 km.] Fork right on the P3.

[45 km.] **Nzala des Beni Ammar**; a turning left 17 km. to Moulay Idriss (see p. 285) and Volubilis (see p. 276).

[50 km.] A turning right (P28) 84 km. to Ouezzane (p. 288).

[58 km.] A second turning left 14 km. to Moulay Idriss, as above.

[61 km.] *Col du Zeggota* pass (Monday market at the village).

[82 km.] **Sidi Kacem**.

This modern township has little enough to offer. 2 km. away, the *zawiya of Sidi Kacem* stands in an old oasis of olives, poplars and fig trees. A moussem is held here in October. Extensive irrigation and planting has utterly transformed previously unproductive areas around this neighbourhood.

From Sidi Kacem the P3 continues (84 km.) to Kénitra. 16 km. along it the P4 from Meknes joins it on the left. A further 16 km. along this latter road stands the *tomb of Sidi Moulay Yaacub*, where the remains of a *thermal establishment* of the Roman era, rebuilt in early Islamic times, have been discovered. These are believed the most likely baths to have been the lost Aquae Dacicae.

At 22 km. is **Sidi Slimane**. 8 km. north of Sidi Slimane, excavations at **Rirha** have disclosed the remains of the Roman colony of *Babba Campestris*, a settlement that was probably inhabited from the second century B.C. until the Roman withdrawal. The broken foundations of walls, houses and baths survive.

[129 km.] **Mechra Bel-Ksiri**.

[143 km.] Souk el-Arba du Rharb, where routes 2 and 3 join to continue to Tangier by the P2. For this road, see p. 155 where it is described as being followed in the other direction.

[303 km.] Tangier (see p. 142).

FES TO TANGIER:
Route 3 (via Meknes and Kénitra)

Route Leave Fes by the P1 from the top of Avenue Hassan II (Route Exit B). Take the P1 to Sidi Allal-Bahraoui where it branches along the P29 to Kénitra, there joining the P2 for Souk el-Arba du Rharb, after which continue along the P2 to Tangier. [See Route Map for Northern Area (pp. 298–9).]
Rail As for Route 2.
Bus Fes to Rabat and change for Tangier; on either stage there are numerous services.
Accommodation and food At Meknes, Kénitra, Arbaoua, Ksar el-Kebir, Larache Asilah.

For Fes to Meknes, see p. 265.

[49 km.] Fork left for Meknes by-pass (P34).

[60 km.] Meknes (see p. 267).

[71 km.] Junction of the P1 with the P4 on the right and, left, the Meknes by-pass.

[78 km.] **Aïn el-Orma** where there is an old caravanserai.

[117 km.] **Khemisset** — a township of some 8,000 people.

The S205 runs north from here to Sidi Slimane, by **Khemis Aït Yadine**, a Thursday market-place and a turning right — 36 km. in all — to the artificial lake made by the *dam of El-Kansara* where there is water ski-ing under the auspices of the Club Auto-nautique de Meknès.

[142 km.] **Tiflet** (Wednesday market).

The road south to **Maaziz** leads on to **Tedders** in 46 km. where there is a September moussem noted for its horsemen, and on to **El-Harch** in 71 km., where there are wild boar, and panthers have been reported, and to **Oulmès** (90 km.) near the small spa of **Tarmilate** or **Oulmès les Thermes** (whose waters, bottled, are the most commonly sold throughout Morocco as Vichy water is in France).

Hotel (at Oulmès les Thermes)
   ***A   *Hôtel Les Thermes* (tel. 901).

[158 km.] **Souk et-Tnine** (Monday market-place).

[168 km.] **Sidi Allal-Bahraoui**. Fork right by the P29.

[196 km.] Kénitra (see p. 162). Turn right along the P2 for Souk el-Arba du Rharb and Tangier. This section of the route is described in the other direction on p. 155.

[433 km.] Tangier (see p. 142).

THE NORTH

This section embraces those roads which in a general way encircle the Rif mountains. The road linking the Mediterranean ports is described as far as the Algerian border (where Oujda is the principal town) and a return route is described via the historic 'Taza Gap' road to Fes.

TANGIER TO OUJDA

Route Much of the road (606 km.) — P38, P28, P39 and P27 — is excellent. Over the Pays Jebala and the Rif this is a glorious drive: the Plain of Gareb and the valley of the Moulouya is rich country and the last lap over the pass across the Beni Snassen range carries you into virtually desert country in which Oujda lies as in an oasis.
   Leaving Tangier, make your way to the 'Toutes directions' roundabout at Place Helvetia, south of the town, or make your way direct to Route Exit C.
Rail See p. 23 for the line Tangier–Fes and Fes–Oujda.
Bus Various buses ply over the whole way described, by stages served with varying frequency.
Accommodation and food At Tetouan, Chechaouen, Ketama, Al-Hoceima, Nador, Saïdia, Oujda.

This road is described above (pp. 289–94) from Tangier as far as Chechaouen, though as if travelled in the opposite direction.

[116 km.] The junction of the P28 and the P39. From here the P39 makes its exhilarating way over the Rif, 213 km. to Al-Hoceima, the coast between being inaccessible for the most part, so steep are the mountains, and another 167 km. to Nador, most of them fairly level.

The Rif is one of the few great strongholds of the Berber way of life, immemorial and self-engrossed, proud and obstinate. Superb to look at, old in conformation, tilled to an extraordinary extent, forested in other parts, the mountains – and their inhabitants – seem remote; not inimical, or even discouraging, but as if one were an irrelevance. This region was a core of the *bled es-siba* and only the slow extension of roads into it and the joy of achieving their Moslem and Moroccan independence have induced the Rifi to come to terms with the state. The Rifi country-man does not live in the past but in a timeless present old as all the past and constituting a summation of it. It is odd that Abd el-Krim could have adapted North Africa's first modern state out of such material; Targuist, along this road, was his last refuge (p. 111); but there was no road here then. The road from Ketama south to Fes – the Route de l'Unité (S302) – was built by voluntary national effort after Independence, even more as a symbolic gesture to link the ex-Spanish zone with the ex-French than as a means to open up the area and include the Rifi in the new Kingdom. It traces an old caravan route from Fes to the sea at Torres de Alcalà.

[215 km.] **Ketama.**

Junction of the P39 with the Route de l'Unité. Ketama consists of little save the *parador* which is the nucleus of a ski-resort and summer-station. The situation is marvellous, and this is cedar country. It is also the centre of the *kif* trade and has a number of sad tales attached to it. Overcome any good Samaritan instincts should someone flag down your car, and keep your doors and windows locked. Stop and you may be invited, or worse, forced at gunpoint, to buy kilogramme quantities and, likely as not, the information passed on to the police. There are other towns in the Rif more suitable for casual visitors.

Hotel
****A   *Hôtel Tidighine* (tel. 10).

Route Map for Northern Area

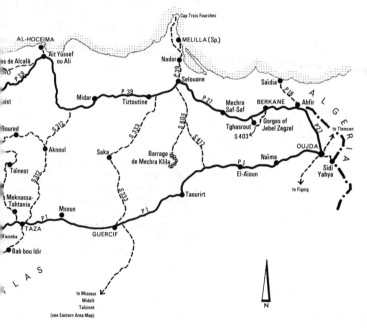

The Route de l'Unité (S302 to Fes via Aïn Aïcha) is 164 km. long
to Fes. It crosses magnificent country. There is a Sunday market
at **Souk el-Had**, a Friday one at **Taounate** (where there is a
moussem in September). A few kilometres before the last village
a road, S304, leads left to **Tahar Souk**, which is in a bad state for
the next 70 km. to **Aknoul** where it joins the S312 for Taza 63 km.
south. 15 km. after Taounate a road on the right leads 30 km. to
Ouartzarhr, whence on 37 km., the last 23 km. by rough piste on
a steep gradient, to the stupendous belvedere of mount *Lalla
Outka* (1,610 metres), and 17 km. more to the Ouezzane-to-Fes
road. At 92 km. is **Aïn Aïcha** village; 114 km. a turning to the
village of **Tissa** where there is a moussem in August/September.
In 143 km. you reach **Aïn Kansara** village, in 164 km. Fes.

[227 km.] A turning left 60 km. to **El-Jebha**, a tiny fishing-port.

(A track before Ketama 8310 via **El Had**, though shorter, is less
easily negotiated.)

[252 km.] A road left 33 km. to **Torres de Alcalà** or, in Arabic,
Kala Irir; a fishing-village with a history. It was called Bades in
Merinid and Saadi times and was used as the nearest port to Fes,
trading with the maritime states of the Mediterranean, with
Venice in particular, the Venetian fleet making regular biannual
calls. The Spaniards were allowed to set up a commercial base
here in 1564 in exchange for their help to Sultan Abdullah against
the Turks. Off the port lie the **Rhomara** (or **Ghomara**) **Isles**,
formerly known as the **Peñon de Velez de la Gomera**. In 1508
these were seized by the Portuguese who lasted there only till
1522. In 1554 the Turks seized them and held them as a base for
piracy until into the nineteenth century, their predatory presence
there effectively discouraging foreign shipping from using Alcalà.

[257 km.] **Targuist** — 1 km. to the right; an administrative centre.

[321 km.] **Aït Yussef ou Ali** where the P39 continues on to Melilla
and a branch road (P39a) to the left lead in 8 km. to Al-Hoceima.
Aït Yussef was the home village and birthplace of the Abd
el-Krim brothers.

Al-Hoceima is a small town, nicely situated above its port,
which was founded by the Spanish in 1928 (when they called it
Villa Sanjurjo). It has modern hotels, a yacht basin and centre for
underwater fishing. The near-by airport is used for direct holidaymakers' flights and internal connections (see p. 23).

Hotels
****B   *Hôtel Mohammed V*, Avenue Mohammed V (tel. 22.33).
***A   *Hôtel Quemado*, Plage de Quemado (tel. 23.71).
**A   *Hôtel National*, 23 Rue de Tetouan (tel. 24.31).
**B   *Hôtel Karim*, 27 Avenue Hassan II (tel. 21.84).
Club Méditerranée (tel. 22.22).
Camping
Plage El Jamil (tel. 20.09).
Cala Iris
Information *O.N.M.T. Tourist Office*: by the Hotel Quemado.

The name of the town is taken from the island in the bay, known to Europe as **Peñon de Alhucemas** since the period during the mid seventeenth century when England, France and Spain squabbled as to which should grab it as a trading-post. Spain won in 1673, though it never became an important place.

After returning the 8 km. to Aït Yussef to rejoin the P39, this road presently turns almost due south to pass up the valley of the Nekor River — passing an extremely beautiful landscape.

[386 km.] On the right a poor road to Taza via **Akhnoul**, 116 km.

[415 km.] **Midar** (Tuesday market).

[430 km.] **Driouch** and a left turn on to road 8112 for Ben Tieb and ultimately connecting Nador via Segengane over a rough track and an alternative route to Melilla via road 8106. None of these roads is recommended.

[452 km.] **Tiztoutine** (Thursday market).

[459 km.] On the right the S333 leads to Jebel bou Haidoun and over a poor road to **Saka** and thence to Guercif (p. 307), 111 km.

[468 km.] **Monte Arruit** (Sunday market).

[472 km.] On the right a road 56 km. to *Barrage de Mechar Klila*, a dam on the Moulouya River which greatly increases the fertility of the plain. This road forks, the left-hand direction leading to the Fes–Oujda road, 72 km.

[477 km.] **Selouane** — casbah built by Moulay Ismaïl in the seventeenth century and restored in the nineteenth. Here you turn right for Oujda or left 11 km. to Nador.
Nador — 10,000 inhabitants; a scruffy, semi-industrial settlement handling goods to and from Melilla. To the east lies the shallow lagoon of *Sebka Bouareq*.

Hotels
****B *Hôtel Rif*, Avenue Youssef Ibn Tachfine (tel. 36.37).
 ***A *Hôtel Mansour Ed-Dahab*, 101 Rue de Marrakesh (tel. 24.09).

Camping
Karia Plage, Kariat-Arekman (30 km. on the 8101 overlooking the *Sebka Bouareq*).

13 km. beyond Nador lies the frontier of **Melilla**, a Spanish colony since 1479. Its old quarter — the *Medina-Sidonia* — is still largely walled and contains some pleasant old streets; the rest of the town resembles nothing so much as the run-down Andalusian provincial town that it is. Since the French evacuation of Oran Melilla has gone from bad to worse, the garrison of that base having been in the habit of crossing to shop on the cheap here — the last people to see any point to this anachronistic colonial outpost. To enter Melilla you need your passport and car papers and must change money into pesetas in the teeth of hostile officialdom.

Just before the frontier, a road on the left circles Melilla to reach the promontory of *Guelaïa* and the *Cap Trois Fourches*, a poor though a pretty road 19 km. long.

From Nador you return by the P39 to the junction of this with the P27, which branches leftwards.

[516 km.] **Mechra Saf-Saf** at the crossing of the *Moulouya River*. The river was the frontier between the ancient Mauritania and Numidia as also between the French and Spanish zones under the Protectorates.

The Moulouya rises south of Khenifra, far away in the heart of the Middle Atlas and up a well-defined valley. The desert corridor which comes to the Mediterranean at Oujda has proved a less effective political frontier between Morocco and Algeria than this valley, the two combining, the one to allow nomadic Saharan tribes to reach the coast and the other offering them an easy path into the centre of Morocco. Only the strongest sultans have been able to straddle these rifts and combine under their authority the lands east and west of them while, when the central Moroccan governments have been weak, intrusive tribes have made this valley a part of the *bled es-siba*. One such tribe was the Beni Merin who entered the country in this way and based their growth into the Merinid dynasty upon Adjdir (between Boured and Akhnoul) whence they could command the Moulouya valley and cut the route through the Taza Gap. The Alaouites also used this means to attack Fes from the Tafilelt.

[536 km.] A detour right on the S403 returning the same way 34 km. through the beautiful hill-country of the *Beni Snassen* range. Off the road, right, 10 km. away, lies **Taforalt** a summer resort and Wednesday market. At 17 km. is a path to the cave of *Tghasrout* where there is a stalagmite which vaguely resembles a camel and which is credited with curing sterility. (There are many caves hereabouts, and many of them have yielded prehistoric remains.) You may continue into the *Gorges of Zegzel*, left, by a poor track and rejoin the P27 at Berkane.

[546 km.] **Berkane**, a modern agricultural centre. Roads, left, lead by various ways through cultivated land to the sea-coast and Saïdia (see below).

[568 km.] **Ahfir** (on the left) − a modern agricultural centre with markets on Mondays and Thursdays.

From here the P18 road leads, left, 20 km. to **Saïdia**. This is a charming little seaside resort on a splendid sandy beach. The *River Kiss* − a mere stream − marks the frontier with Algeria; it enters the Mediterranean at Saïdia, beside a *ksar* built late in the last century by Moulay el-Hassan.

Hotels (at Saïdia)
    **A *Hôtel Hamour*, Place du 20 Août (tel. 51.15).
    **B *Hôtel Al Kalaa*, Saïdia Plage (tel. 51.23).
    *A *Hôtel Select*, Boulevard de la Moulouya (tel. 51.10).
Front de Mer, Saïdia Plage (tel. 51.55).
Camping
Essi (tel. 82).
Centre Autonome, Saïdia Plage.

Turning right at Ahfir − still on the P27 − you reach [606 km.] Oujda.

Oujda

Population 260,000
Air For connections by air, see p. 23. *Angads* airport 15 km. north on the P27, about 30 DH by taxi.
Rail Three trains daily for Casablanca, two for Tangier and one slow train south to Bouarfa by night twice weekly. Railway information bureau telephone 27.01.
Bus Connections from Rabat, Fes, Nador Figuig, etc. C.T.M. garage in Rue Sidi Brahim, other carriers at the *Gare Routière*, Place du Maroc.
Taxi Ranks at the station, Hôtel de Ville, etc. Those intending to travel to Algeria by

train can complete the final 15 km. to the border by *grand taxi* from the Gare Routière (or by unpredictable local buses).

Car Hire *Avis*, 110 Avenue Allal Ben Abdellah (tel. 39.93) and at the airport.
Hertz, 20 Boulevard Fetouaki (tel. 21.15) and at the airport.

Hotels

****A   *Hôtel Al Massira Salam*, Boulevard Maghreb Al Arabi (tel. 53.00).
****A   *Hôtel Terminus*, Place de l'Unité Africaine (tel. 32.11).
****B   *Hôtel Oujda*, Boulevard Mohammed V (tel. 40.93).
**B   *Hôtel Lutetia*, 44 Boulevard Hassan Loukili (tel. 33.65).
*A   *Hôtel Simon*, Boulevard Tarik Ibn Ziad (tel. 58.26).
*A   *Hôtel Royal*, 13 Boulevard Zerktouni (tel. 22.84).
*B   *Hôtel Ziri*, Boulevard Mohammed V (tel. 43.05).

Information *O.N.M.T. Tourist Office*: Place du 16 août (tel. 43.29).
Consulate Algerian: 11 Boulevard de Taza.
Banks, Post Office and Shopping All are centred on Place du 16 août.

This is a brisk modern city, a French creation built around a small medina.

HISTORY

Oujda has had a long and largely unhappy history. The plain of Oujda was once fertile and cultivated by sedentary Berbers. There was a Roman town near by, at Marnia, which seems to have been established at the beginning of the third century. Oujda itself was founded in 994 by Ziri ibn Attia who created a small state for himself out of the surrounding country. Later the Magrawa tribe held it, their dominions reaching as far as the Tafilelt, but Yussef ibn Tashfin the Almoravid conquered them in 1070. The Almohads took it in 1206 and built walls for it. After bitter and protracted fighting over decades, the Merinids finally established ownership of Oujda despite the claims to it of the Ziyanid dynasty of Tlemcen. Abu Yaacub rebuilt the walls, mosque, baths, etc., in 1296. Again in 1352 the Merinids had decisively to beat off invaders from Tlemcen. By this time, however, the rich plain had been laid waste by incursive nomadic tribes coming from the south. The Saadi used the town as a base from which to attack Fes, as did the Alaouites later. But during the reigns of both dynasties Oujda was several times taken by the Turks established in Algeria. After the Turkish threat was removed it was the French in Algeria who bedevilled Oujda; they took it in reprisal for the acts of Moroccan sultans in 1844 and 1857; in 1907 they retook and held it until the end of the

Protectorate. It has, therefore, been a French town longer than any other in Morocco.

PRINCIPAL SIGHTS

There is really nothing to see of interest in the *medina* save the markets and the life led there. The *Great Mosque* was founded by the Merinids, though it has been much altered since first built. The *Bab Sidi Abd el-Wahab* is the best of the gates.

ENVIRONS OF OUJDA

Sidi Yahya

6 km. distant down a wide, ceremonial road. This is very much something to see. Great springs arise in an empty plain, shaded by vast old baobabs and immense palms. The clear water runs in streams and there is grass and flowers in bloom. There is almost a village of *koubbiyet* over the graves of saints and holy men who have lived as hermits here or been buried in this very holy place.

Sidi Yahya is traditionally identified as St John the Baptist. He is buried here, though there is doubt as to exactly where, under the trees hung with clothes whose colour lends the grove a magical aspect or in the *koubba* where animal sacrifices are made. He is revered here alike by Moslems, Jews and Christians — an oecumenical figure. In such a spot one is not surprised to find so great a concentration of holiness — sacrifice, entombment, vague memories of fertility cults (the cloth-hung trees), holy men living apart from the world, many women washing in the streams — or a cave of the houris, the *Ghar el-Houriyat*, who bring blessings and good fortune. This is a classic place; it is also very beautiful.

Among the hermitages here is one once used by Sidi bel-Abbes, the patron of Marrakech (p. 220).

Keen students of Maghrebi architecture might cross into Algeria to see the great Almoravid *mosque* of **Tlemcen** and the huge *Merinid ruin* at **Mansoura**, the mosques of *Sidi Achmed bel Hassan* and *Sidi Haloui*. Into all these an infidel may penetrate. Tlemcen is only 85 km. away over a good, scenically splendid road, the town attractive and the hotel adequate. Bear in mind that relations between Morocco and Algeria are tense and the crossing beset with officious observance of regulations. Although Britons and Americans do not require visas, all but minors and students with supporting identification are required to change a large sum of money, currently nearly £140, into Algerian currency at a very disadvantageous rate.

Oujda to Fes

Route Excellent roads all the way. Leave Oujda by the Boulevard du Taza, and take the P1 to Fes (344 km.).
Air See p. 23.
Rail Five trains daily.
Bus Three buses daily in either direction via Taza.
Accommodation and food At Guercif and Taza.

[612 km.] 2 km. up the road on the left, by the stream of the *Isly*, Moulay Abd er-Rahman was disastrously beaten by the French in 1844 (see p. 104). The valley had, however, previously under the Merinids twice seen the Moroccans victorious in battles against Algerian invaders.

[627 km.] The S403 right leads to Sidi Bouhouria, Taforalt and the Zegzel Gorges (p. 303).

[637 km.] **Naïma** (Thursday market-place).

[665 km.] **El-Aïoun** (on the left).
A large village with a big *ksar* built by Moulay Ismaïl in 1679, restored by Moulay Hassan in 1876. The 5318 road right from here leads to the Zegzel gorges and Berkane (p. 303).

[687 km.] The S412 on the right leads to Nador (p. 301).

[715 km.] **Taourirt** − Sunday market.
In early Arab times this was on a cross-roads between the Taza Gap road between east and west and the caravan route from Sigilmassa in the Tafilelt and the sea at Melilla, a position of importance which ensured it a violent history and virtual destruction by the fifteenth century. The S410 left goes in 53 km. to **Debdou**.

[761 km.] The S329 left up the Moulouya valley is difficult and slow so far as Missour (183 km.) but considerably less so following the S330 73 km. to the P20, the 100 km. to Talsinnt or the 100 km. to Midelt via Ksabi. **Outat Ouled el-Haj** (160 km.), an oasis of thirty *ksour* belonging to an Arab tribe, and **Missour**, where there are nine *ksour*, are not very interesting places but the country is beautiful thereafter. **Ksabi**, with a dozen *ksour*, is best visited from Midelt.

[765 km.] **Guercif**.

Camping *Camping de Guercif.*

A large village which was important in early Arab times and is recorded by the geographer Ptolemy as *Gelafa*. Only tumbled ruins remain of the various fortifications that were built here between the ninth and eighteenth centuries.

The 4940 track south-west over the *Jebel bou Iblane* is, as ultimately all other tracks to Talzemt prove, virtually impracticable for ordinary vehicles.

[802 km.] **Msoun**, by a short turning right.

This is the base and storage-place of the nomadic, sheep-herding Haouwara tribe. The *ksar* was built by Moulay Ismaïl in the seventeenth century.

[829 km.] Turning right on to the S312 for Akhnoul.

[830 km.] You reach Taza.

TAZA

Hotels
   ***A *Hotel Friouato-Salam* (tel. 25.93).
   **A *Hotel du Dauphiné*, Place de l'Indépendence (tel. 35.67).
Camping *Zeitoun*, Avenue de la Gare (tel. 26.76).
Information *Syndicat d'Initiative*, Avenue de Tetouan (new town).
Post Office Rue de Fes.
Almost all facilities and restaurants are found on Avenue de Tetouan and the most useful bus and taxi connections can be made at the terminus by the railway station (tel. 20.19).

An airy town of 50,000 inhabitants, Taza stands on the two levels of a hill 585 metres high rising out of the valley leading to the Touahar pass. The older part of the town, the medina, occupies the hill-top and is separated from the new town and the large ex-French military camp by rather more than a kilometre of climbing road.

History
Possession of Taza has usually been the key to eventual power in Morocco. It was held by the Meknassa tribe in the early days of the Arab invasion and it was to a great extent Meknassa recogni-

tion of and alliance with the first Idrissids that enabled those to form their kingdom of inner Morocco. After the weakening of the Idrissid kingdom the Meknassa were conquered by the Fatimids in 933 at Msoun. Yussef ibn Tashfin, the Almoravid conqueror of northern Morocco, had to take the town from the west, in which he succeeded in 1074. Abd el-Mumin took it for the Almohads in 1132, fortified it, built the first Almohad mosque in it and used it as his capital until he became master of Marrakech and Fes. When the Beni Merin began to threaten the Almohads, coming into Morocco by Figuig and Oujda, then up the Moulouya valley, Taza was their first goal, as it was also the sultans' chief bastion against them. Although the Merinids won their first victory over the Almohads in 1216 they could not take Taza until 1248, and it was more than a quarter of a century again before they were masters of all the country. Abu Yaacub built up the walls and made much of the town, giving it mosques, *medersa* and so on, and indeed the Merinid sultans were always at pains to secure Tazi goodwill. As the dynasty declined and the country fell into anarchy, Taza suffered depopulation and poverty although at the beginning of the sixteenth century Leo Africanus could still be struck by its fortifications — the best-defended town in Morocco. Taza does not, however, seem to have been so vital in the establishment of Saadi rule over the north, though Ahmed el-Mansur was careful to see to its fortifications and built the southern bastion on a somewhat European design whose name, el-Bastioun, too is a European importation into Arabic.

When the Alaouites followed the Merinids' tracks into inner Morocco, Taza played much the same role as before. Moulay er-Rashid took it in 1666 and made it his base against Fes; Moulay Ismaïl built it up — so long as there were Turks in Algeria its position was one of great strategic importance.

But with the general weakening of the Government in the latter nineteenth century Taza began to slip away into the *bled es-siba*; Abd el-Aziz made a *harka* into the area in 1895, but in 1902 'bu Hamara was able to proclaim himself sultan here. Though he was soon dislodged from the town itself he was able for seven years to threaten it from an Algerian base, until returning to Taza, he was defeated and captured by Moulay Hafiz in 1909. The French did not occupy it until May 1914 — the very last year, militarily speaking, of the ancient world. However, neither the Moroccans, nor, altogether, the French were aware of the new era that had dawned and Taza became the main French base for the prolonged fighting necessary to subdue both the Middle Atlas and the Rif — both sides using pre-1914 techniques of warfare.

Principal sights

The interesting part of Taza is the *medina*. Outside the walls, on the east, stands the *Koubba of Sidi Aïssa*. The Merinid Abu Inan built a *zawiya* and hostel for poor travellers which has since disappeared, though tradition suggests it stood here. The main road to the medina passes it and bends back to the *Bab el-Guebour*. On the left of this gate stands Ahmed el-Mansur's '*Bastioun*' built at the end of the sixteenth century. A massive building in brick, it could mount artillery as well as withstand bombardment. Inside it there are some delightful contemporary graffiti of ships on the walls. In the cliff on its farther side are the caves of *Kifan el-Khomari*. These are natural cave chambers in which evidences of Paleolithic, Mousterian habitation were found in 1916.

Inside the town, the *Mosque of el-Andalus* has an Almohad, twelfth-century *minaret* — a modest monument, though well-proportioned. Near by is 'bu Hamara's *house*, late-nineteenth- or early twentieth-century and for the most part wanting its decoration. A Merinid *medrassa*, built by Abu el-Hassan in 1323 — while he was still a cadet — is a very fine little building for a provincial *medrassa* and has some excellent details, as the *mihrab* in the *prayer-hall*. The *Market Mosque* has an odd *minaret* whose upper part is wider than its base; that of the *Mosque of Sidi Azouz* (patron of Taza) belongs also to the twelfth century. The *Great Mosque* is the most important monument in Taza. It was begun by the Merinid Abu Yaacub in 1291 and finished the following year. Its *mihrab* is faced with carved stucco of extreme delicacy and rises to a dome of the same material based upon sixteen ribs and sixteen panels intricately carved into an amazingly complex interlacing of script and floral motives. This rib vault begins in a plain, structural form at Cordoba; here, in its ultimate, purely decorative form, it reaches a lacy culmination of great beauty. Unfortunately one can see little of the building and nothing of the *mihrab's* splendour or the rich Merinid furnishings which are still in use. The *royal palace* — probably dating from the seventeenth century and perhaps built by er Rashid — is a ruin. The north gate — *Bab er-Rih* ('of the wind') — was originally Almohad, as at the extreme western bastion, is the tower called '*Saracen*'. The

Bab Djemaa, facing the new town, is largely of Merinid construction, as is the greater part of the fabric of all the walls. Though there is nothing very special to be seen in Taza medina, the ensemble has much character and gives a strong sense of the past.

Excursion from Taza

A very beautiful drive round the *National Park of Jebel Tazzeka* may be made from Taza. The tracks in the mountainous part of this drive, through marvellous country, are impracticable in wet weather. In fine, the 103 km. back to the P1 are quite possible and are asphalted. **Bab bou Idir**, 32 km., is a small summer-resort. The tracks leading from this way south into the mountains are very bad.

[836 km.] A turning right on the S328 14 km. to **Meknassa-Tahtania**, where people of the Meknassa tribe have lived since the seventh century. The road continues into the Rif, 58 km. to **Taïnest**, after which it becomes a poor track.

[849 km.] *Touahar pass*, 558 metres high.

Crossing this you pass into inner Morocco, geographically. The pass itself is, however, less strategically important than the town.

[863 km.] Road on the left which ends the circuit of the National Park of Jebel Tazzeka (see under Taza).

[896 km.] On the left 1 km. **Sidi Abdeljalil**.

[917 km.] **Ras Tabouda** (Thursday market).

[928 km.] On the left the *Koubba of Sidi Abd er-Rezzak* where ex-voto offerings of calves' muzzles of plaited palm are made — an unexplained custom.

[936 km.] A road left 1 km. to Sidi Harazem (see p. 265).

[944 km.] Turning right on the S302 (see p. 298), which provides access to the Barrage Idriss I (turning right 23 km. north).

[950 km.] Fes (p. 237).

For Fes to Tangier, see pp. 287–94.

THE WEST

The main body of this section continues our description of the Atlantic coast-road south from Casablanca as far as Agadir. (For Tangier to Casablanca, see the Main Centres section beginning on p. 155. South from Agadir (Aït Melloul) is described in the South section beginning on p. 335.) Since it is most easily visited from Agadir, the Sous valley is also described here and, to complete a very attractive round of the western plains and mountains, the route crossing the High Atlas from Taroudant in the Sous to Marrakech by the Tizi n'Test pass and an alternative way from Marrakech to the Atlantic coast at Rabat are also given here. The total distance by the main roads is 1,262 km.

Casablanca to Agadir

Route 557 km. by the main P 8 road and 15 km. shorter taking the coast-road (S 121) between El-Jadida and Safi. The P 8 is a good road, excellently engineered for a cruising speed of 40 miles per hour even over the winding and rather arduous section between Essaouira and Agadir. The long straights of the northern parts are faster and there are few places where it is necessary to slow up. However, it is by no means always a broad road and since it passes through populous regions the hazards with which it is beset are many and various. We describe the route of the P 8 and interpolate a description of the alternative coast-road between El-Jadida and Safi, which is the more attractive way. Between Casablanca and Azemmour there is also an alternative road close to the sea (S 130); it passes several bathing-places, etc., but is not otherwise an interesting road.

Leave Casablanca from the Central Post office (*Map* 4) going north-west on the Boulevard de Paris. At the far end of the place Oued el-Makhazine branch left along the Boulevard d'Anfa and keep straight over the crossing into Boulevard Alexandre I following signs (Route Exit A).

Bus See p. 23. From Casa to El-Jadida, three per day; El-Jadida to Oualidia and Safi, three; Safi to Essaouira, two daily; Essaouira to Agadir six daily.

Accommodation and food At El-Jadida, Oualidia and other sea-food restaurants (on the coast-road), Safi Essaouira, Simimou (food only).

[46 km.] **Bir Jdid** (Thursday market).

[83 km.] **Azemmour**.

Perhaps the most spectacular of Moroccan coast-towns, this is a small one whose white, flat-roofed houses overtop old walls of yellow stone rising above the great river of *Oum er-Rbia* as it flows among fields and gardens. The walls were largely built by the Portuguese — there are quite massive fortifications in ruin to the south, where the *casbah* stands.

The Portuguese had a factor living in the town under a treaty arrangement from 1486, but finding themselves unwelcome from 1502 onwards, they attacked the town in 1510, were turned out the following year and came back in force in 1513 to colonize it.

En-Nasser was beaten off in 1514 when he tried to oust the intruders, but the fall of Agadir to the Saadi in 1541 forced the Portuguese to withdraw from Azemmour. Previous to the Portuguese period little is known of its history; it was probably a Barghawata village and it was fought over by rival Merinids in the middle of the fourteenth century. After the Portuguese withdrawal, Azemmour appears to have led an uncommonly placid existence.

It is very pleasant to walk round the ramparts from where one can see all, really, that there is to see. Although this is so very Moroccan a town, the street-doors of the houses are generally round-arched and have a carved keystone — a legacy from the Portuguese to be noticed all along the Atlantic coast where it has become quite assimilated into local traditions of building.

In the town stands the *sanctuary-mosque of Moulay 'bu Chaïb*, its holy patron since the twelfth century; the town itself is often called locally by his name. There is also the *sanctuary* of another sherif, Moulay Abdullah ben Achmed, though the one who draws a pilgrimage to his tomb in May and has the honour of a moussem in August is a certain Rbi Abraham Moul' Niss — presumably a holy rabbi. (You may still be shown the interior of the rather drɛb little synagogue whose congregation has all but vanished to Israel.)

Friday and Tuesday are both market-days.

From some 5 km. before El-Jadida is reached the road passes by the splendid beach that goes by the town's name.

[99 km.] You arrive at El-Jadida.

EL-JADIDA

Bus C.T.M. station near the junction with Avenue Mohammed V on Rue Abdelmoumen El Mouahidi.

Hotels
- ****A   *Hôtel le Palais Andalous* (tel. 39.06).
- ****B   *Hôtel Doukkala-Salam*, Avenue El Jamiaa Al Arabia (tel. 36.22).
- **A   *Hôtel Dounia*, Avenue El Jamiaa Al Arabia (tel. 25.91).
- *A   *Hôtel Royal*, 108 Avenue Mohammed V (tel. 28.39).
- *A   *Hôtel Suisse*, 147 Boulevard Zerktouni (tel. 28.16).
- *B   *Hôtel de Bruxelles*, 40 Rue Ibn Khaldoun (tel. 20.72).
- *B   *Hôtel de Provence*, 42 Avenue Rkih Rafy (tel. 23.47).

Village de Vacance Amal, Avenue El Jamiaa Al Arabia (tel. 26.39).
Camping *International*, 1 km. south on Avenue des Nations Unies (tel. 27.55).

Information *O.N.M.T. Tourist Office*: 33 Place Mohammed V (tel. 27.04).
Post Office Place Mohammed V.

El-Jadida — 'the new' — has more commonly been known in Europe as Mazagan, its Portuguese name. It is a town of some 70,000 people that has long ago overflowed the enceinte of splendid Portuguese fortifications protecting the port.

The site was almost certainly that of a Phoenician settlement called Rusibis, not founded perhaps before the fifth century B.C. It owed its importance — even to some extent its present prosperity — to the Portuguese who built a fort here in 1502 (which the locals called el-Brija el-Jadida, the contraction of which has stuck) and enlarged this to a fortified town in 1506. It was their most successful Moroccan venture and although Moulay Abdullah, the Saadi, made a determined attack on it in 1562, the Portuguese were able to hold it until 1769, when Sidi Mohammed ben Abdullah finally dislodged them. They had during that time created a pattern of commerce which flowed from the interior through the port and though this languished after their departure — and the town with it — Abd er-Rahman was able to revive it after 1815 when he settled men of the Doukkala tribe, and a colony of Jews from Azemmour, in the half-abandoned town.

As at Azemmour, a walk round the four bastions is rewarding, but the great thing to see is the underground *Portuguese cistern* in Rue Carriera, a catchment-tank that was sunk below governmental buildings. Its vaulted and groined roof is carried on square pillars and round columns — very simple yet, lit both by a shaft of light from the well-head above and by brilliantly placed artificial lights, the vaulting reflected in the sheet of water shallowly covering the floor, it is one of the most dramatically and surprisingly beautiful sights you can see anywhere.

The Church of Our Lady of the Assumption has an arcaded front, simple and still Gothic in feeling. It was restored by the French in 1921. It stands on a little square still called the *Praca do Terreiro*. There are also a couple of rather tumble-down houses dating from Portuguese days and many later ones, like that immediately opposite the entrance to the cistern — late nineteenth-century.

Rue Carriera ends at a battery, built to defend the port, in which there is nowadays a bakery. People prepare their own bread dough and bring it here for baking, as they do roasts and

Route Map for Western Area

Legend:
— Routes
--- Link Routes and Detours

Scale: 0 — 50 kilometres

N ↑

ATLANTIC OCEAN

Place names:
RABAT · SALÉ · to Kenitra · Sidi Allal-Bahraoui · Souk et-Tnine · P1 · Tiflet · to Khemisset Meknes · Nkheila · P22 · Rommani · Ezzhiliga · Moulay Bouazza · S131 · OUED ZEM · Boujad · P13 · KASBA TADLA · to Khenifra · BENI MELLAL · P22 · Fkih ben Salah · Khouribga · P13 · Temara · Aïn Attig · Skhirat · Skhirat Plage · Bouznika · Ben Sliman · Louizia · Tit Mellil · MOHAMMEDIA · CASABLANCA · Berrechid · SETTAT · S114 · P7 · Mechra Benaïbou · Kasbah de Boulaouane · S127 · S105 · Dam of Imfout · S128 · Boulaouane · Skhour des Rehamna · 8d · Bir Jdid · S130 · Azemmour · EL-JADIDA · Moulay Abdallah (Tit) · Sidi Bennour · P9 · Sidi 'Smaïl · Oualidia · S131 · Cap Cantin · Beddouza lighthouse · SAFI · P12 · 8d · P8

their delicious *tangiier*, mutton stews sealed into special vase-shaped pots for baking.

[149 km.] You continue inland along the P8 to **Sidi 'Smaïl** (52 km.) where there is a very large Monday market.

The P9 branches left to join with the Safi-to-Marrakech road. There is nothing of interest about this beautiful road except **Sidi Bennour**, 71 km. from El-Jadida, where there is a Tuesday market and the *zawiya of Sidi Bennour* where a large moussem is held in November.

[230 km.] **Souk et-Tleta de Sidi Bouguedra** (Tuesday market). A turning right to Safi.

[256 km.] Safi (see p. 318).

ALTERNATIVE ROAD FROM EL-JADIDA TO SAFI

Distances from El-Jadida (142 km. in all as against 157 km. by the P8).

This coast-road — the S121 — is officially regarded as panoramic, which is no less than its due. But it is a quiet panorama of wide, rolling plain and lagoon-fringed ocean; a good enough road surface and little traffic. You can either follow the coastal route all the way from Casablanca or join it at El-Jadida. From Casablanca to El-Jadida the route is not an interesting one.

At 13·5 km. is **Moulay Abdullah**, a fishing-village partially occupying the site of ruined **Tit**.

This was probably a *ribat*, founded before 1060, enlarged under Abd el-Mumin to become a fortified town capable of dominating the Doukkala tribes of the region. The origin of Tit is obscured by legend — in response to a vision, it is said, a holy man of Medina, Ismaïl Amghar, travelled as far west as he was able before founding his *ribat* here — and little enough is known of its history while it acted as capital of the region. However, its end is recorded: Mohammed esh-Sheikh, the first Wattasid ruler, transplanted its inhabitants to the neighbourhood of Fes, presumably the better to be able to control them.

The ruined circuit of 'the walls with their seven crumbling *towers* and two *gates* has a desolate grandeur. The real interest of the site is largely concentrated, however, upon the two *minarets* standing inside the walls. The isolated one (which has lost both its lantern and the mosque to which it belonged) dates from about 1060 and is the only Almoravid minaret to have survived. Built of small, dressed stones, it has only one chamber in its height, the windows of which are set in carved, recessed panels framing decorative mouldings supported by engaged pillars that are also carved into the stone-work. The north-west and south-east faces, into which double, arched lights are set, resemble one another; the north-east and south-west faces have rather more elaborate, matching string-mouldings around single arched lights. Much the same type of external decoration is known to have decorated the external walls of the first Almohad Koutoubia Mosque at Marrakech (see p. 207).

The other, whitewashed *minaret* still serves the *zawiya of Moulay Abdullah*, for which it was built. The rest of the buildings are comparatively modern, but the minaret dates from the twelfth century, having been built under the Almohad Abd el-Mumin. It has two superimposed *chambers* and an unusually tall *lantern*. Again it is built of dressed and carved stone and the window-lights are set in recessed panels and decorated with fan or arched mouldings much resembling, in a simpler form, those of the Koutoubia minaret and the Hassan Tower. The development in style between these two minarets is interesting. Unfortunately the decoration of the later has suffered from inexpert restoration and is in any case blurred by many coats of whitewash picked out in bright emerald paint. There is a large moussem here in late August or early September.

At 76 km. you reach **Oualidia**.

Hotels
  **A *Hôtel l'Hyppocampe* (tel. 111).
  *A *Auberge de la Lagune* (tel. 105).
Camping *International* (tel. 24).

A small village largely confined to a Saadi *casbah* and a seaside resort upon a lagoon. The entrance to the sea is largely silted up and the place no longer the small port which el-Walid thought it worth while building the casbah to protect in 1634. This is a delightful place. It has royal approval of its charms: Mohammed V built the near-by *summer villa*; both hotels serve good sea-food.

Cap Beddouza is reached in 117·5 km. This fine Cape has been identified as the *Cape Soloeis* where, according to ancient authors, Hanno, the Carthaginian credited with pioneering the

Phoenician route to the Gold Coast, built an altar to the sea-god — 'Poseidon' in the Greek text. And, indeed, this is a headland where it would be easy to believe in Poseidon's existence and, believing it, to be moved to build upon it an altar to the sea.

In 142 km. you come to Safi.

SAFI

Hotels
****B *Hôtel Atlantide*, Rue Chaouki (tel. 21.60).
 ***B *Hôtel les Mimosas*, Rue Ibn Zaidoun (tel. 32.08).
Camping *Sidi Bouzid*, 2 km. north (tel. 28.71).

This is a town of more than 100,000 inhabitants, built over hills facing the ocean — the older parts of it, that is; the vast growth and industrialization of this town is impressive, though unlovely. Pollution has followed industrialization and the beaches north of Safi are preferred.

The port is both an important fishing-centre and cannery (try the local, piquant sardines) and the chief exporting-point for phosphates. The new chemical factory here is one of the more important industrialization projects in the country, precursor of all the development you have passed through to arrive there. It is good to see its towers risen beside those of the old Portuguese castles; they look curiously well together and their symbolic significance is heartening.

History

Safi may possibly stand where a Punic colony called Mysokaras stood, though as yet there is no archaeological evidence to support the supposition. Nothing in fact is known about the foundation of the town; el-Bekri, the geographer, provides first mention of it in the eleventh century. It was then called Asfi. It was a busy port in the next century — it served Marrakech and its fortunes were somewhat dependent on that city's national status — but was closed thereafter to European shipping until the fifteenth century. By 1480 the Portuguese Crown had established a representative here; though his office was a commercial one, he appears to have had great political influence over the local ruling family. When in 1508 a member of this intrigued dangerously with the king of Castille, the Portuguese governor of Essaouira (then the Portuguese colony of Mogador) was ordered to seize the town. A Moroccan attempt to recapture it failed and the Portuguese fortified it heavily as a base from which they were briefly successful in dominating the interior almost as far as Marrakech. The fall of Agadir in 1541 necessitated its abandonment, the fortress having been blown up by the retiring garrison. At the beginning of the seventeenth century Safi was the main port of Morocco, doing considerable trade, first with France and later with England and Holland, and from 1751 exclusively with Denmark for a time, a cunning Marseillais having secured the Danes a monopoly. But by 1767 the French were able to return and post a consul here.

Principal sights

The walled *medina* slopes down to the sea — which it faces with large old warehouses. At the top of the town stands the *Kechla*, a noble and even palatial Portuguese fortress which one may visit. At the sea's edge there stands the great shell of the *Dar el-Bahr* or 'Château de la Mer' which was most likely the governor's fortified palace. On the southerly hill near by, where the main square — *Place de l'Indépendance* — is situated, a *ribat* was built by Abu el-Hassan towards the end of the fourteenth century, presumably to put a curb on Portuguese activity. The Dar el-Bahr is particularly well defended against this hillside where a suburb, still called *Rbat*, later grew up. The *ribat* has disappeared and is now recorded only in the name of the quarter and that of a small *mosque*.

Both the Kechla and the Dar el-Bahr still carry the carved arms of Portugal; the small vaulted *chapel* in the medina which was formerly the choir of the cathedral is blazoned with those of King Manuel, the Order of Christ, the arms of the Holy See and of the Bishopric of Safi — all nicely Manuelian in style, as befits their early-sixteenth-century date (the chapel is of 1519), and all looking extremely foreign under the African sun.

The Kechla contains some semi-ruinous rooms constituting the *Dar el-Makhzen* of the eighteenth century; they have splendid views over the town. But it is more likely that Sidi Mohammed ibn Abdullah spent his short exile from Marrakech (when he ruled Safi so well that the rebellious Marrakchi invited him back to his viceregal post over them) in the Dar el-Bahr. Among his works in the town were the building of the *Great Mosque* with its annexes, but these seem to have been built during his subsequent sultanate.

The potters of Safi are famous. Their *quarter* lies on the hillside north of the medina, outside the *Bab Chaba* or Valley Gate, a warren of primitive workshops among the white domes of marabouts' tombs. They make green-glazed tiles and the patterned vessels of which one can get so tired because the designs are perfunctory and the colours, these days, inferior. But it is certainly fascinating to watch the master-potters, their assistants and apprentices at work.

The markets are busy places — in short, white and yellow Safi has a great deal of breezy charm.

The more northerly Atlantic ports have an air of unspoken assurance which must derive from their old connection with the Iberian peninsula; the southerly ones, of which Safi is the first we come to, all have a brave and rather lonely air, facing Uqba ben Nafi's ford-less ocean and away from all the world they knew and relied upon. Only at Casa does the existence of a trans-Atlantic world seem credible. At Safi you begin to be aware of the gallantry necessary ever to have sailed into the Atlantic blue, out of the sight of land. And it was from here in 1969 and 1970 that Thor Heyerdahl launched his papyrus boats *Ra* and *Ra II* to substantiate the theory that prehistoric Egyptian sailors could have reached Central America.

From Safi it is not difficult to follow the coast south as far as **Souira Guedama** — 'old walled place' — where there was an eleventh-century *ribat* called *Agouz* and where the sand drifts over the ruins of a Portuguese settlement which lasted only from 1521 to 1525; but you should rejoin the P8 at Tnine Rhiate by way of the 6531 road (12 km. back along the road to Souira Guedama), as the farther tracks back along the sea are very bad. However, it is along them, or others equally bad from the P8 or Essaouira, that you must persevere to reach **Dar Caïd Hadji** and the ruins of *Casbah Hamidouch*, the *Zawiya of Sidi Aïssa*, the *Zawiya of Sidi Ali el-Kourati*, the *Zawiya Akermoud*, and that of *Moulay Bouzerktoun*, dramatically sited on a low cliff at the sea's edge — which you may well want to do in order to attend the moussems held there during the spring pilgrimage of the Seven Saints Regraga (see below).

From Safi, the P8 for Essaouira can be regained by returning 26 km. to **Souk et-Tleta de Sidi Bouguedra** by the P12 — a good road which continues over the high plains to Marrakech without incident or interest — or by cutting the corner to Sebt des Gzoula.

[283 km.] **Sebt des Gzoula** (Saturday market).

[314 km.] **Dar Tahar ben Abbou.**

A village from which a track on the right leads into the valley of the *Tensift* and over the river into the heart-land of the *Jebel Habid*, scattered over which all seven of the Masmuda Saints Regraga have their shrines.

It will be appropriate to introduce these *Sebatou Rijal* here. The Masmuda are as good as indigenous Berbers over the Jebel Habid. This was an isolated region and from a very early period of the Christian era they adhered to a heretical, monotheistic Christian cult of their own which approached close to Arianism. They believed Sidi Aïssa — Jesus — to be the prophet and herald of the Paraclete — 'the Illustrious One' — who would bring full revelation. They based their creed on the text of John XVI, 7–8, 'Nevertheless I tell you the truth; it is expedient for you that I go away: for if I go not away, the Comforter [Paraclete] will not come unto you; but if I go, I will send him unto you. And he, when he is come, will convict the world in respect of sin, and of righteousness, and of judgement . . .' This text has always been claimed by Moslems to announce the advent of Mohammed (indeed he claimed it himself by taking the name Mohammed, which means 'illustrious'). The Masmuda lived on in their generations in the expectation of this coming and when first news reached them of Mohammed's ministry — so the legend holds; though credence has made something more than legend of it — seven members of the Regraga family of Masmuda at once set off to seek him in Arabia. When they arrived at Mecca they demanded to know, 'Which of you was sent by God?' They spoke Berber and were not understood except by Mohammed who answered, 'I, come!' One of them, Sidi Wasmin, was charged with an epistle to the Berbers written or dictated by the Prophet himself. When the seven returned home they travelled the country preaching the new religion and thus became apostles of Islam as well as Companions of the Prophet. This tradition suggests that the seven (at least) belonged to a circle practising a mystical quest equivalent to Mohammed's own. They being masters in their disciplines, Mohammed would have had no need to know Berber dialects to communicate with the seven, nor they with him in Arabic. There is a faint resemblance here to Jesus calling on his disciples one by one to follow him, and to their understanding response.

During forty-four days in spring an annual pilgrimage is made to the shrines of the seven saints. Besides enabling each to receive the pilgrims' homage, this re-enacts symbolically their apostolic journeying. At each shrine a moussem is held, that on the twelfth day, at the *Zawiya Akermoud* (above), being the most important. Buried there are Sidi 'bu Beker and his son Sidi Salih; Sidi Ali el-Kourati and Sidi Aïssa 'bu Khabia lie in the *zouawi* called after them; Sidi Abdullah ben Adnas is buried under a *koubba* by the Tensift, Sidi Wasmin on the far north-east of the Jebel Habid and, in the *zawiya* of the same name, Moulay 'bu Zerktoun whose grave is twice visited during the pilgrimage and to visit freely whose moussem no man may deny his wife since the saint protects her virtue absolutely.

[353 km.] *Zawiya ben Hamida*, whence a track leads in 9 km. to the *Zawiya Sidi Ali el-Kourati*.

[368 km.] A turning right for 16 km. to the *Ziwaya Zerktoun*.

The *Jebel Habid*, or 'iron mountain', will be your first sight of the southern Moroccan landscape, a rocky one covered by maquis out of which grow thuya and argan trees. Foxes, jackals and wild boar live among the rocks. The Masmuda are today mostly represented by families claiming descent from the Seven Saints (they are the organizers of the pilgrimage) for the whole region was settled in the sixteenth century by the Chiadma tribe.

[385 km.] You reach Essaouira.

ESSAOUIRA

Bus C.T.M. station on Avenue Okba Ibn Nafia, just off Place Moulay El Hassan which leads to the harbour. Other carriers on Boulevard Moulay Youssef at Bab Doukkala.

Hotels
- ****A *Hôtel des Iles*, Boulevard Mohammed V (tel. 23.29).
- ***A *Hôtel Tafoukt*, Boulevard Mohammed V (tel. 25.04).
- **B *Hôtel Sahara*, Avenue Okba Ibn Nafia (tel. 23.79).
- *A *Hôtel du Mechouar*, Avenue Okba Ibn Nafia (tel. 20.18).
- *A *Hôtel Tafraout*, 7 Rue de Marrakech (tel. 21.10).
- *B *Hôtel des Ramparts*, 18 Zankat Ibn Rochd (tel. 22.82).

Camping *Municipal*, 500 m. from Place Moulay El Hassan (the centre of the town functionally) along Boulevard Mohammed V.

Information *Tourist Office*: Place Moulay El Hassan.
Post Office Avenue Lalla Aicha (between Bab Marrakech and Boulevard Mohammed V).

Essaouira 'the walled' — is still often called by its Spanish or
Portuguese name of Mogador, a corruption perhaps of *amogdoul*
or 'mooring'. It stands on a rock promontory loosely embracing a
large bay in which lie islets. The bay is lined by a marvellous
sand-beach and to the south are sand-dunes. Smaller than Safi,
Essaouira is perhaps the most attractive place in which to spend a
few days on the Atlantic coast.

The walled town we see was founded in 1760 by Sidi Mohammed ben Abdullah. It belongs almost entirely to the later
eighteenth century and is extraordinarily uniform in style. It is
quite beautiful. The tall white houses have blue-painted wood-
work and ochre bandings. Pepper trees grow in the more open
places, and palms. Apart from the *North Bastion*, where the
Sqala de la Casbah is dramatically lined with old cannon, many
of British manufacture, Essaouira has no 'sights'; the town
itself, however, and the bustling sardine-fishing port being
major ones. The children here are anxious to take charge of you
and march you around, but they are nice about it and therefore
welcome.

The islands over the bay were frequented by Phoenician
traders during the seventh to the fifth centuries B.C. but they do
not appear to have settled a permanent colony there. They were
simply used as a 'counter' for trading during what were probably
annual voyages. This trade seems to have diminished very much
thereafter. Juba II, however, built permanent dwellings and
factories on the larger island for the manufacture of a purple dye
derived from shell-fish. This was probably a royal monopoly; the
dye and products coloured with it were in demand in Rome and
Juba's son Ptolemy was wearing a cloak of this purple when he
entered the theatre at Lyons to be so vociferously acclaimed by
the people as, it was said, fatally to arouse Caligula's jealousy
(p. 63). It is pleasant to visit the islands, though the first-century
A.D. remains are not in themselves greatly interesting. In Juba's
time they were called the Insulae Purpurariae after the dye
which, like that of Tyre, may have been more red than the colour
we call purple.

King Manuel of Portugal had a fort built — perhaps where the
present small casbah now stands in the town — in 1506. This was
most probably designed to give some protection to shipping using

the anchorage. It would have had to be evacuated in 1541 after the fall of Agadir. Moulay Abd el-Malik repaired it in 1628. Sidi Mohammed's reasons for founding his fine city here are a bit obscure. It was partly, for certain, to serve Marrakech and southern Morocco. It may have been somewhat to spite the Agadiri, who had revolted, but since only four years after its foundation he attracted foreign trade to it by removing all taxes upon imports passing through the port he can hardly have designed it, as it suggested, as a secure base and arsenal for Moroccan pirates preying upon foreign ships. As a port handling foreign trade, Essaouira was a success. Sidi Mohammed set up a Jewish colony in the town particularly to handle it. Isaac Disraeli, father of the English prime minister, was born here, or brought here in infancy, where his father was serving some years as his international family's representative. The Jews of Mogador particularly fostered British trade which presently grew considerable as the demand for wool increased in industrial England.

From the crowded municipal beach below Avenue Mohammed V the sand extends more than ten kilometres south to the dunes of *Cap Sim*. To reach Cap Sim and Diabat, notorious in the sixties and seventies for hippies, take the road to Agadir and turn right at 7 km.; a short way after, the track forks left for Cap Sim and right for Diabat. The area is popular with windsurfers.

From Essaouira the P10, a fine road, runs to Marrakech — 171 km. Along it there is a Wednesday market at **Sidi Mokhtar** (68 km.) and a Sunday market at **Chichaoua** (93 km.), where there is a co-operative weaving establishment; the Chichaoua carpets, made to the traditions of the Ouled Bousseba tribe of hereabouts, are of good quality and often characterful in design and colour, while nearer Marrakech (148 km.), by the bridge over the Nifs River, is the Monday-market enclosure of the Oudaïa tribe.

The P8, onwards to Agadir, crosses the comparatively low, western extremities of the High Atlas range. It is an almost exclusively Berber area; though there are few villages along the road, many lie higher on the slopes inland. The tracks up to them are practicable for ordinary motors and the countryside often beautiful, but there is not enough general interest to warrant describing them here.

[424 km.] **Smimou**.
  The only village on the road with a bar (and restaurant).

[502 km.] **Tamri** — the road makes a detour inland to cross the wide valley of the *Aït Ameur*, a watered river-bed green with bananas and fields. Rainfall is scant hereabouts and the water in the seasonal torrents flowing from the higher mountains is carefully conserved for watering oases like this. At a pinch, one might be able to get a room in this village; ask at the café.

[514 km.] You can see the lighthouse of *Cape Ghir*, most westerly point of the High Atlas.

[529 km.] *Paradis Plage* summer café and sandy bathing.

[545 km.] A turning left into the mountains by a pretty road to **Imouzzer des Ida Outanane** (49 km.) where there is a fine waterfall.

Hotel
  ***B *Auberge des Cascades* (tel. 16).

[557 km.] You reach Agadir.

AGADIR

Air *Agadir-Inezgane Airport* is 8 km. south leaving Agadir by Boulevard Hassan II. *Royal Air Maroc* has an office on Avenue Général Kettani (tel. 227.93).
Bus Main bus station at Place Lahcen Tamri but airport buses leave from Place Salam, near the Royal Palace.
Taxi Also use Place Salam for local destinations. Agadir taxi drivers are some of the most truculent in the country.
Car Hire *Avis*, Avenue Hassan II (tel. 233.42) and at the airport.
Budget, Bungalow Marhaba, Avenue Mohammed V (tel. 237.62).
Europcar, Cnr. Avenue du Prince Moulay Abdellah and Avenue des F.A.R. (tel. 230.90).
Hertz, Bungalow Markaba, Avenue Mohammed V (tel. 239, 39) and at the airport.
Hotels
  ***** *Hôtel les Almohades*, Quartier des Dunes (tel. 232.33).
  ***** *Hôtel Sahara*, Boulevard Mohammed V (tel. 206.60).
  ***** *Hôtel Europa-Maroc*, Boulevard du 20 août (tel. 212.12).
  ****A *Hôtel Argana*, Boulevard Mohammed V (tel. 220.70)
  ****A *Hôtel Atlas*, Boulevard Mohammed V (tel. 232.32).
  ****A *Hôtel El Oumnia*, Chemin Oued Souss (tel. 233.51).

****A   *Hôtel Adrar*, Boulevard Mohammed V (tel. 214.17).
****A   *Hôtel Marhaba*, Boulevard Mohammed V (tel. 226.70).
****B   *Hôtel Ali Baba*, Boulevard Mohammed V (tel. 233.26).
****B   *Hôtel Sud Bahia*, Rue des Administrations Publiques (tel. 237.41).
****B   *Hôtel Tagadirt*, Boulevard du 20 août (tel. 215.30).
***A   *Hôtel Royal*, Boulevard Mohammed V (tel. 224.75).
***A   *Hôtel Kamal*, Boulevard Hassan II (tel. 228.17).
***B   *Hôtel Mabrouk*, Boulevard du 20 août (tel. 226.06).
***B   *Hôtel Talborjt*, Rue de l'Entraide (tel. 206.71).
***B   *Hôtel Aladin*, Rue de la Jeunesse (tel. 232.28).
**A   *Hôtel Sindibad*, Quartier Talborjt (tel. 234.77).
**A   *Hôtel Miramar*, Boulevard Mohammed V (tel. 222.73).
**A   *Hôtel Atlantic*, Boulevard Hassan II (tel. 236.61).
**A   *Hôtel les Palmiers*, Avenue du Prince Héritier.
**A   *Hôtel Ayour*, Rue de l'Entraide (tel. 249.76).
**A   *Hôtel Cinq Parties du Monde*, Boulevard Hassan II (tel. 225.45).
*A   *Hôtel de Paris*, Avenue Kennedy (tel. 226.94).
*A   *Hôtel Petite Suede*, Avenue Général Kettani (tel. 228.79).
*A   *Hôtel Tifawt*, Rue Yacoub El Mansour (tel. 243.54).
*A   *Hôtel Bahia*, Rue Mehdi Ibn Toumert (tel. 227.24).
*B   *Hôtel Amenou*, 1 Rue Yacoub El Mansour (tel. 230.26).
*B   *Hôtel de la Baie*, Rue Allal Ben Abdellah (tel. 230.14).
*B   *Hôtel Excelsior*, Rue Yacoub El Mansour (tel. 210.28).

Club Méditerranée and other similar establishments. O.N.M.T. can supply details of the multitude of self-catering apartments available.

Camping *International*, northern end of Boulevard Mohammed V (tel. 209.40).

Information *O.N.M.T. Tourist Office*: (Map **2**) Immeuble A, Avenue du Prince Héritier Sidi Mohammed (tel. 228.94).

Syndicat d'Initiative: Avenue Mohammed V (tel. 226.95).

Banks and Shopping Principally on Avenues du General Kettani and des Forces Armées Royales and Boulevard Hassan II.

Sports and Clubs *Riding*: *Club Equestre*, opposite the golf club.

Tennis: *Royal Tennis Club*, Avenue Hassan II.

Golf: *Royal Club de Golf*, 12 km. on the road to Aït Mellou.

Yachting: *Yacht-Club d'Agadir*, Port.

Flying: *Aéro Club d'Agadir*, Airport.

Post Office (Map **3**) Corner of Avenue Sidi Mohammed and Avenue du Prince Moulay Abdellah.

Emergencies *Hospital Hassan II*: Route de Marrakech (tel. 224.77).

Police: telephone 19.

Since the appalling earthquake of 1960 Agadir has been steadily growing up an entirely modern and well-planned town with an industrial area separated from the pleasure resort that runs beside its marvellous, mimosa-lined beach. All new buildings are constructed to resist earthquake shocks.

In mid-winter the sea here is warmer than it is in the Channel during a summer's heat-wave. This is almost enough, but there is

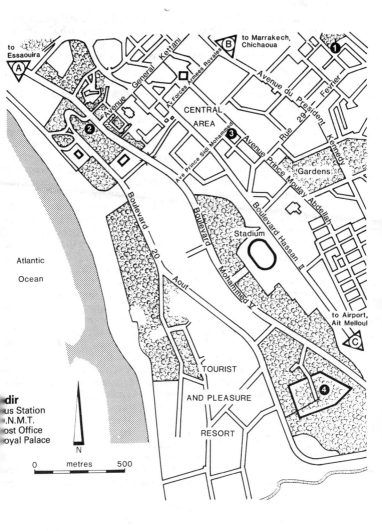

to Essaouira

A

to Marrakech, Chichaoua

B

1

Avenue du President Kennedy

Avenue General Kettani

Av Forces Armees Royales

Rue 29 Fevrier

2

Avenue

CENTRAL AREA

3

Avenue Prince Moulay Abdellah

Gardens

Ave Prince Sidi Mohammed

Atlantic Ocean

Boulevard 20

Boulevard Mohammed V

Aout

Stadium

Boulevard Hassan II

to Airport, Ait Melloul

C

TOURIST AND PLEASURE RESORT

4

dir
us Station
.N.M.T.
ost Office
oyal Palace

0   metres   500

N

too, an air about Agadir which already makes it a delightful and light-hearted town. The people of the Sous valley, which Agadir serves as chief town and port, are particularly lively and open in character — I cannot believe the present air of the place will die away when the spur of rebuilding no longer goads them to a gallant spirit. The clear, dry air becomes contemporary buildings very well; and nobody is going to allow a repetition of the southern Spanish coastal slums here.

It could be that this was the site of the Phoenicians' Rusadir — they would have been likely enough to have had some station near the mouth of the Sous and this is its likeliest spot. However, the people of the valley do not seem to have been interested in the sea until comparatively recent times. Agadir was a Portuguese foundation. An adventurous man called João Lopes de Sequeira built himself a fort around a seaside spring, lying a little to the north of the present town, in 1505. It was called *Santa Cruz de Narba*, or *de Capo Gere*, and was sold to the Portuguese Crown in 1513. It was soon made into the chief Portuguese colonial enclave, built upon the higher ground immediately to the north of the present town centre (the site had to be bulldozed in 1960 and planted with trees as a mass grave for both the town and its citizens). The Saadi family from Taroudant, fifty miles up the Sous valley, made Portuguese Agadir the first goal of their nationalistic and, to some extent, holy war against the country's invaders. In 1531 Mohammed esh-Sheikh built a base camp at Tamraght, a dozen kilometres to the north, from which in 1533 he made a near-successful assault on the town that failed only because the Portuguese were able to seize the hill above the fort of Santa Cruz, forcing him to retreat. Seven years later Mohammed was able to make another outright assault on the town, this time from what is now the Casbah of Agadir, high on the hillside above, which he had fortified for the purpose. But this attempt also failed. The next year, though, in March, a third attack was successful and, El-Jadida only excepted, the Portuguese were forced to evacuate all the Moroccan gains on the Atlantic coast. This spectacular success laid the foundation of Saadi fortunes and had members of the family not fallen soon into fratricidal rivalry they had not needed another twenty-five years to secure the entire sultanate for themselves.

In Moroccan hands, Agadir became a thriving port. It was a chief outlet for the produce of Saharan Morocco and even for trans-Saharan trade. Sugar was then a valuable commodity and the Sous produced a lot of it; but the opening up of the Caribbean in the middle of the seventeenth century put an end to its profitability. In 1751 Denmark gained a brief monopoly over Agadir's foreign trade, as over that of Safi. The following year Sultan Abdullah reconstructed the casbah for fear of renewed Portuguese threats to the port. Soon after, the Sous and the port rebelled against Abdullah's son Sidi Mohammed; Essaouira was built in 1760 and the sultan deliberately discriminated against Agadir. A French traveller, Cochelet, found only some dozen houses inhabited in 1819. However, the port revived considerably and it was to Agadir that the German Government sent the warship *Panther* in 1911 (see p. 109).

For a description of the routes south of Agadir see the South section (p. 335).

Agadir to Marrakech via Taroudant

Route 303 km. by the P 32 to Taroudant and the S 501 to Marrakech. The roads are good.
  Leave Agadir by the south.
Bus Six services a day between Agadir and Taroudant: one daily from Taroudant to Marrakech.
Accommodation and food At Ouled Teïma, Taroudant, Idni, Ijoukak, Ouirgane, the *Grand Hôtel du Toubkal* and Asni.

[567 km.] **Inezgane** lies to the right of the road.
  This walled village is the address rather than the centre for several seaside hotels lining the great beach south from Agadir.

Hotels
  ****A *Hôtel Club Hacienda*, Route Oued Souss (tel. 301.76).
    ***B *Hôtel les Pyramides*, Route Oued Souss (tel. 307.05).
    ***B *Hôtel Provençal*, 9 km. on the Route d'Inezgane (tel. 312.08).
      **A *Hôtel la Pergola*, 8 km. on the Route d'Inezgane (tel. 308.41).
      **B *Hôtel Essafen*, Route de Chtouka (tel. 304.13).
        *A *Hôtel Orient*, Route de Tiznit (tel. 305.48).

It is possible to skirt Inezgane by a short detour which is well signposted.

[570 km.] **Aït Melloul** — the P 32 forks left from the P 30.

[597 km.] **Oulad Teïma** (Thursday market).

[637 km.] You reach Taroudant.

Taroudant

Hotels

**** *Hôtel la Gazelle d'Or*, set in its own grounds outside the town. Note that the hotel closes during the summer. Telephone 20.39.

****A *Hôtel Salam* (tel. 23.12).

**A *Hôtel Saadiens*, Borg Ennassim (tel. 25.89).

*A *Hôtel Taroudant*, Place Assarag (tel. 24.16).

Buses, banks, shopping and people all concentrate on the two central squares — Place Tamoklate and Place Assarag — they are not difficult to find.

A walled town of some 40,000 inhabitants and old capital of the Sous valley district, beautifully placed between the High and the Anti-Atlas and surrounded by ancient olive-groves. It is quite a busy centre with some likely shops for Berber wares, and one of the most exclusive hotels in Morocco, the Gazelle d'Or.

Taroudant became the capital of a Shiite state, ultimately of Fatimid origin, in 1030 or thereabouts. This was overthrown by the orthodox Almoravids in 1056 — early in Abu Bekr's reforming crusade. The Almohads appear to have had little authority over the Sous, which was governed by a local family who were nevertheless forced to accept Merinid suzerainty in 1306. The walls of Taroudant were then destroyed, though rebuilt soon after — and with their protection the town was again soon independent. Now it was governed by an oligarchy whose members presided turn and turn about for six months at a time; a remarkable experiment which apparently endured some decades at least. The Sous was certainly a virtually independent part of Morocco until the Saadi, coming from here, gained the rest of the country and by doing so included it in their sultanate. The history of the sixteenth century, dominated by the Saadi (who had been invited to Taroudant to make the date crop prosper with the blessing of the *baraka* they possessed) is given in the History section (p. 88). The Saadi period was a very prosperous one for the town; the valley produced sugar and cotton in demand in Europe. But disaster overtook the area, beginning with the revolt of Moulay Ismaïl's nephew Ahmed ibn Mahrez, which he based upon the support he found at Taroudant. Ismaïl put down this insurrection in 1687, taking the town and massacring most of the inhabitants. The creation of Essaouira and closure of Agadir port, with the loss of the sugar trade to the West Indies, prevented all hope of re-establishing the old prosperity either of the Sous or of Taroudant. After Moulay el-Hassan's death in

1893 the town became a hotbed of discontent and revolt against both the later sultans and the French. It was not until el-Hiba was cleared from Taroudant in 1913 that it returned to the *bled el-makhzen* and a new prosperity became possible.

There is little to see in the town save the *walls*, particularly those of the *casbah quarter*, in a corner of which the *Hôtel Salam* occupies a not very old palace. The walls of this area are largely early-eighteenth-century, much restored; those of the outer enceinte go back to the Merinid rebuilding, though they too have been repaired often enough until modern times. A certain vivacity and individuality, however, to be sensed throughout the town, compensates for its want of conventional 'sights'.

[645 km.] A turning right for **Freïja** and **Tiout**, the latter a particularly picturesque village guarded by a ruined *ksar* from which there is a noble view. Beware of deep sand crossing the bed of the Oued Sous; the bridge is down.

[689 km.] You branch off the P 32, which continues to Ouarzazate, taking the S 501 or left-hand fork. For Ouarzazate to Taroudant see p. 352.

[725 km.] *Café du Tizi n'Test* − An irresistible halt for the sake of its view.

[726 km.] *Tizi n'Test Pass*.
This is 2,120 metres high though it is claimed to be a little lower than the actual highest point on the road 5 km. ahead. This remarkable spot has, however, all the drama that could be asked of a pass over the High Atlas: the valley of the Sous, almost at your feet, lies 2,000 metres below you.

[744 km.] **Idni** village.
Here, there is the little restaurant and hotel *Alpina* which is the customary halting-place in this pass.

[749 km.] **Casbah Taoundaft**.
The peak you see ahead is *Jebel Toubkal*, highest of the High Atlas range; 4,165 metres.

[755 km.] **Mzouzit** village and *ksar*. Tinmel can be seen on the left, across the torrent bed of the *Nifiss*.

[757 km.] There is a turning leading towards **Tinmel**. One must cross the Nifiss on foot and walk by the village to the ruined *mosque*. Your appearance will be sure to be noticed and the key will be produced from the guardian's house in the village.

Tinmel was perhaps founded by ibn Tumart as the head-quarters of his sect, in 1125 (see p. 78). When the Almohads had taken control of all Morocco Tinmel remained their sacred cult centre and, for a time perhaps, their treasury. Abd el-Mumin built the mosque as a shrine and burial-place for himself. His two successors were also buried here. It was the retreat of the last Almohad in the face of the Merinids' advance and did not fall to them until 1276. The town and its fortifications were then largely destroyed.

Now only scattered piles of masonry remain of the outer walls; an inner ring probably stood around the eminence on which the mosque stands.

The now ruined mosque was built between 1253 and 1154. Its redoubtable external walls suggest that it was actually a part of the town's western defences. The eccentricity of this building consists in the placing of the *minaret* behind and in part over the *mihrab*, so that the sanctuary abuts it and the *quibla*–wall is incorporated in its northern side.

After all that has been said about Maghrebi mosque architecture in the section upon architecture (p. 121) and Almohad mosques — in particular in the description of the two Koutoubias (p. 207) — it is unnecessary to describe what here, for once, you can see for yourself. The *mihrab* is extremely close to that of the existing Koutoubia — which was built a little later than this — and is almost certainly by the same architect. The beautifully sculpted arches here also resemble those of the Koutoubia though in this mosque the engaged columns and capitals adorning their pillars are more slender and delicate — indeed this whole building has the delicacy of a miniature, and its richness. Anyone at all interested in Islamic architecture must wish to see it — a marvellous building in a setting of great beauty.

[763 km.] Across the bed of the Nifiss stands **Talaat n'Yaacub** and the *Kasba Goundafa*, called after the tribe which has for centuries held this approach to the pass. Moulay el-Hassan was obliged to visit here on *harka* in order to assert his authority over this tribe.

The *Agadir n'Gouj*, standing over to the right of the road, was built as recently as 1907.

[766 km.] **Ijoukak** village; tiny hotel and mountain hut.

[798 km.] **Ouirgane** village.

Hotels
****A *Résidence de la Roseraie*, B.P. 769 Marrakech (tel. 4 & 5).
 **B *Sanglier qui fume* (tel. 09).

[811 km.] ***A *Grand Hotel du Toubkal* (tel. 3 via Marrakech).

[812 km.] A track fork right to **Imlil** — 17 km. — which lies just outside the *National Park of the Jebel Toubkal*. There is a *refuge* at Imlil, one at **Aremd** and another at **Neltner**, all stages leading to the summit of *Toubkal*.

[813 km.] **Asni** village in the centre of the '*cirque de Tamarout*', a bowl in the hills forming a kind of oasis of fertility.

[822 km.] The *Gorges of Moulay 'Brahim* extend for 3 km. A large moussem is held close to the *zawiya of Moulay 'Brahim* during Mouloud.

[824 km.] An old road on the right — narrow and poor — 41 km. to Oukaïmeden (p. 230).

[826 km.] **Tahanaoute** (Monday market).

[829 km.] The 6034 crosses right to the Ourika valley road at **Dar Caïd Ouriki**. The same road, left, leads (16 km.) over a poor road to **Oumnast** with its imposing *ksar*, where, left (23 km.), there is the *Barrage Cavagnac reservoir*, and near by, the *zawiya of Lalla Takerhoust*; 46 km. farther on, you come to **Amizmiz**, a large village in a most agreeable setting. The ancient city of *Nifs* may have stood hereabouts, but the place owes its modern foundation to the *zawiya of Sidi el-Hussein ben Messaoud*. There is a *casbah* and an old *mellah*. The Tuesday market is a pleasant one. Beyond the village the track for **Azgdour** — 21 km. — commands fine views.

From here you can return to the Barrage and continue into Marrakech by the S507 road, another 32 km. distant. A left-hand turning off this road leads in 4 km. to **Tameslocht** where there are two sixteenth-century *zouawi* founded by the miracle-working sherif Abdullah ben Hussein el-Hassani; a picturesque spot.

Continuing direct by the S501:

[855 km.] Junction with the S507 from Amizmiz.

[860 km.] Marrakech (see p. 193).

Agadir to Marrakech via Imi-n-Tanoute

Route 259 km. by the P40 to Chichaoua and the P10 to Marrakech. No accommodation along the way.

The P40 to Chichaoua, a recent development, greatly shortens the distance to Marrakech. For much of the way following stream beds, this is a scenically varied and quietly beautiful road rising to the watershed pass of Tizi-Maachou where the slopes, lightly wooded with the argan trees of outer Morocco, abruptly give way to almonds and the deciduous trees typical of inner Morocco.

Officially, the P511 runs into Inezgane (p. 329) rather than Agadir, from which you can reach it at the crossroads south of the airport. (Turn away from Inezgane.) However it is generally more convenient to take the road inland opposite the entrance to Agadir port and join the P40 close to Ameskroud — about 30 km. Several small villages lie beside the road before it runs through **Imi-n-Tanoute** (127 km.), a local administration centre. At Chichaoua (184 km., see p. 324), turn right towards Marrakech on the P10.

[259 km.] Marrakech.

Marrakech to Rabat via Oued Zem

Route 402 km. by the P24 and P22 to Rabat. the roads are good.
    Leave Marrakech by Route Exit A.
Bus Eight daily to Rabat.
Accommodation and food At Oued Zem (food only).

The first 152 km. of this route are described on p. 232, the road being the P24.

[1,012 km.] Fork left on the P22 for Oued Zem. This road onwards is a most attractive drive.

[1,020 km.] **Souk es-Sebt des Oulad Nemaa** (Saturday market).

[1,044 km.] **Fkih ben Salah** (Wednesday market).

[1,090 km.] **Oued Zem.**
A mining-centre of some 15,000 inhabitants. Its chief attraction is the excursion into the hills by the S131 (asphalted) 65 km. to

Moulay Bouazza, named for one of the first Sufi preachers who lived under the Almoravids and Almohads, dying in 1176. His tomb and *zawiya*, rebuilt in 1691 by the Moulay Ismaïl, attract thousands of pilgrims.

The P13 leads eastwards from here towards Kasba Tadla, and passes at 22 km. **Boujad**, a holy town where the large *zawiya of Sidi Mohammed ech-Chergui*, founded in the sixteenth century by that 'patron of horsemen', has spawned a number of other shrines. It is an attractive town of white buildings, those of the *zawiya* dating only from the nineteenth century, being a rebuilding after Mohammed ben Abdullah had had to destroy the old in the late eighteenth century.

[1,132 km.] **Souk el-Arba** (Wednesday market-place).

[1,149 km.] **Ezzhiliga**; the name means 'ex-Christian' (Thursday market close by).

[1,180 km.] **Rommani**.
    Wednesday market and a moussem in September at the *tomb of Sidi bou Amar*, an Andalusian saint of the fifteenth century.

[1,213 km.] A road leads left in 1 km. to **Nkheila** (Monday market).

[1,221 km.] You cross the *Oued Korifla* on the banks of which, fighting the Barghawata, Abdullah ibn Yasin, founder of the Almoravid movement, was killed in 1059. His *tomb* stands near by.

[1,262 km.] Rabat (See p. 163).

For Marrakech to Casablanca, see pp. 192–3, where route instructions for the opposite direction are given.

For Rabat to Casablanca, see pp. 184–6.

THE SOUTH

Here, we take Ourzazate as our central point — it was founded by the French to be just that. From there you can turn towards the Atlantic by a very beautiful road into the Sous, push on down the valley of the Draa to M'hamid, or turn east to Er Rachidia (Ksar es-Souk) and south again into the Tafilelt.

Also described here is the trail south from Taroudant following close by the Atlantic coast to the country's south-western end.

If you are attracted to explore beyond Tan Tan or to visit the oases, *please* also read the section on Motoring (p. 24). There you will be in the wilds. You will be lucky to find petrol or food; accommodation will be problematic and never remotely comfortable; the tracks are abominable — and dangerous unless you are a skilled desert-driver and for preference have a four-wheel-drive vehicle. This warning issued yet again, it must be said that the lonely parts of the far south are marvellously beautiful. You enter another world, seemingly more remote than it is in fact by distance. Here lives are led in other ways, both of the desert and the town; fascinatingly intermingled. (See Introduction, p. 15.)

Marrakech to Ouarzazate

Route P31 (198 km.) (Route Exit F).
Bus Four buses daily.
Accommodation and food At Aït Ourir, Taddert and Ouarzazate.

[30 km.] After crossing the Haouz plain you reach **Aït Ourir** where there is a most charming Tuesday market. From here the road climbs into the mountains. The *Atlas Mountains* are more abrupt on their northern side and subject to quite heavy rainfall. The *hamsin*, a hot south wind off the Sahara, sweeps up to a height of over 4,000 metres (Jebel Toubkal, due south of Marrakech and highest peak of the range is 4,165 metres high) to cause precipitation on the northern side only. Rain is a rare occurrence on the southern side. Hence the valleys here are watered and green with vegetation while the southern slopes are arid. The col of this, the *Tizi n'Tichka pass* (2,260 metres), rises only a little above the height at which no vegetation grows, stunted, scattered junipers reaching almost to its summit. The peaks around it are barren and snow lies there until quite late in the year, yet the pass is now rarely closed for long since ploughs soon clear it. Very well engineered, the road tends to make light of this tremendous barrier; even buses cross in six hours. High as the pass is, there is nothing with which to compare its altitude, and this too tends to make the mountains seem less formidable than they are. It took ten days to a fortnight to cross before the road was built; the tracks were precipitous and dangerous, many torrents had to be forded and travellers were the prey of bandits and toll-extorting tribes inhabiting the high valleys.

Hotel
   **A   *Auberge l'Hermitage*, Pont du Zat (tel. 2).

[67 km.] Across the valley after the pass of *Tiri n'Aït Inguer* there is a *ksar* in the village of **Arhbalou**, which is in fact a fortified granary or *agadir*. These were common, a tribe or confederacy of groups holding their stocks communally and sharing the defence of the *agadir*. Alas, now falling into ruin, this lies behind a new, arcaded building. The village houses hereabouts are built of pisé, or *tabia* as it is called, and roofed with wooden beams on which an overlay of twigs is set before earth is rolled into them. The eaves are deep so as to protect the mud walls which are impervious to everything save water — the classic Berber method of mining an enemy's stronghold was to divert a stream or irrigation-ditch to melt its walls.

Climbing here in the spring, you will see how, having left the plains enjoying early-summer weather, the season recoils until you find almond-blossom round the higher villages. The process reverses if you continue into the desert, where they will already be harvesting barley in the oases.

[90 km.] **Taddert**.

This is the resting-place of buses and most cars crossing the pass. Although 1,650 metres high, this is a sheltered and verdant spot.

Accommodation
The café sells alcohol and plain meals, and has a few simple bedrooms.

[100 km.] Refuge.

[104 km.] *Tizi n'Tichka pass*: 2,260 metres.

[108 km.] On the left, a road leads to **Telouet** in 21 km.

The native stronghold of the Glaoui family, Telouet was the eyrie from which they were able to dominate several routes across the range. (The adventurous could push farther into the mountains from this high valley, into others little visited though notable for the *ksour* and villages they contain.) The *ksar* or *Dar* ('palace') *el-Glaoui* rides picturesquely and imperiously over this valley where there are several hamlets. There are really two *ksour* here; the lower, more ruinous and older is the *Ksar of Caïd*

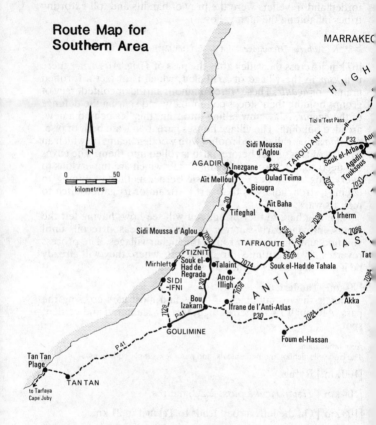

HIGH

Tizi n'Test Pass

P32

Sidi Moussa
d'Aglou

TAROUDANT

Souk el-Arba

AGADIR Inezgane   P32

Agadir
Touksous

Aït Melloul   Oulad Teima

T025

T091

Biougra

Aït Baha

Irherm

T088

T086

P30 Tifeghal

S509 T040

Sidi Moussa d'Aglou   T1055

TAFRAOUTE   A   T   L   A   S

Tat

TIZNIT   T1074   S509

Mirhlett   Souk el-
Had de   Talaint   Souk el-Had de Tahala
Regrada

Anou-
Illigh   T078

SIDI
-IFNI

Bou   Ifrane de l'Anti-Atlas   Akka
Izakarn

T129   P41   P30   T094

GOULIMINE   Foum el-Hassan

Tan Tan   P41
Plage

TAN TAN

to Tarfaya
Cape Juby

0   50
kilometres

N

Hammou; the high *Ksar of Caid 'Brahim* is newer and owned by
the Government. This was built about the turn of the century by
Medani and T'hami el-Glaoui after their phenomenal rise to
power following their rescue here of Sultan Hassan in the last
days of 1893. One can visit its grand, vulgarly decorated rooms
and walk on the battlements. (Give a dirham or so to the guide
who will show them to you.) The unusual sight of green-tiled
roofs indicates the great state to which the brothers aspired; they

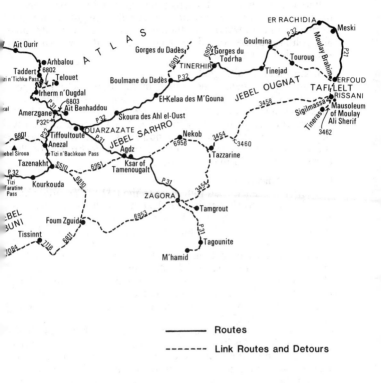

are more usually reserved for royal or religious buildings. Floods have damaged the house considerably. It is not a monument that anybody really wants to endure.

Back on the P31, a few kilometres bring one to the long slopes and wide views sinking towards the confluence of the *Imini* and *Dadès* rivers which, joined, form the *Draa*. The road follows the course of the Imini, into which other streams flow. All this is a dry, sun-exposed land where vegetation is confined to river-beds.

Where these flow slowly the irrigation channels have to be long if they are to water higher ground. Thus a village might be far from its main source of water even though it stands beside the stream, and solitary towers sometimes guard this point of weakness so vulnerable to enemy attack.

[132 km.] Irherm n'Ougdal.

It stands just below the source of the Imini, a prominent, ruinous *ksar* guarding the village. It is high here — 1,970 metres. This too is a traditional halt where refreshments are available.

Here you see your first of the several new mosques recently built in the villages. This one is nothing special, though some show a pleasing fantasy, particularly in the decoration of the minaret — a new form of pop art.

[162 km.] Amerzgane.

There is a branch-road right here to the P32 to Taroudant and Agadir and a track on the left leading to the village of **Aït Benhaddou**, though this is perhaps better reached by the track off the P31 (see below at 176 km.). Do not fail to make the detour necessary to see this village which lies some 15 km. from the road. The track is not a difficult one. Standing across a wide stream, this village is composed of several *ksour*, walls and tall village-houses climbing the steep side of an escarpment, the whole making one of the most satisfactory architectural unities conceivable — and yet it is wholly inadvertent and adventitious. It is also outrageously picturesque.

Here one sees the altered style in which pre-Saharan buildings are raised. The paucity of rainfall allows of pisé building without eaves. Endemic tribal warfare dictated a defensive form and the rest followed upon the limitations of the materials employed — *tabia* walls and split palm-trunks for roofing-beams — and the climate, one which people are naturally at pains to keep out of their houses. The style is not unlike that in which all building on a similar scale has always been done in these materials; sometimes it recalls ancient Egyptian temples, sometimes more a Gothic castle — for there is a fancy and a romance about the detail which, with a barbaric simplicity, echoes the Gothic taste in the same way that the form of a *ksar*, keep and walled court, mirrors that of a Gothic castle. There are stables on the ground floors (animals being perpetually stalled except when rain produces a scant grazing) and dark living-quarters above. Most of life is led on the roof-tops. Walter Harris describes a roof-top dinner-party sheltering against one wall from the rifle-fire of his hosts' immediate neighbours with whom they were at loggerheads (see also p. 132).

The lower and ceremonial-seeming buildings here are new, being built for filming a Biblical epic — a happy occurrence which accounts for the smart new houses on the west bank of the river and the fact that the inhabitants of the village are well used to foreigners in the place. (It is not a bad idea always to be armed with a supply of sweets or fruit with which to reward the children who will everywhere in the country constitute themselves your guides.) The river is easily forded anywhere when in low water and by stepping-stones a little upstream when in spate.

[172 km.] Back on the main road, there is a junction right with the P32.

[176 km.] A turning left, sign-posted for Aït Benhaddou, 10 km.

[192 km.] The road to Ouarzazate branches left from the P31 which continues over the Draa to Zagora. 2 km. along the P31, on the north bank of the river stands the *ksar* of *Tiffoultoute*. This magnificent and classic *ksar* has been partly restored and forms an annexe to the Hôtel Azghor at Ouarzazate, an extremely pleasant place to lodge although no food is served beyond breakfast fare. The decorative brickwork on the older tower is notable and may be as early as the seventeenth century.

[194 km.] On your left is the village of **Tiseltoy**, where the new minaret is positively exuberant.

[198 km.] You reach Ouarzazate.

Ouarzazate

Air See page 23 for details of internal connections.
Hotels
  ****A   *Hôtel Azghor* (tel. 20.58).
  ****A   *Hôtel le Zat* (tel. 25.58).
  ***A   *Hôtel Tichka*, Avenue Mohammed V (tel. 22.06).
  **B   *Hôtel la Gazelle*, Avenue Mohammed V (tel. 21.51).
Club Méditerranée (tel. 22.83).
Camping *Municipal* (tel. 005).

A provincial capital, this town has suffered two transformations in fifty years. It is based upon a fair collection of older *ksour* and some streets that are almost towny (with several Jewish families still living in these), to which the French added an attractively Beau Geste settlement to support their garrison stationed in the fort overlooking the town and river valley from above the main street. The Draa winds beside the town and, in very recent years, the completion of a dam a short way upstream, creating a serene lake, has brought a wholly new prosperity based upon agricultural expansion throughout the neighbourhood. Twenty years ago you would have found it hard to find anywhere poorer or sadder than Ouarzazate; now all is activity, rebuilding and cheer. The only 'sight' of the town is the newest of the *ksour*, a Glaoui house which has been most inappropriately tarted up and labelled '*Hôtel de la Casbah*'. It contains one quite pretty, if crudely done room, said to have been the harem, though it is more likely to have been the master's cool retreat.

The valley of the Draa and the scattered, southerly oases are the home of a curious people called the Haratin. (They are also found along much the same latitude across Algeria and are numerous in the Libyan Fezzan.) Long-headed, dark-skinned, fine-boned, either sex frequently produces individuals of startling good looks. They are not organized in tribes; they own no hereditary lands, but have traditionally worked the lands of others, sometimes in a form of vassalage. Poverty made them a source of slaves, for it was a charity to buy a distressed person's child (incidentally ensuring its future well-being since slaves were, however menially employed, cared for all their lives). The Haratin blood group is shared by nobody else in the pre-Sahara — a fact which has contributed to the suggestion that they represent the survivors of the original population of the desert, those herders of the savannahs and agriculturists of the age of better weather over all the Saharan desolation. Haratin freemen have for centuries monopolized the water-selling trade in Morocco's cities.

Berbers inhabit most of trans-Atlas Morocco. Peaceful modern conditions have gone some way to break down strict tribal divisions though fractions of various tribes still inhabit this or that area or village. Here and there, there are Arab tribes settled among the Berbers and there are fairly frequent settlements of sherifian families, usually living in lone 54ksour. Respect for their holy descent and their *baraka* allowed them to subsist, and sometimes to mediate, among their warring neighbours. There are also small colonies of Jews (who may be native Berbers converted to Judaism in the early centuries of the Christian era).

They are usually metal-workers and gunsmiths though some are mountain-farmers. The population of the modern townships is often mixed, Haratin usually predominating since they are the least firmly rooted of peoples in the region.

Ouarzazate to Zagora

Route P31: 171 km. to Zagora (261 km. to M'hamid). The road is now asphalted. It is one of great scenic beauty, first crossing the Jebel Sarhro which, with the Jebel Ougnat, forms the easternmost part of the Anti-Atlas range, and then, the longer part, beginning after Agdz, following the course of the Draa, under cliffs, beside palm-groves, passing many *ksour* and villages until the valley opens at Zagora.
Bus Two or three buses daily to Zagora, about six hours.
Accommodation and food Except at Agdz (see below) food and accommodation are to be found only at Zagora.

[73 km.] **Agdz**.

A small modern settlement where refreshment of a sort can be had at an exorbitant price. Mint tea in the market shops is to be preferred — and do not be put off by the flurry your arrival in such places may cause: you may be segregated in a sleeping-room and left to sit on the matting floor-covering, but this is out of respect for you, not hostility — you have done the unexpected thing and must not cavil at the sometimes eccentric response it elicits. Take your shoes off on entering such a room.

Agdz is overlooked from across the river by the huge *ksar* of *Tamenougalt*, the former stronghold of the powerful Mezguita tribe which dominated these parts.

[104 km.] A track on the left leads to **Nekob** and **Tazzarine**. This track continues to the Tafilelt (p. 348) but should not be under-taken except with suitable transport and preparation. Petrol available at Tazzarine; thereafter uncertain.

There is a chain of markets along the road held on successive days. While all are interesting and worth while stopping to visit, that held near the most impressive village of **Dar Sheikh el-Arabi** — as its name states, a sherifian household — is perhaps the best.

[171 km.] You reach Zagora.

Zagora

Hotels
***A   *Hôtel Tinsouline* (tel. 22).
  *A   *Hôtel Vallée du Draa*, Avenue Mohammed V (tel. 10).
  *A   *Hôtel la Palmeraie*, Avenue Mohammed V (tel. 08)].
Camping *la Montagne*.

This is another modern administrative township, nicely situated and rather agreeable. There is little to do here except to climb to the very ruinous remains of an Almoravid fortified position on the height across the Draa. It was built *circa* 1080. There is also a large Saturday market here. A signpost set by an ambitious roundabout in the town reads: TIMBUCTOU 52 JOURS — by camelback.

EXPEDITION FROM ZAGORA TO TAMGROUT

Tamgrout — 22 km. downstream from Zagora and over the other side of the Draa.

Here, there is a *zawiya* (one of many in the valley where, there being little alternative entertainment save sex and vendettas, matters of the spirit are a major interest). This has been found to contain a *library* including a number of Korans written on gazelle-skin, the earliest dating from the thirteenth century. These will be shown to you. There are *potteries* in the village, but their products are not remarkable. With a stout car you can circle back to the Draa near Tansikht, by Tazzarine and Nekob, a rather splendid journey of 154 km.

EXPEDITION FROM ZAGORA TO M'HAMID

It is worth while pushing on the 90 km. to M'hamid. Some of the most dramatic and beautiful *ksour* and villages can be seen from the road. Permission must be sought from the military authorities to travel to M'hamid. The road is tarred and very fast. The journey can be made there and back to Zagora in an easy day, and indeed one must return to Zagora as there is nowhere to stay in M'hamid.

[56 km.] **Tagounite**.

A Monday market and a mint-tea café. There is a campsite here.

[90 km.] You reach **M'hamid**.

This is a sandy oasis where the water of the Draa becomes exhausted. Only in some years, and then for a few days, is the seasonal flood sufficient to flow beyond this point into the desert. The *Draa valley* continues westward to the Atlantic, 750 km. distant, its course having been made during the most humid era of the European Ice Ages. When the Draa does flow a little farther into the *Dabaia plain* the river-bed is cultivable and proves fertile. The M'hamid oasis is a strange one with sandy fields, palms and scattered *ksour*. One of these, now a ruin, is of Saadian construction, built to serve Ahmed el-Mansur's communications with the Niger valley that he had conquered. The southernmost point of the oasis, on the right bank of the Draa, is crowned with a *fort* where you must sign the visitors' book. This is the very tip of the long promontory of habitable land that the Draa sustains; beyond it lies a sea of sand, a view of nothingness where busy squalls blow — but a place where nomad tribes wander like mariners. These come to the Monday market and among them you may see the 'Blue men', their skin tinted by the garments they wear, dyed to tones of the lovely indigo blue. Even their heads are blued with the dye from their turbans and their faces by the ends of these which they wrap around themselves as a protection against the sand. These are rarely true Tuareg, though in many respects all these Berber nomad tribes resemble one another. The desert-men seem more foreign to oneself than any other in the world and we seem to them so improbable that they usually ignore us completely.

EXPEDITION FROM ZAGORA ACROSS THE OASES

Only with proper organization and a suitable vehicle would it be wise to attempt the track leading westwards from Zagora to **Foum Zguid** and **Tissint** and on to **Tata, Akka** and **Foum el-Hassan** right over in the west, linking up with **Bou Izakarn** (p. 357). You will also require the permission of the military command in Zagora. All these are administrative centres with petrol and some form of accommodation. Foum Zguid, Tissint, Akka and especially Tata, are all perfectly beautiful places. Their remoteness, the light, the extraordinary bare landscapes and contrasting fertility of the oases enchant and amaze. Do not let anyone tell you that when you have seen one oasis you have seen the lot; in their differences and those of the people who inhabit them, in the altered detail of their architecture, there is the same magic as among Aegean islands — which nobody has ever suggested are monotonously alike.

But take any journey to the oases *seriously*. See p. 25.

Ouarzazate to Er Rachidia

Route P32, 309 km., without excursions up the Dadès and Todrha gorges.
Bus Two buses daily over the stages: Ouarzazate — Tinerhir, Tinerhir — Er Rachidia.
Accommodation and food At El-Kelaa des M'gouna, Boulmane du Dadès, Tinerhir and Er Rachidia.

From Ouarzazate the road holds to the course of the Dadès to

[41 km.] Skoura des Ahl el-Oust.
Club Méditerranée.

An Arab settlement where thousands of roses are grown for making attar. This will be your first sight of very many fine *ksour* together.

[83 km.] El-Kelaa des M'gouna.

Hotel
***A *Hôtel les Roses du Dadès* (tel. 18).

This is extraordinarily beautiful, a long, strung-out collection of *ksour* along a tributary of the Dadès called the *Asif M'Goun* which makes this a fertile rose-growing place. It is about 2,000 metres above sea-level, a height which allows deciduous trees to flourish and therefore El-Kelaa is an oasis of fruit and nut trees rather than the usual date-palms. Rose Festival in May/June.

The way that new prosperity alters life is to be seen for miles along this road where houses in a quite new and well-found style, gaily painted, line it with a ribbon-development replacing the old villages lying off its path.

[115 km.] Boulmane du Dadès

Hotel
****B *Hôtel El Madayeq* (tel. 31).

An administrative centre with its own market. The huge Glaoui *ksar* is splendidly sited above the entrance to the *Gorges du Dadès*. The road up the gorge passes a number of imposing *ksour* which vary in aspect from the strategic medieval fortress to the palatial villa. It is barely practicable to go farther than the *Pont du Dadès* — 23 km. — although the track leads on into a network of others among the mountains, to a pass across the range, one connecting with the head of the Todrha gorge — explorers' country one would dearly like to travel.

The P32 crosses the watershed between the Draa and Ziz drainage areas, arriving at Tinerhir.

[168 km.] **Tinerhir**.

Hotels
* ***A   *Hôtel Sargho* (tel. 01).
* *A   *Hôtel Todrha* (tel. 09).

A very large oasis of olives above which palms wave and crops are grown underneath. It is an administrative centre with a fantastically imposing Glaoui *ksar* which one may visit, although it begins to lapse into disrepair. This is really a palace and not representative of *ksour*; an interesting building in that it demonstrates the possibilities of *tabia* as a building material sophisticatedly used.

The short trip up the *Gorges du Todrha* (14 km.) should be made if possible. There are one or two villages in this valley walled by mountains dramatized by the amazing stratification of their rocks. This is more of a conventional gorge than that of the Dadès — or rather than as much of that gorge as one can easily visit — and the road ends at a very narrow point where there is a spring which is classic and beautiful. Geological faults form the gorges, but here the rock splits and the water comes forth clear and bubbling, and tiny fish and small *écrevisses* inhabit its cold pools. One can stay here or camp in the gorge and walk farther into the mountains. It is said that the mouflon and even panther can sometimes be seen here. The mountain Berbers come down from the farther reaches of the gorge with their donkeys and women equally laden with kindling.

[223 km.] **Tinejad** lies across an empty, upland road in the big Ferkla palmery. An empty road but not a dull one. The wonderful spaciousness of Africa opens as you travel it. The wastes of the *hammada*, the stony or gravel-encrusted desert, here somewhat invaded by sand, are alive with creatures. There do not seem to have ever been enough people here to have alarmed the wild-life seriously. One has to sit still for only a few minutes in places like this for all sorts of birds, insects, lizards to appear as if spontaneously generated by the barren land. Many are strange to us, some larger varieties of ones we know, or differently coloured species — always fascinating. The African scale is hard to become accustomed to; the light plays the oddest tricks upon one — so that a child on a rise on the straight road ahead looms enormous until you approach quite near, and you cannot always be sure whether hills are near or far off, but the ravens *are* the size of geese, the buzzards and falcons big as small turkeys.

[247 km.] **Goulmina**.

A large oasis with some twenty fortified villages or *ksour* whose towered *gates* are notably tall. The Aït Morghad inhabiting Goulmina were at constant war with the Aït Atta who live farther downstream on the Gheris besides spreading over the Jebel Ougnat and the Jebel Sarhro. The stronghold of the horse-breeding Aït Atta was **Touroug**, a very strongly fortified town rather than a village, lying on the Rheris some forty-odd kilometres south-east of Goulmina, best reached by the track branching from the P32 about 10 km. back. It is a rough ride, but worth while. Touroug is still a most imposing place. Here Harris saw the boys of the tribe practising running with galloping horses, holding their tails, a skill which enabled the tribe's infantry to retreat as fast as its cavalry — one of the reasons that at the end of the last century the Aït Atta were so great a power hereabouts that the Haratin of the Draa paid them tribute. After Touroug, the track worsens as it leads to Erfoud, but some at least of the other imposing villages it connects can more easily be reached from Erfoud itself.

[309 km.] You arrive at Er Rachidia (formerly known as Ksar es-Souk).

Er Rachidia

Hotels
****B   *Hôtel Rissani* (tel. 21.86).
  **A   *Hôtel Oasis*, 4 Rue Abou Abdellah (tel. 25.26).
  **B   *Hôtel Meski*, Avenue Moulay Ali Cherif (tel. 20.65).
Camping *Municipal*, just beyond the town on the road to Erfoud.

This is a neat little administrative capital for the Talfilelt. In a way, still a very French colonial place; a frontier-town behind a wall with self-congratulatory gates in it. But it expands and booms as a result of the dam built a little higher up the Ziz river, which flows here in quite a deep bed. The *market* of the old name stands outside the town, though there is another in the square. A brave place, jaunty; the ghost of the Foreign Legion seems substantial here and it is a jolly, drinking town with the raffish air of being on the edge of nowhere.

People driving round Morocco often return north from Er Rachidia to Fes. This route is described on p. 365.

Er Rachidia to Erfoud

Route 99 km. a good road, the P21 — and a beautiful drive. Cross the river at Ksar and turn right.
Bus Several daily.

The Ziz carries a lot of water and has carved a wide bed in the desert. This is intensively cultivated and very populous. A flash flood (of which happily there was forewarning) recently carried away all the interesting *ksour* and hamlets built in the valley bottom and the people are now housed above it in rather bleak, if adequate, housing blocks. Sand rather than gravel covers the desert on either side; Rissani stands, so to speak, ankle-deep in sand. All this riverine activity leads to a widening area of cultivation among the sand since the Gheris comes close to the Ziz and although their courses are mapped as running far beyond, their waters are exhausted here in a kind of delta of irrigation trenches extending south of Erfoud. You have entered a new and quite different world — the Tafilelt, the desert Kingdom of Sigilmassa; it is as startling to see as it is romantic to think of.

[11 km.] A road on the right leads in 2 km. to the *Source Bleue de Meski*, a spring which gushes with Mosaic-drama blue from the rock into a pool in which one should refrain from bathing on account of the danger of contracting bilharzia, prevalent also in the Ziz. Organized camping under Berber tents is offered here, and a café provides food and drink (tel. 249).

[77 km.] You reach Erfoud.

Erfoud

Hotels

****B *Hôtel Sijilmassa* (tel. 80).

  **A *Hôtel Tafilalet*, Avenue Moulay Ismaël (tel. 30).

This is another French creation, shaded by tamarisks and eucalyptus, colour-washed an ox-blood red relieved by dazzling blue
paintwork which gives an extraordinary and dramatic effect.

ENVIRONS OF ERFOUD

Rissani

19 km. south from Erfoud, Rissani is less a place than a collection
of fortifications. Casbahs and barracks, a few houses standing
without wall protection, and a very pretty market-place, form a
sort of town square of sand where a few eucalyptus trees and
French administrative buildings attempt to lend the scene an air
of peace and order. The ox-blood colour of Erfoud is here
deepened to that of dried blood. The many small elegances about
denote both that this is a great terminal for desert trade and the
seat of the long-established dynasty. It was by this route and by
Taouz, 80 km. away to the south, that el-Mansur sent his troops
to the Niger. All the Tafilelt has style; Rissani has it the most. The
main *casbah* with the white and tiled gateway was built by Moulay
Ismaïl in the seventeenth century. He must in fact have restored a
Merinid one since traces of thirteenth-and fourteenth-century
work have been found in it. The tunnelled lanes inside are almost
frightening to walk in, though the children are friendly.

The new *sanctuary-mosque* is something of a pious mistake,
aesthetically speaking.

The *Mausoleum of Moulay Ali Sherif* stands 2½ km. away to
the south-east. It was he who was the ancestor of the Alaouite
dynasty, the descendant of the Prophet who came from Arabia to
this asylum in the west. The building has been many times
restored, most recently after a flood in 1955. It is possible to enter
the shrine. Beside it stand the imposing towered ruins of the *Ksar
d'Abbar*, built about 1800 as the abode of redundant members of
the Filali family, princes and widows, ex-concubines. A very big
affair, it contains a large and a small palace within its double
defence. Some of its former graces persist, particularly the carved
plasterwork in the little palace. No trace has yet been found of a

similar establishment that Moulay Ismaïl is known to have built in the oasis on what is reported to have been a still more magnificent scale.

Another *ksar* 1 km. south-east of the above, the *Ksar d'Oulad Abd el-Halim*, was built as the residence of Sultan Hassan's elder brother who was governor of the Tafilelt. It is the most splendid of them all and was built about 1900.

Tineras, a ruined *ksar* on a knoll which commands a wonderful view over the desert and the oasis, lies south-west of Rissani and is about 11 km. away over a bad track.

Sigilmassa

Sigilmassa — or *Sigillum Massae* which, according to Leo Africanus, was named after the Roman general who founded a camp here — lies a spare and scattered ruin immediately west of Rissani. (The P21 crosses its edge as it turns sharp east to the town.) It is the ruin of a medieval town restored by Moulay Ismaïl.

It was founded by Musa ben Nasser in 707 during the first certain Arab incursion so far south as this. For centuries it was the chief northern terminal of the western trans-Sahara trade. The whole art of *tabia*-building may have then been introduced by the Arabs and (though it is perhaps not really relevant) it is here that the buildings made of it most closely resemble those of Mesopotamia and Egypt. The history of Sigilmassa is given in the History section on pp. 65–76.

Rissani has only comparatively recently supplanted it as the capital of the Tafilelt, and more recently still Er Rachidia. The region has always had a natural tendency to separatism. This has perhaps been strengthened under the Alaouite dynasty which formed the habit of sending surplus male members of the family back home here where they would not be such a serious threat to the ruling sultans as they might be elsewhere. The Filali — another name for the dynasty, referring to the family's having originated here — still inhabit most of the single *ksour* of the region. The large ones near Rissani and the founder's sanctuary were built especially to house extra princes and the harems of deceased sultans. Here Harris found the ailing Sultan Hassan, come, he thought, more to pray at his ancestor's grave than in the hope of asserting his authority or extorting much revenue. He describes the sultan setting out from camp to make his pilgrimage to the tomb of Moulay Ali esh-Sherif near Rissani (Harris had been ill and could not accompany him):

The background of palms and desert, the thousands of tents [of the sultan's encampment], the gay uniforms — though the word is ill-applied to costumes of every hue and colour — of the foot-soldiers, the long white robes of the cavalry, the gorgeous velvet saddles and still more gorgeous banners of gold brocade and embroideries — all formed one of those strange scenes that one can witness now and again at the court of the Moorish sovereign, so much in contrast to the usual dull colouring of the country and its inhabitants.

Nothing more beautiful could be imagined than the long procession of cavalry and infantry, of wild Berber and Arab tribesmen. A gentle wind unfurled the banners to the breeze, and raised the dust under the horses' feet just thickly enough to cast a white glamour over the whole scene, through which sparkled and glistened the flags and the golden globes of their poles, the bayonets and rifles of the infantry, and the heads of the spears of the guard. Then, mounting on his great white horse, saddled and trapped in green and gold, with the canopy of crimson velvet held over his head, rode the Sultan, while huge black slaves on either hand waved long scarfs to keep the flies from his sacred person. In and out of the city of tents, for such the *mahalla* is, wound the procession, the line of march guarded by troops on either side.

It was a last glimpse of the past.

Merzouga

Merzouga lies 59 km. beyond Erfoud on a track which is passable, or by a far more dubious path from Rissani. Both it and the *Erg Chebbi* are on the tourist route, the latter a popular place to observe the desert dawn, four-wheel drive vehicles carrying their cargo of tourists to and fro. The most basic accommodation is available at a café. Travel further south is impracticable for political reasons.

Ouarzazate to Taroudant

Route 297 km. over the P32, a good road and a remarkably beautiful one. It is, however, extremely lonely and ill served by public transport. You leave Ouarzazate by the Marrakech road.
Bus Twice daily.
Accommodation at Taliouine.

[26 km.] Junction of the P32 and P31 from Marrakech; turn left for Taroudant.

[39 km.] A road on the right leads to Amergane and Marrakech.

[65 km.] **Anezal**.

[78 km.] You cross the *Tizi n'Bachkoun* pass; 1,700 metres high. There is a beautiful view over the *Jebel Siroua* on the right.

[93 km.] **Tazenakht**.
   By the *ksar* a Sunday market is held. The turning left for **Agdz** forks after 22 km. to **Foum Zguid** also. It is a bad way to Agdz, but the Foum Zguid track is possible for ordinary cars: a lovely drive of 92 km. and a beautiful oasis at its end − but see p. 25 and p. 345 and inquire at Tazenakht before proceeding.

[117 km.] **Kourkouda**.

[139 km.] You reach the *Tizi n'Taratine* pass.
   At 1,886 metres high this is the highest of the four crossed by this road, the ultimate watershed between the Sous and the Draa.

[178 km.] **Taliouine.**

Hotel
   ****B   *Hôtel Ibn Toumert* (tel. 1).

   A superb *casbah* dominates the town and holds this dramatically beautiful pass. The track, left, for Irherm in the Anti-Atlas is not to be recommended.

[211 km.] **Agadir Touksous** and **Souk el-Arba** (Sunday and Wednesday markets).

[215 km.] **Aoulouz**.
   A wicked track branches right to cross north of the Jebel Siroua towards Ouarzazate. It leads through the Ouzguita tribe's country where the black *burnous* with red or orange decoration on the back is worn and where some fine carpets and stuffs are woven.

[221 km.] A hard to find, stony track leads right to the village of **Sidi Amel** which you can spot on its rise by the sight of a fine minaret and large *koubba*, then houses and a large and imposing casbah in ruins. The view of the Sous valley is wonderful from here.

[245 km.] The S501 to Marrakech turns right from your road; you keep left on the Agadir road.

[289 km.] A road to the left which starts off promisingly but deteriorates would bring you in 89 km. to **Irherm**, an administrative centre in the Anti-Atlas. From there an equally rough track connects up in 86 km. with Tafraoute (p. 355). Although this 'short cut' to Tafraoute probably takes longer, and is certainly much rougher on your vehicle, than the roads via Aït Melloul and Tiznit, it allows you to drive through some extraordinarily wild and desolate country.

[297 km.] Taroudant (p. 330).

Taroudant to Tiznit via Aït Melloul

Route P32 to Aït Melloul, thereafter the P30 to Tiznit, 148 km. Good roads all the way. If you pick this route from Agadir, take the P8 15 km. south to Aït Melloul and branch right by the P30.
Bus Six a day between Taroudant and Agadir; four a day between Agadir and Tiznit.
Accommodation and food At Tiznit.

[40 km.] **Oulad Teïma** (Thursday market).

[67 km.] **Aït Melloul**. Branch left by the P30.

[102 km.] **Tifeghal** (Monday, market-place).

Just outside Tifeghal, on the estuary of the River Massa, is a bird sanctuary with flamingoes, osprey, many species of geese, ducks and waders. There is no accommodation here, but camping and caravanning are permitted.

[148 km.] You reach Tiznit.

Tiznit

Hotels
  ***A *Hôtel de Tiznit*, Rue Bir Inzaran (tel. 24.11).
    *A *Hôtel Mauretania*, Rue de Guelmim (tel. 20.72).
Camping *International*.

Founded in 1882 by Moulay el-Hassan to be the administrative capital of the area during the *harka* he made into the Sous and Anti-Atlas, this is a town of some 20,000 inhabitants. Enclosed by five kilometres of towered walls, Tiznit looks more glamorous than it is, and a great deal older. But its red-washed walls and ochre and blue colours — a certain spaciousness about its streets and squares overlooked by machicolated gates — give the town a delightful appearance. You go to see the *Lalla Tiznit spring*; a photogenic pool beside a sanctuary. The *minaret* near by is a curiosity with its many water-spouts. When Mohammed V visited the town after Independence the entire *mechouar* was carpeted with rugs to receive him. There is a lively market on Thursdays and, every day, the market-streets are interesting since the wares sold show a marked difference from those offered farther north. The *jeweller-shops* are intriguing, although the desert-women's finery is scarcer now than formerly, and this is one of the few places where traditional local Jewish clothes are still sold.

Tiznit was made El-Hiba's capital when he rose in rebellion against the sultan's misrule and the French occupation. The French ended this brief independence in 1917.

From Tiznit you can go down to the sea in 14 km., at **Sidi Moussa d'Aglou** where several marabouts' *koubbiyet* stand above the beach. There is a small summer *bathing-establishment* there. The road passes a Monday market-place. Pleasant bathing is to be had at **Mirhleft**, which lies south and is best reached by the 7064, 45 km.

Tiznit to Tafraoute

Route A good road, the 7074, climbs 111 km. through remarkable country and into the different world — it seems — of rich valleys lapped in the Anti-Atlas mountains.

Tafraoute

Hotel
****B   *Hôtel Les Amandiers* (tel. 8).

Tafraoute lies in a valley in which stand curious rock pinnacles, some of them crowned by *agadirs* looking like the monasteries of Meteora. It is an exotic landscape of rock and palms and gardens which can be seen to the best advantage in almond-blossom time — around the middle of February. Almond-pink is the key colour among the earthy tones with which the buildings hereabouts are washed. The houses are very sophisticated and although one clearly sees their affinity with other southern buildings the tradition in which they are built is strongly local and individual. The inhabitants of these valleys had little to fear from invaders and did not build defensively, but threw open many windows to the outside, decorating the surrounds and inventing symmetrical façades in a manner reminiscent of Victorian villas, seeming eccentric here and fashioned, as they are, with a certain barbaric directness and simplicity. The manifest prosperity of these houses is not based upon the fertility of the valleys so much as on the enterprise of the Ammeln tribe that inhabits them. The tribesmen are the grocers of Morocco. Their shops — often stocked with the range of wares common to 'general stores' and 'village shops' — are usually also their homes and close only when the proprietor can no longer keep awake. Relays of sons and brothers keep them all over the country, particularly in Casablanca where they constitute a political power block, while yet others pioneered Moroccan emigration to France and Belgium, working in commerce or the mines.

ENVIRONS OF TAFRAOUTE

Beyond the town, which grows lively on Wednesday market-days, lie further valleys and more fine villages. If you are staying at the hotel they will help you to visit these and see to it that you have every opportunity to attend any celebration that may be held in them. The music, dances and songs of the Anti-Atlas are as different from those elsewhere as the houses are.

There is a Sunday Market at **Souk el-Had de Tahala** and a Wednesday one at **Arba n'Tafraoute**, both along the road from Tiznit.

From Tafraoute a sometimes narrow, but metalled road leads through rather wonderful passes to **Aït Baha** and **Biougra**, whence a metalled road leads to Agadir. Another bad track leads to **Irherm** (p. 354), whence a partly metalled road goes to Taroudant — all wild and lovely country but scarcely practicable for the ordinary holidaymaker, or his motor-car. In this category, too, is a track which leaves the Tiznit-to-Tafraoute road about 60 km. out from Tafraoute and takes you south to **Ifrane de l'Anti-Atlas** from where it links up with a metalled road to **Bou Izakarn** (p. 357). Ifrane is a remote outpost with a toy fort and tiny café with rooms. On the way you pass some classic oases, startlingly green, set among the stony barrenness of the mountains.

Another excursion from Tafraoute may be made to **Anou-Illigh**, south from the Tiznit road, along 25 km. of rough track. This village used to be the capital of a small sherifian state founded by marabouts of the Idrissi family, established locally by Sidi Mohammed ou Moussa who died in 1563. Partly religious, partly political, the little principality of this Tazeroualt district was typical of the *bled es-siba*. Sidi Mohammed's son extended it into the Sous Valley and even to the Draa. It was primarily to end this state that Moulay el-Hassan came on *harka* into these parts in 1882. A *zawiya* exists near the village, surrounded by the tombs of the Idrissid warrior-saints. The village and district is the home of the Moroccan acrobats whom you may see as far off as the United States, always wearing their traditional red and green clothes. The *zawiya* is most impressive and there is a spring moussem. However, in these parts the people still remember the cruelty of the French 'pacification' and would often rather not meet those foreigners whom they identify with the killers of their fathers.

Tiznit to Goulimine

Route 110 km. The P30 is a good road as far as Bou Izakarn, as is also the P41 to Goulimine.
Bus Six a day to Goulimine.
Accommodation and food At Bou Izakarn and Goulimine.

[13 km.] **Souk el-Had de Regrada** (Sunday market).

[20 km.] **Talaint**.
   A fortified village where there is a Wednesday market.

[67 km.] **Bou Izakarn**.

Hotel
   **B   *Hôtel Anti-Atlas* (tel. 41.34).

   A little place with petrol, a café and a few shops.
   From here the P30 continues — becoming a track — to **Foum el-Hassan**. The road runs south of the Anti-Atlas and tracks run on to **Akka**, **Tata** and the other oases, eventually arriving across the miles of desert at Zagora (p. 344). There are many prehistoric rock-carvings in the neighbourhood of Foum el-Hassan — less

arduous to reach than many others, but still no picnic excursion to see.

[110 km.] You reach Goulimine.

Goulimine

Hotel
　　**B　*Hôtel Salam*, Route de Tan Tan (tel. 20.57).

A romantic desert-edge town of 3,000 people, centred on pink, arcaded market-squares with a view to the south that seems to consist of nothing until faint hills show in the evening light. The big occasion at Goulimine was the great annual camel-market. The war has prevented camelherds from bringing their animals from Mauritania, reducing the event to a spectacle for tourists. Desert-men attend it to supply their wants. In their blue and white clothes, the citizens as well as the shoppers make a brave sight, especially in the dramatic setting of the square: these garments are cut in much the same way as those Nigerians and Ghanaeans wear. At Goulimine you feel you have very much arrived in Africa, something that you know intellectually but do not feel emotionally over much of Morocco, where the strongest links are with the Near East and with Spain and not, as here, with black Africa to the south.

Guedra-dancing is sometimes put on for tourists' entertainment at Goulimine. This is a curious dance form performed on the knees and relying for its movement on the action of the arms and shoulders of the women who perform it. This was evolved, it is said, so that the dancing could be done under the low roofs of tents. It is accompanied by music and wild, taut singing, hypnotic in rhythm and so erotic as to make quite understandable the puritan reformers' zeal against it. However, an hour's performance for a party of rather frigid, if curious tourists is not the way to see the Guedra at its best; it needs the right ambience and half the night really to get in the mood. If you get a chance to be at such a party, seize it.

EXPEDITION FROM GOULIMINE TO TAN TAN AND BEYOND

Route The road is metalled as far as Tan Tan and beyond Tan Tan to Tarfaya and

Laayoune. The distance to Tarfaya is 405 km. but for most purposes, to Tan Tan, 145 km.

Bus Two or three buses daily to Tan Tan. They are very slow and unreliable, so a *grand taxi* may be a better prospect.

Accommodation and food At Tan Tan and Laayoune.

If you decide to essay this region by road you must be prepared for delays caused by military checkpoints, the sparsity of facilities, potential danger and tedium of an area which hardly varies. Given this, we advise travel by air on one of Air Maroc's frequent flights to Dakhla and Laayoune. See p. 25 for warning.

The road goes south-west to Tan Tan, through that nothingness of the view from Goulimine which turns out to be a dry, empty land of low hills and shallow valleys, one of which is the bed of the *Draa* which here contains water laboriously gathered over a wide drainage area including the southern slopes of the Anti-Atlas. It only ever flows for some forty kilometres and is reduced to stagnation in summer.

[145 km.] **Tan Tan.**

Hotels

> *Hôtel Royal* (not yet classified; telephone 71.86).
> *A *Hôtel Etoule du Sahara*, 17 Rue El Fida (tel. 70.85).
> *A *Hôtel Amgala*.

A small garrison-town standing on a hill with the sand desert beyond, Tan Tan is now a provincial capital. Its development is largely political and based on Moroccan claims to the desert regions to its south. Primitive lodging and basic food is available but small hotels provide better comfort and more palatable fare.

In May a moussem is held not far off which is a camel-herders' celebration. Tan Tan Plage, 28 km. further on; bathe there if you must.

Tan Tan seems really over the end of the world, yet the track continues 260 km. to **Tarfaya** and *Cape Juby*, and another 100 km. to **Laayoune.**

Hotels

> *Hôtel Al Massira* (not yet classified; telephone 31.60).
> ****B *Hôtel Parador* Rue Okba Ban Nafia (tel. 22.45).
> **A *Hôtel Residencia*, Rue Prince Moulay Abdellah (tel. 38.29).
> *A *Hôtel Marhaba*, Avenue Hassan II.

EXPEDITION FROM GOULIMINE TO SIDI-IFNI

Happily returned to Morocco in 1969, this little port-town is still somewhat cut off from the country, and more Spanish than Moroccan in flavour.

From Goulimine, the road, 45 km. (of which 30 km. are at present metalled and the rest a not bad *piste*), leads north-west from the town; it is clearly marked. Buses ply between Goulimine and Sidi-Ifni and there are seats to be had in taxis.

It comprises an older quarter and, across the valley, a small new 'European' town, largely made up of villas. The place has a poorish beach on which stands the *Hôtel Ait Ba-arman* *A (tel. 51.73). In the town there is also the *Hôtel Bellevue* *A (tel. 50.72) in the Place Hassan II.

It is quite possible to return via Tiznit; 45 km. of rough *piste* passing sandy coves and a lonely countryside where big cacti grow.

THE EAST

This section is based upon a possible tour of the eastern, empty quarter of Morocco. It is approximately 1,500 km. long and not a tour to make without proper preparation. The Fes-to-Oujda and Er Rachidia-to-Fes stages are, of course, perfectly good main trunk-roads, though around Midelt and Boulmane snow can block the latter in winter. We describe the route going by Boulmane here, though that by Azrou and Ifrane is a popular alternative and scarcely longer. This alternative route is described from Azrou to Fes on p. 236. Of the section from Midelt to Azrou there is little to say beyond that, like all the Middle Atlas roads, its beauty is breathtaking.

The stage between Oujda and Figuig is now over a metalled road. However, it is 383 km. long without any amenities, either along the road or at its end, save very rare petrol pumps.

Fes to Oujda

See pp. 306–10, where information is given for the opposite direction.

Oujda to Er Rachidia

Route You can count on nothing at all on this section of road — intermittent petrol supplies, yes; food-shops of a local kind also; but no beds, restaurants, service garages, signposts, etc.

From Oujda take the P19 for Figuig.
Rail A single freight train runs from Bouarfa to Oujda, a poor alternative to the bus.
Bus One daily between Er Rachidia and Figuig via Bouarfa through which the four buses between Figuig and Oujda run.

The P19 crosses over passes and through valleys; a long, straight slog for much of the way, most of it over true desert-country, not all of which, anywhere, is all sand. There is nowhere to stay, either in the Figuig oasis or along the road, except as the guest of administrative officers. You don't want to run out of petrol or water en route. The climate of Figuig is generally held to be insupportable except from October to April, when it is delightful and the light exquisite.

This said, the person whose sense of adventure does not urge him to go to Figuig if he can is hard to imagine. It is a thrilling journey to make.

[634 km.] **Guenfouda** (Saturday market).

[652 km.] *Jerada pass*, 1,140 metres high.

[689 km.] **Berguent** (Monday market).

[804 km.] **Tendrara** (Thursday market).

[874 km.] **Bouarfa** — a manganese-mining centre.

Figuig — an oasis of some 200,000 date-palms and seven *ksour* housing 15,000 Berbers, which stands on a plateau some 900 metres high — is 115 km. distant from Bouarfa. These fortified villages used generally to be at war with one another. All built of *tabia*, their architecture is rather different from that elsewhere and not wanting in style. **Zenaga** is the largest of the villages. A *hot spring* rises in **El-Hammam el-Foukani**, where there is a *zawiya* also. The administrative centre stands apart. The fields are not open as those of the Tafilelt, but enclosed by high mud-walls. The *koubba* of the patron of Figuig stands by itself; his name is Sidi Abd el-Kader Mohammed.

But it is the wild scenery around the place which pleases most; bare, abrupt, astonishingly colourful. There is not much to do here except to explore this barren world — the *Jebel Grouz*, the *Jebel Maïz* and the *Jebel Malah*. A few small, scattered oases lie beyond the horizon.

It is hard to convey the extraordinary sensation one receives when visiting such utter ends of the familiar world as this.

Route Map for Eastern Area

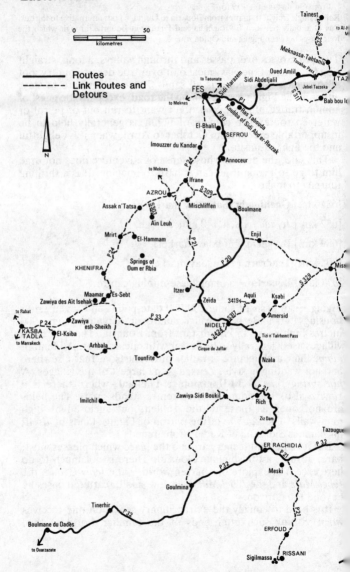

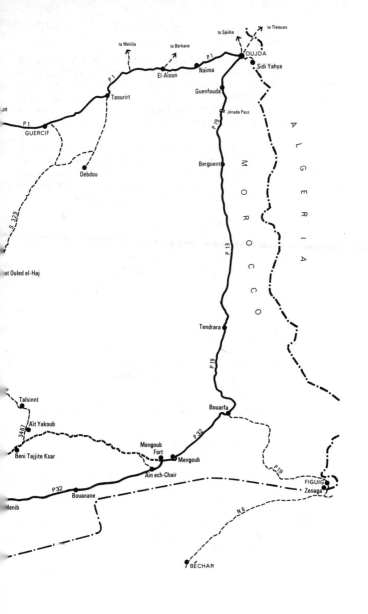

Everything is already so very changed and the desert outlook is altogether unexpected and surprising — such a landscape as might occur in the netherworld, though some find so great a peace and freedom in bareness, brilliantly lit, that they would liken it to Heaven. There is no telling whether you will be gladdened or appalled until you have experienced the desert for yourself.

At Bouarfa (see above), when returning from Figuig, turn left. It will be as well to make sure that frontier relations are quiet even should you drive by the P32. There is no longer a bus to the border or Béchar in Algeria; the last 8 km. can be travelled by the occasional taxi, though. See page 305, note on crossing.

[924 km.] *Mengoub*; turn right for the P32.

[934 km.] Right turn for a very bad track which used to be the main road and is still a possible alternative route for Er Rachidia, if you have a four-wheel drive. Described below.

[942 km.] **Aïn ech-Chair**, where there is a *spring* and a *ksar*.

[1,009 km.] **Bouanane**; another large oasis.

[1,066 km.] **Boudenib**; an administrative centre where there is medical aid, a post office, telegraph and telephone. Boudenib consists of a palmery of 26,000 trees and a large *ksar* — an interesting building — housing 2,500 people of the Chorfa of Boudenib tribe.

[1,137 km.] Junction with the Er Rachidia-to-Erfoud road; turn right.

[1,155 km.] Er Rachidia (p. 348).

EXPEDITION TO BENI TAJJITE AND TAZOUGUERTE

Instead of turning left after Mengoub at 934 km., follow the track left. After 114 km. of bad road you arrive at a track right for *Aït Yacoub ksar*, a further 29 km. to **Talsinnt** and 129 km. to **Missour** on the Guercif-Midelt road, S329 (see p. 306). A few kilometres further on from the Aït Yacoub turning, is the *ksar* of **Beni Tajjite**; lead is mined in the area.

Crossing the *Plaine de Snab* and *Col de Belkassem*, you arrive after 43 km. at the village of **Tazouguerte** where you turn left, rejoining the P32 10 km. later.

Er Rachidia to Fes

Route 350 km. Take the P21 and P20.
Bus Three buses daily, which normally go by Azrou. Change at Midelt if you want to follow this route by Sefrou.
Accommodation and food At Midelt, Sefrou.

The P21 runs through a district of *ksour* and palm plantations growing in the valley of the Ziz. The narrow Ziz Gorge has been dammed enormously to increase the usefulness of its waters in the Tafilelt generally. The dam is called the *Aït Atmanes Dam.*

[1,223 km.] **Rich**.

A modern administrative centre and old *ksar* lying just west of the road − a bleak place inappropriately named for English-speakers. This is Aït Haddidou country, a nomadic Berber tribe who were the terror of travellers by this route.

20 km. away over a poor track, at **Zawiya Sidi Boukil**, there are Monday and Thursday markets of some interest.

[1,253 km.] **Nzala**.

An old French military post with a *fort.*

[1,283 km.] *Tizi n'Talrhemt pass* over the High Atlas range: 1,907 metres.

The name means 'the pass of the she-camel' − you are on the caravan trail to the desert. The *Oued Nzala* trickles beside the road back towards its confluence with the Ziz.

[1,295 km.] **Midelt**.

Hotel
***A *Hôtel Ayachi*, Rue d'Agadir (tel. 21.61).

This is a sizeable mountain centre, market town and chalet-type summer resort. It stands at 1,500 metres amid splendid scenery. There is an old *casbah* here also. The comfortable hotel and an alternative restaurant make it either a good halting-place or centre for exploring the tracks of the near-by *Jebel Ayachi* (3,737 metres), the *Cirque de Jaffar* and on to **Imilchil** (p. 234) or to **Tounfite**; to **Ksabi**, **Aquli** or **Amersid** − all wonderful if rather rough drives, some of them. The markets at Itzer (see below) can also be visited easily from here.

[1,325 km.] **Zeïda**, junction with the P33 from Khenifra (p. 235).

[1,335 km.] The P21 continues along the left-hand fork to Azrou; from here onwards your road is the P20, by the right-hand fork.

If you follow the P21 for about 9 km. from here and turn left you can reach **Itzer** in about another 10 km. This is the great *ksar* of the maraboutic family of the Aït Sidi 'bu Moussa, where big markets are held on Saturdays and at **Boumia** nearby on Thursdays; both are worth visiting. Boumia is reached either by the continuation of the track beyond Itzer or following the P33 left at Zeïda and rejoining the route from Itzer at a point 18 km. along.

[1,381 km.] The road on the right by Enjil and Missour is partly described, from the other direction, on p. 306.

[1,404 km.] **Boulmane**.

Administrative centre and group of *ksour*. The tracks running into the *Jebel Bou Iblane* from hereabouts cannot be recommended for ordinary vehicles.

[1,429 km.] A turning left 30 km. to Ifrane (p. 236) by a spectacular road.

[1,452 km.] **Annoceur**, where 4 km. to the right is the village of **Aïn Khalifa**.

The discovery here of some *Roman inscriptions* led to the belief that there must have been a Roman post here but, nothing further being found after much searching, it is now supposed that these blocks were abandoned during transport to the Tafilelt around 1787 when Mohammed ben Abdullah was building in those parts. This village was on a caravan road to the Tafilelt and the Sahara routes generally. There is a spring here called the *spring 'of the Idols'* — *Aïn Sname* — by which there was a temple in antiquity where, during annual fertility ceremonies, men and women copulated at random in the darkness of one night, the women thereafter remaining continent for a year during which any children born to them were taken to be brought up as servants of the temple — a very Neolithic rite which persisted until the coming of the Moslems in the eighth century.

[1,477 km.] **Sefrou** (Thursday market).

Hotel
   **A *Hôtel Sidi Lahcen Lyoussi*, Ville Nouvelle (tel. 604.97).

A small town with a Jewish colony still surviving. The town had been wholly Jewish before Idriss II converted the people to Islam (a near-by stream is still called the *Oued Youdi*) but Jews from Algeria and the Tafilelt came here in the thirteenth century and have been here ever since. The walls of the *medina* are nineteenth-century ones.

Near by are a number of caves in the *Aggai Gorge*, particularly the *Kef el-Youdi* (or *el-Mumin*) which is a centre of pilgrimage even more popular with the Jews than the Moslems where once again there is a legend of Seven Sleepers. At the *shrine of Sidi 'bu Ali Serghin*, by a spring, the people of Sefrou annually sacrifice a black he-goat, a black hen or a white hen, or one of seven colours, in honour of 'the genies of the spring' with whose water they mingle the blood of the sacrificial animals.

[1,481 km.] A turning 3 km. left to **El-Bahlil** village, splendidly sited over great views. Parts of the village consist of troglodytic houses.

[1,505 km.] Fes (p. 237).

GLOSSARY

For days of the week see p. 39.

Achoura	'New Year' feast; held on the tenth day of the year.
agadir	Fortified silo.
agdal	Garden
Aïd el-Kebir	Religious feast-day
Aïd es-Seghir	Religious feast-day
aïn	Spring.
Aïssawa	A confraternity of followers of Sidi Aïssa.
akhbar	Venerable; great.
Allah	God.
anazah	Screen in mosque.
Andalus, el-	Moslem Spain.
artesonados	Style of decorative work in wood, of Spanish Moslem origin (Sp.).
attawriq	Stylized foliage as used in decorative designs.
bab	Gate.
baraka	Charismatic power.
bayt	Living-quarters, suite of rooms.
bled el-makhzen	Governed lands.
bled es-siba	Ungoverned lands.
burnous	Hooded cloak.
cadi	Judge, of matters under religious laws.
caïd	Magistrate, Government, executive.
casbah	Citadel.
dar	House; in Maghrebi, palace.
dghoughia	Confraternity of followers of Dghoughi.
Djemaa	Assembly; mosque; Friday.
faqih	Canonical lawyer.
faradis	Walled-in (garden) plot (Persian word from which we derive 'paradise').
Fasi	Adjective derived from Fes, meaning 'man of Fes'; plural *Fasiyin*.
Filali	Adjective derived from the Tafilelt; the Alaouite dynasty is also called 'the Filali'.
foundouk	Inn with stabling and stores to rent.
garum	Salty extract from fish intestines used in Roman cooking (L.).

Gnawa	Confraternity; Negro sect.
guich	Tribal troops or soldiers in Government employ.
Hadj	Pilgrimage (to Mecca).
hadji	Pilgrim; honorific title of one having made the pilgrimage to Mecca.
hammada	Stony desert.
hammam	Steam-bath.
hamsin	South wind.
Haratin	People of mixed Negro and Berber blood having no tribal affiliations.
harem	Forbidden; women's quarters.
harka	Burning; punitive expedition.
hezzab	Reciter of the Koran.
horm	Right of sanctuary.
Hornacheros	Immigrants from Hornachos in Spain.
imam	Prayer-leader.
iwan	Reviewing-post.
jebel	Mountain.
jebilet	Hills.
Kaba	Shrine of Islam at Mecca.
khan	A fortified caravanserai on a trade route.
khatib	Preacher.
khettara	Underground water-conduits.
kotbiye	Book; plural *kutubiyyin* (possessive case).
koubba	Domed building.
ksar	Stronghold; plural *ksour*.
litham	Veil.
liwan	Ceremonial room, generally open on one side.
Maghreb	The west; Morocco; adjective *Maghrebi*.
mahallah	Royal encampment.
makhzen	Government.
maqsura	Royal 'pew'; protective partition
marabout	Holy teacher and/or religious leader.
maristan	Hospital (a Persian word).
Marrakchi	Adjective derived from 'Marrakech'; man of Marrakech.
mechouar	Assembly area.
mechra	Dam.
medrassa	Theological college; plural *medersa*.
medina	Township.

Meknassi	Adjective derived from 'Meknes'; man of Meknes (also man of Meknassa tribe).
mellah	Jewish quarter of city.
mida	Ablutive installation (washing-place, lavatory, etc.).
mihrab	Niche in *quibla* giving direction of Mecca.
mimber	Approximating to a pulpit.
minaret	Mosque tower.
Moriscos	Moslem refugees from Spain (Sp.).
moujehaddin	Soldiers engaged in a holy war or *jehad*.
Moulay	Maghrebi expression for a descendant of the Prophet; a sherif.
Mouloud	Anniversary of the Prophet's birth.
moussem	Festival in a holy man's honour (we use the hybrid term '*moussems*' as its plural).
Mozarab	Christian inhabitant of el-Andalus (Sp.).
msalla	Prayer area.
Mudejar	A Moorish style of woodwork carried on under Christian rule in Spain (Sp.).
muezzin	Prayer-caller.
Mulaththamun, el-	The veil-wearers; Almoravids.
muqarnas	Stalactitic type of decoration in domes or on ceilings.
oued	Stream, valley of stream or torrent-bed.
pishtaq	The raised frame surrounding the entrance of an important building.
quibla	'Direction of Mecca'; wall representing it.
Ramadan	Month of fasting.
ras	Head.
ribat	Monastic stronghold.
Rifi	Adjective derived from 'Rif'; man of the Rif mountains.
riwaq	Arcade surrounding the *sabn* of a mosque.
sabil	Public drinking-fountain.
Sidi	Honorific title of respect; as 'sir'.
Shia	Member of Shiite sect.
souk	Market (we use as its plural the hybrid term '*souks*').
Sufi	Religious mystic.
Sunna	Orthodox Islamic dogma; *sunni* means orthodoxy or orthodox believer.
tabia	Mud or adobe used in building; pisé.

tabib	Doctor.
tablinum	Archive room (L.).
Taïbia	Confraternity.
triclinium	Dining-room (L).
Ulema	Council of elders; a religious body.
Wahabi	Member of a sect of Islam.
Yemani	Adjective derived from 'Yemen' or south-west Arabia; a man from Yemen.
zawiya	A cult or confraternity centre; plural *zouawi*.
zekkat	Tithe.

SELECT BIBLIOGRAPHY

ENGLISH

The following books are in print and useful.

Arturo Barea, *The Forging of a Rebel* (Fontana, London, 1984). The second book of the trilogy, 'The Track', describes the Spanish army's struggle against El-Raisani. A brilliant first-hand account of the colonizing war, Chechaouen as the Spanish found it and Tetouan in its squalid heyday as capital of the Spanish zone. Not for the squeamish.

Walter Harris, *Morocco That Was* (Eland, London, 1983). Includes material mentioned below in books no longer in print.

Richard Hughes, *In the Lap of the Atlas, Stories of Morocco* (Chatto and Windus, London, 1979). A charming tribute to the author's long-term enthusiasm for the country. Only one story is fictional, and highly romantic.

Gavin Maxwell, *Lords of the Atlas* (Century, London, 1983). An illuminating study of the el-Glaoui brothers and, in effect, therefore of the last years of the last sultans before the French Protectorate, and of that weird period itself; very readable.

Douglas Porch, *The Conquest of Morocco* (Jonathan Cape, 1986). An absorbing and exciting account of France's last colonial enterprise.

Titles out of print:

Eugene M. Anderson, *The First Moroccan Crisis* (Archon Books, Hamden, Conn., 1966). A detailed study of European infighting for the 'right' to colonize Morocco. A hair-raising account, it ends with the Conference of Algeciras and, incidentally, that fatal alignment of the Powers which led to the 1914 war. Citizens of ex-colonial powers should read it; not for fun however.

Neville Barbour, *Morocco* (Thames and Hudson, London, 1965). An able historical survey up to recent times.

Ernest Gellner, *Saints of the Atlas* (Weidenfeld and Nicolson, London, 1969). An intensely interesting anthropological study of sherifs in the High Atlas, but not for popular reading.

Walter Harris, *The Land of an African Sultan; Travels in Morocco, 1887–9* (Low, London, 1889).

Walter Harris, *Tafilet; Journey in the Atlas and the Oases of the North-West Sahara* (Blackwood, London, 1895).

Rom Landau and Wim Swaan, *Morocco* (Elek Books, London, 1967). More valuable for Swaan's photographs, which include mosque interiors, than for a text adding little to what is not better handled by Barbour.

Budgett Meakin, *The Moors; a comprehensive description* (Sonnenschein, London, 1902).

Budgett Meakin, *Life in Morocco and Glimpses Beyond* (Chatto, London, 1905).

Henri Terrasse, *History of Morocco* (Édit. Atlantides, Rabat, n.d.). Not a lucid history in French, it conveys little in this execrable translation.

David S. Woolman, *Rebels in the Rif* (Oxford University Press, London, 1969). A sober and scholarly history of Abd el-Krim's resistance to the Spanish Protectorate, but far from sober reading, so extraordinary were the events it describes.

Anthology of Islamic Literature, ed. James Kritzeck (Penguin Books, London, 1964). Excellent companion-reading to any visit to a Moslem country.

FRENCH

Jérôme Carcopino, *Le Maroc Antique* (Gallimard, Paris, 1943; revised edition, 1947). As fascinating as it is learned, and enlivened by bitchiness towards rival scholars.

Gaston Deverdun, *Marrekech dès Origines à 1912* (Édit. Techniques Nord-Africaines, Rabat, 1959). For enthusiasts for that city; a labour of love, it is partisan, but adds too to our knowledge of Moroccan history as a whole.

Z. Guinaudeau, *Fes Vu Par Sa Cuisine* (J. E. Laurent, Rabat, 1966). Not the easiest cookery-book to work with but, between the waffle, interesting in itself and worth mastering for the deliciousness of the results. There is an English translation of this work − J. E. Harris, *Fez: traditional Moroccan cooking* (J. E. Laurent, Oudaia-Rabat, 1957) − which does not clarify its obscurities.

INDEX